The Structure of Digital Partner Choice

Andreas Schmitz

The Structure of Digital Partner Choice

A Bourdieusian perspective

Andreas Schmitz
Sociology
University of Bonn
Bonn, Germany

ISBN 978-3-319-43529-9   ISBN 978-3-319-43530-5   (eBook)
DOI 10.1007/978-3-319-43530-5

Library of Congress Control Number: 2016956103

© Springer International Publishing Switzerland 2017
This work is subject to copyright. All rights are reserved by the Publisher, whether the whole or part of the material is concerned, specifically the rights of translation, reprinting, reuse of illustrations, recitation, broadcasting, reproduction on microfilms or in any other physical way, and transmission or information storage and retrieval, electronic adaptation, computer software, or by similar or dissimilar methodology now known or hereafter developed.
The use of general descriptive names, registered names, trademarks, service marks, etc. in this publication does not imply, even in the absence of a specific statement, that such names are exempt from the relevant protective laws and regulations and therefore free for general use.
The publisher, the authors and the editors are safe to assume that the advice and information in this book are believed to be true and accurate at the date of publication. Neither the publisher nor the authors or the editors give a warranty, express or implied, with respect to the material contained herein or for any errors or omissions that may have been made.

Printed on acid-free paper

This Springer imprint is published by Springer Nature
The registered company is Springer International Publishing AG Switzerland

Foreword by Richard Münch

It might be assumed that modern online dating markets correspond better to the ideal, free matching type of supply and demand than offline dating markets do and that they are less subject to socio-structural restrictions. Based on a set of empirical studies, Andreas Schmitz proves that this assumption is not tenable. The practices involved in online dating depend to a great extent on the user's socio-structural position and the habitus associated herewith. Throughout this work, it is shown that online dating is largely determined by offline structures, (dis)positions, and practices of positioning.

Andreas Schmitz provides a suitable theoretical explanation for this empirical finding that is based on Pierre Bourdieu's relational sociology. According to this approach, the socio-structural position of an agent corresponds to dispositions comprising cognition, preference formation, and agency. The relation between two agents' (dis)positions within the social space is constitutive for interaction processes. This is not only confirmed within the framework of online dating, which is demonstrated by the empirical analyses of observational and survey data – in fact, these factors are actually *reinforced* in this digital partner market.

It is a special achievement of the author to have provided us with such a broad and profound empirical basis and its comprehensive, extensive, and detailed theoretical explanation, methodological clarification, and methodical illustration. Hence, a work has been created on the subject of online dating that sets new standards and significantly advances research from a theoretical, methodological, and empirical point of view. Research on partner markets and partner choice will not be able to get around this innovation.

The book proceeds along a systematic structure. The core element of the theoretical argumentation is the development of a relational theory of mating based on Bourdieu, which is compared to the paradigm of 'Mate Choice as Agency in Structures' (MAS), in order to improve the latter's potential for understanding and extending the relational structuration of couple emergence. In a very convincing manner, the author develops a relational theory of mating processes, while at the same time offering an equally convincing interpretation of MAS as an analytical subcategory of a relational theory of mating.

The empirical studies demonstrate the different aspects of societal structuration of the dating market, namely, its chance structure, mating preferences, mating strategies, and processes of *reciprocal classifications*. The analyses are based on process and survey data and are carried out applying both traditional and innovative quantitative techniques. They offer abundant empirical evidence for the assumptions of a Bourdieusian theory of mate choice. The conclusion combines the lines of argumentation and develops a perspective on online dating as a digitally *unified and unifying market of symbolic goods*. This work convinces with its extremely high standard of theoretical reflection and the very close linkage of theory and empirical analysis and takes a substantial step forward for the theory and empirical analysis of mating processes.

Professor Emeritus of Sociology (University of Bamberg)   Richard Münch

Preface

"You are doing research on Online Dating? Oh – how interesting!" I often heard statements like these whenever I revealed the *area of application* of my research. Whereas it is a pleasant feeling to receive attention for one's activities, I never really understood the enthusiasm by media folks and some of my colleagues regarding the mere fact of digitalized ways of finding one's partner. Of course, the realm of love, intimacy, and togetherness has always been relevant for our personal and social lives. Also, still today, the Internet might be seen by some as an entirely new *fait social* which turns society on its head and forces us to call not only our stock of knowledge but even our ways of assessment into question. Considering these two things together, online dating in itself probably makes the impression of a fascinating peculiarity. Yet, the idea behind this book grew on different considerations.

Whereas some social scientists tend to throw their analytical toolbox overboard and feel compelled to develop completely new approaches in the light of a seemingly new phenomenon, others rather treat the web as new bottles for an old wine. When analyzing digital partner markets, most research is based on an individualistic epistemology. There is, however, not only a notable dominance of individualistic and rationalist approaches to online dating. The field of family sociology and *mate choice* is thoroughly dominated by a rationalist and individualist paradigm. This is not to say that this paradigm per se is problematic or to be rejected, but – as long as one sees theoretical and methodological pluralism as sociology's strength rather than as its stigma – one must diagnose a certain analytical impoverishment in the field. To ground one's research on the "micro-macro-distinction," the "actor-structure-dichotomization," and, ultimately, within the analytical framework of Coleman's "bathtub" is a plausible and surely legitimate approach. However, it is by no means the only axiomatic system within the field of modern social sciences.

The idea behind this work was to make a contribution to the field of mating theories, by proposing and developing a *relational* approach. Whereas relation has always been a constitutive for sociological reasoning (one need only think of Karl Marx, Georg Simmel, or Norbert Elias), it is in the last decades that relational sociology as a modern framework emerged and consolidated. There are great many approaches of modern relational social sciences such as the works of Michel Foucault, Harrison White, Neil Fligstein, Douglas McAdam, and – in a certain sense – Peter Hedström. Whereas these and other authorities benefit from specific theoretical conceptions and methodological implementations of 'relationality' in their particular interpretations, the most consistent modern variety of relational reasoning can be found in the works of Pierre Bourdieu and the many further developments of his successors.

In empirical terms, throughout this book I try to accomplish a modest goal. I want to make the small argument that 'structure' in a relational sense can (and from a Bourdieusian viewpoint: must) be located within the agents and their practices themselves. This insight will be regarded as more or less worthy of discussion according to the readers' personal and paradigmatic background. But the evidence of structured partner choice, in a sphere seemingly less affected by structures known from the offline world, may make relational sociology a dialog partner for general partner market sociology and family sociology.

In a broader context, relational sociology, for example, providing us with the concept of habitus, addresses several modern developments within the individualist paradigm to correct its analytical blind spots. This consideration might reveal a connection between rational action theories and relational sociology. This is not to say that the instruments of habitus-field theory could be reduced to an individualist and rationalist framework. On the contrary, from the viewpoint of habitus theory, models of (bounded) rational choice are empirical and theoretical special cases of a general theory of practices. The same applies to the logical relation between concepts such as preferences-dispositions, market-field, exchange-reciprocal classification, etc.

Demonstrating the genuine structuration of dating site users, their habitus, practices, and interactions may be seen as unsatisfying for someone who wants to test different hypotheses or even theories against each other. For example, it might be an interesting question (from a very specific scientific viewpoint!) to test 'Bourdieusian' vs rational choice predictions. However, one must ask how it might be even possible to directly (a) test theories at all and, even if one could do it, how (b) to realize such a test within a *common* statistical model that, for example, holds the causal impact of the "Bourdieusian" variable (lifestyle?) constant for the effect of an independent variable which could be associated with rational choice (education?).

Such discussions may tacitly suggest to the reader that the analysis of partner markets could only be led using quantitative models. This, of course, would be wrong from (virtually) any sociological viewpoint. Apart from the fact that the distinction in quantitative and qualitative methods itself already represents a logical problem, the dichotomization between qualitative and quantitative data and analysis is – from a relational perspective – pointless. However, in order to strike up a conversation with mate choice theorists, who clearly prefer quantitative empirical analysis also throughout this book, a strong emphasis was put on quantitative modeling, whereas qualitative information is only used here and there.

Within the quantitative framework applied throughout this book, several restrictions were made. Regarding dyadic classification, processes were not modeled in a dynamic way (although possible via longitudinal finite mixture modeling), and no hypotheses were tested (although possible via restricted finite mixture modeling). Such extensions, however, may well be applied in further research. More severely, I reluctantly decided to remove the parts on field-theoretical implications, for the sake of the visibility of my main arguments. As a matter of fact, a future project should focus on mobilizing a Bourdieusian generalized theory of fields for the conceptualization and analysis of mating processes. Despite these and other severe restrictions of this work, my hope is that this book represents a small contribution to the field of partner market research.

Bonn, Germany Andreas Schmitz
Spring 2016

Acknowledgments

This book evolved from different projects and scientific investigations I have been working on in the last few years. I am grateful for the generous funding the German Research Foundation (DFG) granted to me and my colleagues for the realization of two research projects on online dating. In view of the project work, I would like to express my thanks to Doreen Zillmann, Jan Skopek, Olga Yanenko, Marcel Hebing, and William Tayler for their prolific, committed, pleasant, and very appreciated cooperation. We enjoyed a stimulating exchange of ideas between methodological individualism and methodological relationism, uninhibited by paradigmatic barriers. Within this research context, we not only had to handle complex data structures but also the nomos of the field of media and of the economic field. I owe gratitude to the principal investigator Prof. Dr. Dr. (h.c.) Hans-Peter Blossfeld for his unprecedented competencies as research manager and his indefatigable efforts in organizing excellent research conditions. I would like to express my very sincere gratitude to the supervisor of my dissertation, Prof. Dr. Richard Münch, for his constant encouragement, his epistemological open-mindedness, and his ways of leading nonhierarchical discourse. I am also particularly thankful for the many great substantial discussions I had in Bamberg with Christian Baier, Michael Bayer, Stefanie Beyer, Christoph Gaasch, Vincent Gengnagel, Frank Grimes, Julian Hamann, Raphael Heiberger, Lydia Kleine, Martin Messingschlager, Caroline Näther, Tobias Phillip, Jan Riebling, Susann and Sebastian Sachse-Thürer, Christian Schmidt-Wellenburg, Sebastian Wenz, Knut Wenzig, Oliver Wieczorek, Erbil Yilmaz, Markus Zielonka, and many others. These discussions without fear or favor with colleagues from rational choice, analytical, network, and discourse-theoretical approaches were and still are essential for my work and the enjoyment it entails. I would also like to thank my colleagues from the field of online dating research Marie Bergström and Bernie Hogan, as well as the Oxford Internet Institute for the many fascinating and entertaining conversations. Another word of thanks is addressed to Prof. Dr. Susanne Rässler and Prof. Dr. Jeroen Vermunt for their profound and valuable feedback on my quantitative developments regarding the dyadic classification and Eigenwert analysis of interactional data. I would also like to thank

Prof. Dr. Jörg Blasius for his kind support and for familiarizing me with geometric data analysis and Daniel Witte for the many years of concerted effort dedicated to the further development of the habitus-field theory, as well as Alice Barth, Felix Lesske, Miriam Trübner, Christian Heuser, Silvia Arnold, Christian Dickmann, and Andreas Mühlichen for the productive collaboration in Bonn. Finally, I want to thank and express all my love to my mother Susanne and my grandmother Anneliese Schmitz, to whom I dedicate this book.

Contents

Foreword by Richard Münch		v
Preface		vii
Acknowledgments		xi
1	**Introduction**	1
	References	9
2	**Online Dating – A Meeting Point for the Modern Individual and Traditional Individualism**	13
	Online Dating as Manifestation of Modernity	13
	The Societal Prevalence of Online Dating	16
	Basic Principles of Online Dating	17
	Online Dating Between Euphoria and Dysphoria	19
	Analytical Perspectives of Digital Mating	20
	The Cult of the Individual 2.0	22
	References	24
3	**The Market Character of Online Dating**	29
	What Is a Partner Market?	29
	Online Dating – An 'Ideal Type' Partner Market	32
	The User's Phenomenological Perception	39
	Interim Conclusion	40
	References	41
4	**Classical Theories of Mate Choice and the Relational Deficit in the Study of Relationship Formation**	43
	Classical Theories of Mate Choice	44
	Mating Preferences and Mate Choice	44
	Mating as Social Exchange	45
	'Erotic Capital' and Couple Formation	46

	Family Economics	47
	The Blau Space	48
	Mating as Agency in Structures (MAS) – The Paradigmatic Core of Current Research	49
	MAS as Variant of Methodological Individualism and Rational Choice	52
	Structure as Externality?	54
	The Structuration of Mating	56
	The Heteronomous Structure of the Partner Market	56
	Transverse Structures of the Blau Space	57
	Situational Logics of Partner Choice	57
	Structures of Biography	59
	Mating Utility and Mating Preferences	60
	Mating as Decision	63
	Structures of the Actor	67
	Structures of Partner Choice	67
	Interaction Process	68
	Structured Logics of Aggregation	71
	References	76
5	**A Bourdieusian Approach to Mating Processes**	85
	The Relational Architecture of Pierre Bourdieu's Sociology	85
	The Partner Market as Social Space	90
	The Social Space as Partner Market	92
	Mating Utilities and Preferences as (Dis-)positions	94
	Mating Rationalities as Dispositions	99
	Mate Choice as Classification Practice	102
	Mating as Reciprocal Classification	103
	Mating as (Symbolic) Domination	107
	MAS as Special Case of a Relational Theory of Mating	109
	References	116
6	**Methodological Implications**	121
	The Relational Methodology of Pierre Bourdieu	121
	Methodological Dimensions of Online Dating	123
	Surveying the Users' Perspectives: The Online Questionnaire	124
	The Methodological Restrictions of Questionnaire Data	124
	Observing the Users' Practices: Web-Generated Process Data	126
	Web-Generated Process Data in the Present Study	127
	Profile Data	128
	Relational Data Integration	129
	Qualitative Interviews	129
	Relational Methods	129
	The Geometric Construction of Space	131
	A Finite-Mixture Model of Dyadic-Classification	133
	References	137

7 Empirical Analyses 141
The Online Dating Market and the Social Space 141
    The Online Space of Lifestyles 141
    Erotic Capital as Dimension of the Digital Partner Market? 143
    The Structure of Chances for Awareness and Exchange 145
The Relational Structure of Mating Preferences 150
    Relational Mating Preferences: The Case of Age Preferences 150
    Structured Systems of Mating Preferences 154
    The Positional Character of Mating Dispositions 156
The (Dis-) Positional Character of Rationalities in Mating 160
    Deceptive Practices and Market Position 160
    An OLS Regression of Deceptive Practices 162
    A Latent Class Regression Model of Mate Value
    and Deceptive Practices 164
    Rationality Types Within the Social Space 166
Structured Reciprocal Classification in Mating Interactions 170
    Lifestyle Homogeneity as a Process 170
    A Dyadic Finite Mixture Model of First and Last Observed
    Contacts 172
    A Dyadic Finite Mixture Model of 6th Contacts 173
References 178

8 Online Dating – A Unified and Unifying Symbolic Good Market 181
The Ongoing Unification of the Market of Symbolic Goods 182
Digital Classification Practices 183
Equal Opportunity as Illusion and Symbolic Violence 186
Re-Traditionalizing Effects of Modern Technology:
    The Case of Gender 187
Acquired Digital Space and Physical Space 189
Structuration Trough Neutralization of Structure 190
Areas of Rationality 192
The Structure of Digital Partner Choice 193
The Mate Choice Paradigm as Special Case of Practice Theory 195
References 197

Appendix 199

Bibliography 203

List of Figures

Fig. 2.1	Idealized process of dating site usage	18
Fig. 3.1	Theoretical comparison of ideal-typical partner markets (Biplots)	37
Fig. 4.1	The MAS paradigm as micro - macro - micro representation	54
Fig. 5.1	The MAS model within the social space model	112
Fig. 7.1	The space of lifestyles	143
Fig. 7.2	Physicality within the social space	144
Fig. 7.3	Ego's ingoing contact network	146
Fig. 7.4	Subjective and objective mate value within the social space	148
Fig. 7.5	Conditional effect of age on preference outcomes in men and women	152
Fig. 7.6	Classes of mating dispositions within the social space	157
Fig. 7.7	Passive projection of rationality-deception types and illustrative variables	167
Fig. 7.8	Correlation between sender's and receiver's cultural capital	171

List of Tables

Table 6.1	Data structure of HTTP status messages	128
Table 7.1	Regression model of users' mate value (centrality)	147
Table 7.2	Latent classes of mating preferences and underlying dispositional principles	155
Table 7.3	OLS – model with logarithmized count of deceptive practices	163
Table 7.4	OLS – model with logarithmized count of deceptions incl. subjective chances	163
Table 7.5	Latent class regression of deception as function of subjective chances	165
Table A.1	Profile parameters for dyadic classes	199

Chapter 1
Introduction

Online dating is sometimes seen as differing from traditional mating contexts by a relativized relevance of structures familiar from the offline world. Seemingly, the users of dating sites find themselves in a sphere with fewer institutional, geographical, temporal, social, or normative restrictions, thus being enabled to realize their preferences and make their choices comparatively less affected by immediate distorting structural conditions. Whereas the internet in general and online dating in particular may be seen as a playground *par excellence* for analysis based on rational choice theories and methodologies, this introductory chapter motivates a Bourdieusian approach to (digital) partner markets.

The internet and social media have cemented their position as an integral part of society and our everyday lives. While no longer extraordinary for most of our everyday practices, such as acquiring information, communicating, or shopping online, searching for a partner on the web still seems to constitute a particular challenge for the modern Western conception of mating and intimacy, which is essentially grounded in ideas of romantic love, spontaneity, and 'destiny'. Nevertheless, today, finding a partner online is a relevant phenomenon in quantitative terms. Online dating and matchmaking services are used by a great number of people around the world, as multiple international studies have shown (see Hogan et al. 2011; Ben-Ze'ev 2004; Schmitz et al. 2011). Whether these specific indicators are exact or not, it can be asserted without question that finding a partner online is anything but a peripheral social matter. On the contrary, it represents a "significant trend in modern courtship" (Illouz and Finkelmann 2009: 414), a trend which is likely to experience a further increase in relevance, given the growing availability of stationary and mobile internet access.

It comes, then, as no surprise to find that in recent years scientists have invested considerable effort in analyzing this modern social and technological manifestation of the 'perennial' subjects of intimacy, love, relationships, and marriage. Regarding judgments of a general societal nature, some social scientists praise the potential of the digital partner market for the allocation of romantic love and happiness (cp. Whitty 2008: 1837; Finkel et al. 2012: 49). The web in general and online dating in particular are seen as providing free access to the rest of the world for everyone, thus not only relativizing the offline restrictions of time and space, but also potentially transcending social barriers. Others paint a rather gloomy picture of the online dating phenomenon. They tend to see it as an intrusion of market logics into the last and most intimate sphere, thus constituting a rationalist threat to romantic authenticity (cp. Illouz 2007; Žižek 2010; Wetzel 2013).

Nevertheless, online dating is particularly appealing for the traditional sociology of mate choice, which sees in this modern partner market an innovative tool for the assessment of established research questions: the character and impact of mating preferences; mating strategies; individual success and failure in mating; and assortative mating, the supra-individual consequences on the partner market and ultimately on the societal level. From this perspective, online dating can help to answer long-standing questions by analyzing the data and the specific social constellations of users searching for a mate online, information which was unavailable or inaccessible in traditional offline partner markets. In particular, the observability of a mass of people explicitly looking for a partner, people who furthermore are encountering one another for the first time, constitutes a promising methodological basis for partner choice research. It does not surprise that scientists essentially approach the sphere of digital mating markets equipped with the theoretical and methodological concepts they acquire in the course of their scientific socialization. The observation which primarily motivates this work is the fact that research on online dating – just like research on traditional mating processes, for all their differences – is strongly dominated by an individualistic mode of thought. There are many studies from the perspective of psychology or communication sciences which, for example, attempt to deduce strategies for online dating from the personalities of the users in question, or to trace their success on the partner market back to psychological characteristics. In a similarly epistemological vein, most genuine sociological approaches to online dating are characterized by an explicit individualistic perspective. This manifests itself perhaps most clearly in the widespread and widely unquestioned terms of *mate choice*, leading to a model of a (more or less) rational actor confronted with choice opportunities external to him or her.

The vast majority of traditional offline research applies a strict dichotomization between actor and structure. This dichotomization between structure and subject, and between choice and opportunities, is also the paradigmatic premise of most research on dating phenomena. 'Structure' in mate choice research is widely considered to be the mere opportunities of choice. In this context, the structuralistic concept of the 'Blau space' (McPherson 1983: 519–532) is sometimes used as structural complement to individualistic choice models. From this point of view, online dating is no more than a "new approach to study [...] issues of opportunity structure and individual preferences" (Blossfeld 2009: 526). This has led many researchers to investigate the users' preferences and to focus on individual choices rather than on structure. The traditional dichotomization between actor and structure has yielded countless analytical insights for online mate choice research (Caspi and Gorski

2006; Ellison et al. 2006; Hancock et al. 2007; Lee 2008; Fiore et al. 2010; Hitsch et al. 2010a, b; Skopek 2011; Skopek et al. 2011a, b; Zillmann et al. 2011; Rosenfeld and Thomas 2012; Hertog 2012; Lin and Lundquist 2013; Portaca and Mills 2013; Zillmann et al. 2013).

However, the structural element of mating processes is systematically reduced to an analysis of the choice opportunities of individual actors, resting on the assumption that in the digital partner market structural mechanisms are relativized or can be controlled by design (e.g. Lin and Lundquist 2013: 188). Relying on offline research tradition and focusing on structure in this sense leads to ignoring structure in other possible senses: Class structures, mental structures, normative structures, cultural structures, structures of actors, etc. are assigned a secondary role, if at all, and, in most analyses, neglected in favor of the explanatory primacy of the subject exercising its free will. In doing so, the latent and indirect relations between different subjects, their differential societal positions, and different and differentiating practices are systematically put in the background in favor of the analytical starting point of the individual actor. These conceptual blind-spots in contemporary empirical research on mating processes can be seen as an individualistic bias, or *a relational deficit in the research on relationships* in modern partner market research.

The approach of this work is to accomplish an objectivizing "epistemological break" (Bourdieu 1990: 26) from the individualistic partner choice perspective, by putting an emphasis on the relational implications of couple formation. This work sees online dating as embodying an exemplary opportunity for such further development of the very theorization and conceptualization of mating processes themselves. The fact that a new context for mating and dating has emerged in the last two decades could thus represent the starting point for further development of mating theory itself.

Within the field of the social science, 'structure' has a wider notion and is not necessarily thought of as being external to the individual actor and his actions (e.g. Durkheim 1964; Parsons 1937; Bourdieu 1977; Münch 1987; Adloff and Wacquant 2015; Schmitz et al. 2016). The approach proposed in this book, however, is not to lapse into the other extreme by simply proclaiming a "structural turn" in partner market research. Reflecting on mate choice theories, Skopek (2011: 295) postulates a stronger *integration* of structure and individual explanations in partner choice research. Essentially, we agree with the critique of the individualist perspective on the limited analytical value of mere structural explanations for mating processes, for example regarding the structuralist approach of Peter Blau (1977, 1984 et al.). Therefore, an intermediating, *relational* approach will be developed in this work.

Pierre Bourdieu is the most prominent proponent of relational sociology in contemporary social sciences. Whereas the issue of relationality has experienced a remarkable upturn in the field of social sciences in the last decades, Bourdieu's implementation of relational reasoning is presumably the most consequent one. Like adherents of the individualistic partner choice paradigm, he criticizes the tradition of structuralism in the social sciences, but he also systematically relates the structural traditions of the social sciences to individualistic conceptions of action and praxis. The starting point of his approach is to transcend the fundamental paradigmatic distinctions in the social sciences, such as those between 'subject' vs.

'structure' or 'micro' vs. 'macro'. In place of subject and structure, Bourdieu develops relational concepts such as 'habitus', 'practice' and 'field', which emphasize the structural implications of subjective phenomena as well as the subjective dimension of structural phenomena. Whereas his concept of "genetic structuralism" (Bourdieu 1989: 19) is usefully applied nowadays in the most diverse research contexts, he never developed a systematic concept of partner markets and mating phenomena. As there is also little research based on the works of Bourdieu systematically conceptualizing processes of mating, this work is dedicated to developing a sociology of mating which mobilizes the concepts developed by Bourdieu.

For this purpose, the predominant model of *partner choice as agency in structures* will be systematically extended to a relational model of *structures within partner choice*. In doing so, this work builds on key works by Blossfeld (Blossfeld 1995a, b, 2009), Blossfeld and Timm (1997, 2003), Blossfeld and Drobnič (2001), Kalmijn (1991, 1994, 1998), Kalmijn and Flap (2001), Mare (1991), and Oppenheimer (1988), who have made considerable advances in offline partner market research with their numerous empirical studies and the underlying coherent individualistic conceptualization of partner choice.

The rationale for choosing the context of an online dating platform is that, at first sight, it constitutes the ideal playground for the theories of partner choice and partner market. Conventional offline partner markets (like schools, nightclubs, or personal networks) as usually analyzed by empirical research represent strongly structured social spheres. Not everyone frequents the same nightclub, schools are segregated by education, mating in an academic context has its own norms, and so on. In consequence, the objective constitution of a couple and the subjective development of reciprocal feelings can be traced back to the structural impacts of institutional settings, geographic characteristics, and normative standards to a large extent. It is thus quite natural that recent individualistic partner choice research sees online dating markets as comparatively *unaffected* by such structural impacts. Many mate choice theorists share the view that the users of a dating site can efficiently realize their personal preferences, as the barriers of geography or social class and the risk of contravening normative rules or third party expectations are lessened by design. Observed practices on a dating site are then interpreted as being driven by the individual intentions, preferences and rational choices (e.g. Fiore and Donath 2005; Lee 2008; Rosenfeld and Thomas 2012). This individual and rational perspective is also constitutive for the public discourse and the self-presentation of dating companies. Online dating platforms are designed for the very purpose of efficient partner choice: "I think we can help people find choice and make better choices" (an employee of an American dating site interviewed by Roscoe and Chillas 2014: 806). Apparently, online dating represents a *prime example* for the application of individualistic partner choice research, which makes use of the traditions of rational choices theories, exchange theories, and market theories.

At the same time, however, the analysis of a digital partner market allows partner market research to assess the structural dimension of mating dispositions, practices, interactions, and outcomes, by using the seemingly *least likely case* of effects and manifestations of structural implications of mating processes. If, therefore, a

Bourdieusian view of this phenomenon offers analytical insight, it might also be worth including it in the canon of the sociology of offline mating, dating, marriage, etc. Thus, the objective of this study is to elaborate the principles of a Bourdieusian theory of mating and to thereby enrich the field of mate choice theories.

To fulfill these research perspectives, our line of reasoning is as follows: Mobilizing classical sociological theories, we will argue in Chapter 2 that the emergence of digital dating practices can be seen as a manifestation of different modernization processes that give 'market' and 'individual choice' their empirical significance in today's Western societies. The chapter then outlines the basic forms and principles of online dating. Furthermore, the significance of this subject area will be elaborated by providing quantitative evidence of its societal prevalence, with an emphasis on the Western world in general and Germany in particular. Subsequently, an overview of the different kinds of scientific reception of online dating will be given, ranging from general societal diagnoses to analytical approaches of mate choice theorists. It will be shown that online dating research is essentially characterized by the strong influence of individualistic and rationalist theories.

Chapter 3 starts with a clarification of the meaning of the term 'partner market', due to the fact that there is both little systematic conceptualization of the partner market in empirical research (Schwartz 2013: 464) and of the basic term 'market' itself in sociology as a whole. Deriving a Weberian concept of the market as a competition for exchange chances, a relational definition of the partner market will be developed. Based on this definition, findings from research, and illustrating qualitative interview material, it will be shown that online dating markets actually are no exceptional phenomenon in the context of couple formation, but can be analytically located within a continuum alongside conventional partner markets such as nightclubs, offline 'lonely hearts' ads, and speed dating events. However, online dating sites do seem to be – in comparison to other contexts of interaction – strongly structured by market principles such as competition for partners, the induction of conscious rational mate choice, and exchange logics. It will be shown that the 'real type' market of online dating can be seen as being particularly close to an 'ideal-typical' partner market. Therefore, everything seems to suggest that online dating can be conceived of as a paradigmatic textbook example for analyses in the spirit of individualistic mate choice tradition.

Chapter 4 inspects the intellectual architecture of the theories that underlie traditional research on online dating processes. It takes a closer look at the most prominent explicit theories of mating processes, including preference theories, exchange theories, and theories of partner markets. Despite the fundamental differences between these approaches, it will be shown that they share a common paradigmatic core: the analytical distinction between agent and structure, which was formulated in its most explicit form by Blossfeld and Timm (see e.g. 1997, 2003), using the label of 'mate choice as agency in structures' (MAS). In this paradigm, structure essentially means the opportunity to meet and choose a partner, e.g. in the sense of geographic, institutional conditions or in the sense of a choice set consisting of eligible and potentially willing men and women. It will be argued that this dominant paradigm is an empirical variation of the predominant syndrome of methodological individualism and modern rational choice theories. The core of this paradigm is constituted by the epistemological agent-structure dichotomization and by the explanatory emphasis on individual rational choice for the assessment of social phenomena.

In the next step, the mate choice paradigm will be examined with regard to the ways structure can be conceptualized. It will also be shown that most individualistic mate choice research tries to overcome the narrow framework of the methodological individualism/rational choice-syndrome and thus indicates the need for further consideration of structural and historical mechanisms. In sum, however, it will be argued that the very starting point of methodological individualism and the predominant influence of rational choice theories inhibit a wider understanding of the structural mechanisms effective in mating phenomena. This relational deficit in the conceptualization of relationship formation will motivate a Bourdieusian approach to (online) partner markets.

Due to the necessity of a foundational social theory which could provide the potential for the mobilization of structure in a wider sense, and in order to avoid replicating the deficiencies of genuine structuralistic theories, Pierre Bourdieu's theories will be invoked in Chapter 5, since it consequently combines subjectivist and objectivist notions of the social. The chapter first gives an overview of the basic principles of Bourdieu's sociology. Based on this theoretical foundation and the contributions from partner market research, a Bourdieusian conceptualization of mating will be developed by contrasting the MAS model's theoretical components with the more general sociological approach of Bourdieu. It will be shown that Bourdieu's conceptual tools (in particular 'social space', 'habitus', and 'practice') enable both the utilization of the insights of the MAS model and the generalization of its analytical concepts. We will argue that from a practical perspective, both approaches can be productively combined and, from a theoretical perspective, the individual mate choice paradigm can be interpreted as an analytical special case of Bourdieu's social theory.

The next Chapter 6 is dedicated to questions of methodology. First, the basic principles of Bourdieu's relational methodology (cp. Bourdieu and Waqcuant 1992; Schmitz 2009) will be outlined. In the next step, we will discuss the core characteristics of the web-generated process data and online survey data which have been collected on a heterosexual, non-specialized major German dating platform. The methodological potential for research examining processes of couple formation is outlined, arguing for a relational integration of the data. The methods used in this work are based, on the one hand, on procedures usually applied by empirical analyses of mating processes (uni-directional regression models), but also on specific *relational* procedures and their integration. The underlying rejection of methodical dogmatism is motivated by the principles of relational methodology, which not only rejects the positivistic identification of variables but also the positivistic approach to their analysis. Bourdieu, for example, envisioned a careful integration of the regression approach as part of his greater theory of social space (see e.g. Blasius and Schmitz 2013). Furthermore, this relational philosophy is also justified by formal statistics: Skrondal and Rabe-Hesketh (2004), for example, show that seemingly opposing models such as class analysis, factor analysis, regressions, IRT models, and MCA can all be applied as part of a generalized linear and non-linear mixture modeling approach, thus enabling new combinations of procedures previously considered irreconcilable. In order to keep sight of the phenomenological dimension of online dating, interview material from different qualitative studies will also be applied.

Both approaches – the individualistic mate choice paradigm and the proposed Bourdieusian approach, as well as the conceptual integration – are confronted with unique theoretical and empirical obstacles when analyzing mating processes in an unknown research setting. In the last section, the methodological challenges and opportunities resulting from web-generated observation will be discussed. Two models will be developed: Firstly, the operationalization and objectification of a user's market value based on the networks of incoming and outgoing contacts, applying an Eigen-value centralization approach of network analysis. Secondly, a model of the statistical classification of dyadic interaction data will be proposed, classifying different couple constellations according to different attributes by applying a finite mixture model approach.

The following Chapter 7 will discuss selected empirical examples of a Bourdieusian investigation of an online dating market. The empirical case of Germany may be seen as particularly relevant given that Hogan et al. (2011: 14) found that Germany had the highest percentage (29%) of couples that met online, when compared to other European countries and Japan. Until recently, empirical partner market research did not have the data necessary to undertake a comprehensive application of a relational conception of the partner market (and its underlying dynamics) to the context of empirical encounters. For the sociological assessment of the character of dating platforms, it is of particular interest that the social web platforms as assessed in this work, which are free of charge, although not ultimately representative for the offline population, do include all social strata of the (German) society (cp. Skopek 2011; Zillmann 2016). From a general mating research perspective, it seems most promising to analyze dating platforms made up of different social strata which are not matched by an algorithm, but require an active process of search, contact, and interaction. This is the specific dating market segment which represents the empirical subject of this work.

In this empirical chapter, we will take up selected theoretical considerations by quantitatively modelling data within the analytical framework of relational sociology. The first analysis presents an empirical construction of the dating market as a social space, showing that the capital structure of German offline society is indeed characteristic for the dating platform analyzed here. Also, by showing that physical attributes and partner market chances correspond to this space, the concept of an autonomous form of "erotic capital" (Hakim 2011) will be dismissed in a context where erotic charisma should be of utmost importance. It will be argued that physicality is a sub-aspect of the user's advertised symbolic goods. The findings will support the conceptualization of the dating site users as agents with particular habitus capable of reproducing the structure of the social space. They also prevents us from assuming a specific habitus of online daters and their symbolic goods as being specifically conditioned and shaped by the logics of the internet and the partner market. In the second step, an objective indicator for market value will be presented and projected into the space, thus illustrating that the objective chances for finding a partner online are a function of this 'market of symbolic goods' and the symbolic goods of the user's habitus.

In the next step, we utilize both observational and questionnaire data in order to scrutinize the widespread practice of ascribing the phenomenon of assortative mating to single homophilous preferences. Starting with the frequently neglected issue of age in mating, it will at first be shown that different mating preferences correspond to each other and form bundles of mating dispositions. Secondly, we will demonstrate that homophily in mating is not a preference characteristic for all users. Thirdly, we are going to confirm that mating dispositions can be seen as a function of the relational position in the social space. In sum, these analyses will highlight the analytical value of the habitus concept.

The subsequent step to be addressed is the issue of strategy in mating, taking deception in online dating as an example. Again, the relational position of the user is utilized for an explanatory model of deception. It is demonstrated that the individual's position in the social space affects not only the quality and quantity of deceptive practices, but also corresponds to different causally adequate rationalities involved in deceptive practices. Thus, this example emphasizes the fact that rationality (in mating) is more a function of the interplay between the user's habitus and the partner market than a general principle of (mate) choice.

Finally, the issue of interaction in mating and reciprocal classification – a differentiated notion of interaction in Bourdieu's work – will be addressed. The theoretical concept of reciprocal classification will be related to the statistical model of dyadic classification using finite mixture models of sender-receiver relations. It will be shown that interaction patterns between online dating users are highly structured and cannot be reduced to any single mating trait such as education, age, income, etc. or to any single kind of disposition such as homophily. Overall, the empirical findings support the argument that 'structure' manifests itself in many ways within the users of a dating platform: within their preferences, rationalities, choices, and interactions.

The concluding Chapter 8 provides a relational reinterpretation of the purportedly unstructured market 'online dating'. The online partner market will be characterized as a digitally unified market of symbolic goods, operating as a *hyperfocus*, by reproducing structuration and social inequality, not despite but because of the relativization of offline structure. In light of the finding that even the near-ideal market of online dating (and the agents using it) is socially structured to the core, this work is intended to foster a scientific reorientation towards 'structure' in a relational sense in the modern sociology of mating processes and beyond.

References

Adloff, F., & Wacquant, L. (2015). For a sociology of flesh and blood. Questions to Loïc Wacquant. In F. Adloff, K. Gerund, & D. Kaldewey (Eds.), *Revealing tacit knowledge: Embodiment and explication* (pp. 185–196). Bielefeld: Transcript Verlag.

Ben-Ze'ēv, A. (2004). *Love online: Emotions on the Internet*. Cambridge: Cambridge University Press. Retrieved from http://www.loc.gov/catdir/description/cam032/2003055129.html.

Blasius, J., & Schmitz, A. (2013). The empirical construction of Bourdieu's social space. In M. Greenacre & J. Blasius (Eds.), *The visualization and verbalization of data* (pp. 205–222). London: Chapman & Hall.

Blau, P. M. (1977). *Inequality and heterogeneity: A primitive theory of social structure* (1st ed.). New York: Free Press.

Blau, P. M., Beeker, C., & Fitzpatrick, K. M. (1984). Intersecting social affiliations and intermarriage. *Social Forces, 62*(3), 585–606.

Blossfeld, H.-P. (1995a). Changes in the process of family formation and women's growing economic independence: A comparison of nine countries. In H.-P. Blossfeld (Ed.), *The new role of women: Family formation in modern societies* (pp. 3–32). Boulder: Westview Press.

Blossfeld, H.-P. (Ed.). (1995b). *The new role of women: Family formation in modern societies*. Boulder: Westview Press.

Blossfeld, H.-P. (2009). Educational assortative marriage in comparative perspective. *Annual Review of Sociology, 35*, 513–530.

Blossfeld, H.-P., & Drobnic, S. (2001). Theoretical perspectives on couples' careers. In H.-P. Blossfeld & S. Drobnic (Eds.), *Careers of couples in contemporary societies. From male breadwinner to dual earner families* (pp. 16–50). New York: Oxford University Press.

Blossfeld, H.-P., & Timm, A. (1997). *Das Bildungssystem als Heiratsmarkt: Eine Längsschnittanalyse der Wahl von Heiratspartnern im Lebenslauf* (Sonderforschungsbereich 186, Vol. 43). Bremen: University of Bremen.

Blossfeld, H.-P., & Timm, A. (2003). *Who marries whom? Educational systems as marriage markets in modern societies* (European studies of population, Vol. 12). Dordrecht: Kluwer.

Bourdieu, P. (1977). *Outline of a theory of practice* (Cambridge studies in social anthropology, Vol. 16). Cambridge: Cambridge University Press.

Bourdieu, P. (1989). Social space and symbolic power. *Sociological Theory, 7*(1), 14–25.

Bourdieu, P. (1990). *The logic of practice*. Cambridge/Oxford: Polity Press/B. Blackwell.

Bourdieu, P., & Wacquant, L. J. D. (1992). *An invitation to reflexive sociology*. Chicago: Polity Press.

Caspi, A., & Gorsky, P. (2006). Online deception: Prevalence, motivation, and emotion. *Cyberpsychology & Behavior, 9*(1), 54–59.

Durkheim, E. (1964). *The division of labor in society*. New York: The Free Press.

Ellison, N., Heino, R., & Gibbs, J. (2006). Managing impressions online: Self-presentation processes in the online dating environment. *Journal of Computer – Mediated Communication, 11*(2), 415–441.

Finkel, E. J., Eastwick, P. W., Karney, B. R., Reis, H. T., & Sprecher, S. (2012). Online dating: A critical analysis from the perspective of psychological science. *Psychological Science in the Public Interest, 13*(1), 3–66.

Fiore, A. T., & Donath, J. S. (2005). Homophily in online dating: When do you like someone like yourself? In G. van der Veer (Ed.), *CHI '05. Extended abstracts on human factors in computing systems* (pp. 1371–1374). New York: ACM.

Fiore, A., Taylor L. S., Zhong, X., Mendelsohn G. A., & Cheshire C. (2010). Who is right and who writes: People, profiles, contacts, and replies in online dating. *Proceedings of the Annual Hawaii International Conference on System Sciences, 43*, 1–10.

Hakim, C. (2011). *Erotic capital: The power of attraction in the bedroom and the boardroom*. New York: Basic Books.

Hancock, J. T., Thoma, C., & Ellison, N. (2007). The truth about lying in online dating profiles. *Proceedings of the ACM Conference on Human Factors in Computing Systems*, 449–452.
Hertog, E. (2012). *Hedged bets: Preferences for future marriage partners' earning power in contemporary Japan*. Unpublished working paper.
Hitsch, G. J., Hortaçsu, A., & Ariely, D. (2010a). What makes you click?—Mate preferences in online dating. *Quantitative Marketing and Economics, 8*(4), 393–427.
Hitsch, G. J., Hortaçsu, A., & Ariely, D. (2010b). Matching and sorting in online dating. *The American Economic Review, 100*(1), 130–163.
Hogan, B., Li, N., & Dutton, W. H. (2011). *A global shift in the social relationships of networked individuals: Meeting and dating online comes of age*. Paper of the "Me, My Spouse and the Internet" project. Retrieved from http://blogs.oii.ox.ac.uk/couples/.
Illouz, E. (2007). *Cold intimacies: The making of emotional capitalism* (1st ed.). Cambridge: Polity.
Illouz, E., & Finkelmann, S. (2009). An odd and inseparable couple: Emotion and rationality in partner selection. *Theory and Society, 38*(4), 401–422.
Kalmijn, M. (1991). Status homogamy in the United States. *American Journal of Sociology, 97*(2), 496–523.
Kalmijn, M. (1994). Assortative mating by cultural and economic occupational status. *American Journal of Sociology, 100*(2), 422–452.
Kalmijn, M. (1998). Intermarriage and homogamy: Causes, patterns, trends. *Annual Review of Sociology, 24*, 395–421.
Kalmijn, M., & Flap, H. (2001). Assortative meeting and mating: Unintended consequences of organized settings for partner choices. *Social Forces, 79*(4), 1289–1312.
Lee, S. (2008). *Preferences and choice constraints in marital sorting: Evidence from Korea*. Working Paper.
Lin, K.-H., & Lundquist, J. (2013). Mate selection in cyberspace: The intersection of race, gender, and education. *American Journal of Sociology, 119*(1), 183–215.
Mare, R. D. (1991). Five decades of educational assortative mating. *American Sociological Review, 56*(1), 15–32.
McPherson, M. (1983). Ecology of affiliation. *American Sociological Review, 48*, 519–532.
Münch, R. (1987). *Theory of action: Towards a new synthesis going beyond parsons*. London: Routledge & Kegan Paul.
Oppenheimer, V. K. (1988). A theory of marriage timing. *American Journal of Sociology, 94*(3), 563–591.
Parsons, T. (1937). *The structure of social action*. New York: Free Press.
Potarca, G., & Mills, M. (2013). *Racial homophily and exclusion in online dating preferences: A cross-national comparison*. Unpublished working paper.
Roscoe, P., & Chillas, S. (2014). The state of affairs: Critical performativity and the online dating industry. *Organization, 21*(6), 797–820.
Rosenfeld, M. J., & Thomas, R. J. (2012). Searching for a mate: The rise of the internet as a social intermediary. *American Sociological Review, 77*(4), 523–547.
Schmitz, A. (2009). Virtuelle Zwischengeschlechtlichkeit im Kontext relationaler Methodologie. Überlegungen zu einer Soziologie der digitalen Partnerwahl. In H.-G. Soeffner (Ed.), *Unsichere Zeiten. Herausforderungen gesellschaftlicher Transformationen; Verhandlungen des 34. Kongresses der Deutschen Gesellschaft für Soziologie in Jena 2008*. Wiesbaden: VS Verlag.
Schmitz, A., Sachse-Thürer, S., Zillmann, D., & Blossfeld, H.-P. (2011). Myths and facts about online mate choice. Contemporary beliefs and empirical findings. *Zeitschrift für Familienforschung, 23*(3), 358–381.
Schmitz, A., Witte, D., & Gengnagel, V. (2016). Pluralizing field analysis: Toward a relational understanding of the field of power. *Social Science Information/Information sur les sciences sociales* (forthcoming).
Schwartz, C. R. (2013). Trends and variation in assortative mating: Causes and consequences. Annual Review of Sociology, 39, 451–470.
Skopek, J. (2011). *Partnerwahl im Internet: Eine quantitative Analyse von Strukturen und Prozessen der Online-Partnersuche*. Wiesbaden: VS Verlag.

References

Skopek, J., Schmitz, A., & Blossfeld, H.-P. (2011a). The gendered dynamics of age preferences – Empirical evidence from online dating. *Zeitschrift für Familienforschung, 23*(3), 267–290.

Skopek, J., Schulz, F., & Blossfeld, H.-P. (2011b). Who contacts whom? Educational homophily in online mate selection. *European Sociological Review, 27*(2), 180–195.

Skrondal, A., & Rabe-Hesketh, S. (2004). *Generalized latent variable modeling: Multilevel, longitudinal, and structural equation models* (Interdisciplinary statistics series). Boca Raton: Chapman & Hall/CRC. Retrieved from http://www.loc.gov/catdir/enhancements/fy0646/2004042808-d.html.

Wetzel, D. J. (2013). *Soziologie des Wettbewerbs. Eine kultur- und wirtschaftssoziologische Analyse der Marktgesellschaft*. Wiesbaden: VS Verlag.

Whitty, M. T. (2008). Liberating or debilitating? An examination of romantic relationships, sexual relationships and friendships on the net. *Computers in Human Behavior, 24*(5), 1837–1850.

Zillmann, D. (2016). *Von kleinen Lügen und kurzen Beinen. Selbstdarstellung bei der Partnersuche im Internet.* [About little lies and small legs. Self-Presentation in Online Dating.] Wiesbaden: VS Verlag (forthcoming).

Zillmann, D., Schmitz, A., & Blossfeld, H.-P. (2011). Lügner haben kurze Beine. Zum Zusammenhang unwahrer Selbstdarstellung und partnerschaftlicher Chancen im Online-Dating. *Zeitschrift für Familienforschung, 23*(3), 291–318.

Zillmann, D., Schmitz, A., Skopek, J., & Blossfeld, H.-P. (2013). Survey topic and unit nonresponse. Evidence from an online survey on mating. *Quality and Quantity, 48*(4), 2069–2088.

Žižek, S. (2010). Time of the monsters. A call to radicalness. *Le Monde diplomatique* 12.10.2010.

Chapter 2
Online Dating – A Meeting Point for the Modern Individual and Traditional Individualism

In the public discourse, online dating is often seen as a unique phenomenon, distinctly different from traditional or 'normal' ways of finding one's partner. Whereas many users worldwide embed online dating into their everyday lives quite naturally, the field of mass media in particular still treats it as a peculiar subject. In the following section, the online dating phenomenon will first be embedded within a historical context. In the context of different long-term societal developments, online dating may be well received as a logical consequence of modernity rather than as an anomaly or singularity. Subsequently, the basic principles of online dating and its societal prevalence will be discussed. In the next step, societal diagnoses of online dating, ranging from euphoric to dysphoric reactions, will be outlined. Finally, research will be reviewed that analyzes processes on online dating platforms, and it will be shown that models of individual (rational) choice play a dominant role in empirical research.

Online Dating as Manifestation of Modernity

Human mating processes have always been in the focus of sociological inquiry, variously described as a core mechanism of the reproduction of social position (Weber 1968), status differentiation (Blau 1964: 127), or class structure (Bourdieu 1983: 188). There is a broad consent that in the premodernity, "connubium and social commercium" (Weber 1968: 1400) between men and women was the result of structural forces predicated on social status, family, religion, and ethnicity (Goldstein and Harknett 2006; Kalmijn 1994; Mare 1991), whereas the modernization of the Western world has largely eroded these traditional structures.

The term 'modernization' comprises, among other concepts, such analytically diverse societal (occidental) developments as 'individualization' (Simmel 2008; Durkheim 1973: 153 ff.), 'rationalization' (Weber 1968), 'commercialization' (Marx and Engels 1848), or 'technologization' (e.g. Postman 1992; Latour 1987). In the context of human mating, 'modernization' can be interpreted as implying multiple processes of social differentiation, reshaping mating processes away from the influence of social origin in favor of individual freedom of choice (see Weber 1947; Simmel 1890; Luhmann 1995; Beck 1992). The process of 'individualization' involves the dissolution of traditional relationships (Durkheim 1992: 162ff.; Giddens 1992: 30). In this process, the actors' scope and necessity for personal decision-making increases, as does the pressure to self-reflexively develop an individual identity and working on new modes of social embedding (Giddens 1991: 258, Beck 1992: 128). Eventually, individualization results in the reorganization of the modern subject in such a way that it feels compelled to seek responsibility in itself, and thus to continually optimize itself according to societal standards (Elias 1997: 119; Foucault 1978, 104ff.; Münch 1991: 31ff.). Rationalization, from the perspective of an individual, is on the one hand characterized by the increasingly instrumental rationality of human agency (Giddens 1991: 52ff.), and on the other hand by an increasing belief in the controllability of the world (Weber 2003, cp. Habermas 1981: 126ff.). As a consequence, everyday practices within the occidental sphere became subject to the dictates of a cost-benefit ratio, turning rational decisions into typical phenomena of "reflexive modernity" (Beck et al. 2004). As a consequence of increased freedom of choice, however, the modern subject became spoilt for choice. The process of rationalization is accompanied by societal commercialization, 'marketization', and 'commodification'. These terms describe the ongoing transformation of "everything, moral or physical" which is "brought to the market", eventually including "the very things which till then had been communicated, but never exchanged; given but, never sold; acquired, but never bought" such as "virtue, love, conviction, knowledge, and conscience, etc." (Marx and Engels 1976: 113). The feelings of modern man (and thereby himself) have become commodified goods, and relinquish their inherent logics in favor of ever advancing market principles.

The institutionalization of technology represents another element of long-term societal diagnoses, distinct from the instrumental rationality of the individual subjects. 'Technologization', as an element of rationalization, can be thought of as the mechanization of everyday life (Degele 2002: 80), as the computerization (Kling 1996) of agency being governed by technology, and finally as the processes of 'algorithmization' and 'digitalization' (Joas 2007: 428; Robinson and Halle 2002: 359ff.). Today, the modern subject can utilize technology to participate in a vast variety of cultural and economic contexts, including the initiation and continuation of social relationships. At the same time, however, the subject becomes used to these possibilities, and by doing so becomes dependent on the digital conditions of its life and eventually transformed by the digital.

Only superficially opposed to these developments is the simultaneous rise in importance – starting during the Enlightenment – of the romantic ideal of love, as described in sociological accounts of human society (e.g. Luhmann 1987). Luhmann conceptualizes *love* as a specific code which accompanies the differentiation of societal sub-systems and individuality as a modern form of communication (Luhmann 1987). The importance of love as part of the process of rationalization grew over time. Weber regarded this process as providing the individual with a sphere of irrationality that enabled an escape from both "the cold skeleton hands of rational orders [and] from the banality of everyday routine" (Weber 1946: 347). Simmel seems to agree by saying "the more individuated life is, the more individual is love" (cp. Bertilsonn 1986: 24). Giddens (1992) and Beck-Gernsheim and Beck (2002) suggest that a process of 'romanticization' inherent to individualization has intensified over the course of the 20st century. Evidently, the modern Western world could never be reasonably described by a categorical opposition of rationality and romantic idealism, as these principles have always been intertwined and co-dependent.

The development of human mating from strong embeddedness within one's closest social circles towards a marketization of love has not begun with the rise of dating platforms. As Bozon and Heran (1989) show, foci of mating developed systematically away from family and neighborhood towards explicit partner markets such as discotheques or balls from the 50s to the 90s. The same applies to the increasing mediability (in its twofold sense) of modern relationship formation. As Giddens (1992) argues, one consequence of modernization processes is that all social relations became increasingly detached from geographical places. In view of these general developments, the phenomenon of online partnership formation can be interpreted as the provisional culmination of different long-term developments inherent to late Western modernity. In fact, the digital dating market – as a technological tool for the rational choice of the subject with particular romantic goals – may be seen as clearly signifying the imperatives and forces of modern Western society.

Although online dating was made for the distribution of romantic luck and togetherness, online dating platforms are designed for the very purpose of efficient partner choice. Rationality also manifests itself in the rhetoric of empowerment, such as the exhortation to invest in one's "erotic capital" (Hakim 2011) in dating markets. The modern occident can be characterized by a particular entanglement of "hyper-rationality" and "hyper-emotionality", "intense emotional rationality" and "rational emotionality" (Illouz and Finkelmann 2009: 417). The online partner market subsists on this modern syndrome as it seems to offer not only modern promises of romantic "salvation" (Weber 1968: 537; Simmel 1985: 177), but at the same time a more efficient use of time and money for the rational individual. Thus, online dating can be interpreted as a striking modern example of the ongoing "commodification of romance and the romanticization of commodities" (Illouz 1997: 26) and "how the boundaries between the social spheres of love and the market are blurred" (Dröge and Voirol 2011: 353) in our times.[1] Up to this point, we assert that the rationalist market environment provided by digital dating markets not only "contributes to the rationalisation (and commodification) of choosing potential partners" (Žakelj

---

[1] However, the (theoretical) challenge that online daters may be confronted with in their practices of using a dating site – the contradictions between romantic ideals and rational calculation – is not a unique feature of online dating, but has been diagnosed by Habermas as early as 1956 for modern mating in general.

et al. 2015), it also *seems to depend on* these very societal and technical conditions. It is no coincidence that we will meet the issues of rationality and individual choice again when looking at the architecture and design from the use's viewpoint, when reflecting on the economic relevance, and, ultimately, when examining the ways online dating is usually approached by social scientists today.

The Societal Prevalence of Online Dating

Today, the increasing social relevance of online dating may be illustrated by our own subjective experience, such as the growing number of users in our own social circles, indicating the declining stigma surrounding online dating. Another indicator is given by the amount and intensity of advertising campaigns, which are inescapable on (German) TV, radio, and websites. Also, the relentless media coverage dedicated to this topic (with a particular upturn in springtime) can hardly be ignored. One might also rely on structural indicators suggesting that using dating sites is a logical consequence of societal conditions. For example, in Germany in 2014, 37.2% of all households were single-person households (Federal Statistical Office of Germany), and estimates suggest that 76% of the adult population are internet users (ARD-ZDF-Online-Study 2012). These societal conditions make the usage of online dating a 'plausible' practice. Reliable indicators on the actual usage of dating sites, in contrast, are more difficult to find. The primary reason is that, as online dating is institutionalized by private corporations, no official data on actual usage, diffusion, and market volume is available. Even if data of this delicate nature is communicated, there is good reason to suspect that the disclosure is part of a marketing strategy. Not least, a dating platform subsists on a high degree of fluctuation, making it difficult to determine the exact number of active customers in contrast to inactive members. In terms of economic revenue, a private research group collected comprehensive data on the German dating market and indicated a growth in revenue from €21.5 Million in 2003 to €202.8 Million in 2011 (Moucha et al. 2012). For the United States, estimations of revenue of $2 Billion (Yoder 2014) are found, and of $4 billion for the worldwide dating industry (cp. Schmitz and Zillmann 2016). With regard to survey research, Rosenfeld and Thomas (2012) can show that, in the US, online dating was the dating market with the biggest increase. Schmitz et al. (2011) show on the basis of a German offline survey[2] that about 9% of all couples consisting of people born between 1990 and 1994 report having met their partner online.[3]

---

[2] The data used stems from the PAIRFAM survey. This survey is being coordinated by Bernhard Nauck, Johannes Huinink, Josef Brüderl, and Sabine Walper (see Huinink, Brüderl, Nauck, Walper, Castiglioni, and Feldhaus 2010). The panel is receiving long-term funding from the German Research Foundation (DFG).

[3] One should note that the distinction between "online" and "offline" dating is only an analytical one and may become increasingly blurred due to the practice of actors using social networking sites. Users may encounter a potential mate offline and use a social network as an opportunity for

Using a sample of German registry offices, Karch et al. (2013: 2) estimate that 16.4 % of all marriages were found online. The German case assessed in this work stands out, as Hogan et al. (2011: 14) found that Germany had the highest percentage (29 %) of couples that met online, when compared to other European countries and Japan.[4] At least, such research can corroborate the idea that traditional dating markets are losing their relative importance in Western societies with the rise of online dating.

Some early research concerns the societal dimension of the spread of online dating (Valkenburg and Peter 2007; Sautter et al. 2010; Skopek 2011) for the United States, Canada, and Germany respectively. Research could show that almost all strata of the societies in question are represented on non-specialized online dating platforms, with a disproportionate amount of highly educated women and less-educated men. For the sociological assessment of dating platforms, it is of decisive interest that social web platforms as addressed in this work – although not ultimately representative for the offline population – comprise all social strata of (German) society (Skopek 2011; Zillmann 2016).

Basic Principles of Online Dating

Two important forms of digital dating and associated different business models exist in the online dating market (cp. Schmitz 2014; Schmitz and Zillmann 2016). The first model is characterized by a matchmaking system. Here, in order to utilize the dating platform, users have to provide personal information in a series of categories and enter this information into a standardized registration questionnaire. This information consists, on the one hand, of socio-demographic attributes like age, gender, religion, lifestyle, education, and career, and on the other hand of physical characteristics such as height, weight, and hair and eye color. Often, a particular emphasis is put on 'psychological' indicators, such as more or less scientific personality traits. Additionally, profile categories cover information such as whether a user smokes, has children, or has previously been married. Finally, users are able to compose texts of their own. These texts might directly address potential partners, or further describe themselves and the characteristics they are looking for – or perhaps wish to avoid – in a partner. As part of the registration process he or she also provides the desired characteristics of a potential mate (e.g. geographic proximity, minimal requirements of age and education, etc.). This information is then presented in the user's profile, a visual overview for other users. In the fundamental

---

a second contact, etc. Accordingly, one can assume that a certain number of respondents will interpret sites such as Facebook as a natural feature of their everyday friendship network.

[4] Due to selective participation in online surveys, especially in this context (Zillmann et al. 2013), the estimate of 29 % should be seen more as an indicator for a maximum proportion, and less as a true population parameter, although other analyses also point towards an increase in couple formation via the internet.

integrative process of the matchmaking business model, using on the information thus collected, a matching algorithm calculates a factor based on which a list of potentially suitable partners will be suggested. The guiding principle behind this matching factor is the similarity of the two participants – usually the greater the better – taking stated or assumed dissimilarities into consideration (e.g. men are not matched with men unless otherwise specified).

A second business model is called simply "online dating", strongly emphasizing the individual search for a potential partner on one's own initiative. Users of a dating site can participate actively and passively on the platform. This comprises browsing for subjectively relevant parameters and contacting other users via short messages or a chat system and selecting promising candidates out of the abundance of contact requests. In the case of a successful contact, messages are exchanged until the interaction ends or intensifies in the form of a change of communication medium, be this email, telephone, or face-to-face encounters. Figure 2.1 gives an idealized overview of the interaction process on a dating platform.

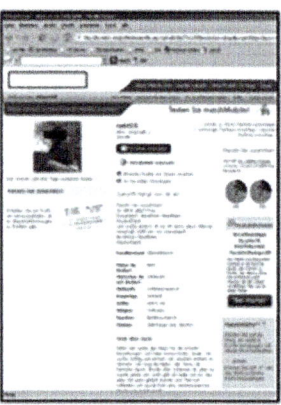

- Registration
- Self-portrayal
- Search
- Contact
- Interaction
- Termination or Stabilization

Fig. 2.1 Idealized process of dating site usage

An ideal-typical interaction process would develop in the following manner: Further exchange of messages – Chat within the platform – Chat outside of the platform (e.g. Skype, Facebook etc.) – Exchange of email address – Exchange of telephone number – Face-to-face meeting – Offline continuation or termination of interaction.

Alongside these two kinds of business models, there exist numerous mixed forms, depending on the characteristics of the particular model in question. Also, one can distinguish between dating platforms which are open to all social strata and those which specialize in market segments such as military dating, religious dating, homosexual dating, dating for older people, etc. A particular transformation of dating has emerged from the increased diffusion of mobile phones, paving the way for genuine 'mobile dating apps', as well as for mixed business models combining online dating and mobile dating (cp. Schmitz and Zillmann 2016). Due to the more general sociological focus of this work, however, a dating platform will be analyzed that comprises (potentially) all the social strata of the German (heterosexual) population and builds on the principle of free choice.

Online Dating Between Euphoria and Dysphoria

Depending on their ideological and theoretical backgrounds, both social scientists and cultural commentators tend to regard the online dating phenomenon as either beneficial or detrimental, notably regarding the particular ideological and normative status assigned to the concepts 'choice' and 'market'.

One perspective frequently encountered both in academia and the media is genuinely positive and favorable regarding digital dating. In a comprehensive review, Finkel et al. (2012: 49) consider "the emergence and popularity of online dating" to be "positive developments" and conclude "that harnessing the power of the Internet is a promising means of improving societal levels of romantic well-being". This assessment is assumed to be especially applicable to singles. In a similar vein, Whitty (2008: 1837) argues that "cyberspace provides a unique environment for people to experience and learn about relationships and sexuality". Also applying a positive connotation, Wetzel (2012: 203) states that "idealization, projection and imagination" are "more encouraged than made impossible" by the technical conditions of online dating. Kauffmann (2011) sees an absence of normative restrictions in dating platforms while Scharlott and Christ (1995: 191) emphasize the diminished relevance of gender norms in online dating as "the safety and anonymity the system offered" helps users to "break free from traditional sex role norms". Also, Cooper and Sportolari (1997: 7) state that online dating "allows men and women more freedom to deviate from typically constraining gender roles that are often automatically activated in face-to-face interactions". Hakim (2013) goes a step further in seeing online dating platforms as a means for women to invest in their 'erotic capital' for the enhancement of their bargaining power, and thus as a means for women's emancipation in general.

The opposing perspective within academia and the mass media seizes upon the narrative of modernization and presents itself as a critical reception of online dating, emphasizing its negative effects on the significance of love (Ben-Ze'ev 2004; Lawson and Leck 2006), society (Caplan 2003; Ellison et al. 2009), and the individual (Yurchisin et al. 2005; Joinson 2004). Its proponents approach online dating primarily in terms of its consequences for the modern individual, and diagnose an emerging "emotional capitalism" (Illouz 2007: 5) promoted by online dating, which some regard as the digital "passion killer par excellence" (Žižek 2010). Frequently, couple formation online is taken as further evidence for the commercialization of love and the self in our modern consumer society (Dröge and Voirol 2011). Other authors go on to suggest that online dating may be causing an overall disintegrative tendency on the societal level, both as a consequence of neglecting offline social contacts and of the involved risk of internet addiction (cp. Wetzel 2012: 200).

Analytical Perspectives of Digital Mating

Alongside critical or optimistic judgments, current researchers try to apply a value-free perspective to online dating processes. A first issue of explicit partner market research is the analysis of processes on dating platforms themselves. Three research trends can be identified in this context (see also Schmitz and Zillmann 2016): The first approach emphasizes the sui generis characteristics of finding a mate online and the specifics of the digital partner market. The second approach examines online dating within the framework of an observational methodology, assuming the potential for offline population inference. The third approach deals with the consequences of online dating in terms of the impact on society, such as the possible reproduction or resolution of class structure.

The *first* research approach takes into account more explicitly the way in which the digital partner market differs from traditional contexts by focusing on the conditions of computer-mediated communication in a market-like encounter. The risk of deception and fraud was one of the first issues that found consideration in research literature (Donath 1999). The highly computerized forms of communication give users increased control over their self-presentation, reducing the necessity for genuinely truthful information, be it in their profiles or in personal messages. This leads to an increased risk of falling victim to deception, for example in responding to a user profile that does not correspond to reality. Hancock et al. (2007) and Toma et al. (2008) examine the significance of deception in online dating, using cross-validation of profile data and survey data from a self-selected sample. They come to the conclusion that deceptive profile data is extremely common, but that the actual discrepancies from users' true characteristics are, in most cases, relatively minor.

Ellison et al. (2006) discuss the specific communicative situation on a particular dating site, and emphasize the fact that, while users are motivated to present themselves as attractively as possible, they simultaneously have to make a realistic, believable impression. By integrating web surveys and group discussion, Caspi and Gorsky (2006: 54) try to explain the subjective motivations for deceptive practices. They show that "the most common motivations to deceive online were 'play' on the one hand and privacy concerns on the other", and that "most people felt a sense of enjoyment while engaging in online deception".

Using survey data, Gibbs et al. (2006: 152) analyze perceived "online dating success" and derive "four dimensions of self-disclosure", namely honesty, amount, intent, and valence. They show that honesty has a negative effect on success in online dating (Gibbs et al. 2006: 170). Gibbs et al. (2006) elaborate further on the increased significance of strategic self-presentation, and analyze perceived success in online dating via a telephone survey. Elements that increased users' own perception of their success included the amount of self-disclosure, the level of intent behind the self-disclosure, and the extent to which disclosed information displayed positive characteristics. Honesty, on the other hand, was not instrumental in increasing users' subjective perception of their success or potential success.

In sum, in this field of research, strategic aspects of presenting oneself online and interacting with potential partners are assessed and conceptualized as a consequence of either the social and technological characteristics of online dating or the psychic traits of the users. Thus, 'structure' here is seen the medium faced by the individual external to him or her.

Some explicit partner market researchers applying the *second* approach put particular emphasis on the new possibilities the internet offers when it comes to surveying and analyzing developing interactional relationships. The first to use so-called "web-generated process data" (Schmitz 2009) seems to have been Fiore (2004). He was able to show that the number of contact requests sent in online dating was significantly dependent on the number of contacts received. Furthermore, his research, theoretically grounded in communication sciences, revealed that men are contacted depending on their age, level of education, and attractiveness, while women are contacted subject to their attractiveness, their figure, and the presence of a profile photograph. Hitsch et al. (2010) and Lee (2008) also employ web-based process data from a dating website in their work, and discuss the phenomenon of assortative couple formation. These authors base their explanation of assortative couple formation on the economic theory of preference, and on the assumed existence of a general, stable utility function. Working from revealed contact patterns, they derive a model of preferences for a potential partner's attributes. Hitsch et al. (2010) apply their preference models to simulate couple formation, and then compare these simulations with empirically observed assortative mating on the dating site they analyze. The key findings of their paper are that the economic Gale-Shapley algorithm predicts observed couples fairly accurately, and that online dating displays market efficiency close to the theoretically postulated reference value. Lee's work shows that, dependent on gender, not only differing attributes but, in particular, similar attributes are subject to preference. Following statistical preference estimates, she proceeds to simulate changes in the structures of opportunity using the same algorithm as Hitsch et al. (2010). The main conclusion is the fact that not only individual preferences but also restrictions in the structures of opportunity can be significant for the formation of patterns of assortative couple formation, even offline. In a different article, however, Hitsch et al. (2010) come to the conclusion that explaining assortative couple formation requires no such further analysis of restrictions, relying instead on the explanatory power of mating preferences alone.

Applying a rationalist framework, Skopek et al. (2011b: 1) – using similar data from a German dating site, and modeling education-based contact patterns – conclude "that educational homophily is the dominant mechanism in online mate choice". Using the same data, it could also be shown that cultural capital (Schmitz 2012) and age (Skopek et al. 2011a) seem to be of utmost importance for the emergence of couples. Alterovitz and Mendelsohn (2013) focus on age preferences of online-daters, whereas Hertog (2012) emphasizes income preferences of online-daters in Japan, while Yancey and Emerson (2014) focus on the relevance of height preferences. Potarca and Mills (2013: 25) focus on ethnic mating preferences using profile data and show for nine European countries that "partner preferences in online dating continue to be racially determined to a large extent". For the U.S.A.,

Lin and Lundquist (2013) show that white users with a college degree are more likely to contact and to respond to white daters with lower education than to black persons with a college degree. A consequence of these contact patterns is the emergence of racial hierarchies. For the same country, Anderson et al. (2014) show that same-race preferences can be observed over different political and ideological groups, leading to racial segregation mediated by online dating. Recently, Huber and Mahotra (2013) assessed political homophily in online dating, and Jackson et al. (2015) emphasized the religious dimension of homophily in the digital partner market. Irrespective of the particular subject, preference-guided choice acts are clearly in the focus of online dating research, highlighting the relevance of homophily for the emergence of homogenous couples. 'Structure' in this research is essentially seen as something that is controlled for by design (as the users enter the dating platform as separated individuals) and as controllable (as the opportunity sets which a user faces can be observed and taken into account in statistical analysis).

The *third*, yet least well-advanced, focus of explicit partner market research refers to the aggregated consequences of online dating. Wang and Lu (2007: 12) assume that, on the internet, "anyone could come, leave, or express themselves in a manner that does not have to heed even the slightest principle of social decency." Maybe due to such impressions, Bühler-Illeva (2006) assumes there to be equalizing effects of dating markets. Schwarz (2013: 458) actually diagnoses a general "dominant view in studies of new technologies" which implies that the "internet promotes diversity" rather than "sameness because of increased contact with people from different backgrounds and the reduced influence of third parties". In contrast, as educational, racial, and age-related homogeneity of online contact patterns is the recurring finding, other positions assume that the patterns found in the offline world are simply transferred to the dating site. This explanatory scheme prompts some scientists to paint a picture of online dating as merely mirroring offline mechanisms of inequality. Overall, there is limited evidence regarding both the degree of the reproduction of social inequality due to online dating and the mechanisms involved. In any case, 'structure' here is seen as the offline social structure emerging from processes on the online dating site.

The Cult of the Individual 2.0

Research on online dating is doubtlessly subject to variations, be it of theoretical, conceptual, or methodological nature. However, diverse the research on finding a mate online may seem, a shared association can be identified. Even under circumstances of ideological, methodical, and theoretical opposition between the various approaches to online dating, the majority of researchers share a clear tendency toward a *generalizing, individualistic* perspective. This is true to some extent for societal diagnoses of online dating. The positive approach emphasizes the efficiency of the market and the potential of free choice for everyone (Stevenson and Wolfers 2007: 47), whereas the critical reception of online dating essentially emphasizes the influence of market-based digital dating on "the modern individual", even to the extent of positing a kind of "Internet self" (Illouz 2007: 81).

More so than in these approaches, the apodictic status of the rational individual with given partner preferences is prevalent in quantitative analyses on processes taking place on dating sites. This manifests itself in the structure and interpretation of the findings, such as online daters in general having generally high mating aspirations (Hitsch et al. 2010), that female users have a "stronger preference for income relative to physical attributes, such as facial attractiveness, height, or body mass index" (Hitsch et al. 2010: 413), that daters "use elaborate rational strategies to achieve their romantic desires" (Illouz and Finkelmann 2009: 416), or that they are "homophilious" (Schulz 2009; Lin and Lundquist 2013: 207). Blossfeld (2009: 526) comes to the conclusion that, in online dating, "individuals have a strong preference for partners with the same educational degree". Likewise, Rosenfeld and Thomas (2010: 5) diagnose an overall "predominance of individual preferences in internet dating".

The specific research context of online dating tends to suggest and legitimize an individualistic interpretation of the empirical findings. The idea of a structure external to the choosing actor may be seen as particularly plausible in the light of the modern narrative of romantic selection. With recourse to Giddens (1992), Chambers (2013: 44) argues, for example, that "in late modernity, intimacy is based on pleasure, autonomy and freedom from constraints." In most research on online dating it is emphasized that dating sites are „much less structured by objective barriers to access or institutional circumstances"than locations for meeting a partner „such as the education system or neighborhoods"(Schulz 2010: 228, o.t.). Hitsch et al. (2005: 9) state that "compared to traditional marriage markets, online dating is characterized by only small search frictions, and the resulting matches are therefore largely driven by preferences and the equilibrium mechanism that brings partners together" (cp. Fiore and Donath 2005; Lee 2008). Wang and Lu (2007:12) even assume that the "lack of spatial confinement makes the cyberspace a free market". Under the assumption that online dating sites are seen as less structured by conditions external to the subject, than in the offline world, the behavioral patterns observed and questionnaire items answered are mostly interpreted as (revealed or stated) preferential realizations. Also, rationality is a recurring explanatory scheme of mating processes online. Illouz states that "in modernity, choice – as a cognized and reflexive category – has become far more salient to the process of looking and finding an object of love" (Illouz 2012: 241). Strongly rejecting structure as an analytical concept, Schulz (2010: 228, o.t.) interprets his findings of educational similarity in first contacts to mean that "the rational intentions of the actors play a significant role for the emergence of the observable patterns of partner selection," and thus that "a structural explanation would be insufficient."

Overall, in the vast majority of research on online dating, structure is treated as an outcome of micro-level (homophilious) preference and (rational) choice acts based upon it. The theoretical basis is strongly dependent on a strictly individualized perspective on 'mate choice', leading to a strong emphasis on generalized individual preferences, strategies, expectations, outcomes, etc. 'Structure', in contrast, is reduced to opportunities, restrictions, norms, institutional settings, places, etc., and thus to entities, which are conceptualized as external to the individual. In consequence, the *differential* aspects of mating markets, mating preferences, and mating processes are not constitutive for most research on online dating, but play something of a secondary role.

This particular way of conceptualizing partner formation processes, starting from the analytical point of the actor who sees himself confronted with an external market structure, is not unique to the digital realm. In Chapter 4, the theoretical foundations for individualistic online dating research will be examined. First, however, the following chapter will show that online dating sites, when compared to other partner markets, do indeed represent an especially appropriate case for the analytical application of research committed to methodological individualism and theories of rational mate choice.

References

Alterovitz, S. S. R., & Mendelsohn, G. A. (2013). Relationship goals of middle-aged, young-old, and old-old internet daters: An analysis of online personal ads. *Journal of Aging Studies, 27*(2), 159–165.

Anderson, A., Goel, S., Huber, G., Malhotra, N., & Watts, D. J. (2014). Political ideology and racial preferences in online dating. *Sociological Science, 1*(1), 28–40.

ARD/ZDF-Onlinestudie. (2012). Retrieved from http://www.ard-zdf-onlinestudie.de/index.php?id=388.

Beck, U. (1992). *Risk society: Towards a new modernity. Theory, culture and society.* London: Sage.

Beck, U., & Beck-Gernsheim, E. (2002). *Individualization. Institutionalized individualism and its social and political consequences.* London: Sage.

Beck, U., Bonß, W., & Lau, C. (2004). Entgrenzung erzwingt Entscheidung: Was ist neu an der Theorie reflexiver Modernisierung? In U. Beck & C. Lau (Eds.), *Entgrenzung und Entscheidung: Was ist neu an der Theorie reflexiver Modernisierung?* (pp. 13–64). Frankfurt am Main: Suhrkamp.

Ben-Ze'ev, A. (2004). *Love online: Emotions on the internet.* Cambridge: Cambridge University Press. Retrieved from http://www.loc.gov/catdir/description/cam032/2003055129.html.

Bertilsonn, M. (1986). Love's labour lost? A sociological view. *Theory, Culture & Society, 3*(2), 19–35.

Blau, P. M. (1964). *Exchange and power in social life* (9th ed.). New York: Wiley.

Blossfeld, H.-P. (2009). Educational assortative marriage in comparative perspective. *Annual Review of Sociology, 35,* 513–530.

Blossfeld, H.-P., & Timm, A. (Eds.). (2003). *Who marries whom? Educational systems as marriage markets in modern societies.* Dordrecht: Kluwer.

Bourdieu, P. (1983). Ökonomisches Kapital, kulturelles Kapital, soziales Kapital. In R. Kreckel (Ed.), *Soziale Welt Sonderband: Vol. 2. Soziale Ungleichheiten* (pp. 183–198). Göttingen: Schwartz.

Bozon, M., & Heran, F. (1989). Finding a spouse: A survey of how French couples meet. *Population. An English Selection, 44*(1), 91–121.

Bühler-Illieva, E. (2006). *Einen Mausklick von mir entfernt. Auf der Suche nach Liebesbeziehungen im Internet.* Marburg: Tectum.

References

Caplan, S. E. (2003). Preference for online social interaction: A theory of problematic internet use and psychosocial well-being. *Communication Research, 30*(6), 625–648.

Caspi, A., & Gorsky, P. (2006). Online deception: Prevalence, motivation, and emotion. *Cyberpsychology & Behavior, 9*(1), 54–59.

Chambers, D. (2013). *Social media and personal relationships. Online intimacies and networked friendship.* Hampshire: Palgrave.

Cooper, A., & Sportolaria, L. (1997). Romance in Cyberspace: Understanding online attraction. *Journal of Sex Education and Therapy, 22*(1), Special Issue: Sexuality and the Internet, 7–14.

Corijn, M. (2003). Who marries whom in Flamish Belgium? In H.-P. Blossfeld & A. Timm (Eds.), *Who marries whom? Educational systems as marriage markets in modern societies* (pp. 37–55). Dordrecht: Kluwer.

Degele, N. (2002). *Einführung in die Techniksoziologie.* München: Fink.

Donath, J. S. (1999). Identity and deception in the virtual community. In M. A. Smith & P. Kollock (Eds.), *Communities in cyberspace* (pp. 29–59). London: Routledge.

Dröge, K., & Voirol, O. (2011). Online-dating: zwischen romantischer Liebe und ökonomischer Rationalität. *Zeitschrift für Familienforschung, 23*(3), 337–357.

Durkheim, E. (1973). *Emile Durkheim on morality and society.* Chicago: University of Chicago Press.

Durkheim, E. (1992). *Professional ethics and civic morals.* London: Routledge.

Elias, N. (1997). *Über den Prozess der Zivilisation. Soziogenetische und psychogenetische Untersuchungen: Erster Band: Wandlungen des Verhaltens in den weltlichen Oberschichten des Abendlandes* (Suhrkamp Taschenbuch Wissenschaft 159, 20th ed.). Frankfurt am Main: Suhrkamp.

Ellison, N., Heino, R., & Gibbs, J. (2006). Managing impressions online: Self-presentation processes in the online dating environment. *Journal of Computer – Mediated Communication, 11*(2), 415–441.

Ellison, N. B., Lampe, C., & Steinfield, C. (2009). Social network sites and society: Current trends and future possibilities. *Interactions, 16*(1), 6–9.

Federal Statistical Office of Germany. (2014). Pressemitteilung Nr. 185 vom 28.05.2014 https://www.destatis.de/DE/PresseService/Presse/Pressemitteilungen/2014/05/PD14_185_122.html.

Finkel, E. J., Eastwick, P. W., Karney, B. R., Reis, H. T., & Sprecher, S. (2012). Online dating: A critical analysis from the perspective of psychological science. *Psychological Science in the Public Interest, 13*(1), 3–66.

Fiore, A. (2004). *Romantic regressions: An analysis of behavior in online dating systems.* Doctoral dissertation, Institute of Technology, Massachusetts.

Fiore, A. T., & Donath, J. S. (2005). Homophily in online dating: When do you like someone like yourself? In G. van der Veer (Ed.), *CHI '05. Extended abstracts on human factors in computing systems* (pp. 1371–1374). New York: ACM.

Fiore, A., Taylor, L. S., Mendelsohn, G. A., & Hearst, M. (2008). Assessing attractiveness in online dating profiles. In Association for Computing Machinery (Ed.), *Proceedings of the SIGCHI conference on human factors in computing systems* (pp. 797–806). New York: ACM.

Foucault, M. (1978). *The history of sexuality volume I. An introduction [La Volonté de savoir].* New York: Random House.

Gibbs, J. L., Ellison, N. B., & Heino, R. B. (2006). Self-presentation in online personals: The role of anticipated future interaction, self-disclosure, and perceived success in internet dating. *Communication Research, 33*(2), 152–177.

Giddens, A. (1991). *Modernity and self-identity: Self and society in the late modern age.* Stanford, Calif: Stanford University Press.

Giddens, A. (1992). *The transformation of intimacy: Sexuality, love and eroticism in modern societies.* Cambridge: Polity.

Goldstein, J. R., & Harknett, K. (2006). Parenting across racial and class lines: Assortative mating patterns of new parents who are married, cohabiting, dating or no longer romantically involved. *Social Forces, 85*(1), 121–143.

Habermas, J. (1981). *Theorie des kommunikativen Handelns*. Suhrkamp: Frankfurt am Main.
Hakim, C. (2011). *Erotic capital: The power of attraction in the bedroom and the boardroom*. New York: Basic Books.
Hakim, C. (2013). *The new rules of marriage: Internet, playfairs, and erotic power*. London: Gibson Square.
Hancock, J. T., Thoma, C., & Ellison, N. (2007). The truth about lying in online dating profiles. *Proceedings of the ACM Conference on Human Factors in Computing Systems, 449*–452.
Hertog, E. (2012). *Hedged bets: Preferences for future marriage partners' earning power in contemporary Japan*. Unpublished working paper.
Hitsch, G. J., Hortaçsu, A., & Ariely, D. (2005). *What makes you click: An empirical analysis of online dating*. Retrieved from https://www.aeaweb.org/assa/2006/0106_0800_0502.pdf.
Hitsch, G. J., Hortaçsu, A., & Ariely, D. (2010). What makes you click?—Mate preferences in online dating. *Quantitative Marketing and Economics, 8*(4), 393–427.
Hogan, B., Li, N., & Dutton, W. H. (2011). *A global shift in the social relationships of networked individuals: Meeting and dating online comes of age*. Paper of the "Me, My Spouse and the Internet" project. Retrieved from http://blogs.oii.ox.ac.uk/couples/.
Huber, G., & Malhotra, N. (2013). *Dimensions of Political Homophily: Isolating Choice Homophily along Political Characteristics*. Working paper. Retrieved from http://huber.research.yale.edu/materials/38_paper.pd.
Illouz, E. (1997). *Consuming the romantic utopia: Love and the cultural contradictions of capitalism*. Berkeley: Univ of California Press.
Illouz, E. (2007). *Cold intimacies: The making of emotional capitalism* (1st ed.). Cambridge: Polity.
Illouz, E. (2012). *Why love hurts. A sociological explanation*. Cambridge: Polity Press.
Illouz, E., & Finkelmann, S. (2009). An odd and inseparable couple: Emotion and rationality in partner selection. *Theory and Society, 38*(4), 401–422.
Jackson, J., Halberstadt, J., Jong, J., & Felman, H. (2015). Perceived openness to experience accounts for religious homogamy. *Social Psychological and Personality Science, 6*, 630–638.
Joas, H. (2007). *Lehrbuch der Soziologie*. Campus: Frankfurt am Main.
Joinson, A. N. (2004). Self-esteem, interpersonal risk, and preference for e-mail to face-to-face communication. *Cyberpsychology & Behaviour, 7*(4), 472–478.
Kalmijn, M. (1994). Assortative mating by cultural and economic occupational status. *American Journal of Sociology, 100*(2), 422–452.
Karch, I., Schaefer, K., Pflitsch, D., & Wiechers, H. (2013). *Vom Dating zum Traualtar. Wie viele der Hochzeitspaare haben sich im Internet kennen gelernt?* Retrieved from http://www.singleboersen-vergleich.de/presse/studie-2013-vom-onlinedating-zum-traualtar.pdf.
Kauffmann, J. C. (2011). *Sex@amour: Wie das Internet unser Liebesleben verändert*. Konstanz: UVK.
Kling, R. (1996). *Computerization and controversy: Value conflicts and social choices* (2nd ed.). Boston: Academic.
Latour, B. (1987). *Science in action: How to follow scientists and engineers through society*. Cambridge: Harvard University Press.
Lawson, H. M., & Leck, K. (2006). Dynamics of internet dating. *Social Science Computer Review, 24*(2), 189–208.
Lee, S. (2008). *Preferences and choice constraints in marital sorting: Evidence from Korea*. Working Paper.
Lee, S. (2015). Effect of online dating on assortative mating: Evidence from South Korea. *Journal of Applied Econometrics, 30*(7) (forthcoming).
Lin, K.-H., & Lundquist, J. (2013). Mate selection in cyberspace: The intersection of race, gender, and education. *American Journal of Sociology, 119*(1), 183–215.
Luhmann, N. (1973). *Zweckbegriff und Systemrationalität*. Suhrkamp: Frankfurt am Main.
Luhmann, N. (1987). *Love as passion. The codification of intimacy* (J. Gaines, Trans.). Cambridge, MA: Harvard University Press.

Luhmann, N. (1995). *Social systems*. Stanford: Stanford University Press.
Luhmann, N. (1997). *Die Gesellschaft der Gesellschaft*. Suhrkamp: Frankfurt am Main.
Mare, R. D. (1991). Five decades of educational assortative mating. *American Sociological Review, 56*(1), 15–32.
Marx, K., & Engels, F. (1848). Manifesto of the communist party. In K. Marx, & F. Engels (1969, 1. ed.), *Selected works* (pp. 98–137). Moscow: Progress Publishers.
Marx, K., & Engels, F. (1976). *Collected works – Volume Six*. New York: International Publishers.
Moucha, P., Pflitsch, D., & Wiechers, H. (2012). *Der Online Dating Markt 2011–2012*. Retrieved from http://www.singleboersen-vergleich.de/presse/online-dating-markt-2011-2012-de.pdf.
Münch, R. (1991). *Dialektik der Kommunikationsgesellschaft*. Suhrkamp: Frankfurt am Main.
Postman, N. (1992). *Technopoly: The surrender of culture to technology*. New York: Vintage Books, Random House.
Potarca, G., & Mills, M. (2013). *Racial Homophily and exclusion in online dating preferences: A cross-national comparison*. Unpublished working paper.
Robinson, L., & Halle, D. (2002). Digitization, the internet, and the arts: eBay, Napster, SAG, and e-books. *Qualitative Sociology, 25*(3), 359–383.
Rosenfeld, M. J. (2010). *Meeting online: The rise of the internet as a social intermediary. draft*. Retrieved from http://web.stanford.edu/~mrosenfe/Rosenfeld_How_Couples_Meet_PAA_updated.pdf.
Rosenfeld, M. J., & Thomas, R. J. (2012). Searching for a mate: The rise of the internet as a social intermediary. *American Sociological Review, 77*(4), 523–547.
Sautter, J. M., Tippett, R. M., & Morgan, S. P. (2010). The social demography of internet dating in the United States. *Social Science Quarterly, 91*(2), 554–575.
Scharlott, B. W., & Christ, W. G. (1995). Overcoming relationship-initiation barriers: The impact of a computer-dating system on sex role, shyness, and appearance inhibitions. *Computers in Human Behavior, 11*(2), 191–204.
Schmitz, A. (2009). Virtuelle Zwischengeschlechtlichkeit im Kontext relationaler Methodologie. Überlegungen zu einer Soziologie der digitalen Partnerwahl. In H.-G. Soeffner (Ed.), *Unsichere Zeiten. Herausforderungen gesellschaftlicher Transformationen; Verhandlungen des 34. Kongresses der Deutschen Gesellschaft für Soziologie in Jena 2008*. Wiesbaden: VS Verlag.
Schmitz, A. (2012). Elective affinities 2.0? A bourdieusian approach to couple formation and the methodology of E-dating. *Social Science Research on the Internet (RESET), 1*(1), 175–202.
Schmitz, A. (2014). The online dating market: Theoretical and methodological considerations. *Economic Sociology The European Electronic Newsletter, 16*(1), 11–24.
Schmitz, A., & Zillmann, D. (2016). Online Dating as a social sciences research tool. In F. X. Olleros, & M. Zhegu (Eds.), *Research handbook of digital transformations*. Cheltenham: Edward Elgar (forthcoming).
Schmitz, A., Sachse-Thürer, S., Zillmann, D., & Blossfeld, H.-P. (2011). Myths and facts about online mate choice. Contemporary beliefs and empirical findings. *Zeitschrift für Familienforschung, 23*(3), 358–381.
Schulz, F. (2009). Bildungshomophilie im Onlinedating. In Deutsche Gesellschaft für Soziologie (Ed.), *Konferenzband der DGS zum Soziologentag in Jena*. DGS Tagung 2009, Jena.
Schulz, F. (2010). *Verbundene Lebensläufe: Partnerwahl und Arbeitsteilung zwischen neuen Ressourcenverhältnissen und traditionellen Geschlechterrollen*. Wiesbaden: VS Verlag.
Schulz, F., Skopek, J., & Blossfeld, H.-P. (2010). Partnerwahl als konsensuelle Entscheidung. Das Antwortverhalten bei Erstkontakten im Online-Dating. *Kölner Zeitschrift für Soziologie und Sozialpsychologie, 62*(3), 485–514.
Schwartz, C. R. (2013). Trends and variation in assortative mating: Causes and consequences. *Annual Review of Sociology, 39*, 451–470.
Simmel, G. (1890). *On social differentiation*. Leipzig: Duncker & Humblot.
Simmel, G. (1985). *Schriften Zur Philosophie und Soziologie der Geschlechter*. Suhrkamp: Frankfurt am Main.

Simmel, G. (2008). *Gesamtausgabe*. Suhrkamp: Frankfurt am Main.
Skopek, J. (2011). *Partnerwahl im Internet: Eine quantitative Analyse von Strukturen und Prozessen der Online-Partnersuche*. Wiesbaden: VS Verlag.
Skopek, J., Schmitz, A., & Blossfeld, H.-P. (2011a). The gendered dynamics of age preferences – Empirical evidence from online dating. *Zeitschrift für Familienforschung, 23*(3), 267–290.
Skopek, J., Schulz, F., & Blossfeld, H.-P. (2011b). Who contacts whom? Educational homophily in online mate selection. *European Sociological Review, 27*(2), 180–195.
Sritharan, R., Heilpern, K., Wilbur, C. J., & Gawronski, B. (2010). I think I like you: Spontaneous and deliberate evaluations of potential romantic partners in an online dating context. *European Journal of Social Psychology, 40*(6), 1062–1077.
Stevenson, B., & Wolfers, J. (2007). Marriage and divorce: Changes and their driving forces. *The Journal of Economic Perspectives, 21*(2), 27–52.
Toma, C. L., Hancock, J. T., & Ellison, N. B. (2008). Separating fact from fiction: An examination of deceptive self-presentation in online dating. *Personality and Social Psychology Bulletin, 34*(8), 1023–1036.
Valkenburg, P. M., & Peter, J. (2007). Who looks for casual dates on the internet? A test of the compensation and the recreation hypotheses. *New Media & Society, 9*(3), 455–474.
van Dijk, J., & Hacker, K. (2003). The digital divide as a complex and dynamic phenomenon. *The Information Society, 19*(4), 315–326.
Wang, H., & Lu, X. (2007). Cyberdating: Misinformation and (Dis)trust in online interaction. *Informing Science Journal, 10*, 1–15.
Weber, M. (1946). From *Max Weber: Essays in sociology*. New York: Oxford University Press.
Weber, M. (1947). *The theory of social and economic organization*. New York: Simon and Schuster.
Weber, M. (1968). *Economy and society: An outline of interpretive sociology*. New York: Bedminster Press.
Weber, M. (2003). *General economic history*. Mineola: Dover Publications.
Wetzel, D. (2012). Ich hab ihn…? Poststrukturalistische Zugänge zu Emotionen/Affekten bei der Online-Partnerwahl. In Deutsche Gesellschaft für Soziologie (Ed.), *Konferenzband der DGS zum Soziologentag in Jena*. DGS Tagung 2009.
Whitty, M. T. (2007). The art of selling one's self on an online dating site: The BAR approach. In M. T. Whitty, A. J. Baker, & J. A. Inman (Eds.), *Online matchmaking* (pp. 57–69). Basingstoke: Palgrave Macmillan.
Whitty, M. T. (2008). Liberating or debilitating? An examination of romantic relationships, sexual relationships and friendships on the Net. *Computers in Human Behavior, 24*(5), 1837–1850.
Yancey, G., & Emerson, M. O. (2014). Does height matter? An examination of height preferences in romantic coupling. *Journal of Family Issues*, forthcoming.
Yoder, S. (2014). *How Online Dating Became a $2 Billion Industry*. Fiscal Times, Retrieved from http://www.thefiscaltimes.com/Articles/2014/02/14/Valentines-Day-2014-How-Online-Dating-Became-2-Billion-Industry.
Yurchisin, J., Watchravesringkan, K., & McCabe, D. B. (2005). An exploration of identity re-creation in the context of internet dating. *Social Behavior and Personality: An International Journal, 33*(8), 735–750.
Žakelj, T., Kocon, D., Švab, A., & Kuhar, R. (2015). Internet dating as a project: The commodification and rationalisation of online dating. *Journal Družboslovne razprave, 78*, 7–24.
Zillmann, D. (2016). *Von kleinen Lügen und kurzen Beinen. Selbstdarstellung bei der Partnersuche im Internet* [About little lies and small legs. Self-Presentation in Online Dating]. Wiesbaden: VS Verlag (forthcoming).
Zillmann, D., Schmitz, A., Skopek, J., & Blossfeld, H.-P. (2013). Survey topic and unit nonresponse. Evidence from an online survey on mating. *Quality and Quantity, 48*(4), 2069–2088.
Žižek, S. (2010). Time of the Monsters. A call to radicalness. *Le Monde diplomatique* 12.10.2010.

Chapter 3
The Market Character of Online Dating

This chapter starts with an excursus on the meaning of the term 'partner market', due to the fact that there is little systematic conceptualization of either 'partner market' in empirical research, or of the basic term 'market' itself in sociology as a whole. Deriving a Weberian concept of the market as competition for exchange chances, a relational definition of the partner market will be developed. Based on this definition, and findings from research and qualitative interview material, it will be shown that online dating markets are not at all an exceptional phenomenon in the context of couple formation. It will be shown that dating site can be analytically located within a continuum alongside conventional partner markets such as night clubs, offline 'lonely hearts' ads and speed dating events. Online dating sites seem to be, in comparison to other contexts of interaction, strongly structured by market principles such as competition for partners, induction of conscious rational mate choice, and exchange logics. Thus, it will be argued that the 'real type' market of online dating can be seen as being especially close to an 'ideal-typical' partner market and, thus, as a paradigmatic textbook example for analyses in the tradition of individualistic mate choice.

What Is a Partner Market?

In the previous chapter, we argued that most research on dating platforms applies a rather narrow concept of structure, by pursuing an individualistic perspective of the user who chooses from extrinsic choice structures. This neglect of the analytical significance of structure in research on online dating particularly manifests in the universal – but ill-defined – application of the term 'partner market' (cp. Schmitz 2014).

Often, a dating platform is simply labeled as a 'market', and seen as the context where actors meet and interact. Yet, what do terms such as 'partner market' or 'marriage market' actually mean in theoretical terms? Surprisingly, this self-evident question is asked relatively rarely. 'Partner markets' are mostly interpreted as a theoretical matter-of-course, without the need for an exact theoretical conceptualization. Schwartz (2013: 464) argues that "the notion of the marriage market underlies most studies of assortative mating" but "the literature has not yet fully grappled with how to conceptualize and measure marriage markets". Usually, no explicit definitions are given and the usage of the term 'market' is essentially metaphorical. In most cases, the term 'partner market' refers to a confined field of social interactions (such as a university or a nightclub) in which mating goals are pursued to a finite degree. However, from a theoretical point of view, such implicit definitions are not satisfactory and, as we will see, not strictly conclusive for empirical work either.

If empirical sociology does not provide a satisfying and manageable operational definition, perhaps we should examine the origins of market terminology, the economic sciences. Equally surprisingly, economic literature also gives no definitive definition of what the terms 'market' and 'market value' mean. This definitional deficit is explicitly stated in *The New Palgrave Dictionary of Economics*: "the concept of the market [...] often goes undefined" (Hodgson 2010: 252).[1] If a 'market' is defined at all in the economic sciences, it is usually as an institution by which a certain good (for example housing, labor, vehicles, etc.) is exchanged between buyers and sellers, who establish prices of one or more commodities via their interactions. Another common definition uses the concept of the 'Walrasian auctioneer market', a theoretical construct that searches for equilibria of actors' preferences in a market with full information and perfect competition. Becker (1974: 300; cp. Chapter 4) postulates the existence of a marriage market, due to his observation that actors compete for the best mate. In a similar vein, rational choice proponent James Coleman (1990: 22; cp. Hodgson 2002: 253) uses the concept of market, as it seems clear to him that "marriage can be seen as taking place in a kind of market", involving men's and women's "barter" of "one commodity – himself or herself". Whereas such definitions might be reasonable within the logic of the economic sciences, they are unsatisfying both from the viewpoint of a sociological theory (of mating), and for empirical work. It is difficult to separate a 'partner market' theoretically from society as a whole due to the difficulty of defining the good being marketed; is the good companionship, a partner, one characteristic of a partner, or something else? This conceptual deficit can encourage *ad hoc* postulates such as the equalization of the components of an individual's mate value (e.g. education) with 'mate value', which may suggest the generalization of the determinants of success chances, preferences, strategies, etc.

---

[1] This remarkable theoretical deficiency has been recognized before, for example by Bourdieu (1997) and Rosenbaum (2000).

What Is a Partner Market?

Another conceptualization of markets in general can be found in the works of the early sociological classicists Max Weber and Georg Simmel.[2] As Weber puts it, a market

> may be said to exist wherever there is competition, even if only unilateral, for opportunities of exchange among a plurality of potential parties.[3]

Simmel gives a similar definition:

> At least three actors are necessary for a market to exist: at least one actor on one side of the market confronted with at least two actors on the other side, whose offers the first actor is able to compare with one another.[4]

These classical approaches to general markets highlight the fact that not only are the specific objects actually being bartered to be understood as the object of competition, but that there is competition for the chances of entering into an exchange at all. Thus, a 'mating market' can be characterized by an antecedent competition for attention (Schmitz 2009). This approach conceptualizes the market via non-realized exchange: The 'price' of an actor on the partner market is a function of actively and passively approved and rejected offers. A 'mate value' can therefore be defined as the relative chance for attention and exchange in a competitive environment with mating goals. Hence, it is not contingent identity elements (for example educational status, attractiveness, etc.) but relational bundles of traits which constitute an actor's exchange chances and, in total, the chance structure of the overall market.

According to Weber's well-known definition of power, we can then understand exchange chances in markets to be a function of power relations, whose origin might lie inside or outside the particular market itself.[5] This approach highlights the relevance of the sociological category of power structures in mating markets, a category that is neglected in traditional economic market conceptions (and sometimes even in empirical sociology). Emphasizing the importance of power relations in and for the market leads to an appreciation of the fact that a partner market should be understood as a *structure of chances*. These chances cannot be reduced to general prevailing traits, as a partner market implies no uniform exchange entity (in contrast to money in a financial market, for example). Chapter 5 will elaborate on a Bourdieusian conceptualization for systematically relating the exchange chances of the partner market to a theoretical concept of society. The methods chapter (Chapter 6) of this work will illustrate the statistical implications for modeling a mate value following the definition proposed here.

---

[2] Of course, there are many alternative definitions in economic sociology (e.g. White 1981; Aspers 2007). However, these works do not really provide an elegant, inclusive definition for mating markets either.

[3] Weber (1922: 382): "Von einem Markt soll gesprochen werden, sobald auch nur auf einer Seite eine Mehrheit von Tauschreflektanten um Tauschchancen konkurrieren".

[4] Simmel (1983: 83f.): "Die Existenz eines Marktes bedarf mindestens dreier Akteure: Mindestens ein Akteur auf der einen Seite des Marktes, der sich mindestens zwei Akteuren auf der anderen Seite des Marktes gegenübersieht, deren Angebote er im Vergleich miteinander bewerten kann".

[5] In most cases, market value is understood as a concept distinct from market price, which is 'the price at which one can trade' – whereas market value is 'the true underlying value'.

Online Dating – An 'Ideal Type' Partner Market

The following section will analytically compare the online dating market to different contexts and principles of finding a partner.[6] In doing so, online dating as well as other important contexts will be constructed *as markets* in an ideal-type (i.e. Weberian) way. Based on our Weberian definition of a partner market, we can infer the central differentiating dimensions of different social contexts in which couples are potentially established. The term partner market can be applied to the extent to which mate search and competition for exchange opportunities with potential partners actually structure practice, and is thus constitutive and specific for the processes of the particular social context itself. To the degree this can be observed, a particular context of couple formation can be thought of as being "*relatively autonomous*" (Bourdieu 1991: 236) from overall society. The specificity level of the objects of interests being competed for (money for instance in a financial market) and the level of irrelevance of the society *outside* the market for the agency *within* the market are two core aspects of the relative autonomy of any market. In other words: the more explicit the good in question is, and the less competition for opportunities of exchange is influenced by external societal conditions, the more applicable the term 'partner market' becomes. Taking these aspects into consideration, the object of online dating exhibits a comparatively high level of relative autonomy.

Unlike offline partner markets, and unlike other online social media, the explicit function of online dating platforms is to realize the formation of couples.[7] The *primary meaning* behind the use of a dating site is to find a partner, whereas – in other contexts of interaction such as the workplace or school – couple formation is for the most part an unintended side-effect of context-specific practice. If applying a conception of the market based around its goods, online dating – compared to traditional contexts of interaction – appears to be oriented towards a *good which is relatively explicit and* universal. In online dating, the objects of supply and demand are (depending on the particular operationalization) clearly defined by (a) the traits of a partner, (b) the partner himself, or (c) the relationships, or (d) the exchange chances as elaborated above. A relatively high specificity of goods can also be attributed to other partner markets, for example prostitution. The degree of specificity is exacerbated by the technical design of dating sites. The users' self-presentation is limited to modular options in various attributes, excluding standard offline forms of self-presentation such as facial expressions, the involvement of third parties, or the use of material objects. Along with the social conventions governing self-presentation (users are expected to present themselves as being 'interesting',

---

[6] See also Schmitz (2009) with an earlier version of this analytical approach.
[7] This also comprises platforms for adultery and sexual affairs which generate short-term togetherness.

'respectable', 'sporty', and so on),[8] online dating has a standardizing impact on its users. In doing so, it forms a relatively homogeneous and structured mass of 'suppliers', who present themselves to other users in the form of choice sets, from which a selection has to be made. In contrast, other partner markets, such as universities or schools, have neither a clear, general good of common interest, nor do they foster a seller-buyer logic of interactions as can be found in online dating, speed dating, or prostitution.

Feld conceptualizes meeting places via his 'focus' theory (Feld 1981; cp. Chapter 4), meaning that particular contexts focalize actors more or less explicitly looking for a partner. For example, a neighborhood will bring together different actors and eventually foster the emergence of some relationships. Against the background of our previous argumentation, online dating can be considered a *hyperfocus*, different from other foci due to its explicit nature of the mate search process, representing the very purpose of the interaction. Due to the high relevance of finding a partner for most social strata, this has implications for the social composition of a non-specialized dating site as considered here. Unlike traditional foci (such as one's workplace or school), which are essentially frequented by socially homogeneous groups, the hyper-focus online dating is characterized by a high level of *socio-structural heterogeneity*. This results from the high accessibility of a non-specialized dating site as well as from the *size of the market*.[9] This can also be seen as a relatively low level of market imbalance, meaning that no particular social strata are extremely over- or underrepresented (cp. Chapter 2). In this regard, online dating resembles online matchmaking (that is, the algorithm-driven system of partner suggestions offered by certain companies), where specific social classes may be structurally over-represented, but all users of all social classes are easily accessible using the search functionality.

Due to the technical architecture of a dating site, users can to some extent ignore physical distances and temporal simultaneity, as they can communicate from different places and in a time-displaced way. This implies a comparatively low level of *co-presence*, when compared with traditional offline contexts, but also when compared to speed dating. As a consequence, a high degree of *parallelity* of interactions is part of the market's logic, being less subject to normative objections (e.g. in contrast to one's circle of acquaintances, where 'dating' multiple partners may be frowned upon).

Because of the market size and the technical design, online dating is less about contacting or selecting *persons*, but rather about perceived combinations of attributes (Lenton and Stewart 2008; Zillmann et al. 2011), and thus *trait-oriented choice*, based on comparisons of multiple alternative user profiles. In contrast to one's family or circle of friends, where the whole person rather than its separate

---

[8] Some dating services even work to identify 'sub-optimal' profiles and pictures, helping users present themselves in the 'right' way.

[9] It is difficult to estimate the true size of online dating sites, as it is of course in the interest of the services' providers to claim to have large numbers of customers. The website we analyzed had over 118,000 registered profiles in 2009.

traits is perceived and evaluated, dating websites notably feature "impersonal market exchange", and thus foster a "considerations for things, not [...] for persons" (Weber 1978: 641). As a consequence of trait-oriented choice, virtual partner markets (but also speed dating, offline matchmaking, or offline advertisements) are characterized by comparatively low transaction and search costs.

However, the relative importance of trait over person, implies a relatively low uncertainty regarding the primary intention of the market participants. Usually, both interaction partners on an online dating site will be looking for a long or short-term relationship, whereas this is usually not that clear in everyday life. This comparatively low uncertainty with regard to the intentions of a potential partner is, however, relativized by the relatively high level of uncertainty regarding the *authenticity* of a communication partner. Just as in the case of speed dating or offline dating agencies, two interacting users on a dating site are unlikely to know each other personally, and are thus mutually *anonymous*. The advantage resulting from the high certainty regarding the goals of a dating site's user is thus undermined by the low certainty regarding his trustworthiness, a problem that prevails to a far lesser degree in everyday offline contexts. Users of online dating sites can exercise extraordinary control over their self-presentation, by using their profile pages and the chat system in a strategic manner. Whereas Goffman's (1959) description of everyday self-presentation is applicable to all social situations, it is particularly apt for online dating platforms. These digital partner markets enable a vast repertoire of deception ranging from minor concealments to the complete falsification of profiles. In computer-mediated communication it is, initially at least, unclear whether one's communication partner actually is who they claim to be.

As the particular degree of anonymity already suggests, online dating is relatively autonomous with regard to direct influences of social structure. The process of couple formation on an online dating site, but also in offline or online matchmaking, occurs in dyadic exclusivity, i.e. *without the direct involvement of third parties or users' social networks*. Impersonality which is a characteristic for market relations in general, precipitates in online dating as a relative "freedom from personal ties and obligations" (Anderson 1993: 145). The paradigmatic inverse of this context might be marriages arranged by the families of the two partners, or – more recently – Facebook's 'Spotted' groups, which mobilize users' social networks to establish contacts with potential partners.[10]

The particular detachment from everyday social structures of interaction as a core characteristic of online dating does not simply affect each single interaction in itself, but all subsequent interactions as well. Whereas two people whose interaction did not lead to a relationship might continue to come into contact with one another in typical offline interaction contexts such as the workplace or school, in online

---

[10] 'Spotted' is an app on Facebook with the following function: if a user in a certain location (usually a specific town or university) sees a person they are romantically interested in, they can post a message in the group in an attempt to mobilize the social network (both their own, that of the potential partner, and indeed of the group as a whole), with the nominally ideal end result being contact with the person in question.

dating, much like online matchmaking and perhaps offline markets such as nightclubs, the probability of future encounter is very low. The *"shadow of the future"* (Axelrod 1984: 124) is thus comparatively insignificant for virtual encounters (see e.g. Diekmann and Wyder 2002: 674f.). This relieves online dating users of the necessity of considering the long-term social relationship with each potential interaction partner. Termination of communication, perhaps simply by not replying to an individual message, is considerably less burdened with normative considerations than in the social contexts of the family, school, or the workplace.

Whereas it is true that interactions on a dating site take the form of dyadic relations, and while it is also true that the user's offline social network is not immediately involved in these interactions, this does not mean that third parties are irrelevant for these interactions. Due to the abundance of potentially available partners and competitors (Stauder 2008), online dating can be thought of as being particularly strongly structured by competition. Within this *polypolistic* market structure of online dating, more than two actors are always indirectly involved in any specific dyadic interaction as alternative partners and competitors. Thus, the autonomy of the online dating market does not exclude sociality, but transforms it into a mechanism of competition inherent to any dyadic interaction. This transformation cannot be established for most everyday contexts such as familial interactions.

The extreme level of market competition manifests itself in *competition for attention and exchange chances* among users (Schmitz 2009), especially in the form of the verbal and visual content of the user's profiles (Illouz and Finkelmann 2009: 416). Whereas more long-term and structurally conditioned interactions – at school or work, for instance – also allow for 'love at second sight', online dating users are forced to approach the surplus of potential partners in a manner which reduces complexity. Given the low degree of physical and temporal co-presence, visual (in the profile design) and verbal (in the chat process) stimuli appear as units of complexity reduction, which, together with the anonymity of encounter, enhance the relevance of personal information (cp. Geser and Bühler 2006: 16). These symbolic structurations of profile presentation facilitate and enforce the comparison of "tastes", "family backgrounds", and "hopes and dreams" (Burrell 2004).

Linguistic expression (e.g., via messages) and stylistic self-staging (via profile design) are core aspects that are even more important for online than for offline mating processes. Physicality (as presented on profile pictures) is of particular relevance in online dating, as it is of course in mobile dating, nightclubs, or indeed prostitution. Although physical appearance is also of utmost importance in contexts such as schools, universities, vacations, or the workplace, physicality in online dating is given priority through the profile design and the necessity for complexity reduction. Often, tabloid journalists, and some scientists, even assume that the primacy of physicality (or "erotic capital') represents a fundamental feature of dating sites (cp. Hakim 2011).

As part of the high degree of market competition, users are frequently inundated with incoming contacts, forcing them to apply selective practices of choice. Conversely, in the case of too little attention, they are motivated to rationally reflect on the underlying reasons. Dating sites' very design also induces reflection upon one's own romantic preferences and potential (initially, for example, via filling out one's profile) and a rationalizing approach to both the self (e.g. one's 'market value') and to potential partners. This often results in a search for "the best bargain" (Illouz and Finkelmann 2009: 416), in accordance with the "principle of maximization" (Klein und Stauder 2008: 82, o.t.).

From a market perspective, online dating can thus be taken to be unusually efficient. Users looking for a partner and possessing comparatively clear intentions, prone to applying cost-benefit calculations, are brought together without a great deal of interference from market-exogenous rationalities. The fact that users enter the digital partner market not just with the expectation of realizing their own preferences, but with the expectation of rational expectations on the part of other market participants, further encourages instrumental rationality. Independent of whether a particular user is genuinely predisposed to act rationally as part of the process of online dating, he or she will be clearly aware of, or will at least assume, utility-maximization strategies on the part of the other users.

Take, for example, inauthentic self-presentation, one of many rational strategies used in online dating; this behavior intensifies market competition, because most users will optimize their profiles according to their expectations of the desires of the other market participants, so as not to suffer any competitive disadvantage (Zillmann et al. 2011; Zillmann 2016). The detection of possible deceptions also becomes of considerable importance in online dating; any potential partner automatically comes under suspicion, and must be unmasked quickly in order to avoid misallocation of one's time and attention. Just as in the fundamental axioms of rational action theories in general, and theories of mate choice in particular, a user is prompted to reflect upon the expected utility of each contact event. The fact, for instance, that a man's profile exhibits a subjectively ideal height must be considered in the context of the probability that this particular attribute is actually true. The user is driven, therefore, to set the value of a potential partner's attributes against the likelihood of their veracity. Computer-mediated communication in online dating, which enables a relatively high level of control over the consistency and plausibility of a user's self-portrayal, also fosters rational strategies of creating profile data and of formulating and standardizing text messages. Given the recordability of messages, the process of interaction between two users is constantly accessible for both parties. Also, performing plausibility checks is a valid rational strategy for users (Gibbs et al. 2011). The technical and social conditions of online dating as described here can be thought of as representing a kind of partner market that induces rationality (Illouz and Finkelmann 2009: 415) on the level on the subject, and a particular logic of supply and demand on the market level.

In sum, according to various dimensions, online dating can be considered to represent a partner market, one which is strongly structured by the competition and instrumental rationality in the mate search process. Due to the fact that the mechanisms inherent to online dating are less affected by offline conditions than traditional partner markets, a high operational market efficiency can be said to exist. As a result of the comparatively high level of relative autonomy – in the sense of homogeneous intentions and goods, on the one hand, and the irrelevance of external personal networks on the other – online dating can be justifiably labeled as a partner market.

What Is a Partner Market?

Illouz and Finkelmann's critical perspective even leads them to the conclusion that, before the rise of the internet, the very term 'market' was "largely inadequate" (2009: 409) for the conceptualization of the processes of couple formation. For the purpose of summarizing and consolidating these arguments, Figure 3.1 shows a graphical visualization in the form of ideal-typical biplots (Gower et al. 2010).[11]

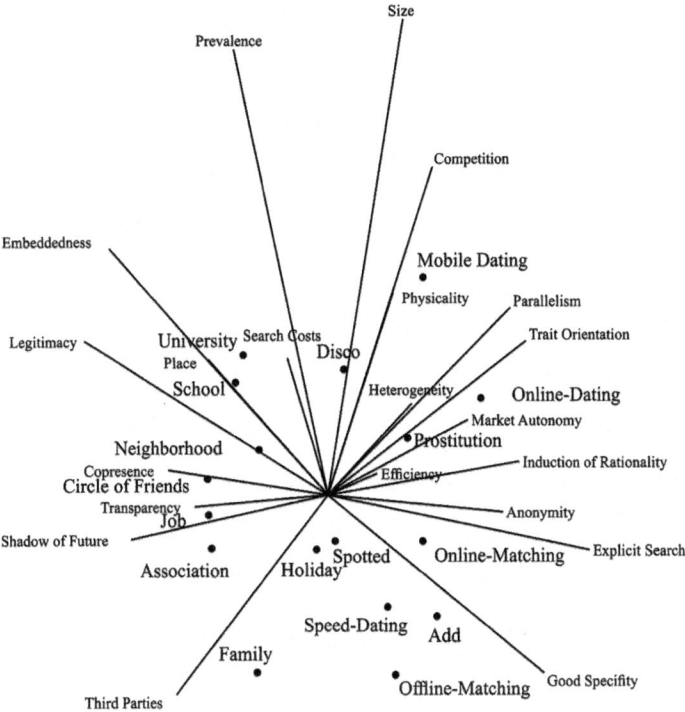

Fig. 3.1 Theoretical comparison of ideal-typical partner markets (Biplots)

In accordance with the ideal-typical approach outlined here, the traditional contexts of encounter (Family, Neighborhood, School, etc.) are to be found on the left-hand side of the diagram. What is common to them is that they represent contexts of encounter that are subject to strong social structuration, characterized by the direct involvement of third parties, highly institutionalized, and often strongly bound to geographic space. Accordingly, they usually do not involve explicit mate search, anonymity, and market autonomy.

An idealized online dating partner market is located on the right-hand side of the ideal-typical diagram, and displays analytical similarities to speed dating, online matchmaking, mobile dating, and offline dating agencies, romantic advertisements, and prostitution. These contexts of encounter are explicit entities of partner

---

[11] The graph is based on a relational table in which each context was assigned an ideal-typical triple-ordinal value.

mediation, unlike the workplace or school, for example. Online dating, and the other contexts in close proximity, differ by way of their exceptional levels of competition and their attribute-driven process of selection. Speed dating differs here, thanks to the manageable number of participants involved, by way of a considerably more person-oriented process of selection and less intense competition. The same holds true for the Facebook's 'Spotted' function, which is used when looking for a specific person. 'Spotted' groups on Facebook share with online dating the fact that they are both explicit and online forms of mate search. 'Spotted' differs from and online dating by its practically absent competition and the strong embeddedness in existing social networks.

Online dating differs from online matchmaking by the fact that the market's size and levels of availability, which initially appear similar, are limited by the matchmaking algorithm, resulting in a smaller 'field of eligibles' in the digital matchmaking market. Online dating also displays proximity to an ideal-typical nightclub, where interaction is similarly characterized by the above-average presence of potentially 'romantic' intentions such as flirting, and by relatively high levels of competition for attention, anonymity, and attribute-oriented selection. Equally, prostitution can be seen as a market with clear intentions and competition for attracting the client's attraction. In an analytical sense, online dating might be even thought of as a particularly extreme form of such mating contexts, as the market character here is even closer to the theoretical reference.

The ideal-typical approach outlined here does not deny that there are empirical differences between different dating sites or different offline mating contexts. It is an idealized representation, which corroborates the argument of Chapter 2, where we argued that online dating can be seen as a confluent consequence of societal developments, such as individualization, rationalization, and marketization. In addition, as the ideal-typical approach shows, online dating sites are certainly not exceptional phenomena in the context of couple formation, but can be located within an analytical continuum alongside conventional partner markets. Online dating sites seem to be, in comparison to other contexts of interaction, particularly strongly defined by the logics of preferences, choice, exchange, competition and market. Applying the definition above, one can say that, in online dating, exchange chances are less affected by societal structure than anywhere else (economists might say they are 'frictionless', and thus close to the economic market model). As for "rational choice theorists, as indeed for 'free-market' economists generally, the market is the site of a certain idealized freedom" where "individual agents are free to pursue their interests, to 'maximize utilities'" (Guillory 2000: 23f.), the online dating market seems to constitute a particularly well-suited area of applicability of individualist and rationalist reason.

The User's Phenomenological Perception

In the following section, a selection of qualitative interviews will be presented which were conducted in the context of this project, as well as some carried out in collaboration with Marie Bergström with the users of German and French dating sites (see also Bergström 2011). The interviewees were contacted and subsequently interviewed via the chat system of the dating site itself. The advantage of this method is the fact that the participants' answers could be collated and analyzed straightforwardly and accurately.[12]

Firstly, many interviewees emphasized the economic advantages online dating represents in comparison to offline dating:

> (Laughing) it is more economical because it's not as cost-intensive. Among other things, going out does cost a lot of money. It's definitely cheaper to register with some online dating service. By the way, men think like this, too, because I also spoke to Tim, you know, why did you register there, and he said he just wanted to meet someone – this way he doesn't have to buy the woman a drink every time (laughing).

The users also remarked upon the extraordinary range of potential partners, although this is accompanied by a high number of unappealing or unfavorable interaction partners.

> There is, of course, an excess supply, there are too many people. I got to know a lot of idiots, total idiots, complete idiots, but I met some nice people, too.

This re-emphasizes the aforementioned pressure to select potential partners according to specific attribute parameters:

> Mate choice and all that, you can do it very fast in an online context, be it in written form, e-mail, or on the phone. You learn to differentiate quickly between who's suitable and who isn't.

The interviewees formulated their own cost-benefit ratios in reaction to the unusually intense choice situation, emphasizing the fact the rationalized search for a partner online is particularly efficient:

> You get involved in a conversation very quickly, you just write something. But these possibilities come with restrictions created by the market.

The relative ease with which a reciprocal exchange can be realized in online dating is affected by the aforementioned fact that the users share the common goal of finding a (short or long-term) partner, which generates an intense pressure to make a decision:

> It leads to inhibitions somehow, when everybody knows that everyone is just talking to you in order to find a mate. And then I feel an extreme pressure to immediately decide whether someone is suitable or not. And I don't like this. I prefer to meet people and to show an interest afterwards. That is, leave it to chance.

---

[12] The actual object of research was the analysis of deception in online dating. The interviews were carried out as part of a dissertation by Eva Peter 2009. The results presented here are a re-analysis of this qualitative data material.

The situation of particular market competition, induced by the excess supply and the pressure of choice, manifests itself in a critical reflection on the character of the institution. Women in particular find themselves in a position of uncertainty regarding men's true motives; women are also contacted by men far more intensively than vice-versa, as has already been demonstrated.

> Well, on these dating sites, there is a surplus of men, and somehow I have the sense that they take it pretty easy. They just click through and, well, if he doesn't fit a hundred percent, then you're just directly eliminated – there's really a kind of consumerist behavior behind that, it's actually kind of embarrassing, I think.

This leads to a discrepancy between, on the one hand, the normative expectations regarding the integrity of a potential partner's motives, in particular exclusivity of interest, and the simultaneous acceptance of the extent to which the encounter conforms to the rules of the market, which are often perceived as resembling supermarkets:

> Yes, well, it's probably true, I think. How you deal with it is something else, but I really kind of found, for myself, that it's really a little bit like shopping in the supermarket." "Well, the negative point in all this is really this shopping mentality.

The interviewees complain about the cold logic of the market, while simultaneously using it as an excuse for higher standards and an almost instant, parameter-driven method of selection. One expectation which seems to appear very frequently as a result of the logic of the market is the desire for a partner who is both outstandingly compatible – pointing towards higher romantic standards – but who also displays spontaneity and sophistication.

> If they don't fit exactly and perfectly, you just look for the next one – it's just like looking through the shelves in the supermarket, where you pick a tin and, well, it's not the one, so you just put it back and take the next one. This – that is, this feeling – has been constant for me all these years. That just being, even after talking on the phone or after writing each other, just like that, without further ado and without any parting words, just being clicked away.

Much more so than for classical mating contexts such as schools, universities, workplaces, and so on, users of dating sites find themselves in a situation which is, from their perspective, comparable to the markets they are familiar with in their everyday lives.

Interim Conclusion

To summarize the overall line of reasoning so far: The historical developments of Western modernity, as outlined in Chapter 2, fostered the rationalized and individualized constitution of the modern subject desiring intimacy, as well as the market-based character of the realization of romantic desires, thus making online dating a plausible consequence of societal development. The analytical conceptualization of online dating and the user's phenomenological perceptions outlined in this chapter go one step further, in that they emphasize the fact that online dating is a context particularly close to the ideal-typical notion of a market.

The arguments mobilized in this chapter seem to sufficiently and effectively legitimize a research practice of applying individualistic and rationalistic models in the context of online dating if 'structure' here is understood as less relevant or being statistically controllable.

In Chapter 6 we will argue that a Bourdieusian approach to online dating and general issues of mating may well offer further analytical insights into this phenomenon, and indeed allows us to systematically integrate perspectives and findings from traditional mate choice research. However, we will first inspect and discuss the intellectual architecture of theories that underlie research on online mate choice in the next chapter, and elaborate the dichotomization of 'structure-agency' as their common paradigmatic core. This undertaking will then indicate the need for a wider notion of 'structure' into research on mating phenomena. It will also provide us with the starting point for a systematic analytical integration of 'structure' into practice, by transcending the opportunity-choice distinction, following the Bourdieusian tradition.

References

Anderson, E. (1993). *Value in ethics and economics*. Cambridge, MA: Harvard University Press.
Aspers, P. (2007). Theory, reality, and performativity in markets. *American Journal of Economics and Sociology, 66*(2), 379–398.
Axelrod, R. M. (1984). *The evolution of cooperation*. New York: Basic Books.
Becker, G. S. (1974). A theory of marriage. In T. W. Schultz (Ed.), *Economics of the family: Marriage, children, and human* (pp. 299–344). Chicago: University of Chicago Press.
Bergström, M. (2011). Casual dating online. Sexual norms and practices on French heterosexual dating sites. *Zeitschrift für Familienforschung, 23*(3), 291–318.
Bourdieu, P. (1991). In J. B. Thompson (Ed.), *Language and symbolic power*. Cambridge: Polity.
Bourdieu, P. (1997). Wie eine soziale Klasse entsteht. In P. Bourdieu (Ed.), *Schriften zu Politik & Kultur* (Der Tote packt den Lebenden, Vol. 2, pp. 102–129). Hamburg: VSA.
Burrell, C. (2004). *Online Dating. Info 311 Term Project*. University of Washington School of Information. Retrieved from http://www.jaamati.info/portfolio/human/info311/Online_Dating.pdf
Coleman, J. S. (1990). *Foundations of social theory*. Cambridge: Harvard University Press.
Diekmann, A., & Wyder, D. (2002). Vertrauen und Reputationseffekte bei Internet-Auktionen. *Kölner Zeitschrift für Soziologie und Sozialpsychologie, 54*(4), 674–693.
Durlauf, S. N., & Blume, L. (2008). *The new Palgrave dictionary of economics* (2nd ed.). Basingstoke: Palgrave Macmillan.
Feld, S. L. (1981). The focused organization of social ties. *American Journal of Sociology, 86*(5), 1015–1035.
Geser, H., & Bühler, I. (2006). *Partnerwahl online*. Retrieved from http://socio.ch/intcom/t_hgeser15.pdf
Gibbs, J. L., Ellison, N. B., & Lai, C.-H. (2011). First comes love, then comes Google: An investigation of uncertainty reduction strategies and self-disclosure in online dating. *Communication Research, 38*, 70–100.
Goffman, E. (1959). *The presentation of self in everyday life*. New York: Doubleday Anchor Books.

Gower, J. C., Sugnet, L. G., & Le Roux, N. J. (2010). *Understanding biplots*. New York: Wiley.
Guillory, J. (2000). Bourdieu's refusal. In N. Brown & I. Szeman (Eds.), *Pierre bourdieu: Fieldwork in culture* (pp. 19–44). New York: Rowman & Littlefield.
Hakim, C. (2011). *Erotic capital: The power of attraction in the bedroom and the boardroom*. New York: Basic Books.
Hodgson, G. M. (2002). *How economics forgot history: The problem of historical specificity in social science*. New York: Routledge.
Hodgson, G. M. (2010). Markets. In J. B. Davis & W. Dolfsma (Eds.), *The Elgar companion to social economics* (pp. 251–266). Cheltenham: Edward Elgar.
Illouz, E., & Finkelmann, S. (2009). An odd and inseparable couple: Emotion and rationality in partner selection. *Theory and Society, 38*(4), 401–422.
Lenton, A. P., & Stewart, A. (2008). Changing her ways: The number of options and mate-standard strength impact mate choice strategy and satisfaction. *Judgment and Decision Making, 3*(7), 501–511.
Rosenbaum, E. (2000). What is a market? On the methodology of a contested concept. *Review of Social Economy, 58*(4), 455–482.
Schmitz, A. (2009). Virtuelle Zwischengeschlechtlichkeit im Kontext relationaler Methodologie. Überlegungen zu einer Soziologie der digitalen Partnerwahl. In H.-G. Soeffner (Ed.), *Unsichere Zeiten. Herausforderungen gesellschaftlicher Transformationen; Verhandlungen des 34. Kongresses der Deutschen Gesellschaft für Soziologie in Jena 2008*. Wiesbaden: VS Verlag.
Schmitz, A. (2014). The online dating market: Theoretical and methodological considerations. *Economic Sociology, 16*(1), 11–25.
Schwartz, C. R. (2013). Trends and variation in assortative mating: Causes and consequences. *Annual Review of Sociology, 39*, 451–470.
Simmel, G. (1983). *Soziologie: Untersuchungen über die Formen der Vergesellschaftung* (Gesammelte Werke: Vol. 2, 6th ed.). Berlin: Duncker & Humblot.
Stauder, J. (2008). Opportunitäten und Restriktionen des Kennenlernens. Zur sozialen Vorstrukturierung der Kontaktgelegenheiten am Beispiel des Partnermarkts. *Kölner Zeitschrift für Soziologie und Sozialpsychologie, 60*(2), 266–286.
Stauder, J. (2011). Regionale Ungleichheit auf dem Partnermarkt? Die makrostrukturellen Rahmenbedingungen der Partnerwahl in regionaler Perspektive. *Soziale Welt, 62*, 41–69.
Weber, M. (1922). *Wirtschaft und Gesellschaft: Grundriß der verstehenden Soziologie. Grundriß der Sozialökonomik* (3rd ed.). Tübingen: Mohr.
Weber, M. (1978). In G. Roth & C. Wittich (Eds.), *Economy and society*. Berkeley: University of California Press.
White, H. C. (1981). Where do markets come from? *American Journal of Sociology, 87*(3), 517–547.
Zillmann, D. (2016). *Von kleinen Lügen und kurzen Beinen. Selbstdarstellung bei der Partnersuche im Internet*. [About little lies and small legs. Self-Presentation in Online Dating.] Wiesbaden: VS Verlag (forthcoming).
Zillmann, D., Schmitz, A., & Blossfeld, H.-P. (2011). Lügner haben kurze Beine. Zum Zusammenhang unwahrer Selbstdarstellung und partnerschaftlicher Chancen im Online-Dating. *Zeitschrift für Familienforschung, 23*(3), 291–318.

Chapter 4
Classical Theories of Mate Choice and the Relational Deficit in the Study of Relationship Formation

The analytical emphasis on the 'individual' within research on online dating markets, as outlined so far, is not a phenomenon unique to this specific subject area. It is also constitutive for a great deal of traditional and current research into the sociology of mating. Although there is no single coherent research program on mating processes in the social sciences, the individualistic paradigm also prevails in empirical research on offline partner markets, above all in its quantitative variation. This section will elaborate on the central components of the approach, constitutive for research on empirical mating processes both on and offline. The way these theoretical foundations are used and integrated by modern individualist mate choice researchers will then be illustrated. This dominant approach in the field of partner market research in contemporary empirical sociology can be characterized as a combination of theories of preference, choice, and social exchange, of several different market-related considerations, and drawing on further theoretical inspirations. Collectively, it constitutes a research paradigm which will henceforth be referred to as "mating as agency in structure", or MAS. Subsequently, MAS will be examined with regard to its potential to include structure into the different models of individual mate choice. It will be then shown that individualistic mate choice research tries to overcome the restrictions inherent to methodological individualism and rational choice. This, in sum, will indicate the need for a relational notion of 'structure' in research on mating processes.

Classical Theories of Mate Choice

Mating Preferences and Mate Choice

A widespread perspective on processes of couple formation is the concept of individual acts of partner selection, acts which are seen as the result of preferences for specific traits in a partner, and as generating in sum the aggregated population patterns. The assumption here is that the selection of a certain partner depends essentially on subjectively (and sometimes consciously) considered preferences for certain characteristics, such as socio-economic status, physical appearance, or age. Preferences are seen as relevant for the *choice* of potential partners, as they guide "behavior by directing" actors to "select and pursue whatever potential romantic partner most closely approximates their [...] ideals" (Eastwick and Finkel 2008: 262). On the one hand, this perspective is based on ideas from evolutionary biology and evolutionary psychology (e.g. Buss and Barnes 1986) assuming "common preferences" (Alpern and Reyniers 2005) – that is, that organisms will not actually differ in terms of their preferred characteristics. On the other hand, the preferential approach is based on a utilitarian theory of action (see e.g. Bokek-Cohen et al. 2007; Witt 1991).

Theories that refer to an actor's choices amongst alternatives as resulting from preferences imply the concept of a subjective maximization of utility, often referred to in the social sciences as theories of "rational choice" (Elster 1986). In its original form, utility theory assumes that actors have transitive preferences; for example, if an actor A prefers actor B over C, and D over B, he should follow the assumption of rationality by preferring actor D over C. Furthermore, actors are defined as being capable of taking a decision characterized by complete preferences: actor A knows whether he prefers actor B over C or whether B and C are equivalent for him. Also, preferences are defined as stable: if actor A prefers actor B over C today, he will show the same preference order tomorrow.

As opposed to the biological theory of "common preferences" and to the economic theories of a general utility function (Sprecher et al. 1994; Schmitt et al. 2012), sociological mate choice theories also take potential variations in partner preferences into account. Of special interest for sociologists are gender-specific and socio-structural differences between partner preferences (e.g. South 1991). In this context, in particular, homophilous preferences (preferring a similar trait), hyperphilous preferences (preferring higher values in certain characteristics) or hypophilous preferences (preferring lower values in certain characteristics) receive special attention (Skopek et al. 2011). Homophilous preferences are also sometimes called "horizontal preferences", and hyper- and hypophilous preferences are sometimes called "vertical preferences" (Hitsch et al. 2010). A further aspect of preference is the desired relationship form itself, be it long or short-term, casual or serious, etc. (Regan et al. 2000; Baker 2005). Women tend to prefer long-term relationships, whereas men are more likely pursue short-time relationships (Stewart et al. 2000; Buss 2006). It has been repeatedly shown that women are more likely – compared to men – to prefer partners who can offer them financial security (Butler-Smith et al. 1998; Hirschmann 1987; Harrison and Saeed 1977; Skopek 2011) and who display subjectively preferable status attributes such as a good education or career (Hassebrauck 1990; Kaupp 1968; Skopek 2011). Research also shows that men have a preference for younger women (Campos et al. 2002; Cameron et al. 1977) and physically attractive partners (e.g. Hirschmann 1987).

In the social sciences, the assumption of individualistic and rationalistic theories is that acts of partner selection are governed by such conscious or unconscious personal preferences.

The decision of choosing a partner is then conceptualized as a (more or less) formal model of expected utility maximization via the realization of mating preferences, and of minimizing costs, such as the costs of a particular relationship or the opportunity costs of the search process itself, with actors gathering information regarding their own structures of opportunity (England and Farkas 1986; Oppenheimer 1988). Stage and filter models of couple formation found in social psychology (Murstein 1970) are often integrated into general models of partner choice, meaning that it is no longer considered a single act, but rather a sequence of choice acts undertaken by two partners (Willoughby and Carroll 2010). In this context, the sociological concept of 'exchange' plays a major role.

Mating as Social Exchange

A common extension of the rationalist approach to mate choice is the conceptualization of couple formation as a specific form of social and material exchange (Blau 1964; Becker 1993; Edwards 1969; Burgess and Huston 1979; Thibaut and Kelley 1959; Brehm et al. 2002). James Coleman (1990) motivates the connection between rational choice theory and exchange theory with recourse to the actor's interest in controlling resources controlled by other actors, an interest which can be rationally realized by offering their own resources in exchange (see also White 2013). The basic assumption here is that men and women are trying to maximize their subjective utility by adjusting the distribution of reciprocal rewards via resource exchange. Two actors reciprocally satisfy their particular desires and needs through their respective partners (Thibaut and Kelley 1959). A relationship is considered worthwhile if the cost does not exceed the benefit (Blau 1964: 114) and thus if it is balanced – that is, if the exchange of advantages is equitable. A particular aspect of exchange is the fairness of the process, as emphasized by equity theory (Walster et al. 1978).

A common example is that of the exchange of male socio-economic status resources for female physical attractiveness (see e.g. Blau 1964; Rosenfeld 2005; Edwards 1969; Elder 1969; Skopek et al. 2011). Special attention has also been paid in research to the status-caste exchange between different ethnicities (Blau and Duncan 1967) and to the exchange of male breadwinning for female homemaking (e.g. Sanchez et al. 1998). Apart from economic exchange, a formal and well-defined interaction, Blau (1964: 94) also conceptualizes *social exchange*, characterized by the rather unspecific and personal nature of interaction, which fosters "feelings of personal obligation, gratitude, and trust", which may emerge due to equity as well as to inequity. Equity of goods is not the only condition of social and economic exchange, but the "imbalance of power and extrinsic rewards" is often "the source and remains the basis of lasting reciprocal love conditions" (Blau 1964: 78). The example perhaps most evident in the context of mating interactions is the power difference between men and women, which traditionally underlies matrimony in many societies and still manifests in myriad phenomena in enlightened Western societies to this day.

'Erotic Capital' and Couple Formation

A current model of exchange-based mate choice is developed by Hakim (2011), who strongly emphasizes the relevance of female physicality as "erotic capital". Although this is not a genuine theory of mating processes, the concept of "erotic capital" is essentially discussed in the context of partner markets, including dating sites. Hakim defines erotic capital as being composed of the seven elements "beauty, sex appeal, liveliness, a talent for dressing well, charm and social skills, and sexual competence", plus – exclusively female – fertility (Hakim 2011: 10ff.). These elements are taken to be independent both from one another and from other forms of capital such as economic capital or Bourdieu's cultural capital (Bourdieu 1986). Hakim considers erotic capital to be empirically independent from other forms of capital; "it can be completely independent of social origin", for example (Hakim 2011: 18). To this end, Hakim offers a plethora of empirical observations regarding the effects of erotic capital, for example with respect to the advantages it brings for one's career or on the partner market (Hakim 2011: 33, 39, 103). Possessing erotic capital is seen to represent a universal advantage in many different activities and interactions. The significance of erotic capital does differ, however, with regards to gender: whereas women are frequently unable to turn their erotic capital to their financial or career advantage, attractive men can increase both income and status via their physical appearance (Hakim 2011: 3ff.). Basing her arguments on secondary analyses of empirical survey research, Hakim postulates that men possess a fundamentally stronger libido than women. Simultaneously, men are seen as less able to satisfy their libidinous drive, and therefore see a threat in female eroticism which must, for strategic reasons, be devalued as a form of capital. This "male sex deficit" (Hakim 2011: 3) prompts Hakim to postulate that women must deliberately and selectively invest in their erotic capital so as to relativize the societal advantages of their male competitors or romantic partners. Hakim assigns tremendous importance to marriage and partner markets in the context of her theory of erotic capital. Along with the workplace, these elements represent the central setting for the deployment and exchange of erotic capital. Erotic capital is at its most effective in these situations – especially in its leveling of the playing field for women, in that they can improve their social status by 'marrying up': "Erotic capital is women's trump card in mating and marriage markets" (Hakim 2010: 510). Playing this "trump card" is conceptualized by Hakim as a process of exchange between male economic capital and female attractiveness (which includes behavior considered to be feminine). She ascribes the relative insignificance of male erotic capital on the partner market to the male sex deficit, and to the potentially greater levels of female erotic capital in general (Hakim 2010: 506). As part of the exchange of female attractiveness and male status, women are able both to secure a desirable male partner and then get their own way in potential conflicts in any resulting relationships. It can be summarized that Hakim's theory essentially conceptualizes both the initiation of processes of couple formation and the dynamics within established relationships in terms of the positive effects of female physical appearance. This resource is not just assigned the role of the central explanatory variable in the process of couple formation – it also fulfils the role of a device to further women's market influence and bargaining power.

Family Economics

Although Gary S. Becker does not present an explicit theory of general mating processes, he does develop a micro-economic model of marriage markets. Becker, based on his readings of the work of Blau and Homans (Becker 1976: 255) and biological findings (Becker 1976: 13f.) makes reference to the prevailing cultural mating conditions at his time (especially the strong gendered division of the labor market, gender norms, heteronormative norms, etc.) and develops formal models of marriage markets.[1]

In terms of his general economic approach, Becker (1976: 5) makes three "foundational assumptions": households maximizing a common utility, market equilibrium over all households, and stable preferences of the actors involved. Becker sees mating processes as a legitimate object for the economic approach due to two reasons. First, as he assumes that "marriage is practically always voluntary […] the theory of preferences can be readily applied" and persons marrying "can be assumed to expect to raise their utility level above what it would be were they to remain single" (Becker 1974: 300). Second, as many "men and women compete" with each other in finding the best mate "a market in marriages can be presumed to exist" (Becker 1974: 300).

In contrast to theories of individual partner preferences and partner choices, the assumption of Becker's early marriage market theory is that two actors achieve, through marrying, a higher common level of utility than possible individually

---

[1] His works, being essentially "concerned with demonstrating the applicability of formal economic analysis to a new, unusual subject" have inspired few empirical studies supporting his "abstract formalisms" (Frey and Eichenberger 1996: 188). Many sociologists refer to the historical and cultural peculiarities of his times and not to his Nobel Prize-winning formal work.

(Becker 1976, 1991). The individual utility function of classical economics is thus replaced by a common household utility. Married couples or families are conceptualized as producers of "commodities" (such as offspring), which are produced in reciprocal exchange for the actors' time within the household and the labor market sector respectively (Becker 1993: 23f.). As a consequence of the intended dyadic productivity and comparative advantage of marriage, the individual utility of a specific marriage is thought of as being dependent on the level of compatibility between man and woman, and on the level of marital specialization. Becker postulates a series of (empirical) 'substitutes' such as gender and income, and 'complements' such as education, age, etc. More specifically, male labor market potential is understood to be a substitute for female (non-market) productivity in the domestic sphere. Thus, one may expect that couple formation should broadly follow a strong negative assortative logic with regard to male and female income potential. In general, Becker postulates a positive sorting of mating on complementary traits, and a negative sorting on traits that are substitutes on the household level over all households.

Becker's theory was developed in the 1970s, and parts of its axioms are still occasionally utilized by some mate choice theorists today. Within the social sciences, however, it is less well known that the 'later' Becker tried to include cultural dimensions of human partner markets (1996), dissociated himself from the foundational assumption of stable preferences, and eventually turned to habits as explanatory concepts. Becker's economic theory can be thought of as a sociologically simplified but formally elaborated specification of sociological theories of exchange. Both theories assume that by exchanging material and immaterial goods, maximization will be realized. However, there are also important differences between those approaches to human agency in general and to mating processes in particular. First, exchange theory locates utility on the level of the individuals involved, whereas Becker's early model leaves the realm of methodological individualism with the concept of utility maximization over the household population. Basing their theories on the distinction between substitutive and complementary traits (Becker) and economic versus social exchange (Blau), both approaches take into account the economic and non-economic dimensions of couple formation, and can conceptualize similarity and dissimilarity in couples. However, due to Becker's emphasis on labor division, i.e. domestic versus non-domestic work, his early economic theory prioritizes economic conditions for the explanation of marriages.

The Blau Space

Both Becker (1976) and Blau (1964), and those who adhere to their theories (see e.g. McPherson 1983), postulate a "marriage market", where men and women compete for the best partners, initiating and participating in processes of exchange. An explicit structural conception of couple formation was first put forward by Peter Blau. He developed – in a theory that would later be named after him, 'Blau space' (McPherson 1983: 519) – a spatial representation capable of visualizing the distribution of traits characteristic for a particular society. The notion of Blau space enables the representation of social structures as a distribution within a multi-dimensional space, where the axes of the space are mapped according to the variation amongst the actors of this space (Blau et al. 1984: 589). Using the Blau space, one can describe populations using distinct nominal parameters (e.g. sex or ethnicity) and gradual parameters, which differentiate between status hierarchies (e.g. education, prestige, power). This spatial model is composed of predefined attribute axes (such as age, career prestige, or income); the distance between the units plotted on the axes illustrates the inverse function of similarity. In this way, human contact behavior is not seen as coincidental, but is described as a decreasing function of distance. The closer persons (or their characteristics) are to one another, the more likely a contact between them becomes (McPherson and Ranger-Moore 1991: 21f.). Blau assumes that actors in similar positions will also be predisposed to having similar experiences and characteristics, therefore leading – thanks in part to the increased likelihood of contact – to increased couple formation between actors with similar attributes (Blau 1977: 37). Accordingly, this model assumes homophilous preferences even more decisively than theories of partner preference.

When compared to Becker's abstract marriage *market* and the assumption of market equilibrium free from external influences, the Blau space is an explicit model of *society*, addressing specific opportunities of mating by principle. This concrete geographic and contextual selectivity has always been central to research on mating (Bozon and Héran 1989). In this context, a specification of the Blau space's general social opportunity structures can be derived by concentrating on the overall likelihood of meeting a potential partner. "Foci" (Feld 1981; Flap 2002: 12) are locations which focalize the encounters of actors and thus also increase the chances of meeting a partner (Stauder 2008). The inherent "processes of focused choice lead to homophily to the extent that people draw their friends from foci, and foci bring homogeneous sets of people together" (Feld 1982: 798). The structural selection of a focus is not neutral, but increases the chances of meeting similar people and decreases the chances of finding dissimilar people. Due to the selective attendance of specific location contexts, the homogeneity of resulting couples is a recurring result of the majority of partner market research (Blossfeld and Timm 1997, 2003; Kalmijn and Flap 2001; Bozon and Héran 1989). Research shows that high homogeneity emerges in school contexts with regard to age and education, in local neighbourhoods with regard to religion, and in the workplace with regard to social class background (Kalmijn and Flap 2001).

Mating as Agency in Structures (MAS) – The Paradigmatic Core of Current Research

These different approaches to theorizing mating processes are integrated and utilized in pragmatic and productive ways by the majority of traditional and current empirical research on online and offline partner markets. Despite many differences in researching human mate choice in detail, a common paradigmatic core of mate choice research can be identified: the strict dichotomization between actor and structure.

According to Belot and Francesconi (2007: 6), mating can be explained "in terms of the preferences of individuals who are choosing one another" and of the "opportunities people have to meet someone". Rosenfeld (2005): 1294f. applies the concepts of "individual utility maximization or exchange", "affinity" (in the sense of homophily preferences), and "propinquity and exposure" (in the sense of structural opportunities). Oppenheimer's theory of marriage timing is based on a conceptualization of couple formation which appraises the individual's search process with regard to "the relative numbers and dispersion of available members of the opposite sex", and the desire to "mate assortatively" (Oppenheimer 1988: 572). In a similar vein, Huckfeld (1983) contrasts meeting probabilities, as a function of a social context structure, with (friendship) preferences. Schroedter and Kalter (2008: 362) approach the issue of mating processes by postulating opportunity structures which define the supply of potential partners; the actor chooses from this pool according to his personal preferences. In the context of migrants' marriage patterns, González-Ferrer (2006: 172) argues that the main theoretical approaches are "individual preferences" and the "structure of the marriage market" – that is, "the constraints for individuals' marital choices that derive from sex imbalances" and "from the size of the own group within the local marriage market". A similar theoretical foundation underlies Carol's (2016) analysis of "partner choice among Muslim migrants and natives in Western Europe". For the explanation of marriage timing, Wiik and Holland (2015: 7) consider "individual preferences and behaviors" and limiting constraints caused by the "partnership market", which is conceptualized by "structural and demographic factors", such as "the population's sex and age ratios".

Norms are often treated as an element effective in the causation of marriage patterns. Kalmijn (1998: 418), for example, speaks of "three social forces": the "preferences of individuals for resources in a partner", "the constraints of the marriage market", and "the influence of the social group". Norms are, following Blossfeld and Timm (1997: 10, o.t.), significant in the decision to marry, as actors are in need of "conscious orientation" towards "socio-cultural norms" which are to be interpreted as "decision support in uncertain, frequently recurring action situations."

Obviously, and despite different theoretical and empirical focuses, the foundations of social scientists addressing mating phenomena share a certain commonality. In all these approaches, the actor and his preferences are contrasted to external structures of the market and the associated opportunity structures. Mating processes are thought of as individual choice acts within a given opportunity structure, which is usually referred to as a "partner market" or "marriage market", constituting the subject's field of eligibles (Winch et al. 1954: 244). This paradigmatic distinction between individual choice and external structure can be identified most explicitly in a formulation by Corijn (2003: 39), stating that

> any explanation of spousal selection has to rely on the dynamic interplay of opportunity structures and marriage markets on the one hand, and of individual preferences and strategies, on the other.

In a similar way, Blossfeld and Timm's (2003: 3) conceptualize mating phenomena as the

> interplay of opportunity structures to meet potential partners in specific phases in the life course – i.e. the chance to meet someone of the opposite sex within the social networks structured through the educational system for example – as well as individuals' preferences determining the choice of partners within these social circles.

This paradigmatic distinction between actor and structure, which underlies the greatest part of research on online and offline mate choice, will be henceforth referred to as *mate choice as agency in structures* or *MAS*.

Using the term 'paradigm' here does not mean that all research on mating is the same in every instance. 'Paradigm' is meant rather in the sense of Kuhn (1962), that is, to describe which techniques, models, problems, solutions, and values are shared among scientists at a given time, despite minor differences in their research. Labeling MAS as a paradigm does nothing more – but also nothing less – than emphasize that a considerable number of social scientists make a dichotomizing distinction between actor and structure for the purpose of assessing mating phenomena. As a consequence of this paradigmatic dichotimization, any explanation of mating is regarded as the result of the additive consequences of decision and choice acts on the individual level. This can be best seen where the fundamental differentiation between structure and choice itself becomes an object of research, determining which of the two may be more important for the explanation of mate choice (e.g. Belot and Francesconi 2007, Blossfeld and Timm 2003).

Regarding preferences in mating, it is frequently "assumed that people have a preference for spouses that are similar to themselves in terms of socioeconomic and cultural resources", due to the fact "the benefits from marriage are thought to be most efficiently utilized when individuals of similar traits match in the marriage market" (Çelikaksoy et al. 2010). Condensing a series of international comparative studies on educational homogamy, Blossfeld and Timm (2003: 331f.) conclude that inhabitants of all countries "seem to prefer to a large extent marrying an equally educated partner". As a consequence, they see this as supporting Becker's hypothesis "that men and women benefit mostly from each other if they resemble themselves as much as possible" as well as Blau's thesis that "the like likes the like." (ibid.). Alongside homophilous preferences, some researchers assume a "competition hypothesis", which emphasizes the "economic rather than the cultural side of socio-economic status, and posits that homogamy results not from a preference for similarity but from a preference for a partner with plentiful socio-economic resources" (Mäenpää 2015: 16).

Structural mechanisms are taken into consideration by research in the MAS paradigm, but they are essentially reduced to individual structures of opportunity and restrictions, which are conceptualized as the marginal distributions of a population structuring the probabilities of encountering actors with particular traits. The structural constraints of the partner market often include the specific, local manifestation of the Blau space (or the 'local field of eligibles') such as spatial proximity (Homans and Aden 1968; Katz and Hill 1958), the normative impact of one's social circles

(Kalmijn 1998), or the structural availability and ratio of particular traits, such as sex (Lichter et al. 1995) or ethnicity (Lewis and Oppenheimer 2000). The paradigmatic axiom of MAS is that these "institutional arrangements" essentially "delimit the pool from which people can choose, and preferences determine how people choose partners out of the pool they face" (Kalmijn and Flap 2001: 1290).

Overall – as in online dating research, as outlined in Chapter 2 – the dominant recurring empirical finding of offline research is that a process of assortative mating takes place over a range of different single variables such as education (Blossfeld and Timm 2003), income (Kalmijn 1994), ethnicity (Chiswick and Houseworth 2011), or weight (Klein 2011). Although there is no doubt that the MAS paradigm provides plenty of valuable findings, we may pose the question whether the scope of theorizing mating processes is ultimately exhausted by this single framework.

MAS as Variant of Methodological Individualism and Rational Choice

The common ground, as outline above, in large parts of traditional and current mate choice research is the consequence of a shared individualistic theoretical epistemology. Kalmijn explicitly emphasizes, in the context of mating processes, the "shift from the aggregate to the individual level" (Kalmijn 1998: 418). In a similar vein, Stovel and Fountain (2009: 367) explicitly treat "matching as a process that must begin at the individual level, and build from there". Also, the model of Huinink and Feldhaus (2009: 313) is deliberately conceptualized for the integration of "sociological, economic and psychological concepts" of "individual action and decision making". Although not necessarily stated quite so explicitly, this approach underlies most quantitative studies on empirical mating research, be it online or offline (Kurzban and Weeden 2007; Schulz 2009; Yang 2009; Blossfeld 2009; Blossfeld and Timm 2003).

The hegemonic status of this particular world view is particularly evident when examining the few explicit theoretical overviews available,[2] which tend to strongly emphasize the individual, implicitly favor individual or even psychological and biological arguments, and thus systematically avoid structural ones (Munck 1998; Surra and Boelter 2013). One of the few examples can be found in Surra and Boelter (2013: 215ff.), who review explicit theories on dating and mate selection and differentiate the literature into three bundles: (1) 'economic theories' (gender specialization, women's economic independence, economic search theory, coupled partners, and economic resources), all of which presuppose the analytical dimen-

---

[2] This scarcity of explicit works on sociological theories of mating processes can be interpreted as tacit consent to seeing individualism as the obvious approach to the realm of mate choice and partner market, thus making it pointless to suggest different theoretical approaches (in contrast to different hypotheses derived from the same paradigmatic foundation).

sion of decision and exchange; (2) 'marriage market and mate availability', addressing the issue of opportunity structure; (3) 'homogamy in dating and mate selection' as "one of the prime motivators for selecting a mate" (ibid. 222).[3] Evidently, even this modern comprehensive overview of different theories of mating confines itself to dichotomizing logic of action and external structure. Just as in many other fields of sociology, contemporary empirical mate choice research is essentially influenced by the action-theory paradigm. Here, the process of couple formation is, despite the theoretical variations, always considered to be a question of individual choice and as a phenomenon which has to take the subject as its starting point.[4] The strong emphasis on individual choice in analyzing mating processes can be seen to be the dominant perspective in a range of different approaches, and it is probably no coincidence that this scientific subject is most frequently referred to as 'mate choice research'.

The MAS perspective corresponds to the family of action-theory approaches, which conceptualize sociological explanations based on methodological individualism as goal-oriented agency, restricted by structural conditions, and actualized by a decision mechanism of (bounded) rationality. Thus, MAS can be seen as a conceptual example of Coleman's (1990) 'macro-micro-macro approach', or of the RREEMM model (see e.g. Lindenberg 2001), or of Boudon's MmSM model (1986), or alternatively of the model of frame selection (Kroneberg 2006). Following Esser (1993: 238, o.t.), models of this kind assume that an "actor is confronted with opportunities for action, as well as restrictions", that he can "select from alternatives", that he always "has the choice", that these selections are "regulated by expectations on the one hand" and "evaluations on the other hand", and – usually – that these selections from the choice sets follow a "rule of maximization".

In the context of mating, the strong emphasis on choice is justified by arguing that "throughout the twentieth century men and women were less likely to have been forced to marry a person of a particular background or social circle" (Corijn 2003: 39). Applying this view, the logic of the mate choice situation is conceptualized by 'bridging hypotheses' (especially regarding available opportunities); the logic of mate selection employs a preference-based decision mechanism (usually the expected utility of a particular choice act); and the logic of aggregation is conceptualized as the collective result of individual acts of partner selection (such as aggregated marriage rates or levels of homogamy) (see Figure 4.1).

---

[3] More recently, in a seminar description, Bruch (2015) states that "social scientists argue that two factors shape marriage and dating patterns: men and women's preferences for partners, and the size and composition of the pool of potential mates". https://www.nico.northwestern.edu/seminar-events/seminar-listings/2015/nov18.html

[4] This also holds true of investigations of subjective structures of meaning, strategies, and self-presentation – some of which are based on the theories of Goffman (1959) – which analytically emphasize the phenomenological perception of the actors involved (Lawson and Leck 2006; Bergström 2011; Zillman et al. 2011).

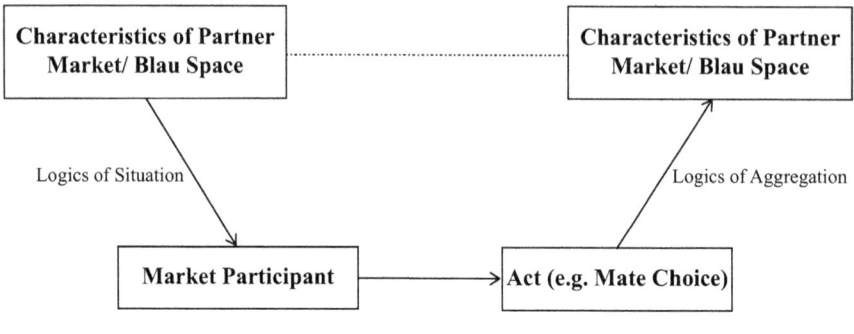

Fig. 4.1 The MAS paradigm as micro - macro - micro representation

Regarding the logics of aggregation, White (2013: 29) provides a comprehensive overview of the "current status of theorizing about families", and about issues of family sociology such as mating. He concludes that any adequate theory of family sociology needs to "identify the social mechanism that is producing the effect" (ibid. 2013: 29). The term 'mechanism' here, however, is not meant as a possible plausible meta-theoretical concept, but explicitly refers to Hedström's (2005) 'analytical sociology', a more recent variety of methodological individualism, which also takes the distinction between agent and structure as its premise.[5]

The argumentation so far is not intended to suggest the existence of an entirely homogenous field of rational action theories, but should serve to emphasize a paradigmatic family resemblance between different sociological theories (which becomes most evident when located within an overall field of sociological theory).

Structure as Externality?

The different varieties of the MAS paradigm, all based on the same strict actor-structure differentiation, can be understood as a variation of methodological individualism and rational choice (in the following, MI/RC). Thus, for the majority of mate choice research, as in many other research contexts, one can follow Adloff and Wacquant (2015: 186), who state that "the predominant conception of social structure locates it squarely outside of the agent". Applying the MI/RC framework in the

---

[5] Very close to the MAS paradigm outlined here, Hedström's 'mechanism approach' emphasizes the same macro-micro/micro-macro procedure. A minor difference seems to be that the nomological core of analytical sociology is defined by the desire-belief-opportunity model, meaning that actors intend to act within their frames of opportunity and based on their beliefs. Similar to the social space approach, analytical sociology emphasizes the relevance of relations for grasping sociological mechanisms. A core methodological difference is constituted by the emphasis on simulation techniques for modeling the logics of aggregation.

form of mate choice essentially conceptualizes structure as *external* structures of opportunity in the sense of eligible alternatives, and as external normative expectations. As this categorical subject-structure distinction reserves the term 'structure' for entities and mechanisms outside the actor, it is difficult to systematically incorporate societal and historical conditions, which may be decisive in shaping individuals' decisions and for actors themselves.

On the other hand, what else could be meant by 'structure', if not the actor's explicit choice opportunities and restrictions of choice, resulting from the distribution of variables in the overall population and their manifestations in the form of potential partners? There is a vast range of understandings of structure in the social sciences: social structure, structure of functionally differentiated societies, structure of societal spheres, structure of markets, network structures, cultural structures, normative structures, knowledge structures, symbolic structure, meaning structures, cognitive structures, structures of action, structures of domination, power structures, ideological structures, etc. In many different theories, the apodictic dichotomizing view of 'actor versus structure' is rejected. Some famous historical examples are Parsons' (1937) "unit act", expressing that "action is system" (cp. Luhmann 2011: 24), Giddens' (1984) "structuration theory", emphasizing the duality of structure and action, or White's (1992: 196) actor, who comes "into existence" and is "formed as overlaps among identities from distinct network populations". In wide parts of the field of traditional and modern social sciences, 'structure' *sensu lato* is seen as integrative element of the actors themselves, as

> Structures do not exist simply as Durkheimian facts that persons encounter in their extant environment, in the form of invisible relations, objective distributions of resources, or systems of constraints and opportunities that press or limit them from without. They are also dynamic webs of forces inscribed upon and infolded deep within the body as perceptual grids, sensorimotor capacities, emotional proclivities, and indeed as desire itself. Structures are internal springs or propellers as much as they are external containers, beams, or lattices. They are limber and alive, not inert and immobile. (Adloff and Wacquant 2015: 186)

Evidently, the dichotomous conceptualization of actor and structure – which is the basic premise of traditional (mate) choice – is anything but unchallenged within the field of social sciences. The same applies to interaction, which can likewise be understood as genuinely structured entity. Münch (1987: 335) emphasizes the "interpenetrative" nature of the relation between "microinteraction and macrostructures".

A comprehensive theory of mating processes may profit from a notion of structure which is constitutive for actors and their interactions. However, any broader notion of structure can be taken into account by MAS only in the context of the underlying action-structure dichotomy, as provided for in the MI/RC tradition. The next section will analyze how 'structure' manifest itself *within* the singular analytical elements of the MAS paradigm as well as *transverse* to them. In doing so, the need and potential for a relational notion of structure in research on mating processes will be emphasized.

The Structuration of Mating

The Heteronomous Structure of the Partner Market

Sometimes, an explicit or implicit assumption of the partner market's autonomy from societal preconditions is made. This can be observed most clearly in the case of Becker's economic theory, where the partner market is defined as relatively autonomous from societal influences. Assuming a partner market equilibrium implies that supply and demand on the partner market are stable and balanced, and not distorted by externalities, i.e. non-market influences. This goes hand in hand with the assumption of the existence of an autonomous and generalizable principle of partner market competition, prevailing in different social contexts (such as universities, schools, nightclubs, etc.) – a principle which is thought of as being decisive for mating processes and their outcomes (i.e. couple constellations). Thus, the interdependencies of the partner market with other social spheres are not a core topic for the neo-classical economic approach.

Also in the context of online dating, some authors strongly emphasize the issue of market-specific and frictionless equilibria. Hitsch et al. (2005: 9) state that "compared to traditional marriage markets", online dating is "largely driven by preferences and the equilibrium mechanism that brings partners together", and Stevenson and Wolfers (2007: 47) state that "the potential of the Internet" is "to increase the efficiency of matching". Wang and Lu (2007:12) even assume that the "lack of spatial confinement makes the cyberspace a free market" where "anyone could come, leave, or express themselves in a manner that does not have to heed even the slightest principle of social decency". Assuming the presence of autonomy allows for an emphasis on market-specific processes, but tends to ignore the external heteronomous structuration of a society of partner market processes, partner preferences, strategies, etc. Likewise, although to a lesser extent, anytime the sociologist conceptualizes a context of encounter such as a university, school, nightclub etc. *as a market*, he also tends to imply the operation of relatively autonomous partner market competition to a certain degree. In the context of online dating, the idea of relative market autonomy is manifested in the widespread distinction between a presumed *everyday life* in the offline world versus processes within an online dating platform.[6] However, the question as to whether autonomy exists in any partner market – that is, regarding the extent to which mate choice is a function of overall societal mechanisms or of societal spheres (such as the economic or religious sphere) – must be explicitly formulated as a question of the degree of a partner market's *heteronomous structuration*. The extent of market heteronomy corresponds to the degree to which the preferences, situations, choices, interactions, etc. of mating processes cannot be

---

[6] The implicit assumption of market autonomy also precipitates within some parts of mate choice, axiomatic when finding that – in online dating – the 'same' empirical patterns of (educational) homophily can be observed as found in offline research and that – to the astonishment of the observer – somehow users "transfer their offline preferences to the online environment" (Schulz 2010: 506, o.t.).

understood as something specific to the market but as structured by society. However, rational choice does not have a theory which addresses different societal spheres with regard to their heteronomous impact on market and market participants.

Transverse Structures of the Blau Space

In contrast to Becker's marriage market, the Blau space describes the societal dimensions of the partner market, and when combined with Feld's focus theory, allows an emphasis on the specific opportunities of encounter. The main problem with the Blau space, which is used as a macro-theory by many researchers, is that it can do little more than operationalize the external "structural conditions" which "generate the alternatives on the micro-level of mate choice" (Blossfeld and Müller 1996: 388, o.t.). Whereas this view might be useful in conceptualizing the structured nature of the 'field of eligibles' (i.e. the structure of potential partners and their traits), it cannot conceptualize the varieties of the subjective dimension which can be associated with objective positions. The reason for this is that the "objective of this theory is to explain patterns of social relations [...] in structural terms, not in cultural or psychological ones" (Blau 1964: xi). The Blau space "ignores cultural differences" (Blau 1977: 245) and postulates "that the structures of objective social positions among which people are distributed exert more fundamental influences on social life than do cultural values and norms" (Blau 1977: 10). This implies not only a severe analytical restriction, but it reinforces the tendency to reserve any notion of 'structure' to mechanisms outside the actors. Thus, it cannot take into account any wider notion of structure, including the interplay of societal and normative conditions with the actors' internal processes. As a consequence of neglecting *structured interdependencies* between structure and action, the Blau space neglects the fact that the structural probability of interaction due to physical proximity does not necessarily mean that the actors involved are motivated to interact and to form a relationship. In fact, structural proximity may well lead to a low willingness to interact and thus operate as a means of dissociation. In the following section, however, we will argue that considering 'transversal' structures such as the interplay of subjective meaning and objective position is of utmost relevance for a sociology of mating processes.

Situational Logics of Partner Choice

'External' Structures of Situation

In the lower left corner of 'Coleman's bathtub', the structural complications of situational elements effective in mating processes appear. The MAS paradigm, and indeed most mate choice research, maintains the assumption that actors are objectively and subjectively located in a *specific market situation*, inducing a general situation of mate choice for all market participants.

As the theoretical focus of choice models is constructed around the actor, the theorization of situational logics on the partner market, and thus any related bridge hypotheses, is seldom given high priority in research. Even the proponents of modern rational choice theories reduce these theoretical components of the 'bathtub' model to "necessary auxiliary assumptions about actors' preferences, beliefs, and constraints" which cannot be derived "from an empirically confirmed general theory" (Kroneberg and Kalter 2012: 80). As bridge hypotheses can not be derived from the theory of action itself, "building rational choice models and explanations" then requires researchers to "turn to a combination of substantive background knowledge, qualitative pretests, and orientating heuristic principles" (ibid.), in order to derive the sociological conditions of choice situations. It is widely recognized that, in terms of objective situational elements, different actors are subject to different restrictions and possess different resources. However, the subordinate theoretical status of the structural conditions of individual mate choice systematically fosters a neglect of the *structural relations between different mating situations*, which cannot be taken into account in a systematic way without a theory of the objective interdependencies between classes of situations.

'Internal' Structures of Situation

With regard to the actor's intentions, just as in the more theoretically-developed models of methodological individualism, in MAS, mating situations are conceptualized by the key characteristic of "one dominant problem" which must be solved by the actors in question (Esser 1999: 358, o.t.). In doing so, mate search, mate choice, self-presentation, marriage, etc., are analytically ascribed to all actors as being the key motivation of their behavior in the general mating situation on the market. In the case of online dating, Skopek et al. (2009: 7, o.t.) argue that,

> from the viewpoint of the actor, looking for a mate is a decision problem, with the only realistic goal being to minimize the probability of serious miscalculations.

Others postulate a general problem of trust inherent to online dating, which is seen as a social fact which every user is confronted with. However, any such generalization of mating as being one dominant problem to be solved by all actors tends to systematically neglect possible systematic deviations from the researcher's individual interpretation of the conditions which underlie the generalized market participant's uniform act of mate choice. Regarding subjective meanings, it cannot be universally inferred that each analytically-defined market participant in a situation of mate choice genuinely and subjectively orientates his agency in the same manner towards a future "romantic" outcome. Take the example of the different 'agendas' users of a dating site may have, ranging from marriage to non-committal relationships to purely sexual affairs, not forgetting mere indecisiveness. Furthermore, meeting people on the online dating market might actually transform the original intentions of users. One the other hand, returning to the example of the trust problem, one could argue that not every user finds himself objectively and subjectively in the same problematic situation of trust versus mistrust. For example, some users may perceive it as difficult to find a communication partner at all, thus making the presumed trust problem insignificant to them. Such subjective aspects of mating situations, however, are hardly independent from various specific socio-structural conditions, as one's market position is not independent from one's strategies (e.g. Skopek et al. 2011). In addition, any situation must be understood as the interplay between object and subject. Take the example of erotic appeal, which cannot be understood unless the interplay between the observer's criteria and the observed's traits are taken into account. This necessitates a way of conceptualizing the differential nature of structured subject-object relations, and thus the (structured) relations between structured cognition and traits.

In sum, the situational logics of mate choice comprise subjective and objective variations to such an extent that the fact of *structured situations* transcends the narrow framework of assuming or modeling a general situational logic effective in all mating processes.

Structures of Biography

Following the tradition of methodological individualism, most mate choice research maintains a notion of the future-oriented subject, which systematically conceals the fact that subjects are socialized agents with different biographies and societal status, which are inferred in any situation of mate choice. Blossfeld and Müller (1996: 394, o.t.) diagnose as a problem of the basic rational choice approach the fact that "most RC researchers apply timeless reconstructions of situations". They also criticize Becker for reducing the decision to marry to the expectations of future outcomes (Blossfeld and Müller 1996: 389, o.t.). In a similar vein, Kok argues "that we can only understand choices and behavior by taking into account experiences in earlier stages of life" (Kok 2007: 208). Situations of mate choice are not only affected by "external" resources and restrictions, but also vastly differ with regard to the *biographical structures* of different actors. This alone subverts the aforementioned idea of one dominant problem to be solved by all actors.

The individualistic life-course perspective (see e.g. Elder 1969) transcends the framework of the MI/RC complex by emphasizing the impact of antecedent life-courses on actors' mate choice timing. For example, particular past experiences of dating site users might be more relevant for their practices online than an assumed future goal. However, there is still the need for an adequate conceptualization of the fact that not only the time point (e.g. of marriage) can be traced back to systematical biographical conditions, but also the internal and external conditions of mate choice situations themselves. In consequence, the internal conditions – like the perceptions and evaluations of the actors – and the external conditions – like resources, opportunities, restrictions and necessities – of any choice act (e.g. contacting a specific user's profile) must also be understood as socially and historically variable. This structural logic, however, comes into conflict with the analytical capabilities of

'Coleman's bathtub', which starts with a general model of internal and external conditions and implies no systematic way of theorizing the various histories of actors.

Mating Utility and Mating Preferences

Structure of Utilities

From an (implicit) assumption of a general mating situation and the concomitant idea of an average, future-oriented actor, individualistic models imply a general utility unit which must be maximized in order to achieve a decision value, ultimately leading to the choice act itself (e.g. approaching a potential partner). For example, Ormel et al. (1999) conceptualize "well-being" as a fundamental unit of utility, whereas Frey and Eichenberger (1996: 194) even discuss "love" as the relevant utility unit in mating. Collins criticizes such practices of merging all possible (partner) market goods into one "abstract utility function", which is sometimes assumed and often modeled as being "maximized by all actors" (Collins 2004: 144) whenever such an (implicit) assumption of a "common metric" for all possible goods is made.[7] First, different actors may consider different goods in a potential mate to be subjectively beneficial – for example, specialization in a married couple, increased reputation resulting from couple formation, or sexual satisfaction. In doing so, actors' expectations also differ systematically in the probability they assign to their desires being satisfied depending on the selection of one particular alternative. Furthermore, the very degree to which the anticipation of the future itself can be applied may vary over different actors. Some may actually anticipate long-term consequences being associated with particular goods, other may be bound in the here-and-now of a romantic experience. Second, like subjectively expected utilities, any objective utility – meaning any advantage of mating apart from the subjective evaluation – can hardly be generalized using a single unit of utility. Even if this insight may be accepted theoretically by individualistic thinking, any averaging specification of a general utility unit still implies a universal objectivity *qua* design. Overall, Oppenheimer (1988: 570) rightfully asserts that there "are numerous returns to marriage that defy easy quantification". Thus, whereas the assumption of a common utility function as part of a consistent economic model may be formally appropriate, the practical danger in sociological research on mating processes remains of falsely assuming that a mass of actors (or an average actor) subjectively or objectively maximize the same utility unit in the course of their mating practices. Peggs and Lampard (2001: 95) come to the same conclusion and state that "one of the major problems with applying utilitarian models of rational choice to decisions concerning couple relationships is that such models are unidimensional", thus postulating a stronger consideration and conceptual development of multidimensional or *structural utilities*.

---

[7] It should be emphasized that within the theoretical framework of the utility model, **Z** is unspecified at the outset and can be made explicit according to very different and multiple criteria.

Structure of Preferences

Synchronically Structured Preferences

The (implicit) assumption of a general utility unit in mating precipitates in the empirical practice of modeling a single mating preference (which is seen as a function of utility) over all actors. In research on partner choice, as in a great deal of orthodox rational choice research, "preferences are often assumed to be the same across persons" (Freese 2009: 11), neglecting differences in mating preferences for classes of actors. MAS researcher Timm (2004: 74), for example, assumes that the preference and utility structures of men and women have an overall inherent tendency to (educational) homogamy (cp. Blossfeld and Timm 2003: 333).

However, like mating utilities, any single mating preference (such as preferring tall men to short men) cannot be generalized as being universally applicable over all market participants. Actors may differ by means of which traits and which trait combinations they desire, ignore, or avoid in a partner. An obvious example is the desired relationship form, be it long or short-term, casual or serious, etc., (Regan et al. 2000; Baker 2005), which prevents there being any 'common preference' in online daters, due to the fact that preferred relationship status correlates with preferred mating traits. Depending on the specific actor's position in the market, and therefore dependent on the mating situation as a whole, a preference for a highly educated partner (for example) may be the decisive preference for a particular actor – but this is not necessarily the case for all market participants. Thus, mating preferences must be seen as *structured preferences*, in that different actors may prefer different mating traits.

Apart from this little-questioned (but seldom theorized) fact, 'structure' manifests in yet another way in mating preferences. Mating preferences are usually assessed in isolation from one another – that is, researchers concentrate on educational preferences (Skopek 2011), or on preferences for age (Kenrick and Keefe 1992; Buunk et al. 2001; Skopek et al. 2011), or on preferences for attractiveness (see Toma and Hancock 2010). There is little scientific discussion of the relationships between the preferences themselves (and thus between the preferred resources on the partner market) and the potential implications for conceptualizing and modeling mate choice (cp. Skopek et al. 2011). In the context of age preferences, Bozon (1991: 142) argues:

> Functioning along informal lines, the marriage market involves procedures of appreciation and selection which are based on 'perception', a synthetic notion combining several registers of classification: thus age is never appreciated per se, but together with the many social, physical and psychological aspects which define a person.

Consequently, the act of assuming or modeling the operation of singular mating preferences actually artificially separates bundles of traits as they appear objectively in the form of potential partners and subjectively within mental representations.

The same applies for homophily, the preference for similarity, which plays a core role in the explanations of most modern mate choice research: homophilous mating preferences (as well as hypo- and hyperphilies) are also rarely assessed and modeled with regard to their interrelations. Taking into account the fact that mating preferences are not empirically distinct. Klein (1996: 211) emphasizes, in reference to Schoen and Wooldredge (1989), the fact that overall attractiveness of a potential mate may be seen as the core sorting market mechanism of couple formation. Nevertheless, questions remain as to which variables actually constitute general attractiveness, and whether all actors base their mating preferences on total attractiveness, or if in fact every indicator of this total attractiveness is itself socio-structurally variable. As the total attractiveness of a particular actor may well be perceived differently by different potential mates, a certain preferential model may be appropriate for the logics and agency of some actors, but less so – or not at all – for others. However, such questions of a varying adequacy of the mating preference model itself are – again – rarely reflected upon in traditional and modern mate choice research.

In sum, emphasizing structures in the context of mating also addresses the *relational structure between mating preferences*. If, however, different classes of actors can be described by different structures of mating preferences, the question arises whether these preferential classes are independent from objective conditions. To the extent that such *social structuration of preferences* can be observed, a theory is required which transcends the categorization between "internal" preferences and "external" position, as methodological individualism and rational action theories are not designed for such purposes.

Diachronically Structured Preferences

As with the conditions of mating situations, mating preferences are not usually assessed according to their biographical and social preconditions in a systematic way in the vast majority of mate choice research. As the origins of mating preferences, being prior to any mating situation, are not the primary task of most analyses, they are sometimes established on the basis of evolutionary psychological assumptions (such as male interest in female physicality). Whereas there is little reason to deny biological conditions for human actions, such perspectives neglect the societal impacts on mating preferences. A more dynamic approach is discussed by Stovel and Fountain (2009: 385), who state that "matching areas may best be understood as settings in which actors' preferences are, at least in some respects, endogenously produced". Here, mating preferences are treated as a function of the autonomous partner market itself, neglecting heteronomous influences of different social spheres. Others argue that it is the "local marriage market" which forms and frames "cultural factors, such as norms and preferences, which influence individuals' marital behaviours through distinctive mechanisms" (Mu and Wu 2015: 5). One is inclined to agree with Blossfeld (1996: 189), who argues that "the historical process is always ongoing", which "poses difficult theoretical and empirical specification problems with regard to the preferences and constraints at any point in time". The resulting question is how to systematically conceptualize these historical developments. Wiik and Holland (2015: 6) argue that children's "own preferences for when and whom to marry" can be understood as an indirect "product of their parents' preferences", as in the course of socialization processes "children internalize parental expectations and attitudes". Mating preferences are also often traced back on the basis of generalized conceptions of society, such as the traditional 'male breadwinner' model, as an internalized normative mechanism of preference (Blossfeld and Timm 2003: 333). Yet again, the problem here is that different classes of actors can have incorporated very different historical conditions during their particular socializations. Thus, a theory seems necessary which considers *diachronic preference structures* and thereby allows researchers to derive the historicity of mating preferences outside of and prior to the partner market and singular sub-segments such as the occupational sphere.

Mating as Decision

Structures of Bounded Rationality

'Structure' may also impact on the logics of mate selection with regard to decision mechanisms. Usually, in the conceptualization of mate choice, some kind of rational choice decision is assumed as the nomological core, generating the actual individual decision value (e.g. for initiating a mating procedure). However, and as a consequence of our argumentation so far, for the assumption of strict rationality in mating, the problem of every rationalistic model arises that "multiple, contradictory interests [for example the presence of multiple, interdependent mating preferences, A.S.] could preclude maximization of interest for all dimensions and thus for the self" (Kara 2009: 71). Even for marriages (which certainly imply a more serious decision situation than, say, mere flirting), it has been shown that "a considerable number of men and women marry their first reasonably serious partner" and not a partner according to an actual maximized utility (Frey and Eichenberger 1996: 189). It thus comes as no surprise to find that modern empirical mate choice research has largely distanced itself from strict forms of utilitarianism and emphasizes the idea of bounded rationality in mating (see e.g. Skopek 2011). The conceptual advantage of the MAS paradigm – which stems from its suitability for the application of further explanatory mechanisms – is its openness and flexibility. For example, findings from cognitive psychology can be applied to enable a more realistic concept of the actor (Miller and Todd 1998). Individuals do not actually think rationally, but rely instead on "fast and frugal heuristics" (Reimer and Rieskamp 2007) – due to both the unavailability of information and to constraints in time and cognitive capacity – rather than on calculations which genuinely maximize utility (Todd and Miller 1999; Heiner 1983; Oppenheimer 1988). The assumption prevalent in earlier forms of rational action theory – that utility is maximized in the form of a partner – is often rejected in favor of the principle of 'satisficing' (Simon 1956), in which a person is considered a potential partner by sufficiently fulfilling one's preferences.

Due to the individualistic concept of the logic of situation, however, research is compelled to assign a generally prevailing 'boundedness' as being inherent to one situation for all actors. The individualistic paradigm sees mental models as characteristics of general situations (and not, for instance, of situation-independent habits, frames, rationality etc.). Take the example of (search) heuristics in mating, using the famous 'secretary problem' (Gardner 1960; Ferguson 1989): How shall an actor choose his partner, given that potential partners appear in a random order and do not reappear when rejected? This generalization of a search problem, and its possible solution, neglects the fact that the quantity and quality of all potential partners vary dependent on the attributes of the actor in question, for example their class background. Thus it can be expected that actors will also differ by means of their search strategies and rationalities, as the problem presents itself differently to different actors. Some actors may indeed try to gather information on the market structure and their own chances, trying to identify an optimum (leading to a few pathological cases, which media and critical theory tend to suggest represent standard practice on online dating sites). Others may consider themselves satisfied with a sufficient mate, and some with a near-optimal mate. Also, some actors might follow a rational model in one sense (e.g. gathering information by browsing all profiles in an area), but not in the other (e.g. systematically reflecting the traits of acceptable profiles). Accordingly, it is a daring thesis indeed to assume that all actors will show the same quality and quantity of boundedness in their rationalities. Against the background of our previous argumentation, we must instead assume that different (classes of) actors will incorporate different bounds of rationality. For example, some users of a dating site are in the situation of having to make a decision quickly due to their own age, whereas for others time is on their side.

The concept of *structured boundedness in mating* has consequence for the aforementioned preferences. If different actors can be characterized as being differentially bound in their rationality, it is even more problematic to postulate a set of generally prevailing mating preferences which are processed by all actors in the same (bounded) rational way. Thus, the fact that mental processes do usually not follow the logic of maximization has implications for the generalizability of the aforementioned utility metric, and for its contingent preferential manifestations. Only if all actors under- and overemphasize mating traits in the same way could the concepts of preference and (bounded) rationality be modeled equally for all actors on the partner market.

Normative Structures of Decision

A particular constraint for free mate choice from the viewpoint of MAS is that decision processes in mating are dependent on norms. The traditional normative approach in social sciences is to see rules of endogamy (or exogamy) as the core mechanism of mate choice (see e.g. Stovel and Fountain 2009: 367). For example, age patterns of marriage partners have been explained in terms of societal norms regarding an acceptable age relation within a couple (e.g. Lewis and Spanier 1979; Spanier and Glick 1980). It is true that mating norms can enter into decision-making processes, for example in the case of older women hesitating to contact a younger man online (cp. Skoepk et al. 2011). However, even if norms are built in to individual models they are usually trivialized by "subsuming them under one single preference ranking for each agent." (Peter and Spiekermann 2011: 229). On a methodological level, this ignores the fact that different cultural and economic conditions are associated with different mating norms, such as flirt rituals specific to particular social classes. Furthermore, even if a particular class of actors orient their mate choice decisions according to normative demands, it does not follow that the mechanism of normative orientation underlies the mating practices of all actors. Consequently, the degree to which *structured norms of decision* are considered to exist in an individualistic model of mate choice, corresponds to the leverage of the assumption of generalized 'normative preferences' or 'norm-based preference distortion' effective in mating decisions.

Norms effective in mating processes tend to be treated as external restrictions in mate choice research, so that the normative structure is treated as a set of external conditions defining which practices are legitimate or not. For example, Çelikaksoy et al. (2010: 67) assign norms to "third party involvement" which "can influence marital choice within the social/ethnic group or family to which an individual belongs". Likewise, Mäenpää (2015: 17) assumes that actors may "follow the social norms and rules of the surrounding community that prescribe what kind of partner is proper and desirable". Here, mating norms are seen as *regulative rules* and not as *constitutive* rules (e.g. Searle 1969). However, norms do not only operate as mere external decision guides. They structure the cognitive and mental apparatus of (classes of) actors, as well as the meaningful dimension of practice, a fact that points to *normative structure of decisions* in mating. For example, the fact that the man 'should' be taller than the woman in a relationship is also clearly manifested in online dating. But do we need to assume that women orient their interaction practices according to a given rule of height, in order to fulfill social standards and prevent feelings of shame? Norms in mating may also operate as constitutive due to the fact that a plethora of historical preconditions will impact on pre- and semi-conscious emotional states in many women when encountering men with particular physical seizes. As a consequence of this constitutive nature of norms, it also hardly plausible to assume that "social norms are changed by rational actors" in reaction to perceived "costs and benefits to an extent that these norms do not facilitate the actor's means-ends relationships anymore" (Blossfeld and Timm 2003: 9). Norms must be understood as being effective in the form of inert *structured orders of implicit or tacit knowledge*, rather than as volatile reflected orientations towards external expectations. But furthermore, to the extent that these orders of knowledge show a relation of order between each other, a theory would be needed which would allow us to grasp the *structure of knowledge structures*.

Dispositional Structures of Decision

This critique of a general (bounded) rationality and normative orientation underlying mate choice can be further extended by focusing on 'unconsciousness' as the analytical endpoint of boundedness. For example, with relevance for online dating, with its profile structure, Willis and Todorov (2006: 592) show that "trait inferences from faces" do not operate via "slow, effortful, and deliberate" processes, but can be characterized as "fast, intuitive" and "unreflective" and that as soon as 100 milliseconds after seeing a person's face, an impression of trustworthiness, competence, sympathy, attractiveness, and aggressiveness emerge in the human brain. As a consequence of such findings, not only must we reject instrumental rationality as a general decision mode in mating, we also must refuse to accept the idea that any mate choice act is the factual result of conscious rational choice. This insight indicates the need for a conceptualization of subconscious decision processes.

This is widely recognized by mate choice (and rational choice) researchers; however, as Andersen and Hansen (2010: 26) argue, one important implication of introducing subconscious decision making is that partners sort according to preferences "without observing this trait consciously or rationally considering its implications". Accordingly, sorting processes, the core explanatory goal of the individualist mate choice paradigm, cannot be traced back to any unitary decision mechanism.

Yet again, the problem would be less severe if all actors would be alike in their deviation from the ideal-type model as constructed by the researcher. As this is not reasonably to be expected, the analytical MI/RC framework begins here to show its limitations.

However, the concept of rationality in partner choice must not be dismissed. Rather, rationality must be understood as one possible emanation of underlying dispositions. Hodgson (2009: 10) argues that

> experiments since the 1970s show that conscious sensations are reported about half a second after neural events, and unconscious brain processes are discernable before any conscious decision to act, [which] suggests that our dispositions are triggered before our actions are rationalized: we contrive reasons for actions already under way.

Just as bounds of rationality must be seen as variable and affected by social influences, all such unconscious processes are anything but free from historical, structural, and normative preconditions;, instead, they take the form of *differentially structured mating decisions*.

In fact, rationality may be best understood as one emanation of a multitude of dispositional mechanisms, as the very "capacity for deliberation and choice" depends on "habits and instincts, inherited respectively through our culture and our biology" (Hodgson 2009: 2). Accordingly, one has to follow Illouz, arguing in the context of mating processes, that "choice is far from being a simple category and is no less shaped by culture than are other features of action" (Illouz 2012: 19). Again, as "habituation and sociality are linked together" Hodgson (2009: 6f.), actors must be understood as differing in their dispositions, prior to any situation of mate choice. One may then think about actors who are predisposed towards rationality, equity, submission, domination, etc.

Structures of the Actor

As we have shown above that the realm of habits is prior to (partner) choice, and that habits must be understood as being genuinely structured by societal impacts, the need for theorizing *structured actors* arises. Coming from the starting point of a rational choice approach, Kara (2009: 71) argues that "the possibility of preference patterns incapable of being represented by a unified preference ordering" requires "an alternative framework which posits the self as a multidimensional complexity as opposed to a one-dimensionally representable simplicity". The framework of rational choice theory and methodological individualism does not provide a multidimensional actor and thus cannot grasp the varieties of different societal impacts which may be constitutive for the structuration of actors.

The tendency to apply a generalized logic of agency in mating is a result not least of one of the fundamental problems of all individualistic approaches. In focusing on future-oriented decisions, one has no coherent concept to systematically handle the historically induced trans-situationality of a specific (mating) situation.[8] MAS, as is the case for most rational action theories, has no systematic historical conceptions of 'actor' or 'situation' which transcend the situation itself. Thus, MAS has no theoretical solution to the problem of "the co-ordination of past, present, and future cognition, and of orders of preference as consecutively occurring sets of beliefs and desires" (Wiesenthal 1987: 446, o.t.). Remarkably, some evolutionary psychologists came to the same conclusion. Gustavsson et al. (2008: 580) argue that the finding of the "plasticity" of human mating preferences requires "a shift in research focus to emphasize the dynamics of mating strategies as outcomes of past selection and interactions between individuals and their social and asocial environment within societies". However, there is no theoretical sociological framework inherent to the MI/RC complex which could provide a conception of the actor as temporally structured.[9]

Structures of Partner Choice

A partner market may well be perceived as being a structured complex of actors following different dispositional logics, with rational or bounded rational modes being special cases. We can then speak of *structured mate choice*, not only due to the fact that dispositions are structured by means of different mental knowledge systems and by means of different class backgrounds. Structure in mate choice also manifests in form of the empirical interdependence of the choice objects (i.e.

---

[8] The tendency to abandon the strong assumption of stable preferences comes at the price of a lack of pre-situational mechanisms, which could explain non-contingent patterns of agency in mating.

[9] One could think of mobilizing the individualistic life-course approach here, however, this further development of rational action theories has no theoretical concept for historizing the actor himself.

partners). Any act of mate choice is not only based on differentially structured dispositions, but is also situated within particular classes of eligibles, comprising particular combinations of choice sets. The consequence of *structured choice sets* is a strong indication of mating as (partially) unintended practice. Kalmijn (1998: 400) argue that, as

> preferences for socioeconomic and cultural resources do not by themselves translate into homogamy and endogamy with respect to social characteristics", but because "social characteristics are correlated with such resources", outcomes of mating always imply "the unintended by-product of individual preferences for resources in a partner.

Due to the fact that unintended elements of mate choice may be the result of very different underlying opportunity and meaning structures, it is difficult to postulate a general intentional structure for the average actor. This is of utmost relevance for the preferential element in modeling mate choice. The empirical relationship between particular mating preferences and mating behavior is weak, as Wood and Brumbaugh (2009), Todd et al. (2007) and Schmitz et al. (2009) show, in the context of stated and revealed mating preferences. Desiring particular traits in a potential mate does not mean that a partner of this nature is actually contacted. Likewise, one cannot derive or reveal 'true' preferences from the observation of a choice act, as different structural mechanisms may be at work. Analyzing, for example, the choice of a partner as a function of educational degree, subjects the practices of all actors to a uniform post-hoc logic, which may approximate the situation for some (non-random) actors, but fails to recognize the logics underlying the choice practices of others. Consequently, modern mate choice research requires a reorientation towards structural preconditions, subjective implications, and differential interdependencies between structure and subjectivity of different mate choice acts.

Interaction Process

Synchronic and Diachronic Structures

The arguments so far should already motivate a stronger consideration of structure in mate choice research, but the necessity for integrating structural concepts becomes of even higher priority when taking into account the fact that mating processes comprise two actors, choosing each other. When it comes to interaction, some authors no longer consider mate choice to be a single act, but rather a sequence of choice acts undertaken by two partners (e.g. Willoughby and Carroll 2010; Skopek et al. 2009). Mating is also often conceptualized as a two-sided extension of the rational actor model or even as "one two-sided choice act" (Schulz 2010: 229, o.t.). As shown above, for mate choice research, the concept of 'exchange' is the central concept for the purpose of conceptualizing mating interactions.

Individualistic models often assume the existence of, and subsequently model, 'average' relationship types, such as an exchange between highly educated actors, or between an actor with a high income and one who is physically attractive. A pertinent question, however, is whether a general model of exchange can be imposed on the variation of different *exchange* logics. For example, a particular observed dyad in online dating may be described in terms of economic exchange, whereas another may be better described in terms of social exchange, etc. The same applies to Becker's theory, which postulates the existence of general resource relations of substitution and complementarity. Substitution and complementarity are understood as being essential characteristics of specific variables, which Becker's model generalizes or averages over household members. This rather obscures the fact that very different (exchange) relations may result in a lasting couple formation, and exchange in mating must be understood in terms of *synchronic and diachronic structures of exchange*.

Another problem is determining the extent to which the concepts of exchange are appropriate for the conceptualization of interaction (in mating) at all. Mating is often associated with the idea of actual exchange between two potential partners. If, for example, user A contacts user B and User B sends an answer, they are seen as exchanging parties. 'Exchange', however, is a processual term that can hardly be equated with the concept of choice acts. The sociological term 'exchange' actually refers to more than a simple principle of *quid pro quo* which the actors involved were both themselves aware of and immediately affected by. On the contrary – an objectively attributable exchange in mating is likely to be imperceptible to the actors in question, as the involved actors (e.g. in flirting) scarcely orient their current interactions towards future exchange profits.

Exchange may only retrospectively appear as the implied logic of interaction, as opposed to an actual act of exchange in the here and now of the observed interaction. Thus, when observing aggregated outcomes on the market level, which speak of underlying exchange logics, one may assume "that capital marries capital", but nothing entitles us to conclude "that individuals marry in order to unite or exchange their capital" (Bozon and Héran 1989: 117). Accordingly, mating-related interactions can be differentiated according to the *exchange structure of interaction*, i.e. to the degree that exchange logics are subjectively relevant categories for the particular actors.

Evidently, 'exchange' as a model may only be appropriate to a sub-quantity of interactions; for example, Blossfeld and Drobnič (2001) critically discuss Becker's "specialization of labor", and contrast its explanatory power with those of competing explanatory mechanisms, such as "role specialization", "power structures", "male oppression of women", "economic exchange", "non-economic exchange", "doing gender", "symbolic exchange", "identity-formation", "social class", and "country contexts". These structured logics in interactions also point to the fact that society impacts on interaction in a fundamental way. The interactional situation of two particular actors on a partner market is more than a situation of direct interdependency between the actors. However, neither Becker's nor Blau's theory focus on the fact that "each single case of social interaction is determined simultaneously by characteristics of the interacting units and by properties of the social system in which the interaction occurs" (Haller 1981: 775). More specifically, "each individual social exchange [...] does not simply imply a relationship between the two exchanging parties, but also implies their connection to a group, an organization, or a society, and to further structures of exchange, power, community, and culture" (Münch 2002: 86, o.t.). In fact, Blau's conceptualization of exchange in mating was not conceptualized to systematically assess 'macro-sociological' conditions, just as his Blau space was not able to consider exchange processes:

> I must admit [...] that I was more successful in analyzing exchange processes themselves than in using them as the basis for a theory of macro-sociological structures. For this reason I altered my approach; instead of assuming that macro-and micro-sociological phenomena can be explained by the same theory, I now assumed that the two require different, though complementary, theories (Blau 1989: 16).

Overall, there seem to be very different *structures of exchange* and, more generally, *structures of interaction* underlying mating processes, all of which are socially structured even before the first moment of encounter. Accordingly, in the case of an emerging couple, the subjective meanings involved (such as mating intentions) and the resources invested are to be derived from the particular social position of the two agents, including various "ecological factors", "motivational factors" and "material resources" (Collins 1990: 34f.), factors which cannot be generalized for all dyadic constellations.

Interaction and Recursive Structuration

The fact that mating is characterized as a reciprocal and temporal process of structured agents within a structured social environment has further analytical consequences for the MAS concepts discussed so far. Take the example of preferential explanation in online dating. Even if mating preferences, such as educational preferences in online first contacts, statistically explain a certain amount of actual mating interactions, it does not follow that this particular preference is also causal for the process of stabilization of couples. Interacting with a potential partner transposes the active agent into a new situation, with new decisions to be made and different relevant preferences, intentions, rationalities, and choice sets. For example, whereas female attractiveness in a profile picture might be a major determinant of male first contacts, the subsequent communication processes puts different preference dimensions into play, such as the intended form of relationship. Thus, the fact that mating implies interaction processes means that 'structures' manifest themselves in the form of *sequential structures of partner preferences*.

Not only do different preferences play different roles depending on the phase the two actors are in, as has been addressed by stage and filter models – they can also change due to this very interaction. As Frey and Eichenberger (1996: 198) argue, "preference changes" can emerge during the course of interaction. One important mechanism is that the emotional initiation of a relationship, when perceived as romantic, systematically "leads to a systematic overemphasis of a partner's characteristics related to love" while other traits are "underemphasized or sometimes even completely ignored" (Frey and Eichenberger 1996: 194). If in a developing relationship based, say, on preferences for age, a situation of commitment emerges which is constitutive for the continuation of the relationship, this can make other potential partners seem less attractive. The emergence of commitment might also be conceptualized and modeled as a preference. However, the particular preference object is now a different one, meaning that a preference considered relevant for a first contact cannot be assumed to be constantly influencing behavior throughout the subsequent process of couple formation. This, however, further challenges the element of rationality in the choice paradigm. Assuming that the same situational logics and preferences apply to the process of interaction over time implies that prior investment "does not influence one's consideration of current options", but that "only the incremental costs and benefits of the current options" affect decision making (Arkes and Ayton 1999: 591). The currently relevant "endowment effect" of an existing partnership (Simpsons 1987) and the "sunk cost" (Arkes and Blumer 1985) effect of past investments speak against the analytical transference of first-contact choice situations to subsequent interactional steps in mating.

Sen argues that commitment involves "counter-preferential choice", thus "destroying the crucial assumption that a chosen alternative must be better than [...] the others for the person choosing it" (Sen 1977: 328). Likewise, the insinuated logic of exchange is incrementally subverted by emerging commitment, which inhibits the logics of direct reciprocity. If the interactional character of couple formation is reduced analytically to individual preference-based choice acts or general logics of exchange, this makes it difficult to adequately take into account the different mechanisms of reciprocity inherent to mating processes. The concept of reciprocity relativizes the idea of single, causally relevant mating preferences, as it amalgamates the individual contingent preferences of an interaction into a kind of 'unified preference unit', the relationship itself: the interaction itself receives its own value as part of the process of interaction. For an individualistic conception of mate choice, this again turns out to be problematic if the probability and character of reciprocity – and hence any 'unified preference' – varies between different types of interactions, e.g. as a function of social class background and different associated traditions. Apart from the probability of the emergence of reciprocity between two potential partners, fundamental questions – such as when and how they describe their relation as "love" – arise. The danger again is in ignoring the socially differential character of *structures of commitment and reciprocity* in couple formation.

Structured Logics of Aggregation

Remarkably, the logic of aggregation and the concomitant structural outcomes are often *not* treated as distinct from the micro-level of mate choice behavior. As the value-expectation theory of MAS is often applied using the 'logic of as if' within a formal modeling strategy of observed outcomes, the structural consequences often tend to be simply analytically equated with aggregated choice acts. In doing so, the logic of aggregation is reduced to the summation of the same type of acts, such as marrying, contacting according to specific traits, deception, etc. (see Hedström 2005: 101ff. for a similar critique). For example, the macro-explanandum of marriage rates is seen simply as a direct consequence of individual acts of marriage. Classical methodological individualism in general does not usually reflect upon the question as to whether this reductionism is justified or not. On the contrary, Coleman sees it as "especially important that the individual-action component remains simple" (Coleman 1990: 19). Likewise, many mate choice researchers reduce *a priori* such macro-explananda to a question of the totality of summarizable acts. However, a collective marriage rate may be better conceived of as the result of myriad different acts and underlying meanings. In this case, it represents a methodological (not a logical) problem for methodological individualism and mate choice research to simultaneously grasp different meanings and different behaviors which generate one macro-phenomenon. Each structural explanandum may represent a set of unintended consequences – an insight which is otherwise constitutive for methodological individualism.

For example, the rate of educational homogamy in a society may be the structural outcome of culture-oriented mate choice, age-related mate choice, etc., and hence may represent a 'structural by-product' of acts which imply the most diverse underlying meanings. Some proponents of the MAS model tend to analytically conflate the phenomenological perspective of the assumed average actor, the model of agency itself, and the structural outcome. In doing so, the structural outcome of mating – most prominently assortative mating – is reduced to a function of one type of mating preferences, mating utility, mating rationality, mate choice acts, exchange in mating, and rule of aggregation: homogamy is the function of selection, being the function of homophily, given a set of alternatives (cp. de Singly 1987 for a critique).

A particular problem is that different sorting mechanisms may underlie one and the same variable. On the market level, education, for example, may imply a positive sorting with regard to homophily and social exchange or negative sorting due to couple-level division of labor and economic exchange. Furthermore, multiple mechanisms of aggregation beyond mere addition can be assumed to be operating, as for example escalation, inhibition, accumulation, etc. Ultimately, neither the simultaneity nor the interdependence between such different aggregation mechanisms can be grasped when taking a single bathtub as one's analytical basis.

From Externalized Structure to Structural Relationism

Against the background of our considerations so far, one can clearly state that the paradigm of mate choice as agency in structures leaves plenty of room for a wider notion of 'structure'. This is not to say that social reality must be understood as a chaotic complex of arbitrary structures. On the contrary, accepting the genuine and multidimensional structuration of mating processes ultimately poses the question of structured interrelations between and within actors, interactions, mating preferences, mate choices, mating rationalities, mating preferences, etc. to such an extent that the combined framework of methodological individualism and rational choice becomes questionable regarding its analytical scope.

The paradigmatic core of the MAS perspective reduces the notion of structure to a structure of opportunity in the sense of alternatives, resources, and restrictions such as normative expectations, which are seen as external to the 'subject'. In reducing structure to what Illouz (2012: 19f., 242) labels *"ecology of choice"*, that is, the environment (including normative restrictions and cultural conditions), MAS mirrors the MI/RC complex, with its strict actor-structure distinction. In the context of mate choice, the resulting scientific practice of conceptualizing and modeling an average actor is to assume a generalized logic of mate choice, averaged modes of decision making, generalized mating preferences, generalized mating strategies, and mating interactions; analytical elements which are contrasted with an external structure. Structural relations between and within these concepts (i.e. mating resources, mating rationalities, specific mating preferences and utilities, specific mating habits, specific exchange relations in mating, and specific structural conditions of mating) are not the analytical focus of the MAS model. As a consequence, of the MI/RC framework, mating preferences and utilities, or rationalities, situations, opportunities, etc. are rarely discussed as being empirically variable. They are, instead, lashed prior to empirical analyses. Such practice neglects the possibility that not only the contingent variables of the decision model (say income preferences) but also the very conceptual elements themselves may vary in their applicability according to social structural conditions. This is not to say that the old objections to unrealistic models of rational action are to be repeated here. One may well accept that a sparse model need not grasp the complexities of reality. However, even more problematic than any unrealistic model of (bounded) rationality is the potentially *structural differential applicability* of any model. For example, rational conduct in mating might be an appropriate description of one class of actors, but not necessarily of all actors. Also, the degree to which an actor can be located in a situation of mate choice may well be seen as variable.

Ultimately, this raises the question of the conceptualization of the actor himself. In the context of mating, Peggs and Lampard (2001: 109) see a "multidimensional approach to analyzing decision-making as a necessity" and state that such an approach "needs to be operationalized in a way which is sophisticated enough to accommodate the complexity and heterogeneity of the influences involved and to address the interplay between structure and agency in real rather than additive terms". A core implication of such pertinent questions is that structure must be located within the actor. This addresses the "architecture of choice" (Illouz 2012: 20) – that is, "mechanisms that are internal to the subject and shaped by culture" affecting "cognitive and emotional processes" which are constitutive for the variety of mate choice processes. If, however, classes of actors do systematically differ from each other by means of these concepts, a structural theory seems necessary which could provide concepts of 'functionally' differentiated societies generating these structures as well as their synchronic and diachronic interdependencies. To the extent that these considerations hold empirically, the analytical framework of methodological individualism and (bounded) rational choice are put into question.

An individualist approach, applying 'Coleman's bathtub' to exchange processes, would be to simultaneously think of a multitude of bathtubs, including the multitude of individual mating preferences and decisions. However, even if one could imagine and model hundreds of bathtubs, due to the fact that every bathtub enters into the situational logics of another, the limits of methodological individualism would soon be reached. This has consequences a fortiori for the interactional dimension in mating, such as 'exchange'. If different constellations of interaction and exchange underlie empirical mating processes, the bathtub-model must be rejected.

To the degree to which these considerations are taken seriously, the very epistemological foundation as provided for by methodological individualism is called into question, entailing the need for an alternative underlying epistemology. Scott (2000: 136) argues "that rational choice theorists do tend to deny any autonomy or constraining power for social structures" which is "not inherent in rational choice theory but in the methodological individualism that, for most of its advocates, is adopted as a philosophical underpinning." Methodological individualism postulates that any sociological explanation requires micro-foundation (see e.g. Coleman 1986): this means that a sociological explanation can only be said to possess an explanatory status if it is possible to model social phenomena in terms of individual behavior. In perhaps its most clear form, Homans, an early proponent of this epistemology, states: "If you look long enough for the secret of society you will find it in plain sight: the secret of society is that it was made by men, and there is nothing in society but what men put there" (Homans 1961: 385). In doing so, as with individualistic research in general, large parts of mate choice research identify "micro with the actions of individuals" and thus tends to eliminate "structural features conceptually from the core of the mechanism directly responsible for a macrophenomenon" (Mayntz 2004: 251). In the context of mate choice some authors explicitly postulate to study mating phenomena on the macro-level via "independently taken individual marriage decisions at the micro level" (Blossfeld and Timm 2003: 3). This view reduces the explanation of social forces to 'individual' acts which are conceptualized as isolated events.

The manifold developments within mate choice research have shown that most sociologists not only dissociate themselves from the basic rational choice model, but also implement structural considerations into their particular models and research. Indeed, some mate choice authors indeed indicate the need for further developments in the sociology of mating in a structural direction. In the context of online dating, Skopek (2011: 331), for example, postulates an integration of the "macro-structural paradigm of opportunity structures" and "the micro-paradigm of individual preferences" in order to assess the "mutual dynamic of relationship formation".

Regarding fundamental social theory, some modern methodological individualists try to transcend the "traditional notions of methodological individualism by emphasizing the explanatory importance of relations and relational structures" (Hedström and Bearman 2009: 8). A relational mechanism – including "basic mechanisms as competition" – involves a "process linking two or more unconnected social sites by a unit that mediates their relation with one another and/or with yet other sites" (Mayntz 2004: 250; cp. McAdam et al. 2001: 26)". However, even the most modern variant of methodological individualism, "analytical sociology", tends to reduce the notion of relations in a Weberian manner to the orientation of action towards others (Hedström and Bearman 2009: 8). This notion of relation also manifests in the context of mate choice research. Huinink and Feldhaus (2009: 310f.) begin their life course framework of family sociology with the idea that "individuals act in a given situation which is structured by opportunities, restrictions and exigencies", and additionally postulate "information from the interrelated life course of partners", which is interpreted as "part of the external opportunity structure of the target person" (ibid.). In a similar way, Huston (2000: 298f.) adds the "relationship" as a third level of the analysis of mating processes to the "societal level" and the "individual". Transcending the dyadic relationship, Kalmijn (1998: 418) rightfully argues that third party effects, such as the "influence of the social group", are also mechanisms of high relevance for conceptualizing mating processes. Apart from the fact that it is difficult to adequately integrate interrelated actors (influenced by third parties) within the framework of MI/RC, latent relational mechanisms *within and between* (classes of) actors are not constitutive momenta. Even in modern Western societies, there is a vast majority of possible third parties, social groups, and societal spheres directly and indirectly involved in mating processes. Thus, classical sociological questions of domination and power underlying partner market processes (which may precipitate in the very relations and interdependencies between different actor's mating preferences, mating situations, mating strategies, mating practices, success chances etc.) can hardly be incorporated as systematic element of MAS. Overall, one may well diagnose a *relational deficit in the analysis of relationship formation* in large parts of current research on mate choice.

This also applies to research on modern dating phenomena such as online dating. Focusing on structure in the sense of the Blau space, its regional or institutional concretizations, normative regulations, and the concrete choice opportunities an actor faces, leads to ignoring structure in a relational sense. As online dating research essentially rests on the dichotomization of macro versus micro, it is systematically compelled to observe preferences rather than structures at work on dating sites. The analytical and explanatory focus of general partner market research requires a completion of the model of 'structures of selection acts' with a model of 'structures within selection actions and interactions'. This implies taking into account the socio-structural and historical preconditions and variations of the MAS model and its analytical elements. Acknowledging that structure can also manifest itself as the differential relation between these conceptual elements, the *a priori* differentiation between actor and structure must be abandoned in favor of a relational notion of structure. Recourse to modern developments of methodological individualism, however, is only partly able to supply the latter principle.

The general epistemic principle of a relational perspective is to start any research with "the relations and think from there towards the related" (Elias 1978: 127) – or, as White puts it, the actor "should be a construct from the middle of the analysis, not a given boundary condition" (White 1992: 196f.). This idea can be found in the works of early sociologists such as Karl Marx, Georg Simmel, and Leopold von

Wiese. There are also several more recent works which are grounded in the relational paradigm (e.g. Donati 2010; Crossley 2010).[10] A specific conceptualization of the relational paradigm in social sciences is represented by the notion of "field" (Lewin and Cartwright 1952; Elias 1978; Bourdieu and Wacquant 1992; Martin 2003; Fligstein and McAdam 2012) or "space" (see e.g. Bourdieu 1985), being instances which induce the linkage of its entities (including actor and structure). In this paradigm, the concept of 'relation' is set at the beginning of the operation. Consequently, not only are actors' direct relations analyzed, but also the indirect relations between agents and their traits.

Without reproducing the one-sided structuralism which is convincingly criticized by some authors (see e.g. Skopek 2011; Stauder 2008), in the next chapter, the relational sociology of Pierre Bourdieu will be elaborated. This theory is designed to transcend the subject-object distinction characteristic of the MI/RC complex. The integration of structure and agency will allow us to augment the perspective of 'mate choice as agency within structures' with the addition of a perspective which could be labeled as *mating as structures within agency*, thus providing an alternative theoretical framework for 'mate choice' research. In doing so, as Bourdieu did not develop a systematic approach to this subject area, the different mate choice theories outlined so far will be used to inform and develop a Bourdieusian theory of mating processes. Conversely, this Bourdieusian theory will be applied to structurally augment the MAS paradigm discussed so far.

References

Adloff, F., & Wacquant, L. (2015). For a sociology of flesh and blood: Questions to Loïc Wacquant. In F. Adloff, K. Gerund, & D. Kaldewey (Eds.), *Revealing tacit knowledge: Embodiment and explication* (pp. 185–196). Bielefeld: Transcript Verlag.

Alpern, S., & Reyniers, D. (2005). Strategic mating with common preferences. *Journal of Theoretical Biology, 237*(4), 337–354.

Andersen, S. H., & Hansen, L. G. (2010). The rise and fall of divorce – A sociological adjustment of Becker's model of the marriage market. *FOI Working Paper*. Retrieved from https://core.ac.uk/download/files/153/6480754.pdf.

Arkes, H. R., & Ayton, P. (1999). The sunk cost and Concorde effects: Are humans less rational than lower animals? *Psychological Bulletin, 125*(5), 591–600.

Arkes, H. R., & Blumer, C. (1985). The psychology of sunk cost. *Organizational Behavior and Human Decision Processes, 35*, 124–140.

Baker, A. J. (2005). *Double click: Romance and commitment among couples online*. Cresskill: Hampton Press.

Becker, G. S. (1974). A theory of marriage. In T. W. Schultz (Ed.), *Economics of the family: Marriage, children, and human* (pp. 299–344). Chicago: University of Chicago Press.

Becker, G. S. (1976). *The economic approach to human behavior*. Chicago: University of Chicago Press.

Becker, G. S. (1993). *A treatise on the family*. Cambridge, MA: Harvard University Press.

Becker, G. S. (1996). *Accounting for tastes*. Cambridge, MA: Harvard University Press.

---

[10] For a discussion of relational epistemology see Cassirer's work 'Substance and function'.

References

Belot, M., & Francesconi, M. (2007). *Can anyone be "the" one? field evidence on dating behavior*. ISER Working Paper, 17.
Bergström, M. (2011). Casual dating online. Sexual norms and practices on French heterosexual dating sites. *Zeitschrift für Familienforschung, 23*(3), 291–318.
Blau, P. M. (1964). *Exchange and power in social life* (9th ed.). New York: Wiley.
Blau, P. M. (1977). *Inequality and heterogeneity: A primitive theory of social structure* (1st ed.). New York: Free Press.
Blau, P. M. (1989). Reciprocity and imbalance. A citation classic commentary on exchange and power in social-life by Blau, P. M., *Current Contents/Arts & Humanities, 25*, 16.
Blau, P. M., & Duncan, O. D. (1967). *The american occupational structure*. New York: Wiley.
Blau, P. M., Beeker, C., & Fitzpatrick, K. M. (1984). Intersecting social affiliations and intermarriage. *Social Forces, 62*(3), 585–606.
Blossfeld, H.-P. (1996). Macro-sociology, rational choice theory, and time. A theoretical perspective on the empirical analysis of social processes. *European Sociological Review, 12*(2), 181–206.
Blossfeld, H.-P. (2009). Educational assortative marriage in comparative perspective. *Annual Review of Sociology, 35*, 513–530.
Blossfeld, H.-P., & Drobnic, S. (2001). Theoretical perspectives on couples' careers. In H.-P. Blossfeld & S. Drobnic (Eds.), *Careers of couples in contemporary societies. From male breadwinner to dual earner families* (pp. 16–50). New York: Oxford University Press.
Blossfeld, H.-P., & Müller, R. (1996). Sozialstrukturanalyse, Rational Choice Theorie und die Rolle der Zeit: Ein Versuch zur dynamischen Integration zweier Theorieperspektiven. *Soziale Welt, 47*(4), 382–410.
Blossfeld, H.-P., & Timm, A. (1997). *Das Bildungssystem als Heiratsmarkt: Eine Längsschnittanalyse der Wahl von Heiratspartnern im Lebenslauf* (Sonderforschungsbereich 186, Vol. 43). Bremen: University of Bremen.
Blossfeld, H.-P., & Timm, A. (2003). *Who marries whom? Educational systems as marriage markets in modern societies* (European studies of population, Vol. 12). Dordrecht: Kluwer.
Bokek-Cohen, Y., Peres, Y., & Kanazawa, S. (2007). Rational choice and evolutionary psychology as explanations for mate selectivity. *Journal of Social, Evolutionary, and Cultural Psychology, 2*(2), 42–55.
Boudon, R. (1986). *Theories of social change*. Oxford: Polity Press.
Bourdieu, P. (1985). The social space and the genesis of groups. *Theory and Society, 14*(6), 723–744.
Bourdieu, P. (1986). The forms of capital. In J. Richardson (Ed.), *Handbook of theory and research for the sociology of education* (pp. 46–58). New York: Greenwood.
Bourdieu, P., & Wacquant, L. J. D. (1992). *An invitation to reflexive sociology*. Chicago: Polity Press.
Bozon, M. (1991). Women and the age gap between spouses: An accepted domination? *Population. An English Selection, 3*, 113–148.
Bozon, M., & Heran, F. (1989). Finding a spouse: A survey of how french couples meet. *Population. An English Selection, 44*(1), 91–121.
Brehm, S., Miller, R. S., Perlman, D., & Campbell, S. (2002). *Intimate relationships* (3rd ed.). Boston: McGraw-Hill.
Burgess, R. L., & Huston, T. L. (1979). *Social exchange in developing relationships*. New York: Academic.
Buss, D. M. (2006). Strategies of human mating. *Psychological Topics, 15*(2), 239–260.
Buss, D. M., & Barnes, M. (1986). Preferences in human mate selection. *Journal of Personality and Social Psychology, 50*(3), 559–570.
Butler-Smith, P., Cameron, S., & Collins, A. (1998). Gender differences in mate search effort: An exploratory economic analysis of personal advertisements. *Applied Economics, 30*(10), 1277–1285.

Buunk, B. P., Dijkstra, P., Kenrick, D. T., & Warntjes, A. (2001). Age preferences for mates as related to gender, own age, and involvement level. *Evolution and Human Behavior, 22*(4), 241–250.

Cameron, C., Oskamp, S., & Sparks, W. (1977). Courtship American style: Newspaper ads. *The Family Coordinator, 26*(1), 27–30.

Carol, S. (2016). Like will to like? Partner choice among muslim migrants and natives in Western Europe. *Journal of Ethnic and Migration Studies, 42*(2), 261–276.

Çelikakso, A., Nekby, L., & Rashid, S. (2010). Assortative mating by ethnic background and education among individuals with an immigrant background in Sweden. *Zeitschrift für Familienforschung, 22*(1), 65–88.

Chiswick, B. R., & Houseworth, C. (2011). Ethnic intermarriage among immigrants: Human capital and assortative mating. *Review of Economics of the Household, 9*(2), 149–180.

Coleman, J. S. (1986). Social theory, social research, and a theory of action. *American Journal of Sociology, 91*(6), 1309–1335.

Coleman, J. S. (1990). *Foundations of social theory*. Cambridge: Harvard University Press.

Collins, R. (1990). Stratification, emotional energy, and the transient emotions. In T. D. Kemper (Ed.), *Research agendas of the sociology of emotion* (pp. 27–67). Albany: State University of New York Press.

Collins, R. (2004). *Interaction ritual chains*. Princeton: Princeton University Press.

Corijn, M. (2003). Who marries whom in Flamish Belgium? In H.-P. Blossfeld & A. Timm (Eds.), *Who marries whom? Educational systems as marriage markets in modern societies* (pp. 37–55). Dordrecht: Kluwer.

Crossley, N. (2010). *Towards relational sociology. International library of sociology*. New York: Routledge.

de Campos, S. L., Otta, E., & de Oliviera Siqueira, J. (2002). Sex differences in mate selection strategies: Content analyses and responses to personal advertisements in Brazil. *Evolution and Human Behavior, 23*(5), 395–406.

de Munck, V. C. (1998). *Romantic love and sexual behavior: Perspectives from the social sciences*. Westport: Praeger.

de Singly, F. (1987). Théorie critique de l'homogamie. *L'Année sociologique, 37*, 181–205.

Donati, P. (2010). *Relational sociology: A new paradigm for the social sciences. Ontological explorations*. London: Routledge.

Eastwick, P. W., & Finkel, E. J. (2008). Sex differences in mate preferences revisited: Do people know what they initially desire in a romantic partner? *Journal of Personality and Social Psychology, 94*(2), 245–264.

Edwards, J. (1969). Familial behavior as social exchange. *Journal of Marriage and the Family, 31*(3), 518–526.

Elder, G. (1969). Appearance and education in marriage mobility. *American Sociological Review, 34*(4), 519–533.

Elias, N. (1978). *What is sociology?* New York: Columbia University Press.

Elster, J. (1986). *Rational choice*. New York: New York University Press.

England, P., & Farkas, G. (1986). *Households, employment, and gender: A social, economic, and demographic view*. New York: Aldine.

Esser, H. (1993). *Soziologie. Allgemeine Grundlagen*. Frankfurt am Main/New York: Campus.

Esser, H. (1999). *Soziologie: Spezielle Grundlagen. Band 1: Situationslogik und Handeln*. Frankfurt am Main: Campus.

Feld, S. L. (1981). The focused organization of social ties. *American Journal of Sociology, 86*(5), 1015–1035.

Feld, S. L. (1982). Social structural determinants of similarity among associates. *American Sociological Review, 47*, 797–801.

Ferguson, T. (1989). Who solved the secretary problem? *Statistical Science, 4*(3), 282–289.

Flap, H. (2002). No man is an island: The research programme of a social capital theory. In O. Favereau & E. Lazega (Eds.), *New horizons in institutional and evolutionary economics*.

Conventions and structures in economic organization. Markets, networks and hierarchies (pp. 29–59). Cheltenham: Elgar.

Fligstein, N., & McAdam, D. (2012). *A theory of fields*. Oxford: Oxford University Press.

Freese, J. (2009). Preferences and the explanation of social behavior. In P. Hedström & P. Bearman (Eds.), *Oxford handbook of analytic sociology* (pp. 94–114). Oxford: Oxford University Press.

Frey, B. S., & Eichenberger, R. (1996). Marriage paradoxes. *Rationality and Society, 8*(2), 187–206.

Gardner, M. (1960). Mathematical games. *Scientific American, 202*(1), 150–153.

Giddens, A. (1984). *The constitution of society. Outline of the theory of structuration*. Berkeley: University of California Press.

Goffman, E. (1959). *The presentation of self in everyday life*. New York: Doubleday Anchor Books.

González-Ferrer, A. (2006). Who do immigrants marry? Partner choice among single immigrants in Germany. *European Sociological Review, 22*(2), 171–185.

Gustavsson, L., Johnsson, J., & Uller, T. (2008). Mixed support for sexual selection theories of mate preferences in the Swedish population. *Evolutionary Psychology, 6*(4), 575–585.

Hakim, C. (2010). Erotic capital. *European Sociological Review, 26*(5), 499–518.

Hakim, C. (2011). *Erotic capital: The power of attraction in the bedroom and the boardroom*. New York: Basic Books.

Haller, M. (1981). Marriage, women, and social stratification: A theoretical critique. *American Journal of Sociology, 86*(4), 766–795.

Harrison, A. A., & Saeed, L. (1977). Let's make a deal: An analysis of revelations and stipulations in lonely hearts advertisements. *Journal of Personality and Social Psychology, 35*(4), 257–264.

Hassebrauck, M. (1990). Wer sucht wen? Eine inhaltsanalytische Untersuchung von Heirats- und Bekanntschaftsanzeigen. *Zeitschrift für Sozialpsychologie, 21*(2), 101–122.

Hedström, P. (2005). *Dissecting the social: On the principles of analytical sociology*. Cambridge: Cambridge University Press.

Hedström, P., & Bearman, P. S. (Eds.). (2009). *The Oxford handbook of analytical sociology*. Oxford: Oxford University Press.

Heiner, R. A. (1983). The origin of predictable behavior. *The American Economic Review, 73*(4), 560–590.

Hertog, E. (2012). Hedged bets: Preferences for future marriage partners' earning power in contemporary Japan. Unpublished working paper.

Hirschmann, E. C. (1987). People as products: Analysis of a complex marketing exchange. *The Journal of Marketing, 51*(1), 98–108.

Hitsch, G. J., Hortaçsu, A., & Ariely, D. (2005). *What makes you click: An empirical analysis of online dating*. Retrieved from https://www.aeaweb.org/assa/2006/0106_0800_0502.pdf

Hitsch, G. J., Hortaçsu, A., & Ariely, D. (2010). Matching and sorting in online dating. *American Economic Review, 100*(1), 130–163.

Hodgson, G. M. (2009). Choice, habit and evolution. *Journal of Evolutionary Economics, 20*(1), 1–18.

Homans, G. C. (1961). *Social behavior: Its elementary forms*. New York: Harcourt Brace & World.

Homans, P., & Aden, L. (1968). *The dialogue between theology and psychology* (3rd ed.). Chicago: University of Chicago Press.

Huckfeld, R. R. (1983). Social contexts, social networks, and urban neighborhoods: Environmental constraints on friendship choice. *American Journal of Sociology, 89*(3), 651–669.

Huinink, J., & Feldhaus, M. (2009). Family research from the life course perspective. *International Sociology, 24*(3), 299–324.

Huston, T. L. (2000). The social ecology of marriage and other intimate unions. *Journal of Marriage and the Family, 62*(2), 298–320.

Illouz, E. (2012). *Why love hurts. A sociological explanation*. Cambridge: Polity Press.

Kalmijn, M. (1991). Status homogamy in the United States. *American Journal of Sociology, 97*(2), 496–523.
Kalmijn, M. (1994). Assortative mating by cultural and economic occupational status. *American Journal of Sociology, 100*(2), 422–452.
Kalmijn, M. (1998). Intermarriage and homogamy: Causes, patterns, trends. *Annual Review of Sociology, 24*, 395–421.
Kalmijn, M., & Flap, H. (2001). Assortative meeting and mating: Unintended consequences of organized settings for partner choices. *Social Forces, 79*(4), 1289–1312.
Kara, A. (2009). Implications of multiple preferences for a deconstructive critique and a reconstructive revision of economic theory. *Journal of Economic and Social Research, 11*(1), 69–78.
Katz, A. M., & Hill, R. (1958). Residential propinquity and marital selection: A review of theory, method, and fact. *Marriage and Family Living, 20*(1), 27–35.
Kaupp, P. (1968). *Das Heiratsinserat im sozialen Wandel*. Stuttgart: Ferdinand Enke.
Kenrick, D. T., & Keefe, R. C. (1992). Age preferences in mates reflect sex differences in human reproductive strategies. *Behavioral and Brain Sciences, 15*(1), 75–91.
Kincaid, H. (1995). *Philosophical foundations of the social sciences: Analyzing controversies in social research*. Cambridge: Cambridge University Press.
Klein, T. (1996). Der Altersunterschied zwischen Ehepartnern. Ein neues Analysemodell. *Zeitschrift für Soziologie, 25*(5), 346–370.
Klein, T. (2011). Durch Dick und Dünn. Zum Einfluss von Partnerschaft und Partnermarkt auf das Körpergewicht. *Kölner Zeitschrift für Soziologie und Sozialpsychologie, 63*, 459–479.
Kok, J. (2007). Principles and prospects of the life course paradigm. In *Virtual knowledge studio for the humanities and social sciences*. Retrieved from https://www.cairn.info/revue-annales-de-demographie-historique-2007-1-page-203.htm
Kroneberg, C. (2006). *The definition of the situation and variable rationality: The model of frame selection as a general theory of action* (Sonderforschungsbereich 504, No. 06–05). Mannheim: University of Mannheim.
Kroneberg, C., & Kalter, F. (2012). Rational choice theory and empirical research: Methodological and theoretical contributions in Europe. *Annual Review of Sociology, 38*, 73–92.
Kuhn, T. S. (1962). *The structure of scientific revolutions*. Chicago: University of Chicago Press.
Kurzban, R., & Weeden, J. (2007). Do advertised preferences predict the behavior of speed daters? *Personal Relationships, 14*, 623–632.
Lawson, H. M., & Leck, K. (2006). Dynamics of internet dating. *Social Science Computer Review, 24*(2), 189–208.
Lewin, K., & Cartwright, D. (1952). *Field theory in social science: Selected theoretical papers* (1st ed.). London: Tavistock.
Lewis, S. K., & Oppenheimer, V. K. (2000). Educational assortative mating across marriage markets: Non-Hispanic whites in the United States. *Demography, 37*(1), 29–40.
Lewis, R. A., & Spanier, G. B. (1979). Theorizing about the quality and stability of marriage. In W. Burr, I. Reiss, R. Hill, & F. Nye (Eds.), *Contemporary theories about the family: General theories and theoretical orientations* (pp. 268–294). New York: Free Press.
Lichbach, M. (2003). *Is rational choice theory all of social science?* Michigan: University of Michigan Press.
Lichter, D. T., Anderson, R. N., & Hayward, M. D. (1995). Marriage markets and marital choice. *Journal of Family Issues, 16*(4), 412–431.
Lindenberg, S. (2001). Social rationality versus rational egoism. In J. H. Turner (Ed.), *Handbook of sociological theory* (pp. 635–668). New York: Springer.
Luhmann, N. (2011). *Einführung in die Systemtheorie*. Baecker, D (Ed.). Heidelberg: Carl-Auer Verlag.
Mäenpää, E. (2015). Socio-economic homogamy and its effects on the stability of cohabiting unions. In The Population Research Institute Väestöliitto (Ed.), *Finnish Yearbook of Population* (pp. 32–34). Turku.
Martin, J. L. (2003). What is field theory? *American Journal of Sociology, 109*(1), 1–49.

References

Mayntz, R. (2004). Mechanisms in the analysis of social macro-phenomena. *Philosophy of the Social Sciences, 34*(2), 237–259.

McAdam, D., Tarrow, S., & Tilly, C. (2001). *Dynamics of contention*. Cambridge: Cambridge University Press.

McPherson, M. (1983). Ecology of affiliation. *American Sociological Review, 48*, 519–532.

McPherson, J. M., & Ranger-Moore, J. R. (1991). Evolution on a dancing landscape: Organizations and networks in dynamic Blau space. *Social Forces, 70*(1), 19–42.

Miller, G. F., & Todd, P. M. (1998). Mate choice turns cognitive. *Trends in Cognitive Sciences, 2*(5), 190–198.

Münch, R. (1987). The interpenetration of microinteraction and macrostructures in a complex and contingent instituional order. In J. C. Alexander, B. Giesen, R. Münch, & N. J. Smelser (Eds.), *The micro-macro link* (pp. 319–337). Berkeley: University of California Press.

Münch, R. (2002). *Soziologische Theorie. Band 2: Handlungstheorie*. Frankfurt am Main: Campus.

Murstein, B. (1970). Stimulus – value – role: A theory of marital choice. *Journal of Marriage and the Family, 32*(3), 465–481.

Mu, Z., & Wu, X. (2015). Residential concentration and marital behaviors of Muslim Chinese. *Population Studies Center Research Report 15*.

Oppenheimer, V. K. (1988). A theory of marriage timing. *American Journal of Sociology, 94*(3), 563–591.

Ormel, J., Lindenberg, S., Steverink, N., & Verbrugge, L. M. (1999). Subjective well-being and social production functions. *Social Indicators Research, 46*(1), 61–90.

Parsons, T. (1937). *The structure of social action*. New York: Free Press.

Peggs, K., & Lampard, R. (2001). (Ir)rational choice. A multidimensional approach to choice and constraint in decisions about marriage, divorce and remarriage. In M. S. Archer & J. Q. Tritter (Eds.), *Rational choice theory. Resisting colonization* (pp. 93–110). New York: Routledge.

Peter, F., & Spiekermann, K. (2011). Rules, norms, commitments. In I. C. Jarvie & J. Zamora-Bonilla (Eds.), *The Sage handbook of the philosophy of social sciences* (pp. 216–238). Thousand Oaks: Sage.

Regan, P. C., Levin, L., Sprecher, S., Christopher, F. S., & Cate, R. (2000). Partner preferences: What characteristics do men and women desire in their short-term sexual and long-term romantic partners? *Journal of Psychology & Human Sexuality, 12*(3), 1–21.

Reimer, T., & Rieskamp, J. (2007). Fast and frugal heuristics. In R. F. Baumeister & K. D. Vohs (Eds.), *A Sage reference publication. Encyclopedia of social psychology* (pp. 347–349). Los Angeles: Sage.

Rosenfeld, M. J. (2005). A critique of exchange theory in mate selection. *American Journal of Sociology, 110*(5), 1284–1325.

Rosenfeld, M. J., & Thomas, R. J. (2012). Searching for a mate: The rise of the internet as a social intermediary. *American Sociological Review, 77*(4), 523–547.

Sanchez, L., Manning, W. D., & Smock, P. J. (1998). Sex-specialized or collaborative mate selection? Union transitions among cohabitors. *Social Science Research, 27*(3), 280–304.

Schmitt, D. P., Jonason, P. K., Byerley, G. J., Flores, S. D., Illbeck, B. E., O'Leary, K. N., & Qudrat, A. (2012). A reexamination of sex differences in sexuality: New studies reveal old truths. *Current Directions in Psychological Science, 21*(2), 135–139.

Schmitz, A. (2012). Elective affinities 2.0? A bourdieusian approach to couple formation and the methodology of E-dating. *Social Science Research on the Internet (RESET), 1*(1), 175–202.

Schmitz, A., Skopek, J., Schulz, F., Klein, D., & Blossfeld, H. P. (2009). Indicating mate preferences by mixing survey and process-generated data. The case of attitudes and behaviour in online mate search. *Historical Social Research/Historische Sozialforschung, 34*(1), 77–93.

Schoen, R., & Wooldredge, J. (1989). Marriage choices in North Carolina and Virginia, 1969–71 and 1979–81. *Journal of Marriage and the Family, 51*(2), 465–481.

Schroedter, J. H., & Kalter, F. (2008). Binationale Ehen in Deutschland. Trends und Mechanismen der sozialen Assimilation. In F. Kalter (Ed.), *Migration und Integration* (Sonderheft 48 der KZfSS, pp. 350–379). Wiesbaden: VS Verlag.

Schulz, F. (2009). Bildungshomophilie im Onlinedating. In Deutsche Gesellschaft für Soziologie (Ed.), *Konferenzband der DGS zum Soziologentag in Jena*. Jena: DGS Tagung 2009.

Schulz, F. (2010). *Verbundene Lebensläufe: Partnerwahl und Arbeitsteilung zwischen neuen Ressourcenverhältnissen und traditionellen Geschlechterrollen*. Wiesbaden: VS Verlag.

Scott, J. (2000). Rational choice theory. In G. K. Browning, A. Halcli, & F. Webster (Eds.), *Understanding contemporary society. Theories of the present* (pp. 126–138). London: Sage.

Searle, J. R. (1969). *Speech acts: An essay in the philosophy of language*. Cambridge: Cambridge University Press.

Sen, A. K. (1977). Rational fools: A critique of the behavioral foundations of economic theory. *Philosophy & Public Affairs, 6*(4), 317–344.

Simon, H. A. (1956). Rational choice and the structure of the environment. *Psychological Review, 63*(2), 129–138.

Simpson, J. A. (1987). The dissolution of romantic relationships: Factors involved in relationship stability and emotional distress. *Journal of Personality and Social Psychology, 53*(4), 683–692.

Skopek, J. (2011). *Partnerwahl im Internet: Eine quantitative Analyse von Strukturen und Prozessen der Online-Partnersuche*. Wiesbaden: VS Verlag.

Skopek, J., Schulz, F., & Blossfeld, H.-P. (2009). Partnersuche im Internet. Bildungsspezifische Mechanismen bei der Wahl von Kontaktpartnern. *Kölner Zeitschrift für Soziologie und Sozialpsychologie, 61*(2), 183–210.

Skopek, J., Schmitz, A., & Blossfeld, H.-P. (2011). The gendered dynamics of age preferences – Empirical evidence from online dating. *Zeitschrift für Familienforschung, 23*(3), 267–290.

South, S. J. (1991). Sociodemographic differentials in mate selection preferences. *Journal of Marriage and the Family, 53*(4), 928–940.

Spanier, G. B., & Glick, P. C. (1980). Mate selection differentials between Whites and Blacks in the United States. *Social Forces, 58*(3), 707–725.

Sprecher, S., Sullivan, Q., & Hatfield, E. (1994). Mate selection preferences: Gender differences examined in a national sample. *Journal of Personality and Social Psychology, 66*(6), 1074–1080.

Stauder, J. (2008). Opportunitäten und Restriktionen des Kennenlernens. Zur sozialen Vorstrukturierung der Kontaktgelegenheiten am Beispiel des Partnermarkts. *Kölner Zeitschrift für Soziologie und Sozialpsychologie, 60*(2), 266–286.

Stevenson, B., & Wolfers, J. (2007). Marriage and divorce: Changes and their driving forces. *The Journal of Economic Perspectives, 21*(2), 27–52.

Stewart, S., Stinnett, H., & Rosenfeld, L. B. (2000). Sex differences in desired characteristics of short-term and long-term relationship partners. *Journal of Social and Personal Relationships, 17*(6), 843–853.

Stovel, K., & Fountain, C. (2009). Matching. In P. Hedström & P. S. Bearman (Eds.), *The Oxford handbook of analytical sociology* (pp. 365–390). Oxford: University Press.

Surra, C. A., & Boelter, J. M. (2013). Dating and mate selection. In G. W. Peterson & K. R. Bush (Eds.), *Handbook of marriage and the family* (pp. 211–232). New York: Springer.

Thibaut, J. W., & Kelley, H. H. (1959). *The social psychology of groups*. New York: Wiley.

Timm, A. (2004). *Partnerwahl- und Heiratsmuster in modernen Gesellschaften. Der Einfluss des Bildungssystems*. Wiesbaden: DUV.

Todd, P. M., & Miller, G. F. (1999). From pride to Prejudice and Persuasion. In G. Gigerenzer & P. M. Todd (Eds.), *Evolution and cognition. Simple heuristics that make us smart* (pp. 287–308). New York: Oxford University Press.

Todd, P. M., Penke, L., Fasolo, B., & Lenton, A. P. (2007). Different cognitive processes underlie human mate choices and mate preferences. *Proceedings of the National Academy of Sciences of the United States of America (PNAS), 104*(38), 15011–15016.

References

Toma, C. L., & Hancock, J. T. (2010). Looks and lies: The role of physical attractiveness in online dating self-presentation and deception. *Communication Research, 37*(3), 335–351.

Walster, E., Walster, G. W., & Berscheid, E. (1978). *Equity. Theory and research*. Boston: Allyn & Bacon.

Wang, H., & Lu, X. (2007). Cyberdating: Misinformation and (Dis)trust in online interaction. *Informing Science Journal, 10*, 1–15.

Wendt, A. (1999). *Social theory of international politics*. Cambridge: Cambridge University Press.

White, H. C. (1992). *Identity and control: A structural theory of social action*. Princeton: Princeton University Press.

White, J. M. (2013). The current status of theorizing about families. In G. W. Peterson & K. R. Bush (Eds.), *Handbook of marriage and the family* (pp. 65–89). New York: Springer.

Wiesenthal, H. (1987). Rational Choice – Ein Überblick über Grundlinien, Theoriefelder und neuere Themenakquisition eines sozialwissenschaftlichen Paradigmas. *Zeitschrift für Soziologie, 16*(6), 434–449.

Wiik, K. A., & Holland, J. A. (2015). Partner choice and timing of first marriage among children of immigrants in Norway and Sweden. *Discussion Papers No. 810 of the Research Department*, Statistics Norway.

Willis, J., & Todorov, A. (2006). First impressions: Making up your mind after a 100-Ms exposure to a face. *Psychological Science, 17*(7), 592–598.

Willoughby, B. J., & Carroll, J. S. (2010). Sexual experience and couple formation attitudes among emerging adults. *Journal of Adult Development, 17*(1), 1–11.

Winch, R. F., Ktsanes, T., & Ktsanes, V. (1954). The theory of complementary needs in mate-selection: An analytic and descriptive study. *American Sociological Review, 19*(3), 241–249.

Witt, U. (1991). Economics, sociobiology and behavioral psychology on preferences. *Journal of Economic Psychology, 12*(4), 557–573.

Wood, D., & Brumbaugh, C. C. (2009). Using revealed mate preferences to evaluate market force and differential preference explanations for mate selection. *Journal of Personality and Social Psychology, 96*(6), 1226–1244.

Yang, C. (2009). Looking online for the best romantic partner reduces decision quality: The moderating role of choice-making strategies. *Cyberpsychology & Behavior, 13*, 1–4.

Zafirovski, M. (1999). What is really rational choice? Beyond the utilitarian concept of rationality'. *Current Sociology, 47*(1), 47–113.

Zillmann, D., Schmitz, A., & Blossfeld, H.-P. (2011). Lügner haben kurze Beine. Zum Zusammenhang unwahrer Selbstdarstellung und partnerschaftlicher Chancen im Online-Dating. *Zeitschrift für Familienforschung, 23*(3), 291–318.

Chapter 5
A Bourdieusian Approach to Mating Processes

In this chapter, by reflecting upon the structural dimensions of the previously outlined paradigm of "mate choice as agency within structures" (MAS) and its core analytical elements, a Bourdieusian conceptualization of mating will be developed. The purpose of this procedure is twofold. The potential of a Bourdieusian approach to mating processes will be motivated by illustrating its theoretical and conceptual spectrum compared to the MAS model. At the same time, the well-defined traditions of MAS are used to concretize Bourdieu's somewhat sporadic and unsystematic reflections on couple formation. The main argument will be that the conceptual building blocks of MAS – such as mating preferences, utilities, strategies, chance, mate choice, dyadic exchange, and markets – can be conceptualized as functions of the social space. It will be shown that the conceptual tools of 'social space', 'habitus', and 'practice' enable both the utilization of the insights of the MAS model and the relational generalization of its analytical concepts. Consequently, the model of mate choice as agency in structures will be characterized as an analytical subcategory of relational structuralism.

The Relational Architecture of Pierre Bourdieu's Sociology

Before we compare the logics of the MAS paradigm with Bourdieu's relational theory, the following section shall give a brief introduction to the basic principles of this sociological research program. There are great many introductions to and expansions on his works, and as such we will only outline the most important key points, and those aspects most relevant for the subsequent discussion of mating phenomena.

The genuine relationality of the Bourdieusian approach is manifested in its *relational epistemology*, which underlies the theoretical concepts as well as practices of research. The ontological premise is that "the real is the relational", and relations are the 'material' out of which social reality is built (cp. Bourdieu and Wacquant

1992: 97). Questions regarding the substance or the 'essence' of a thing tend to veil that the essence of any one thing may represent itself very differently in different historical and social contexts. Thus, all the analytical concepts of the relational approach serve the purpose of *(re-)constructing* social facts, rather than postulating their existence *a priori*. In doing so, this relational thinking intends to transcend the positivistic differentiation between traditional "paired concepts" such as the "basic dichotomy" of objectivism versus subjectivism, and – corresponding to this differentiation – "materialism versus idealism, economism versus culturalism, mechanism versus finalism, causal explanation versus interpretive understanding" (Bourdieu 1988: 780). Thus, for modern sociological theory, this particular *constructivist* structuralism represents an alternative to both the methodological individualism as usually applied in sociological (mate) choice research and to methodological holism, which has been profoundly criticized by many (mate) choice researchers.

'Structure', from the relational point of view, is not reduced to infrastructure, normative structure, physical place, or actual contact opportunities, but is a *relational* entity. 'Society' is conceptualized as a relational entity – called social space – which comprises the interrelations between (classes of) agents and social spheres – i.e. social fields such as the economic or the scientific field. Social spaces and fields are defined by their relational structure, that is, their effective capital dimensions, their positional structure, the relevant objects of interests and competition, unquestioned beliefs, structures of meaning, etc. On the face of it, the social space may seem to resemble the Blau space, which has been discussed as an important structural 'complement' of individualist mate choice conception in the previous chapter. For Blau (1987: 76), social structure is "a multi-dimensional space of positions among which people are distributed", a space which "cannot be operationally represented by a single variable". He emphasizes the fact that "the various dimensions of differentiation are not necessarily orthogonal", and that some indicators "such as education and occupational status tend to be closely related" (Blau 1987: 75f.). This idea of a multidimensional model of space and the spatial position of agents is also fundamental to Bourdieu's theoretical approach, although it differs conceptually and methodologically with regard to the construction of the axes. Whereas the axes in the Blau space are represented by several dimensions (and their covariations) defined *a priori*, Bourdieu constructs them *a posteriori*, in form of a dimensional space on the basis of empirical data from particular societies in a certain epoch. The conception of capital, by designating society's structural axes in this way, reduces the complexity of the myriad resources in Blau space (and their covariations) to a latent, less dimensional social space, itself structured by the axes of capital.[1] Furthermore, Blau's structural parameters – heterogeneity, "the extent of differentiation of the members of a collective into nominal groups" and inequality, "the extent of differentiation of a population in terms of resources or ranked status"

---

[1] In fact, the 'Blau space' must be seen as a series of uni- and bivariate distributions, as Blau sees "covariation" of social differences as an additional structural parameter (Blau 1987: 75 f.), and not as an object of multivariate construction (cp. Chapter 6).

(Blau 1987: 77) – imply a certain proximity to a relational approach, which locates social classes within the social space. However, the Blau space also displays a clear difference here when compared to the social space, as no elaborated concept of agency or practice is implied in the former. Although Blau refers to "social relations between positions", which correspond to roles, he contests the significance of "internalized cultural values and norms [and] psychological preferences" (Blau 1987: 75) and rejects them as explanantia for (mating) processes. For Blau (1964: xi), "the explicans [...] is not some element of the cultural system [...] but some aspects of structural differentiation defined as the distribution of people among different positions along various lines". Within the social space approach in contrast, structure is conceptualized in a wider sense, meaning that 'culture' itself may operate as a capital form constitutive for the agents' dispositions. The Bourdieusian conception of society comprises cultural, normative, and psychic moments as structural aspects of the social space, which is thus characterized both by 'objective' positions and by 'subjective' position-takings.

As a consequence of this relational epistemology, the differentiation between the actor and the society external to him is set aside.[2] Relational constructivism implies relating the 'subjective' dimension to objective circumstances. The relational paradigm introduces the phenomenological perspectives of the agents by way of an "epistemological rupture" (e.g. Bourdieu 2010: 5 f.), that is, by locating the dispositions of the agents within the structure of the society – the social space. Consequently, 'structure' is seen as a constitutive moment for agents, regarding not only their objective position within the social space, but indeed the corresponding dispositional structures, comprising preferences, (ir-)rationalities, evaluative and cognitive mechanisms, 'personality', etc. In order to express these fundamental interrelations between 'societal' and 'mental' entities, the concept of 'habitus' was developed, which is conceptualized as structured structure (Bourdieu 1977: 72 ff.; Wacquant 2016). Habitus comprises bundled schemes of perception, evaluation, and practice that are specific to particular positions in the social space. The relationship between these schemes and the social space is not one of direct one-to-one correspondence, but:

> The habitus and the field maintain a relationship of mutual attraction, and the illusio is determined from the inside, from impulses that push toward a self-investment in the object; but it is also determined from the outside, starting with a particular universe of objects offered socially for investment (Bourdieu 1999: 512).

Thus, the agent does not stand in opposition to society as an external entity; he himself is – by way of his habitus – society. The habitus is the principle which generates practices, in accordance with the practical sense, beyond determinism and freedom of choice. If applied in practice, habitus operates as 'structuring structure', meaning

---

[2] Social space and social fields construct the same thing: society. Whereas the first perspective applies the view point of social inequality, the second one conceptualizes society as (quasi-)functionally differentiated. Schmitz et al. (2016) critically discuss Bourdieu's concept of the 'field of power' (Bourdieu and Wacquant 1992: 104 ff.) and elaborate on the relations between social space and the field of power.

that the agent's practices (re)produce and change the overall structure of the social space. Whereas Blau's structuralism is lacking with regard to its conceptualization of conflict and competition, with agents applying certain strategies in order to improve or maintain their position, such issues are at the center of the very notion of social space and fields, which Bourdieu conceptualizes as battlefields. Thus, in contrast to structural theories such as the Blau space, no allegations of structural determinism can be made against relational structuralism, as the concept of habitus clearly emphasizes the active and creative side of practice.

The social space also provides researchers with a model for the emergence of preferences and interests. From this viewpoint, affective bonds to objective structures and other agents are instilled by familial socialization, which transforms the infantine libido from a narcissistic to a social orientation (Bourdieu 2000: 166). Within these processes, class-specific capital endowments are internalized and become constitutive elements of the agents' habitus. In this process, gender operates as an "absolutely fundamental dimension of the habitus that [...] modifies all the social qualities that are connected to the fundamental social factors" (Bourdieu 1997: 128). Accordingly, the expressions 'female habitus' or 'male habitus' are a problematic simplifications; for example, dispositions (including mating preferences) and lifestyle (such as clothing) are the result of gendered habitus (a fact which has been rediscovered by 'intersectional' sociologists in recent times).

The structure of the social space, the specifically gendered class position, and the life-course trajectory are acquired and incorporated to the degree that social structure and history do not only influence the agents' categories of perception, but also their very bodies. The way we eat, our posture, our personal hygiene, and so on – all these elements are essentially the result of "embodied social structures" (Bourdieu 1984: 467f.) and the bodily emanation of the habitus "hexis" manifests in class-specific posture, gestures, facial expressions, speech, and feelings (Bourdieu 1977: 93f.). Accordingly, every form of capital is physical, in that it affects the bodies of the individuals in question.

Agents possess (and are possessed by) not only particular capital assets, but the value of their capital depends on the appreciation shown by others. Here, we differentiate analytically between a resource and its symbolic perception, introducing the term 'symbolic capital'. Symbolic capital is "nothing more than economic or cultural capital [...] acknowledged in accordance with the categories of perception that it imposes" (Bourdieu 1990: 135).[3] For mechanisms of symbolic capital, the categories of perception, the evaluative and moral systems – or, in short, the tastes of the agents – requires a particular cognitive and symbolic structure. At the same time, misrecognition is constitutive for symbolic power relations, as it conceals the arbitrary nature of symbolic goods.

---

[3] Symbolic capital – that is, the acknowledgment of the habitus and hence of the goods of an agent – could be interpreted as what Schoen and Wooldredge (1989) and Klein (1996: 211) refer to as 'total attractiveness'. However, as symbolic capital is structured by social class and gender (amongst other things), it cannot be represented by a linear, unidimensional unit applicable to all classes.

'Power' is not treated as one parameter amongst others, as it is in the Blau space. It is instead a foundational aspect of the social space and inherent to all its structuring dimensions (such as economic, cultural, social, or political capital) – thereby systematically enabling access to both micro and macro-sociological phenomena for the sociological analysis of power and domination. Apart from direct exploitation in the sense of Marx, this view strongly emphasizes the way in which the dominated "actively participate in their domination" by perceiving "the world through the eyes of the dominators" (cp. Lebaron 2001: 125). 'Symbolic domination' depends on the "practical recognition through which the dominated, often unwittingly, contribute to their own domination by tacitly accepting, in advance, the limits imposed on them" (Bourdieu 2000: 169). As a consequence, the objective differences in economic, cultural, or any other capital become intensified, making symbolic capital a core element of class reproduction. This manifests in aspects of our everyday lives such as lifestyle and language, which operate – from the viewpoint of social space theory – as core mechanisms of symbolic power.

In contrast to most individualistic paradigms, Bourdieu's theory locates 'structure', in the sense of the material and symbolic constitution of the social space, not only between agents but also within agents. In contrast to individualistic approaches, 'the individual' is thus not seen as such, i.e. as an *indivisible* entity. It is instead conceptualized as being intersected and formed by both material and meaning structures deriving from the social space (and class relations) as well as from social fields. Thus, the Bourdieusian agent is necessarily a 'plural' or 'hybrid' actor (Schmitz et al. 2016). Accordingly, there are a great many sources of structuring agents' overall dispositions (and indeed the preferences contingent to them). Dispositions are affected by their (and their classes') current and past positions, as well as by their trajectories (connecting the past and the future) within the social space. Dispositions are also differential functions of the effects of different social fields. One may think of the differential impact the economic field has on the emergence of dispositions towards family, marriage, home ownership, etc., or of the impact the state has on the legitimacy of particular sexual orientations and ideal of the family (Bourdieu 1996a).

The internalization of these manifold influences does not follow the logics of mere learning, in the sense of reproducing behavioral patterns, for example, according to familiar conditions. Instead, it follows the dispositional logics of taste. This generative principle of the habitus is of utmost relevance for any sociology which assesses issues of preference and choice. As Lizardo puts it (2014: 11):

> One of the key phenomena that Bourdieu claims the theory of taste is necessary to account for is the fact that choices tend to exhibit higher-order coherence across realms, such that persons tend to choose music, movies, home interiors, clothes, foods, or what have you, using the same set of underlying (but not necessarily consciously accessible) 'criteria'.

The habitus, relatively autonomous to particular situations, is conceptualized as the non-deterministic "tendency to perpetuate itself according to its internal determination, its conatus, by asserting its autonomy in relation to the situation (rather than submitting itself to the external determination of the environment rather as matter does)" (Bourdieu 1996b: 3). In contrast to classical theories which, for example, consider norm-orientation to represent compliance to external rules, the habitus is seen as implying the logics of 'implicit knowledge' and 'knowledge systems'. This implies that "traces of past experiences affect some performance, even though the influential earlier experience is not remembered" (Greenwald and Banji 1995: 4f.). This, however, further implies that agents will infer their overall schemes of perception, evaluation, and practices in such a way that they correspond over a variety of situations, including new situations without 'ready-made scripts or frames'. The 'hysteresis' of the habitus can be observed most clearly whenever societal conditions change and agents tend to follow internalized patterns, no longer matching the altered circumstances.

Accordingly, this practical notion of habitus rejects the idea that utility maximization and rationality are anthropological constants, as well as the assumption that any (bounded) rationality can be generalized to create *a universally valid model*. However, instrumental rationality in decision-making, as well as considering norms, is taken into account by habitus theory. Such manifestations of the practical sense are seen as empirical special cases, which can be understood as functions of the social space. For example, an act of rational choice requires an acquired dispositional habitus, which will lead to a particular class of agents displaying such practices over a variety of different 'choice situations', such as shopping, interacting, dating, etc.

To conclude, in contrast to theories which invest their theoretical efforts on the 'micro-level' of the actor and his choice acts, or on the societal macro-level, and its deterministic influence on individual agency, the concept of relational structure is of utmost importance from the Bourdieusian point of view. Taking these preliminary considerations into account, the following instrumentalization of Bourdieu's theory will develop a relational sociology of mating phenomena.

The Partner Market as Social Space

At first glance it might appear somewhat surprising that it seems necessary to elaborate on Bourdieu's works for the purpose of deriving a theoretical system for the assessment of mating processes. In his early studies in Algeria and the French region of Béarn, marriage strategies were the focus of his research. In these contexts, he found patterns contradicting structuralistic models of (consciously or unconsciously) norm-orientated mate choice, which was an important theoretical watershed, as it fostered the development of a non-finalist practice model of matrimonial and 'choice' strategies stemming from the family's historical and social position (Lamaison and Bourdieu 1986: 117). However, Bourdieu never developed an explicit theory of mating-related interaction mechanisms (Schmitz 2012: 2; Bourdieu 2008).

Following this paradigm, and as we argued in the context of different partner markets, the task of constructing a research object refers to the issue of relative autonomy. Relative autonomy here means the extent to which any specific structure, including its objective and subjective dimensions, can be considered to be independent from external conditions, other contexts, and ultimately society itself (e.g. Bourdieu 2004: 47ff.). This is of particular relevance for a relational assessment of mating processes. Within this approach, the social space – like the Weberian concept of the market – can be understood "as a structure of the probabilities of convergence and divergence of individuals, a structure of affinity or aversion" (Bourdieu 1997: 113, o.t.). However, the specification of the partner market as derived from Weber, which interprets individual chances as a function of a power structure, does not resolve the problem of how to further conceptualize the societal power structure of and mechanisms within the partner market. For Weber, the concept of power is "sociologically amorphous" because "all conceivable qualities of a person and all conceivable combinations of circumstances may put him in a position to impose his will in a given situation" (Weber 1947: 153). Although Weber's work should not be reduced to an individualistic approach, as is often the case (see e.g. Alexander et al. 1987: 16f.), it can be stated that the relational character of the market and society as a whole was not the analytical starting point of his work. As Swedberg notes, Bourdieu directs criticism at "Max Weber's model of a market, which consists of sellers and buyers who first compete with each other and then enter into exchange with each other." (Swedberg 2011: 74; Weber and Roth 1978: 82–85, 635–640). Bourdieu thus emphasizes the fact that the "existence of a market in no way implies that transactions only obey the mechanical laws of competition" (Bourdieu 2008: 181), and that the permanent exchange of "gifts, words, women, etc." (Bourdieu 1986: 52) does not conform to logics specific to an abstract market. By transcending Weber's conception of markets, each exchange (and each interaction) can be better understood as a "two-way relation that is always in fact a three-way relation, between the two agents and the social space within which they are located" (Bourdieu 2005: 148). Thus, the social space is seen as constitutive for each market and antecedent to each (romantic) exchange. The same could be derived via a field-theoretical argument; to the degree a market is relatively autonomous, it may be seen as a field. However, as any field is located in the field of power, society itself must be understood as constitutive for all fields and markets (cp. Schmitz et al. 2016).

The relevance of the social space for the character and outcomes of exchange is even more pronounced in the context of a partner market, whose chance structure must be understood as a genuinely *heteronomous* phenomenon. Bourdieu never spoke of a partner market as a "field", which would imply relative autonomy from the social space by means of a specific illusio, nomos and doxa, and specific capitals. The partner market is – according to this perspective – not a relatively autonomous sphere of meaning and behavior, but rather a key mechanism of the "production and reproduction of symbolic capital" for society as a whole (Bourdieu 2001: 42; Schmitz and Riebling 2013: 18). Each particular sub-market of the "totality of the partner market" must be seen as part of a hierarchically structured partner market as a whole (Bourdieu 2008: 181f.). Even if a nightclub or a university may seem to represent a relatively distinct social context, mating chances and their actualizations are highly dependent on processes in other mating markets. Therefore, a partner market's (chance) structure is interpreted and constructed as a function of the structure of society as a whole, rather than via autonomous markets. This implies that mating processes are to be interpreted primarily in the context of competition between social classes and the different prices they get for the "products of their upbringing and education" (Bourdieu 2008: 184), and not as a form of partner market competition in its own right. Consequently, the partner market is neither conceptualized as an abstract entity separate from society, nor equated ad hoc to a specific social context of society (such as the university), but is constructed from the outset as a genuinely heteronomous object of research.

The Social Space as Partner Market

Having clarified that a partner market is seen as a manifestation of the social space, the question remains as to how processes of mating can be understood within the framework of social space theory. Bourdieu gave few explicit but many scattered ideas regarding the way in which mating processes are to be conceptualized in his theory. Unsurprisingly, mechanisms of mating are understood as functions of the relational position of the agents in the social space:

> People located at the top of the space have little chance of marrying people located towards the bottom, […] because they have little chance of physically meeting them (except in what are called 'bad places,' that is, at the cost of a transgression of the social limits which reflect spatial differences). (Bourdieu 1998: 10)

As we have seen before, the concept of social space can be seen as a more general alternative to Peter Blau's structural space model, representing the structural component for many researchers, seeing as it does agents' probabilities of encounter as functions of the social structure. However, in structuring agents' chances of meeting, the social space does not only correspond to a general space of opportunities, like the Blau space, but also to the habitus-specific "field of eligibles". The structures of opportunity and restrictions are not reduced to conditions for choosing one's mate, but primarily as internalized structures of the habitus. This is because past opportunity structures, in the sense of eligible alternatives, are thought of as constitutive elements of the habitus, which is not systematically taken into account in MAS.

Social space and habitus also analytically comprise particular foci (meeting contexts, as discussed by MAS). In *The State Nobility*, Bourdieu (1996a: 183) discusses academic classes as socially homogenous 'foci' which generate a sense of internal togetherness and serve the function of excluding 'undesirable company'. Here, the habitus can be seen as the *focus-generating instance* which spans contingent geographic locations and social occasions. On this foundation, the concept of 'foci' can also be examined from a field perspective; universities, bars, dating platforms, etc. can be thought of as sub-fields of the partner market (i.e., society) itself. Often thought of as relatively autonomous spheres, fields can also be understood in the sense of institutional settings, such as organizations as fields (Schmitz et al. 2016). The institutional definition of the field then allows for the analysis of actual contexts of interaction with regard to the particular capital structure and interactional processes, without postulating an auto-nomos.

Proximity within the social space, which denotes proximity of class habitus, increases not just the probability of encountering and interacting with similar agents, but also of the formation and institutionalization of couples through dispositional affinities. If two agents from different positions in the space meet, they usually "will not get on together, will not really understand each other, will not appeal to one another. On the other hand, proximity in social space predisposes to closer relations" (Bourdieu 1998: 10). Disparities in lifestyle complicate the agents' conversations, their interactions, indeed their very being together, as there is often little common basis for reciprocally decoding symbolic expressions. Taste ist not confined to decoding similarities, but is also reflected in the dissociation from alternative lifestyles: "Aversion to different lifestyles is one of the strongest barriers between the classes; class endogamy is evidence of this" (Bourdieu 1984: 56).

In contrast to the structuralistic nature of the Blau space, the habitus approach includes the subjective actor perspective, in form of the class-based correspondence of position and disposition within the social space, as capital forms and dispositions constitute a class-based union. Much like the structuralist approach, the relational perspective asserts that "what brings a man and a woman together is mostly the affinity between their habitus, produced by similar social preconditions and conditions" (Bozon and Héran 1989: 92f.). However, whereas the Blau space neglects the fact that probabilities of encounter do not necessarily mean willingness to interact, and that probabilities of encounter may well be accompanied by rejection, the social space also allows us to see objective proximities as a source for subjective distance, just as objective distance may be a source for subjective attraction.

Detecting a compatible habitus (of whichever form) is the start of any relationship, and "spontaneous decoding of one habitus by another is the basis of the immediate affinities [...] encouraging well-matched relationships" (Bourdieu 1984: 243; Schmitz 2012). Lifestyle – that is, the way in which the dispositions of the habitus are expressed in everyday life – is constitutive for a range of mechanisms. Lifestyles as expressions of a position in the social space structure the selection of foci of encounter, as their specific use strongly depends on the agent's (dis)positions. Stylistic and symbolic cues indicate the social price (or distinctive value) of possible partners (Bourdieu 1998: 121). In the 'market of symbolic goods', the agents' social status – and hence the symbolic representation of their capital configuration – are perceived to be, or at least sensed as, the objects of exchange and interaction (Bourdieu 2002a: 229). These symbolic goods operate as everyday expressions of what Goffman labeled the presentation of self, and cannot be reduced to a cluster of single variables such as income, education, age, and so on.

Also, and in contrast to Hakim's concept of 'erotic capital' (cp. Chapter 4), habitus theory does not locate the determining factors of (erotic) appeal in the essence of appearance and behavior. These factors are closely intertwined with the habitual categories of perception and assessment – that is, in the configuration of capital and in the symbolic system characteristic for the class structure of a society. Thus, the human body is not only "the most indisputable materialization of class taste" (Bourdieu 1984: 190), which is accentuated symbolically in "signs of which each body is the bearer – clothing, pronunciation, posture, bearing, manners" (ibid. 241). The body is also the soil where patterns of perception, cognition, and recognition are rooted in.

As a consequence of the societal variety associated with habitus in its objective and subjective regards, lifestyle similarity is only one conceivable 'mode' for successful emergence of a couple. Apart from the fact that lifestyle does not necessarily address manifest similarities (two agents preferring, say, action movies or tennis), but rather shared latent principles (two agents sharing a similar approach to different movie genres or sports), lifestyle can also become an effective factor of couple formation due to systematic differences between two agents and their habitus as explained further below.[4]

In many different ways, distinctions "in the physical order" (i.e. material differences) become, via the practical application of lifestyle, and their appreciation by others, a "symbolic order" (and vice versa), and thus a major factor in the reproduction of social inequality (Bourdieu 1984: 175). This fact is particularly conspicuous and profoundly consequential when it comes to practices of mating. In the following section, the parallels and differences between habitus theory and the agency-related elements of the MAS approach will be examined. For the purpose of clarity, the analytical structure of utilities, preferences, rationalities, strategies, and action as established in the previous chapter will serve as a guideline.

Mating Utilities and Preferences as (Dis-)positions

In many individualistic models, the implicit cause of any agency is the maximization of utility.[5] Within habitus theory, the implicit notion of 'objective' utilities – be it by implying a universal object providing a unit of utility (such as money, in traditional economics) or modeling a common averaged utility function over all actors – is fundamentally rejected. In Bourdieu's constructivist approach, it is not appropriate to assign universal status to a contingent good, which in mating may involve labeling, say, education or income as the fundamental unit of utility. The same applies to subjectively expected and maximized utility. MAS and methodological

---

[4] Thus, lifestyle in mating addresses two aspects: first, lifestyle as one of many 'variables' relevant in mating processes, such as gender, age, income, occupational status, educational degree, etc.; second, as a latent principle of taste comprising and undermining the impact of every single variable.

[5] Usually, the maximization of utility is discussed in the context of two central dichotomies: whether it can be thought of as genuinely factual or merely hypothetical, and whether it manifests itself consciously or unconsciously.

individualism may take into account that "what an individual considers cost and what benefit and the subjective expectations concerning cost and benefits are wide open to social influence" (Lindenberg 2013: 4). But as demonstrated in the last chapter, there is no theoretical conception within the individualistic paradigm for systematically deriving the 'form and substance' of utilities, which are inherent to the plethora of possible (mating) choices. In contrast to perspectives, which assume that all actors perceive and process "the same decisive attributes" (Bourdieu 1984: 100) in the same way, habitus implies a differential perception of potential partners and their traits. This enables a substantiation of the differential character of subjectively expected utilities – that is, which mating trait is perceived as promising depends on the particular interplay between habitus and the good in question.

Agents reproduce objective patterns of relative *(dis)utility* without necessarily consciously optimizing any utility in the actual conduct of mating. The relational perspective conceptualizes the objective utility of mating as the material and symbolic profit of practice, beyond the synchronous fulfillment of the specific agent's goals. One specific explanatory scheme here is the "disinterested interest" (Bourdieu 1977: 177): utility maximizing practice without (and due to the very absence of) subjective utility maximization. The practical sense of habitus does not generally exclude intended utility maximization in mating, seeing it instead as a subordinate phenomenon which itself varies with the habitus of the agent. In other words, there may be systematic mechanisms in the social space which foster or inhibit subjective utility maximization: firstly, locational, by means of a specific habitus, which may feature a particular pre-situational tendency to maximize its utility; secondly, situational, by means of specific social conditions which may induce utility maximization in mating.

However, the concept of habitus rejects the apodictic distinction between "subjective utilities" and "objective utilities", applying instead a *transverse* differentiation: the habitus represents differential products of "unconscious adjustment to the probabilities associated with an objective structure" (Bourdieu 2001: 37). What is perceived as being useful and what is objectively useful for a particular agent are interconnected elements of the specific habitus, and as such dependent on social class. This may be recognized from an individualist viewpoint, habitus theory, however, is more consequential regarding the implementation of this insight. In habitus theory, bundles of subjective and objective (dis)utilities are conceptualized as diverse functions of the social space and correspond in equally diverse ways to mating preferences.

Just as no single utility unit can be claimed within the relational approach, the conceptualization and (implicit) assumption of the existence of common preferences – which motivates early versions of the methodological individualist tradition, and still appears in the practices of modeling within modern mate choice research – is criticized by Bourdieu. This generalizing idea can be identified, in paradigm, in the economists' motto *de gustibus non disputandum* (Stigler and Becker 1977), a maxim which "involves a decision to treat tastes as fixed parameters in their models rather than as variables" (Dupre and O'Neil 1998: 164). Applying the view of social space, in contrast, we can strongly emphasize the social variability of mating preferences, as the dichotomization of objective structures and subjective perceptions is rejected and replaced with the differentiation between class-specific habitus.

The central mechanism of translating an agent's societal position into mating preferences is the societal development of the habitus, which over time adapts to its objective position and thereby to its *societal* chance structure. This view implies a systematic historical component and is thus – more so than even the most enlightened forms of individualism – "distinct from Walrasian atomism, which ignores all economically and socially motivated preference structures" (Bourdieu 1983: 276, o.t.). The issue of the socio-genesis of mating preferences was discussed in Chapter 4, showing that some authors trace mating preferences back to endogenous market effects. However, as the question arises as to the extent to which we are actually dealing with a market with autonomous effects, for example regarding partner preferences, the question must also be asked as to whether these preferences might be better interpreted as a function of the social space which operates prior to any market experience. This relation between preferences and their general societal background is also considered as part of the individualistic paradigm. In particular, the gender-specific character of preferences and romantic exchange relations are considered in most analyses (e.g. Buss 1989; Schmitt et al. 2012; Skopek 2011). These preferences are sometimes ascribed to specific developments in an individual's life (see e.g. Huinink and Feldhaus 2009). Blossfeld and Timm (1997), for example, argue that mating preferences are closely bound up in the life-long process of identity formation. South also analyzes the socio-structural antecedents of mating preferences, which he ascribes to the logic of exchange relations (South 1991: 929f.).

The habitus concept more fundamentally and systematically emphasizes the societal conditions of all (mating) preferences. The socialization process creates the agent's "schemes of perception and appreciation, in other words, their dispositions and tastes" which play "as large a role in their selection of a sexual partner as in other areas" (Bourdieu 2002b: 557). As the agents' habitus adapt to their objective chance structures, preferences are traced back to their synchronic and diachronic position (Bourdieu 1990: 53). Any adaption of preferences (Elster 1986) is, therefore, not to be examined from the perspective of analytically separate contexts (such as opportunities on the partner market), but with regard to positions and trajectories in society. Consequently, adaptive preference formation must be understood of as genuine mechanism of the habitus, preceding any potential situations of mate choice. For example, the "taste of necessity" (Bourdieu 1984: 372f.) – that is, the transformation of external necessities into agents' tastes – may also be applied to explain the mating preferences of agents with unfavorable structures of opportunity on the mating market and in society as a whole.

Furthermore, both the social genesis of singular (mating) preferences and their systematic interrelations are fundamental characteristics of the habitus concept, in contrast to the majority of analyses conducted based on the MAS paradigm. The habitus perspective assumes different classes of systems of preference, which correspond to classes of conditions of existence – that is, of economic and social conditions, which impose different patterns of perception, evaluation, and behavior.

Therefore, mating preferences are not examined in isolation. Instead, they are seen as systems of preferences, or more precisely as systematic bundles of dispositions. Take women's 'overall' preferences for male traits as an example: it is the 'female habitus' which fosters the preferences for taller, older, and wealthy men, preferences which cannot be separated from each other (Bourdieu 2001: 37f.; see also Bozon 1991). The "by-product" hypothesis (Kalmijn 1998: 400) sometimes discussed in mate search literature elaborates on this idea of empirically correlated preferences: the apparent selection of one characteristic (e.g. education) may actually be the by-product of another preference (e.g. income).

The dispositional perspective goes one step further, as it interprets all (stated or revealed) mating preferences manifesting in practice as *usually* being 'by-products' of the habitus, rather than the outcome of actors favoring separate traits as such, be it consciously or unconsciously. For example, preferences for a certain education level, age, income, etc. are primarily a by-product of the disposition towards a certain habitus. Only under certain conditions, specific preferences can attain a relative autonomy from the dispositional system they are a part of. In consequence, the idea of mate choice as a by-product of another preference can be generalized to dispositions. Each analytically-postulated preference must then be suspected of being a manifest by-product of a latent 'meta-preference' or disposition.[6] The dispositional adhesiveness of any (mating) preference supports the argument of the strong heteronomy of partner markets: mating preferences and resources can hardly be assumed to be market-specific, and instead are conceptualized as a function of the relational system of the social classes.

The fundamental basis for habitual preferences is membership of a particular class and the related trajectories in the social space. As argued above, gender is a crucial and constitutive momentum of habitus. That does not imply that all men and women have the same dispositions, but that there is a gendered logics involved in class-habitus, a fact which, for example, manifests in the guise of (mating) dispositions. The example of gendered class-habitus leads to a clear rejection of the concept of any general homophily in mating (Bourdieu 2008: 183f.; Schmitz 2012): contingent, universal preferences for similarity are no explanation for mate selection in practice, or for the resulting outcomes.

At first glance, a similar critique may be aimed at the idea of lifestyle homophily, as prominently discussed in *Distinction* (1984), and seemingly resembling Kalmjin's (1998: 400) approach, who states that "people prefer to marry someone who has similar cultural resources because this enables them to develop a common life-style in marriage that produces social confirmation and affection". However, this would be a misinterpretation of the actual underlying mechanisms within the model of social space. In habitus theory, mating preferences are not conceptualized as

---

[6] A similar development can be identified in modern rationalist approaches. Freese proposes to extend the preference concept within analytical sociology (which is a currently discussed version of methodological individualism), by means of "abstract tastes that are pertinent to choices across many situations" in order "to make sense of heterogeneity in larger individual patterns of action" (Freese 2009: 107).

isolated, but as preferential bundles deriving from habitus and manifesting themselves in a "practical sense" (Bourdieu 1990: 13f.) such as (un)conscious life-style affinities. This necessarily comprises various relational mating dispositions, making homo-, hypo-, and hyperphily respective special cases of particular habitus.

Gender, which shapes the relational structure of preferences, is one potential source for non-similarity-based mating processes. Both mating preferences and favorable capitals are gender-specifically structured and complementary to each other. Couple formation can be understood as a function of "two balanced matrimonial strategies" (de Singly 1987: 188), which can foster similarity and complementary of couple configurations. The example of *Le Bal des Célibataires* gives insights into this analytical view (Bourdieu 2002a, 2008), using the example of Béarnese first-born men, whose symbolic capital had been devaluated in the 1960s through the opening of the marriage market. Here it was shown how technical and social developments in French society led to a unification of the partner market and to a devaluation of rural males' symbolic capital. This comprised "the peasant mode of production and reproduction [...] whether land and country life or the peasant's very being, his language, his attire, his manners, his bearing and even his 'physique'" (Bourdieu 2008: 181). Whereas rural males' symbolic capital was devalued by the expansion of the marriage market, the symbolic capital of urban males was revalued, affecting the relational structure between mating chances and social classes. Women from rural society were more likely, due to their disposition for men of a higher status, to prefer a partner in the increasingly accessible urban environment, or more likely themselves to be selected by an urban male with higher status. Although the female agents certainly possessed particular habitus-based mating preferences, their impact was relativized through the social changes of the time. Overall, the internalized structures and histories led to a significant number of these women preferring men from the city over bachelors from their own rural region. Hence, the taste of these women was not determined by their position in their traditional, local society, but found a new manifestation as a function of their position in the extended marriage market of modernized France.

As one can see that the female expectation of capital conversion had an impact on both their mating preferences and the resulting couple configurations, it turns out that the habitus concept certainly comprises the explanation of heterophilous mating preferences. Heterophilous mating preferences, such as age preferences or height preferences, can be traced back to their social and historical conditions (Bourdieu 2001: 37), and just like homophily, heterophilious dispositions are seen as rooted in objective constraints. The social space generally structures aspirations, that is, "the extent to which they can be satisfied" (Bourdieu 1973: 83) by way of an "adjustment of preference to the objective probabilities" (Bourdieu 2001: 37). These adjustments are also a function of objective or subjective trajectories. The mere expectation of a future position may relativize the connection between structure and aspiration, in the same way that objective advancement, when actually realized, can be associated with an effect of hysteresis (Bourdieu 1984: 142). However, a rational action approach would explain such patterns of female hypergamy with the utility gained by household division of labor, habitus perspective would suggest that hyperphily is already internalized in the earliest phases of socialization. The same applies to hypophily in mating which – as we shall see – can be understood as the disposition towards revaluation through devaluation (one may think of the stable pattern of men's preference for shorter female partners).

In sum, the habitus perspective focuses on the fact that homogamy "can have opposite meanings depending on whether it takes place among the privileged or the dispossessed" (Bourdieu 2008: 183). Homophily, hypophily, and hyperphily are, from this perspective, structures of disposition which can be observed to varying extents in the social space. This empirical finding is also sometimes considered in individualistic research, for example in the way that highly educated women are particularly homophilous with regards to education (see e.g. Mare 1991). However, the social variability of such homophilous preferences is not the analytical starting point within the MAS paradigm, but rather an empirical finding deviating from the rule.

Mating Rationalities as Dispositions

Taking into account our considerations to this point, the habitus concept also challenges the (implicit) assumption of rationality in mate choice, which is frequently implied in various forms in both traditional and contemporary mate choice theory. From a Bourdieusian perspective, (mate) choice is usually not the result of a decision made deliberately. As "the constraints surrounding every matrimonial choice are so numerous and appear in such complex combinations that the individuals involved cannot possibly deal with all of them consciously" (Bourdieu 2002b: 558), decisions are rarely "based on scrutiny of the potential consequences of the decision between multiple alternatives, or on the consideration of the advantages of all possible actions and their consequences" (Bourdieu and Chartier 2011: 282, o.t.). The same applies to processes of partner choice, which, "like many other forms of selection, follows principles of which the individuals concerned are not necessarily conscious" (Bozon and Héran 1989: 92f.). The relational perspective juxtaposes rational calculation and practical sense; Bourdieu's theory of "habitus has the primordial function of stressing that the principle of our actions is more often practical sense than rational calculation" (Bourdieu 2000: 63f.). The "practical sense" (Bourdieu 1990: 13f.) is the principle of all manifestations of evaluation, perception, and practice. It does usually not follow rational considerations, but is a result of the interplay of habitus and structure.

Referring to Goffman, Bourdieu speaks of the "sense of one's place" and the "sense of others' place" (Bourdieu 1985: 728) being effective in mating processes, which implies a clear rejection of the rational processing of contingent variables. The sense of place is "a sense of what one can or cannot 'permit oneself'" and "implies a tacit acceptance of one's place, a sense of limits ('that's not for the likes of us', etc.), or, which amounts to the same thing, a sense of distances, to be marked and kept, respected or expected" (ibid.: 728). This incorporated and largely unconscious sense takes effect as a practical sense of the relational character between one's own position and the position of a potential partner. It is "at the same time a sense of the place of others, and, together with the affinities of habitus experienced in the form of personal attraction or revulsion, is at the root of all processes of cooptation, friendship, love, association, etc., and thereby provides the principle of all durable alliances and connections, including legally sanctioned relationships" (Bourdieu 1987: 5). The position in social space and the corresponding habitus are linked to a sense for an agent's status that becomes manifest in the perception of other people, and influences the willingness, ways, and conditions of interacting with them. The taste for a partner, therefore, not only describes the socio-spatial origins of partnership preferences, but it is the generative principle underlying couple constellations. The practical sense comprises the aforementioned class-based lifestyle disposition to desire one's own habitus mirrored in that of the partner, but also to the disposition towards agents with higher or lower symbolic capital. In doing so, the practical sense manifests itself as a conscious and reflected taste only under certain conditions. This is because the practical sense depends on a "social instinct" capable of reading physical signals "which, unconsciously registered, are the basis of 'antipathies' or 'sympathies'" (Bourdieu 1984: 241; cp. Willis and Todorov 2006).

Although dispositions in mate selection are only accompanied by calculated behavior in exceptional circumstances, it cannot be "ruled out that the responses of the habitus may be accompanied by a strategic calculation tending to perform in a conscious mode the operation that the habitus performs quite differently" (Bourdieu 1990: 53). Intentional, conscious action – such as choosing a partner with certain traits – may indeed be characteristic for certain habitus and situations, but it is not necessarily the dominant logic of practice for all positions. The habitus perspective highlights the "economic and cultural conditions for access to what is regarded as rational economic behavior" (Bourdieu 2000: 70), and specifies the relational conditions of rational conduct, namely being "in the position" to act rationally" (Bourdieu and Wacquant 1992: 131).

As argued in the previous chapter, parts of the individualistic paradigm assume bounded rationality rather than actual rationality in mating. Concepts such as incorporated habits or scripts, are somewhat closer to the habitus model. However, if decisions are made according to bounded rationality, the extent of boundedness und thus the scale of the search process can vary according to habitus. With the concept of habitus, any act of rational processing – just like alternative modes of decision such as the boundedness of rationality – is genuinely specified as a socially-differentiated phenomenon, as different social classes systematically differ by means of their capital and ultimately their (cognitive) restrictions. For example, for a certain segment of the social space, the educational status of a potential partner may represent an objective and subjective goal and an object of rational reflection and choice. Others may show bounded rationality due to the complexity of their field of eligibles, and the next class of agents may be determined to such a degree that rationality does not occur at all. Accordingly, individual rationales and rationality regarding the seemingly same object may well be different.

This leads to a discussion of the degree to which future outcomes are anticipated and considered in (mate) choice. In the context of socially differential, subjectively expected utilities, "it has to be pointed out that the propensity to subordinate present desires to future desires" – for our purposes here, chances for attention and chances for exchange – "depends on the extent to which the sacrifice is 'reasonable', that is, on the likelihood [...] of obtaining future satisfactions superior to those sacrificed" (Bourdieu 1984: 180). The 'practical sense' relativizes the individualistic assumption of an average actor's focus on the future, as the very origin and content of anticipation itself is based on habitus (Bourdieu 2000: 208f.):

> The art of estimating and controlling the chances, to see in the present configuration of the situation the future 'present there'[...], the aptitude to forestall the future by a sort of practical induction or even to play the possible against the probable with a calculated risk, these are here as so many dispositions which can only be acquired under certain conditions, that is to say, in certain social conditions. (Bourdieu 2014: 238).

Being constitutive attributes of the habitus, different trajectories allows us to consider as being habitus specific not only what different agents regard as possible, but also the scope of anticipation itself.

This is of importance for the conceptualization of mating strategies – such as self-promotion, deception, contact initiation, flirting, etc. – all of which have to be understood as differing with regard to the extent to which they are oriented towards the future. Within the Bourdieusian framework, a certain class of strategies may be seen as intentional actions whose goal is the realization of a preferably attractive partner, achieved with the aid of convertible capital. However, given compatibility between habitus and situation, in most cases a strategy must be understood as the habitus-based (or practical) adaptation to objective prerequisites. Consequently, strategies usually occur unconsciously and without deliberate planning on the part of the actors. From a relational perspective, a mating strategy can be considered as "the immediate correlate of a practice [...] not posited as an object of thought, as a possibility envisaged within a project", but as emanation of the practical sense which is "inscribed within the presence of the game" (Bourdieu 1998: 80). Take the strategy of deceptive strategies in mating as an example: Bok, for instance, finds that many lies tend to be unplanned, emerging spontaneously during communication (Bok 1979), and DePaulo et al. (1996) show that, on a psychological level, everyday lies are, as a rule, unplanned. Deceptive practices, nevertheless pertinent in many cases, can be interpreted as practices which take on the form of objectively goal-oriented sequences without necessarily being the result of either a deliberate strategy or mechanical determination. Ultimately, as mating strategies are embedded within "individual dispositions with deep social roots" (Bozon and Héran 1989: 92f.), and due to the different strategic preconditions associated with different habitus, their content and degree of future orientation can be expected to correspond to social classes in much the same way as mating utilities, preferences, and rationalities (and irrationalities) do.

As a consequence, any singular mating strategy must also be understood as elements of the nexus of different strategies specific to particular classes and habitus. Mating strategies must

> not be seen in the abstract, unrelated to inheritance strategies, fertility strategies, and even pedagogical strategies" [but] "as one element in the entire system of biological, cultural, and social reproduction by which every group endeavors to pass on to the next generation the full measure of power and privilege it has itself inherited (Bourdieu 2002b: 558).

Whereas, in traditional societies, families were the executors of marriage strategies, in modern Western societies, the classes take the place of the family, making mating strategies a matter of specific positions and dispositions in the social space.[7]

The complexity of the external influences effecting the various ways of mental processing further demonstrates that any form of rationality can only be assumed for those agents who share both the decision situation in question and an identical habitus.

Mate Choice as Classification Practice

Our line of argumentation so far has shown that – in contrast to the MAS model – for Bourdieu, couple formation is not primarily a result of (intentional) acts of choice based on the preference of individual characteristics. Instead, habitus-based practices actualize the logic of the social space which "brings together things and people that go together" (Bourdieu 1984: 241). The habitus is not only manifested in "the fundamental structures of the socially constituted preference systems", but it represents "the generating and unifying principle of making choices, whether with regard to educational institutions, disciplines, sports, culture, or political opinions", and indeed with regard to potential partners (Bourdieu 1996b: 2). In contrast to MAS and most individualistic approaches, the subjective sense of the habitus – for example the preference for a particular characteristic – and the choice act itself are not analytically separated, but interpreted as a "practical sense" with an incorporated, objective, and historical dimension (Bourdieu 1998: 25). Thus, any act of choosing a mate implies more than just behavior and a synchronic sense of the individual actor. The apparently actively selecting actor of the MAS perspective is "never completely the subject of his practices" (Bourdieu 2000: 138), but is guided by his internalized history and the 'external' conditions which are typical for a certain (class-based) habitus. This, however, cannot be understood as a deterministic mechanism, as the model of habitus takes into account the agents' (limited) potential for creative and reflexive reasoning. It is the models of rational choice that must be criticized for their inherent finalism and determinism:

> If choices are made to depend, on the one hand, on the structural constraints (technical, economic, or legal) that delimit the range of possible actions and, on the other hand, on preferences presumed to be universal and conscious, then the agents [...] constrained by the logical necessity of 'rational calculus', are left no other freedom than adherence [...] to the objective chances (Bourdieu 1990: 46).

---

[7] Here, the perspective of social fields can be useful in further disentangling the impacts of the economic, political, scientific, etc., fields on particular classes and their strategies.

The practical sense of the habitus, in contrast, offers a way of conceptualizing agency beyond the false juxtaposition of determinism and free choice. In habitus theory, practice is conceptualized as *classification* practice: agents who are classified by their position in social space classify themselves and others indirectly via everyday practices, and directly via practices of interaction. Take the example of offline flirting or online chatting: a conversation often revolves around questions of everyday life, and at the same time enables a (not necessarily conscious) 'clandestine scrutiny' of habitus congruency. In these processes of finding common positions, practices, as well as agents and their characteristics, are rated and classified according to differentiated and differentiating taste. Following Bourdieu (1984: 6), "social subjects, classified by their classifications, distinguish themselves by the distinctions they make, between the beautiful and the ugly, the distinguished and the vulgar, in which their position in the objective classifications is expressed or betrayed". In the same way, classification practices in mating mean that a socially-classified habitus actually classifies itself, the potential partner, third parties, and the symbolic goods involved in the practice. However, and as argued above, habitus affinity usually rests on unconscious antipathies and sympathies, so that mate choice is often a by-product of everyday practices which are characterized by many more logics than those purely connected to mating.

Mating as Reciprocal Classification

As with the individual utilities, rationalities, preferences, and choices of the MAS model, the conceptualization of the interactional dimension of mating can also be thought of as a function of social space and habitus. In habitus theory, it is the structure of the social space which underlies and structures every symbolic exchange relation between two agents. Bourdieu (1984: 578) criticizes the "interactionist fallacy", by which processes such as exchange are wrongly regarded as being consciously perceived by the agents involved and independent of their social antecedents. In contrast, "interacting individuals" are seen as bringing "all their properties into the most circumstantial interactions", and their "relative positions in the social structure (or in a specialized field)" as guiding "their positions in the interaction" (Bourdieu 1984: 578–579).

Because a certain structuralist reasoning affects this perspective on interactions, Bourdieu's works do not feature an explicit discussion of processes of mutually interrelated actions and perceptions, which occupy an important position in mating. Interactions are discussed less systematically as an analytical level in their own right in the orthodox reception of habitus theory and – with regard to his empirical work – Bourdieu did not devote himself to the empirical "minutiae of interactions" (Bourdieu 2001: 35). However, for an analysis of mating processes, the categories of interaction and intersubjectivity must be emphasized, at least for 'modern' societies, as the impact of the social space not only precipitates in form of an agent's practice, but also in form of interacting agents' reciprocal practices of reference.

Thus, the question arises as to potential class-specific variations of (symbolic) exchange and interaction in mating.

Although Bourdieu did not put too great of a focus on interactions, it can certainly be inferred that he did not assume a universal form of reciprocity, instead considering there to be variations between, for example, the classification practices taking place in and between different social classes. In his research on the marriage strategies of Kabyle families, it was necessary to analyze the positions of two interacting families with regard to the distribution of economic and symbolic capital. With regard to modernity, he argued that the laissez-faire nature of the free partner market tends to conceal the structural necessities and forces that are constitutive for mating processes in our times. As a matter of fact, habitus mechanisms become the more important the less direct group influences can be made responsible for resulting couple constellations.

As argued above, practices of mating are best understood as habitus-specific classification practices, meaning that agents are classified by the social space and classify objects in the course of their agency. However, in contrast to an inanimate consumer good, a relationship (in the Western modernity) is based on consent and the mutual interest of two agents, meaning that processes of mating do not merge into one-sided practices, but rather take the form of *reciprocal classification* practices (Schmitz 2012). This generalization of mating as a practice of classification emphasizes the fact that socially classified agents classify themselves and their potential mates in the process of mating, and thus reproduce the classified structure of the social space. In this way, the way in which the process of classification works can be generalized to facilitate an understanding of how reciprocal classification works: much in the same way Bourdieu's (1985, 1987) concept of class condenses agents down to imprecise groups defined by probabilities, interactions can be seen as theoretically endless, but methodologically reducible to a finite number of reciprocal classes. The questions of 'who chooses whom', so fundamental in MAS, can then be re-framed into 'how do agents classify themselves and each other into classes of agents'. As reciprocal classification practices are not restricted to habitus similarity,[8] but comprise manifold differences in habitus, a vast range of configurations can be systematically addressed, such as symbolic capital equivalency, cultural submission, exploitation, etc.

A benefit of the extension of the practice model is the resolution of the analytical problem that homophily in one manifest characteristic may be accompanied by heterophily in another. With regard to the example of the marriage market in Béarn, one could state that market conditions had an impact on the females' sense of their place, inasmuch as their scope of what they could achieve changed. Conversely, those males from urban areas who mate with females from rural areas relativized lifestyle similarity, consciously or unconsciously, in favor of other traits (such as

---

[8] Consequently, 'amor fati' (Bourdieu 2000: 143) then means not only seeing one's own trajectory epitomised in a partner, but also seeing one's destiny in the difference another symbolizes.

youth or cultural inferiority). The resulting couples were dissimilar regarding their lifestyle, but they can be ascribed a certain latent trait equivalency that originated through the evaluations and practices of the agents involved. Applying the perspective of reciprocal classification, one can hypothesize that agents who are equivalent in the overall volume of their capital, and hence their symbolic capital, are more likely to start an interaction than those who differ with regard to their capital volume. This means that a comparable symbolic capital, and hence the same (or higher) capital volume, can facilitate a relationship or marriage in relative independence of its composition. Therefore, one can conclude that (gender-specific) equivalency of symbolic capital can relativize the traditional preference for lifestyle similarity under certain circumstances, such as a change in the scope of the partner market or the access to new partner markets.

The concept of strategy can not only be related to individual practices, but also to reciprocal classification practices. As the "convertibility of the different types of capital is the basis of the strategies aimed at ensuring the reproduction of capital" (Bourdieu 1986: 253), a mating strategy can be conceptualized as the (intended or unintended) conversion chances of an agent's capital into another capital. The concept of reciprocal classification then allows for the conceptualization of an operation similar to exchange theory, as it has the potential for including rational, preference-based (exchange) actions.

However, rational choice and rational exchange become a special case of the 'how' of reciprocal classification, just as preferences are a special case of the 'practical sense' within the framework of habitus theory. The question then is: what are the conditions for instrumental rationality and direct reciprocity in mating? To name but a few, if actors perceive and accept the market as such, this will be associated with their submission to the market's imperatives. Regarding the agents' habitus, some may have a disposition to exchange and rationality, even before they meet a potential partner. With regard to reciprocal classification practices, one might expect that dissimilarities between two agents mean that they are not, or not yet, compatible, a fact which will create a friction between habitus and situation, and thus make room for conscious and anticipative logics of exchange.

Reciprocal classification also comprises situations inhibiting rationality and the logics of exchange in phenomenological terms. Whereas exchange theory, in its form of a rationalist reduction, sees it as a prerequisite that the actors involved perceive a specific trait as an exchangeable resource, or that a hypothetical assumption can be generalized for all dyads, the mechanism of elective affinity is based on the (class-specific) misunderstanding of the fact of resource exchange and the symbolic dimension of interaction. It may well be that the emergence of a couple is primarily the result of untroubled interaction, and hence a *systematic inhibition* of situations inducing rational exchange.

In fact, according to Western notions of romanticism, it is a 'norm' to 'find oneself in one's partner' without having to behave rationally. In large parts of modern

Western society, the notion of romantic choice is heavily dependent on concealing individual rationalities and the symbolic character of each couple formation.[9] Processes of symbolic good exchange are characterized by the need for hiding the economic dimension of reciprocity, while emphasizing the symbolic reciprocity. In the case of mating processes, this becomes apparent in the context of scientific terms like 'profit', 'credit' and 'interest', which are used as explanatory concepts for mating outcomes, whereas it is usually taboo for the agents involved to express such considerations. Even more than in gift exchange markets, modern romantic exchanges deny the logics of *do ut des* between the two partners. In the case of mating, agents commonly misjudge the objective relationship between one another by temporarily concealing the logic of gift and counter-gift, although, for example, an invitation to a dinner is *de facto* not unrelated to the probability of subsequent sexual interaction. In an economy of symbolic goods, the "consensus regarding the exchange rate is also present in an economy of symbolic exchanges, but its terms and conditions are left implicit" (Bourdieu 1998: 96). Exchange on the partner market is, as such, not an exchange for profitable gains, but – like the exchange of gifts – an exchange of symbolic goods, in particular of recognition as a potentially attractive partner. Blau also assumes that "in intrinsic love attachments […] each individual furnishes rewards to the other not to receive proportionate extrinsic benefits in return but to express and confirm his own commitment and to promote the other's growing commitment to the association" (Blau 1964: 77). However, there is still a clear intentional concept inherent to any social exchange within Blau's approach. Habitus theory, in contrast, does not assume target orientation as fundamental principle of practices and reciprocal classification. Also, with habitus theory there are different 'classes of exchange' to be expected rather than an overall prevailing exchange principle for all actors.

In applying the concept of reciprocal classification it is not assumed that rivaling theoretical arguments compete for the one appropriate explanation of couple emergence. On the contrary, the fact that different mating interactions involve different logics is an insight constitutive for the relational perspective. Different theories, as contrasted with each other, for example, by Blossfeld and Drobnič (2001) in the context of couple's careers are regarded instead as (analytically overemphasized) conceptions of dyadic configurations, which can be applied to particular empirical couples in a variable extent and cannot be applied without recognizing their interdependence. Any generalized conception of exchange relations, such as Becker's suggestion of their complementary and substitutive character, is best interpreted relationally, as a function of the societal background of the two parties involved. Hertog (2012), for example, shows in the context of online dating that specialization

---

[9] This was also recognized by Thibaut and Kelley (1959: 28), early proponents of exchange theory in mating, who state that "mating is not governed by anticipations or consequences, covert calculation of the relative merits of different actions, or the deliberate attempt to maximize outcomes". However, this concession makes it difficult to conceptualize mating processes as separate from exchange itself, inasmuch as the character of exchange is more imputed theoretically than considered directly relevant for the praxis of the agents involved.

and collaborative theories of marriage explain male and female partner choices of different educational backgrounds and income groups.

Ignoring the variations underlying different interactional elements may lead to fallacies, such as inferring homophilous preferences from observed couple homogeneity, or inferring subjective rationality in the light of apparently appropriate rational behavior during objectifiable exchange.

Mating as (Symbolic) Domination

The relational perspective, in the sense of a Bourdieusian approach, focuses on the structural implications of purportedly subjective entities, and is thus sensitive towards the power and domination inherent to mating processes. Most traditional mate choice research essentially deals with the reproduction of social inequality as an aggregated result of particular preference-guided choice acts. Relational sociology of mating, in contrast, emphasizes that these preferences and perceptions, as well as the opportunities to realize them, are largely socialized, and manifestations of the prevailing circumstances of power and domination. However, for the purpose of assessing relations of domination, the relational view does not – for example – consider it necessary that "all differences between women and men can immediately be attributed to patriarchy" (Blossfeld and Drobnič 2001: 25). It instead treats domination as one aspect of societal relations, which precipitates in the most everyday situations.

Symbolic power and domination is a basic category of the social space and the field of power (Schmitz et al. 2016). It is the field of power (often in guise of the nation-state) where the categories of what is seen as legitimate are defined, for example regarding institutions such as family or marriage (who is allowed to marry whom, gay marriage), with vast implications for socialization (Bourdieu 1996a). Symbolic domination also occurs in form of the structuring effects the dominant class has on the dominated. The standards of the dominant, such as the power to legitimately define the value of symbolic goods, can become constitutive for the cognitive apparatus of the dominated, who apply these standards to themselves.

A core example in the context of mating processes is reciprocal affection, which often manifests itself in the form of disposition-based lifestyle affinities, and can be seen as an emanation of gendered domination (Bourdieu 2001: 36f.). The habitus of the sexes, and hence their mating dispositions, show a complementary interrelation. It is a preliminary simplification (yet not entirely unfounded in our modern Western societies), that men tend to symbolize their societal position by mating with women with a relational deficit in capital endowment. In a complementary manner, women tend to realize their own symbolic subordination by mating with a man who is, for example, taller, better educated, older, and so on. While the relevance of social status has been recognized by all research in the field, an important argument here exemplarily highlights that mating implies more than a subjective and objective optimization: "without any calculation, through the apparent arbitrariness of an inclination that is not amenable to discussion or reason", women "can only want and love a man whose dignity is clearly affirmed and attested in and by the fact that he is visibly 'above' them" (Bourdieu 2001: 36). The cognitive mechanism at work here is based on the fact that many women can identify with the dominant culture, as the submission implied does not conflict with their sexual identity, which predisposes them to submission (cp. Bourdieu and Passeron 1977; Bozon 1991). Consequently, male and female mating dispositions, practices, and strategies must be interpreted as emanations of the symbolic power structure of a society, practices which have been internalized and manifested from early on within and through the family.

The difference between the sexes is reproduced, in particular, by the internalization of two complementary social requirements: whereas masculinity is created by simply 'existing' – through activity, exertion, and even combat – femininity entails the passive "being-perceived (percipi)" by men (Bourdieu 2001: 66; cp. Schmitz and Riebling 2013). This is particularly well-illustrated in the conditions under which couples emerge. Even in our times, women – far more than men – are assigned the status of symbolic goods, their symbolic and marital exchange value essentially ensuing from what Hakim (2010) attempts to grasp, with the term 'erotic capital' as an individual resource. However, the ultimate authority held over their own erotic impact is relatively low for women who conform to the stereotypical expectations of the partner market. The traditional forms of capital which Hakim affirmatively ascribes to male exchange partners can be employed and exchanged in many more situations and in a more flexible manner. The exchange value of economic and cultural capital is relatively independent of the involved relationship constituted by the agents participating in the exchange. This is not the case, thanks to its predominantly feminine connotations, for the resource 'eroticism'. The exclusivity and specificity of the exchange relationship has a great deal of influence on the value of this resource on the partner market. An over-generalized investment in this resource will lead to inflation, and therefore devaluation of the value of one's own body. Masculine domination defines the sexual or marital exchange value of female attractiveness in the aggregate to such an extent that a female body cannot be generalized without paying the price of its symbolic devaluation. Either way, investing in 'erotic capital' will always entail an investment in the existing balance of power between the sexes. The habitus approach casts light on the way the internalization of gender-specific and stereotypical ideals of beauty simultaneously entails the habitualization of the conditions of their reproduction. Any explanation of attraction cannot be reduced to biologically determined preferences, but must take into account that (mating) preferences are structured by the social fact of male domination. In this way, the frequently observed differences in preference for age, education, or height can be interpreted as the expression of internalized structures of power (see Bourdieu 2001: 36ff.).

One may wonder why developments in the labor market which improved women's material status did not immediately lead to a change in women's relational preferences, for example making them desire men with a lower social status. The historical example of Béarn makes clear that societal changes do not necessarily lead to changes either in the structure of the agent's dispositions or in the relational structure between the sexes. The principle of gendered domination, making marriage a problem of 'above and below', remain the same. Only its empirical manifestations change, due to the expanded spectrum of symbolic goods. The gendered hierarchy of society is constituted in such a way that the reversal of traditional patterns, where women in prestigious positions choose a man with lower status, paradoxically will lead to a devaluation of themselves. Applying the explanatory scheme of normative theories – such as the 'male breadwinner' norm – here would obscure the structural logics which actually occur. The dispositional mechanism is that women can identify with the dominant culture, as the submission implied does not conflict with their sexual identity, which predisposes them to submission (Bourdieu and Passeron 1977).

As was argued above, apart from lifestyle homophily, reciprocal classification practices between classes imply symbolic differences as a major mechanism for the conduct and results of interactions between the sexes. In a variety of everyday situations, these differences are reproduced as a function of the interacting individuals' habitus, generating the "transformation of power into charisma or into the charm suited to evoke affective enchantment" between agents differing in power (Bourdieu 1998: 102). Obviously, it is more than a matter of time for this to impact on the inertia of the agent's habitus. An elimination of this basic principle would require radical changes in many social fields and not only in the fields of labor and education.

Symbolic domination and its foundation in the agent's cognitive schemes are anything but restricted to the relation between the sexes.[10] It also operates with regard to class and race, and, given the relational logic of the theory in question, is therefore always 'intersectional', emphasizing the interplay between categories such as gender, race, and class as differential cumulative disadvantages within societies.

MAS as Special Case of a Relational Theory of Mating

The differences between the paradigm of mate choice as agency in structures and Bourdieu's theoretical approach as elaborated in the previous section are far from indicating a theoretical incompatibility. Whereas trying to transfer the relational approach to the logics of 'Coleman's bathtub' would be an endeavor doomed to failure, due its restricted capacities to incorporate structure into its explanatory schemes, an integration of the MAS model into the social space approach is possible, and indeed fruitful.

A relational sociology of mating enables a break with both the researchers' and the observed agents' perspectives, by applying a more fundamental notion of structure. The concept of social space can be seen as an elaborated version of Peter Blau's structural space model (McPherson 1983: 519ff.), which often represents the structural complement to individual mate choice. Both the Blau space and the social space see agents' probabilities of encounter as functions of the social structure. In

---

[10] It would be a comparatively small (but greatly important) analytical operation to extend this analytical scheme to categories of ethnicity, heteronormativity, or age.

contrast to Blau's structuralism, which only offers a way to interpret structure as structures of opportunity (e.g. mate choice sets), the social space approach conceives of structure as operating within the agents and their practices. Here, the construction of a generalized lower-dimensional space, and the identification of relevant (trans-situational) classes of agents within this latent structure of opportunity, is the analytical starting point, as opposed to the idea of an averaged choosing actor in a particular situation of choice.

Mating utilities, rationalities, alternatives, preferences, strategies, choices, interactions, etc., are not assumed for a particular market, but they are primarily seen as a function of differential positions in social space. This insight emphasizes the historical coherence for certain (classes of) agents and the social differences between these (classes of) agents. Individualistic approaches such as MAS have no conceptualization of the conditions structuring the actor prior to the observed mating situation in question. However, some proponents of rational action theory are partly aware of these trans-situational preconditions of mate choice situations. Blossfeld and Timm (2003: 338) refer to "social origin", meaning "a conglomerate of highly correlated economic and social characteristics of parents such as wealth, household income, prestige, jobs, education, etc". In a similar argumentative thrust, Kalmijn (1998: 400) argues that "education is not only strongly related to income and status, but also to taste, values, and lifestyles". The concept of habitus genuinely emphasizes this fundamental intersection of different resources, as well as that of the interplay of objective resources and subjective dispositions. In doing so, it consequently prioritizes the trans-situational and historical coherence of an individual's dispositions, as well as the individual's role as 'symbolic good'. The habitus model is not one of ahistorical actors operating on an autonomous partner market, but of fully socialized agents, as "the past remains present and active in the dispositions it has produced" (Bourdieu 2000: 64). The agent looking for a mate is thus not only seen as being affected by his synchronic relational position, but also by a mechanism of hysteresis or "inertia" (see e.g. Bourdieu 1996c: 346) – that is, by an encroachment of history into the present.[11] Again, a similar consideration can be found in Blossfeld and Timm (1997), who argue that mating preferences are closely bound up in the life-long process of identity formation, but lack a theorization of the structural dimension of history.

Following Blossfeld (1996: 184), the mate choice perspective – like rational choice theory in general – "logically presupposes" a "macro-theory to identify the specific historical structures and processes which produce and change concrete opportunity sets for individuals' actions" and thereby "cut down the set of abstractly possible courses of action to a vastly smaller subset of feasible actions". Whereas the Blau space may fulfill these requirements in a synchronic perspective, it lacks a grasp of the historical dimension of structure. This not only implies the historical development of opportunity sets facing the actor, but also – indeed, especially – the theoretical derivation of historically structured actors. As the Blau space is not built

---

[11] Three forms of historicization can be derived from this insight: the historicization of the agent 'looking for a mate', the historicization of the space of the categories he applies on the market, and the historicization of the space of the positions in the partner market, that is, his structure of opportunity. A fourth historicization is the one of the scientists' categories and their ways of constructing the research object.

for conceptualizing the interplay of structure and actor, it is also hardly suitable for theorizing processes of actor formation, such as the development and change of the actor's (mate) preference structure. Habitus theory, in contrast, puts a particular emphasis on assessing those mechanisms which precede acts of mate choice or simply finding a specific focus. In doing so, this view emphasizes the fact that multiple conditions such as class background and field effects are to be read as part of the habitus itself.[12] For this reason, the habitus also fulfills the requirements of some methodological individualists. Kara (2009: 71) postulates a "framework in which the self is represented by multiple dimensions and hence by multiple preferences", and recognizes that these multiple dimensions "of the self could be taken to indicate the multiple considerations with respect to which alternatives of choice are to be ranked" in such a way that these "rankings may be irreducibly distinct, partly interdependent, possibly conflicting, context-dependent and/or dynamic" (cp. Elster 1986).

The generative principle of the habitus concept includes the 'decision' element of MAS, as "the habitus is the geometric location of determinisms and decisions" (Bourdieu 1974: 40, o.t.) and of the "systematic principle of selection" (Bourdieu 1990: 102). This means that both the alternatives and the methods used to calculate their value can be reconstructed as functions of habitus. Although practices of 'mate choice' usually follow the practical sense of the habitus, rather than a rational calculation or the deterministic influences of norm or societal positions, the habitus comprises traditional, rational, bounded rational behavior, frames, norm-orientation, etc. The notion of habitus interprets concepts such as frames as a systematic part of habitus, and hence with regard to their social differentiality. Whereas modern individualistic research may discuss, for example, the situational conditions under which an actor utilizes a particular pattern or script, the relational approach also enables an analysis of the differential distribution of frames and scripts as functions of the habitus, independent from a contingent mating situation. The activation of frames and scripts is thought of less as a function of specific situations, as MAS would assume, but more as the function of generalized situations where an agent is located – that is, his habitus. One could transfer this idea to the MAS approach by assuming a habitus mechanism affecting which particular socially-different frame or script is transferred in a seemingly comparable mating situation. The habitus concept also comprises the classical sociological conception of role and norms, which are sometimes also used for the description of mating processes. However, anticipated normative expectations are not overemphasized, and a role set which would be indifferently applicable to all agents, is not assumed here. Instead, roles and norms effective in mating are not seen as external orientation, but as internalized elements of the agent's dispositional schemes and knowledge order, thus emphasizing structures of empirical matches between agent and role. Overall, 'mate choice', the core concept of MAS, can be understood as depending on habitus, which generates a multitude of social practices which may be grounded in rational, traditional, role-taking, normative, etc. logics.[13]

---

[12] Lindenberg (2013) also sees the historicization of the actor as a current need for development of rational action theories, and proposes types of personality to this end.

[13] The effects of social fields may serve as a habitus-generating instance within the field of power (cp. Schmitz et al. 2016; Witte 2014).

The same applies to the prices that agents can fetch on the partner market by staking their habitus and the symbolic goods associated herewith. Whereas in "economic theory a valued good has 'a single price' at equilibrium" […] "the values in the space of correspondences that Bourdieu constructs are always polysemous, multidimensional, carrying differing meanings with respect to associated principles of action and contradictions among those principles, and likely to be interpreted differently with respect to actors' distinctive locations in a social or cultural field" (Breiger 2000: 108). The profit deriving from a good is thus not seen as following a linear function over all actors, but rather as a discontinuous function of the position within the social space.

Figure 5.1 underlines the conception of habitus as pattern of internal and external conditions, as well as the interrelations between these patterns: each distinct analytical concept – mating preferences, strategies, choices, opportunity sets, exchange in mating, etc. – can be understood as being simultaneously constituted by and constituents of the relational structure of the social space. As in MAS, 'structure' here comprises opportunities associated with particular positions in the space. Nevertheless, structure is also located within the actors themselves. Each class of agents within the social space is understood as a structured entity with particular originating conditions for practice and interaction, ultimately contributing to the change and reproduction of the social space itself. This does not imply that each position in the social space would be only accessible via its particularities. On the contrary, the social space perspective identifies objective conditions and relations between classes of objective and subjective (dis)positions.

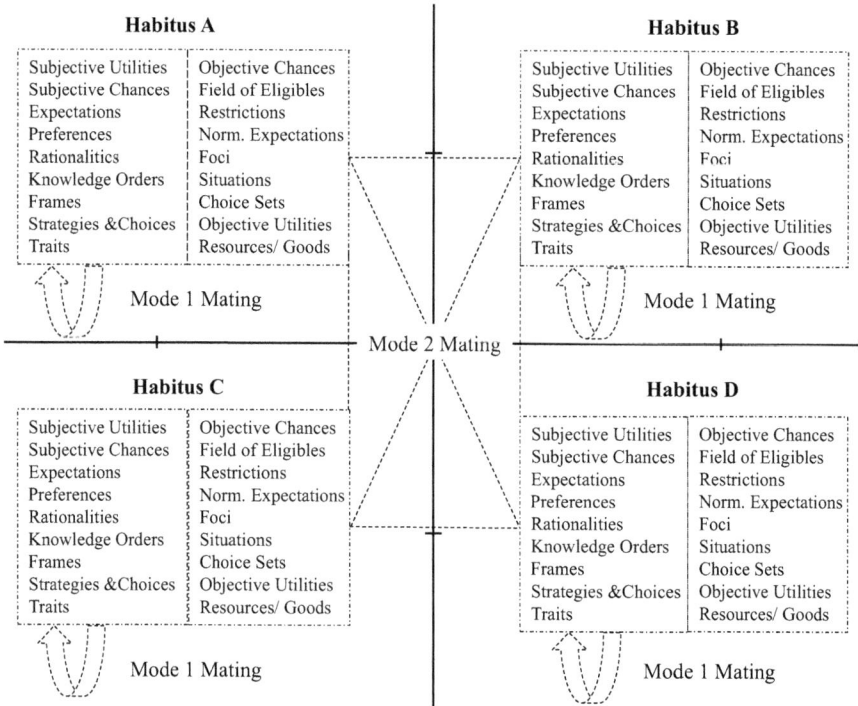

Fig. 5.1 The MAS model within the social space model

Applying the relational concept to mating research not only highlights the fact that agents systematically differ in their preferences, expectations, choices, and ways of internalizing and coping with restrictions and resources. This view also reveals that the very applicability of the individualistic model's concepts itself varies over the social space and hence with the agent's habitus. For example, a particular segment of the social space, such as the middle-classes, could be seen as a 'locus of rationality', as particular trajectories and conditions of this position tend to foster a rational habitus. The relational approach specifies mating situations similar to the individualist notion of situational logics in the sense of Popper, as the habitus comprises the "sum total of the conditions – internal and external" (Popper 2002: 8). The concepts of habitus and situation are closely connected, as it is the habitus that "constitutes the situation", just as the history of situations is constitutive for the habitus (Bourdieu and Chartier 2011: 91, o.t.). According to the habitus perspective, all potential decisions, "and the 'system of preferences' which underlies [them], depend not only on all the previous choices of the decider but also on the conditions in which his 'choices' have been made, which include all the choices of those who have chosen for him" (Bourdieu 1990: 49). This means that the effects of past non-mating related decisions must be taken into account systematically, but also that the probabilities of specific forms and substances of decision vary depending on their position in the social space, and the degree of compatibility between habitus and situation.

The concept of habitus relativizes the situational character of mate choice – thus solving a key problem of mate choice theory – by emphasizing the trans-situational character of mating. Each particular (mating) situation is primarily a function of the societal position of the agents involved. Also, in situations of mating, "the elements which define the setting in which interaction" occurs (the aforementioned foci of interaction) depend on the specific "social background" (Bozon and Héran 1989: 92f.). This particularly includes the involved class trajectories up to the event of interaction and from then on. As a consequence, the analytical juxtaposition of mating opportunities as choice sets and mating as a choice act is not applied here, as the individualist 'logics of situation' and 'logics of choice' both merge in the concept of habitus based practice. Consequently, the extent of the situationality of mating can itself be considered a variable: for example, whether a mating situation is a high cost or low cost situation (or a situation at all) also becomes a question of the position in the social space.

Rather than postulating the existence of a partner market, the habitus view allows researchers to recognize that instrumental rationality will emerge to the degree that the agents themselves perceive a market situation. This extent involves both the differential potential and indeed the differential necessities of choosing between multiple alternatives. For example, the sense of one's own position does not automatically imply the preference for similarity regarding a maximum of characteristics or lifestyle features – when and inasmuch as mating actually constitutes a choice, i.e. if the 'habitus driven' moment takes a back seat to rational calculations. Relational sociology can provide insights into the situational conditions of individual agency, and may also serve as a systematic source for the derivation of 'bridge hypotheses', which serve to "link an actor's 'environment' (institutions, norms, values, communication, symbols etc.) to an actor's 'personal setting' like internalized norms and values, identities, emotions, etc." (Winter and Kron 2009: 4).

The concepts of social space, habitus, practice, and (reciprocal) classification allow us to specify the various logics inherent to interaction processes as the interplay of one agents' habitus with another's, and thus the confrontation of two positions in the social space. This consideration emphasizes the fact that a particular mode of interaction such as exchange is an *analytical* special case. Thus, habitus theory is not a mere "cultural matching theory" which "concludes that class homophily is accounted for by cultural similarities and enabled by the social organization of culture by class" (Streib 2015: 20). The everyday interaction between agents of different social classes is itself essentially a function of said agents' habitus. Such interaction will result in reciprocal routines, depending on the relational structure between the (two) habitus in question. As outlined above, however, this necessarily comprises the manifest dyadic (lifestyle) similarities and (gender-based) dissimilarities, emerging from the respective encounter of homo-, hyper-, and hypophilic dispositions.

Just as in the case of individual practice, rationality in interaction can be thought of in different ways. This includes 'habitual rationality', in the sense that an exchange between two agents from the same or different classes may be based on their dispositions toward rationalizing the other in the context of expected exchange. Rationality and exchange (as meaning and form) might also be evoked by the relational heterogeneity of the two agents. This kind of interaction can cause an "interruption" of the "routine adjustment of subjective and objective structures", and "constitutes a class of circumstances when indeed a rational choice may take over" (Bourdieu and Wacquant 1992: 131).

Thus, rationality in mating may also be thought of as being induced by particular types of encounter within the relational approach, such as the interaction between agents of different or similar positions in the social space. However, the social space also contains a plethora of (situational) conditions that do not foster rationality or even suppress rationality in mating. Think of the encounter of two agents with congruent lifestyles or the case of habitus complementarity due to dissimilarity of symbolic goods. Nevertheless, even those cases of individual agency or dyadic interaction that are closest to the logics of economic rationality will always involve a symbolic dimension (cp. Lebaron 2001: 124). Any choice requires presuppositions regarding the situation, refers to a culturally constituted symbolic order of choice objects, and rests on the recognition of other agents (if one were being old-fashioned, one could say that any practice requires the mobilization of symbolically generalized communication media). The social space approach to the partner market as a symbolic good market thus challenges analytical separations such as dichotomizations into market and non-market traits, as all goods and capitals effective on the partner market imply a symbolic dimension, just as all symbols entail materialistic preconditions and consequences. Examples of this symbolic dimension include the differential capabilities of capital conversion, including the required effort, the involved legitimacy, and the access to different markets as objects of strategic struggles.

Apart from direct reciprocal classification, the social space concept differs in a fundamental way from traditional mate choice approaches, in that its relational structuralism does not assume the operation of isolated concepts such as decisions being independent of each other (Blossfeld and Timm 2003: 3). Agents are – even without living together or seeing, knowing, or affecting each other directly – mutually dependent (or rather non-independent) in a theoretical (and statistical) way. This is of particular interest in the digital context: two users unknown to each other are not only theoretically related due to the inclusive nature of the social space concept, but they also are statistically dependent, as the social space operates as "common fate" (cp. Kenny et al. 2006) for all its agents. In other words: differences and similarities between two agents are neither random, nor a mere result of direct influence, but a logical and statistical consequence of the relational nature of the social space. This social fact finds little consideration in traditional theories of (mate) choice and even less when it comes to the analysis of 'individual' actions. Making reference to relational structuralism allows us to develop the theory of 'mate choice as agency in structures' further towards a theory of 'mating as structures in agency' and 'mating as structures in interaction'. In doing so, the relational perspective can be understood as a generalized perspective of symbolic good markets, which sees not only the direct relations between agents engaged in mate search, but also between the latent structural and sub-individual conditions involved.

Regarding the specific case of online dating, one can argue that the MAS model and its axiomatic system most strongly correspond to the right side of the graphical representation of ideal-type partner markets, as illustrated in Chapter 3 (Figure 3.1), where contexts have been located which are particularly close to the ideal-type notion of an relatively autonomous partner market. In online dating, the opportunity structure, in the sense of external structure, is often seen as relativized due to the technological conditions, leading to a research context only consisting of individuals and their actions. Given a relative absence of distorting offline structure, unlike most offline partner markets, users of a dating site can choose from alternative sets, are required to reflect their preferences, to consider their personal resources, and to develop well-founded decision. Thus, when reflecting on online dating in a spontaneous way, one might be expected to abolish the concept of 'structure', and apply the individualistic model in its purest form. However, if online dating can indeed be thought of as being particularly representative of the abstract concept of 'partner market', it is more than just an appropriate research context for the application of the individualistic MAS model. For the same reason, an online dating platform also represents a particularly good example for highlighting the analytical potential of a relational approach to mating processes. Online dating represents – thanks to its relative autonomy, the purported relativization of structural impacts, and the absence of direct external social structure – a unique opportunity to elaborate on the structural implications of couple formation in a 'least likely' scenario for the application of structural reasoning.

Only if 'structure' is used for addressing entities and mechanisms outside the agent, may online dating be seen as a structure-free sphere. Following Bourdieu (1984: 241) who states that class endogamy "is ensured almost as strictly by free play of the sentiment as by deliberate family intervention", one must expect to find social structure in strong operation on a digital dating platform. This expectation can be derived from the hysteretic nature of habitus, a concept which addresses the thoroughly structured nature of agents themselves. Whereas approaches, such as the focus-theory, address concrete places which enable and structure encounter, the habitus approach replaces the manifest place by a latent space of positions and dispositions. Effects of the physical and geographical space are not denied, but social space and habitus are seen as *prior* to them (cp. Bourdieu 1999: 123 ff.). Physical spaces (in the connotation of both geographical and digital spaces) are seen as *acquired* spaces, involving different conditions and consequences for the particular agents' habitus. Consequently, we must expect that the retranslation of the social space, in the form of a "definite distributional arrangement of agents and properties", is not limited to the "physical space", in the sense of the material offline world (Bourdieu 1996d: 10). The "invisible set of relationships" (ibid.) must rather be expected to manifest itself in the digital space, as constituted by an online dating market. Before we address the empirical manifestations of structure, we will now turn to the methodological and methodical implications of a Bourdieusian approach in general and to the online partner market in particular.

References

Alexander, J. C., Giesen, B., Münch, R., & Smelser, N. (Eds.). (1987). *The micro-macro link* (1st ed.). Berkeley: University of California.
Blau, P. M. (1964). *Exchange and power in social life* (9th ed.). New York: Wiley.
Blau, P. M. (1987). Contrasting theoretical perspectives. In J. C. Alexander, B. Giesen, R. Münch, & N. Smelser (Eds.), *The micro-macro-link* (pp. 71–85). Berkeley: University of California Press.
Blossfeld, H.-P. (1996). Macro-sociology, rational choice theory, and time. A theoretical perspective on the empirical analysis of social processes. *European Sociological Review, 12*(2), 181–206.
Blossfeld, H.-P., & Drobnic, S. (2001). Theoretical perspectives on couples' careers. In H.-P. Blossfeld & S. Drobnic (Eds.), *Careers of couples in contemporary societies. From male breadwinner to dual earner families* (pp. 16–50). New York: Oxford University Press.
Blossfeld, H.-P., & Timm, A. (1997). *Das Bildungssystem als Heiratsmarkt: Eine Längsschnittanalyse der Wahl von Heiratspartnern im Lebenslauf.* Sonderforschungsbereich 186. Vol. 43, Bremen: University of Bremen.
Blossfeld, H.-P., & Timm, A. (2003). *Who marries whom? Educational systems as marriage markets in modern societies* (European studies of population, Vol. 12). Dordrecht: Kluwer.
Bok, S. (1979). *Lying. Moral choice in public and private life.* New York: Random House.
Bourdieu, P. (1973). Cultural reproduction and social reproduction. In R. K. Brown (Ed.), *Knowledge, education, and cultural change: Papers in the sociology of education* (pp. 71–112). London: Tavistock.
Bourdieu, P. (1974). *Zur Soziologie der symbolischen Formen.* Frankfurt am Main: Suhrkamp.
Bourdieu, P. (1977). *Outline of a theory of practice. Cambridge studies in social anthropology* (Vol. 16). New York: Cambridge University Press.

References

Bourdieu, P. (1983). Unpublished interview with Maria Iser. In M. Iser (Ed.), *Der Habitus als illegitimer Normalfall gesellschaftlicher Reproduktion. Die soziale Bedeutung von symbolischer Gewalt und strukturgesteuertem Lernen und Handeln in der Theorie von Pierre Bourdieu*, pp. 242–279.
Bourdieu, P. (1984). *Distinction: A social critique of the judgement of taste*. London: Routledge and Kegan Paul.
Bourdieu, P. (1985). The social space and the genesis of groups. *Theory and Society, 14*(6), 723–744.
Bourdieu, P. (1986). The forms of capital. In J. Richardson (Ed.), *Handbook of theory and research for the sociology of education* (pp. 46–58). New York: Greenwood.
Bourdieu, P. (1987). What makes a social class? On the theoretical and practical existence of groups. *Berkeley Journal of Sociology, 32*, 1–17.
Bourdieu, P. (1988). Vive la crise!: For heterodoxy in social science. *Theory and Society, 17*(5), Special Issue on Breaking Boundaries: Social Theory and the Sixties, 773–787.
Bourdieu, P. (1990). *The logic of practice*. Cambridge/Oxford: Polity Press/B. Blackwell.
Bourdieu, P. (1996a). On the family as a realized category. *Theory, Culture & Society, 13*, 19–26.
Bourdieu, P. (1996b). *State nobility. Elite schools in the field of power*. Stanford: Stanford University.
Bourdieu, P. (1996c). *The rules of art: Genesis and structure of the literary field*. Stanford: Stanford University Press.
Bourdieu, P. (1996d). *Physical space, social space and habitus*. Lecture at the University of Oslo.
Bourdieu, P. (1997). Wie eine soziale Klasse entsteht. In P. Bourdieu (Ed.), *Der Tote packt den Lebenden* (Schriften zu Politik & Kultur, Vol. 2, pp. 102–129). Hamburg: VSA.
Bourdieu, P. (1998). *Practical reason: On the theory of action*. Cambridge: Polity Press.
Bourdieu, P. (1999). *The weight of the world. Social suffering in contemporary society*. Stanford: Stanford University Press.
Bourdieu, P. (2000). *Pascalian meditations*. Cambridge: Polity Press.
Bourdieu, P. (2001). *Masculine domination* (1st ed.). Cambridge: Polity Press.
Bourdieu, P. (2002a). *Le bal des célibataires*. Paris: Seuil.
Bourdieu, P. (2002b). On marriage strategies. *Population and Development Review, 28*(3), 549–558.
Bourdieu, P. (2004). *Science of science and reflexivity*. Chicago: University of Chicago Press.
Bourdieu, P. (2005). Principles of an economic anthropology. In N. J. Smelser & R. Swedberg (Eds.), *The handbook of economic sociology* (2nd ed., pp. 75–89). Princeton: Princeton University Press.
Bourdieu, P. (2008). *The Bachelors' ball*. Chicago: University of Chicago Press.
Bourdieu, P. (2010). Sociologists of belief and beliefs of sociologists. *Nordic Journal of Religion and Society, 23*(1), 1–7.
Bourdieu, P. (2014). The future of class and the causality of the probable. In A. Christoforou & M. Lainé (Eds.), *Re-thinking economics: Exploring the work of Pierre Bourdieu* (pp. 233–269). London: Routledge.
Bourdieu, P., & Chartier, R. (2011). *Der Soziologe und der Historiker*. Wien: Turia+Kant.
Bourdieu, P., & Passeron, J. C. P. (1977). *Reproduction in education, society and culture*. Beverly Hills: Sage.
Bourdicu, P., & Wacquant, L. J. D. (1992). *An invitation to reflexive sociology*. Chicago: Polity Press.
Bozon, M. (1991). Women and the age gap between spouses: An accepted domination? *Population. An English Selection, 3*, 113–148.
Bozon, M., & Héran, F. (1989). Finding a spouse: A survey of how french couples meet. *Population. An English Selection, 44*(1), 91–121.
Breiger, R. L. (2000). A tool kit for practice theory. *Poetics, 27*(2–3), 91–115.

Buss, D. M. (1989). Sex differences in human mate preferences: Evolutionary hypotheses tested in 37 cultures. *Behavioral and Brain Sciences, 12*(1), 1–49.
de Paulo, B. M., Kashy, D. A., Kirkendol, S. E., Wyer, M. M., & Epstein, J. A. (1996). Lying in everyday life. *Journal of Personality and Social Psychology, 70*(5), 979–995.
de Singly, F. (1987). Théorie critique de l'homogamie. *L'Année sociologique, 37*, 181–205.
Dupré, J., & O'Neill, J. (1998). Against reductionist explanations of human behaviour. *Aristotelian Society Supplementary, 72*(1), 153–171.
Elster, J. (1986). *An introduction to Karl Marx*. Cambridge: Cambridge University Press.
Freese, J. (2009). Preferences and the explanation of social behavior. In P. Hedström & P. Bearman (Eds.), *Oxford handbook of analytic sociology* (pp. 94–114). Oxford: Oxford University Press.
Greenwald, A. G., & Banaji, M. R. (1995). Implicit social cognition: Attitudes, self-esteem, and stereotypes. *Psychological Review, 102*(1), 4–27.
Hakim, C. (2010). Erotic capital. *European Sociological Review, 26*(5), 499–518.
Hertog, E. (2012). *Hedged bets: Preferences for future marriage partners' earning power in contemporary Japan*. Unpublished working paper.
Huinink, J., & Feldhaus, M. (2009). Family research from the life course perspective. *International Sociology, 24*(3), 299–324.
Kalmijn, M. (1998). Intermarriage and homogamy: Causes, patterns, trends. *Annual Review of Sociology, 24*, 395–421.
Kara, A. (2009). Implications of multiple preferences for a deconstructive critique and a reconstructive revision of economic theory. *Journal of Economic and Social Research, 11*(1), 69–78.
Kenny, D. A., Kashy, D. A., & Cook, W. L. (2006). *Dyadic data analysis*. New York: The Guilford Press.
Klein, T. (1996). Der Altersunterschied zwischen Ehepartnern. Ein neues Analysemodell. *Zeitschrift für Soziologie, 25*(5), 346–370.
Lamaison, P., & Bourdieu, P. (1986). From rules to strategies: An interview with Pierre Bourdieu. *Cultural Anthropology, 1*(1), 110–120.
Lebaron, F. (2001). Toward a new critique of economic discourse. *Theory, Culture & Society, 18*(5), 123–129.
Lindenberg, S. (2013). Social rationality, self-regulation, and well-being: The regulatory significance of needs, goals, and the self. In R. Wittek, T. Snijders, & V. Nee (Eds.), *The handbook of rational choice social research* (pp. 72–112). Palo Alto: Stanford University Press.
Lizardo, O. (2014). Taste and the logic of practice in distinction. *Sociologický ústav, AV ČR*.
Mare, R. D. (1991). Five decades of educational assortative mating. *American Sociological Review, 56*, 15–32.
McPherson, M. (1983). Ecology of affiliation. *American Sociological Review, 48*, 519–532.
Popper, K. R. (2002). *The poverty of historicism*. London: Routledge.
Schmitt, D. P., Jonason, P. K., Byerley, G. J., Flores, S. D., Illbeck, B. E., O'Leary, K. N., & Qudrat, A. (2012). A reexamination of sex differences in sexuality new studies reveal old truths. *Current Directions in Psychological Science, 21*(2), 135–139.
Schmitz, A. (2012). Elective affinities 2.0? A bourdieusian approach to couple formation and the methodology of E-dating. *Social Science Research on the Internet (RESET), 1*(1), 175–202.
Schmitz, A., & Riebling, J. (2013). Gibt es erotisches Kapital? Anmerkungen zu körperbasierter Anziehungskraft und Paarformation bei Hakim und Bourdieu. *Gender- Zeitschrift für Geschlecht, Kultur und Gesellschaft, 2*, 57–80.
Schmitz, A., Witte, D., Gengnagel, V. (2016). Pluralizing field analysis: Toward a relational understanding of the field of power. *Social Science Information/Information sur les sciences sociales* (forthcoming).
Schoen, R., & Wooldredge, J. (1989). Marriage choices in North Carolina and Virginia, 1969–71 and 1979–81. *Journal of Marriage and the Family, 51*(2), 465–481.
Skopek, J. (2011). *Partnerwahl im Internet: Eine quantitative Analyse von Strukturen und Prozessen der Online-Partnersuche*. Wiesbaden: VS Verlag.

South, S. J. (1991). Sociodemographic differentials in mate selection preferences. *Journal of Marriage and the Family, 53*(4), 928–940.

Stigler, G. J., & Becker, G. S. (1977). De Gustibus non est Disputandum. *The American Economic Review, 67*(2), 76–90.

Streib, J. (2015). Explanations of how love crosses class lines: Cultural complements and the case of cross-class marriages. *Sociological Forum, 30*(1), 18–39.

Swedberg, R. (2011). The economic sociologies of Pierre Bourdieu. *Cultural Sociology, 5*(1), 67–82.

Thibaut, J. W., & Kelley, H. H. (1959). *The social psychology of groups*. New York: Wiley.

Wacquant, L. (2016). A concise genealogy and anatomy of habitus. *The Sociological Review, 64*(1), 64–72.

Weber, M. (1947). *The theory of social and economic organization*. New York: Simon and Schuster.

Weber, M., & Roth, G. (1978). *Economy and society: An outline of interpretive sociology*. New York: University of California Press.

Willis, J., & Todorov, A. (2006). First impressions: Making up your mind after a 100-Ms exposure to a face. *Psychological Science, 17*(7), 592–598.

Winter, L., & Kron, T. (2009). Fuzzy thinking in sociology. In R. Seising (Ed.), *Views on fuzzy sets and systems from different perspectives: Philosophy and logic, criticisms and applications* (pp. 301–320). Berlin: Springer.

Witte, D. (2014). *Auf den Spuren der Klassiker. Pierre Bourdieus Feldtheorie und die Gründerväter der Soziologie*. Konstanz: UVK.

Chapter 6
Methodological Implications

In the first section of this chapter, Bourdieu's relational methodology will be outlined. It will be shown that the principle of relation is constitutive for this research program, and manifests itself in an emphatically empirical constructivism. In a second step, the data which will be used for empirical analyses is discussed. The data are derived principally from a single database, comprising (1), data derived from a questionnaire of the users of a major German dating website (2), user profile data from the website's users, and (3), observed data, especially regarding real-time interactions, from the same site. Further information was gathered from (4) qualitative interviews. This chapter will describe the methodological principles underlying the data of types (1)-(3), representing the core data basis for the various analyses, and their resulting strengths and weaknesses. Furthermore, the processes by which the data were collected and integrated at database level, and the potential for complementary and supplementary data integration, will be discussed. The chapter will end with an overview of the methods used in the empirical analyses. The statistical analyses applied in this work follow the quantitative traditions of methodological individualism (generalized linear and non-linear mixture modeling), methodological relationism (geometric data analysis and network analysis), and propose an integration of both (a new model of dyadic classification).

The Relational Methodology of Pierre Bourdieu

The principle of relation pervades Bourdieu's entire scientific work: his theoretical concepts, his research practice, his fieldwork, and his approach to data analysis. The central element of this research program is the construction analysis of 'fields of relations', i.e. of societal spaces which give categories (such as practices, perceptions, forms of capital, agents, etc.) their particular meaning. The methodological[1] dimension of this sociological paradigm can be understood as "constructivistic structuralism" (Bourdieu 1989: 14), that is, a research practice that sees constructing a research object as the first task of its scientific method. Bourdieu warns against the "scholastic fallacy" (cp. Bourdieu 1998: 199), which conflates the scientists' perspective with the logic of practice of the agents being examined. Taking the economist Gary Becker as an example, whose *Treatise on the Family* (Becker 1993) is highly relevant for traditional mate choice research, Bourdieu criticizes the practice of inference from seemingly objective characteristics. In his view, the way Becker reaches his conclusions is a "merely a thinly disguised projection of the researcher's 'lived experience'" (Bourdieu 1984: 100).

The elementary task of empirical work following habitus/field theory and the theory of social spaces is to construct a common space of traits and agents. This operation facilitates the localization of all entities according to central oppositional structures – the capital forms. Even Bourdieu's earliest field work in Algeria was characterized by an attempt to relationally collect and code of data of different types, in order to identify and represent the common structure of oppositions and similarities (cp. Blasius and Schmitz 2013). Bourdieu applied the logic of relation and the derivable relational concepts as (implicit) hypotheses for controlled observation and questioning. The concept of relation, at first without specific meaning, is thus concretized in the course of empirical application. In doing so, the collection of objective, differential power resources and subjective perceptions are taken into account as necessary conditions for the construction of relational spaces. For this purpose, the phenomenological perspectives of the actors involved are considered by way of surveying their dispositions and by objectifying these subjectivities through reciprocal reference within a common social space.

The construction of fields and spaces is not conducted spontaneously, such as simply claiming the existence of a certain field 'X'; instead, they are only constructible by means of statistics (Bourdieu and Wacquant 1992). For the construction of social space, everyday action routines can be surveyed, which for example manifest in the form of lifestyle practices (Rouanet et al. 2000). The relational system these various stylizations of the agents' everyday lives constitute assigns the meanings and values of the particular symbolic goods. However, 'objective' or material information, as well as discursive information, must also be taken into account and combined in order to construct a research object. In doing so, methodological relationism conceptualizes each form of capital – and each habitus in relation to other forms of capital and habitus – empirically, so as to describe society and its constituent parts. Thus, in contrast to other methodological approaches, the forms of capital and

---

[1] In doing so, the two terms 'methodology' and 'method' are used separately, with the former term referring to the overarching principles that can be derived from a particular theory, and the latter to the concrete techniques of data analysis. The widespread practice of equating 'methodology' and 'method' corresponds to the use of 'methodology' in the singular, and ultimately to the orthodoxy of a particular theory. Only if one believes in the plausibility of a mono-cultural theoretical landscape does the question of various methodologies not arise. The fact is that different methodologies will suggest using different methods.

habitus and their interrelations are not taken as given, with a universal claim to validity independent of spatial and temporal context. These concepts are defined and constructed in a relational and historical manner. Bourdieu elaborates, for example, on the familiar structural principles of economic, cultural, and social capital, describing the French society on the basis of extensive empirical data. However, it does not follow that every society is subject to these hierarchical principles. Bourdieu speculates that, in the case of socialist East Germany, for instance, political capital will have been the central structural principle, requiring careful sociological investigation (see Bourdieu 1991). The same applies to societal areas and contexts of encounter such as dating websites. All spheres of action and interaction must also be seen as matters of relational construction, rather than as positivistic facts with predefined characteristics and intrinsic values. Subsequently, we will give an overview of the data and methods used in this work and, in doing so, we will use the principle of relationality as an analytical guideline.

Methodological Dimensions of Online Dating

The data available for traditional partner market research is highly restricted as, usually, random sample surveys or aggregate statistics regarding marriage rates are the basis for empirical analyses (Schmitz 2009). The research setting 'online dating' comprises the earliest moments of romantic encounter. Thus, when compared to surveys or official statistics which observe the outcomes of mating processes, online dating can be located at the other end of the observational spectrum. The prevalence of the observability of a mass of people explicitly looking for a partner, people who are encountering one another for the first time, constitutes a promising methodological basis for research on reciprocal classification processes of mating. Log file data arising on a dating platform are (unlike survey data) completive, not subject to the logic of random samples in the way survey research is, non-reactive (or unobtrusive), and more reliable. Thus, the research context of online dating represents an opportunity to reveal mating dispositions and to observe practices of competition for romantic exchange chances *in situ*. Furthermore, subjective meanings inherent to usage practices on an actual partner market can be included by surveying standardized (stated mating preferences) and unstandardized information (Zillmann 2016). The data on which this work is based are derived from a single database, comprising (1), data derived from a questionnaire of the users of a major German dating website (2), user profile data from the website's users, and (3), observed data, especially regarding real-time interactions, from the same site. Further information was gathered from (4) qualitative interviews.[2]

---

[2] A comprehensive sample description of the initial survey is given by Zillmann (2016).

Surveying the Users' Perspectives: The Online Questionnaire

The *initial questionnaire* was the first questionnaire that users of the dating website received when registering at the website. The questionnaire comprises questions regarding socio-demographics, hobbies, and lifestyle practices as well as variables on the users' preferences, their strategies and self-perceived chances, their reasons for using this dating site, and the perception of the online dating market in comparison to offline partner markets. The questionnaire was sent both to newly registered users – that is, those users who registered after the start of the survey – and to those users who were already members at the start of the survey.

The design and all technical details of the process of data collection were reviewed in May and June 2009, first in a test environment and then by test users on the live system of the website itself (cp. Skopek 2011; Zillmann 2016; Schmitz 2009). The surveys were brought to an end on April 15th 2010 after a relaunch of the company's website. All registered and active users of the online dating site were invited to participate via e-mail between June 2009 and April 2010. A total of 3535 users took part in the survey, corresponding to a response rate of about 10%.

The Methodological Restrictions of Questionnaire Data

As stated above, a large number of research studies on mating emphasize subjective preferences, and hence data collected via standardized questionnaires. In the specific context of online research, this affords researchers many advantages. Above all, variables can be surveyed and recorded in a flexible and effective way. However, there are also limitations to the online survey data collected on a particular platform, which are threefold (cp. Schmitz 2009).

Firstly, there are the classical restrictions of survey data for mate research, independent from the survey mode. Questionnaire data depicts subjective estimations filtered by perception, not practices, thereby introducing a systematic bias in favor of respondents' conscious (strategic) and unconscious deviations from their 'true behavior'. In the context of mate preference research, unconscious preferences and strategic questionnaire responses become a serious problem for conclusive inference, as we can expect these phenomena to appear frequently and systematically. The very concept of preference rests essentially on the assumption of conscious perception and decision. Thus, applied to human mating practices – which are not necessarily completely conscious – one might fail to assess the genuine importance of specific traits.

Secondly, preferences measured as statements do not necessarily conform to future practices. Stated preferences are biased by intentional and unintentional deviations from 'true' values, and by the actors' cognitive incapacity to reflect on the structural parameters of their agency. The problem is that the actors might be functionally unable to evaluate their orders of preference, i.e. the relevance of specific cues for contact initiation and contact maintenance. Research on mate choice applying the stated preference perspective can never – despite a great deal of time and effort – measure and predict 'true' preferences.

Survey data feature hypothetical decision elements, but do not contain the factual actor's choice set. This, however, is a necessary requirement for a theoretically adequate application of preference-based research. If the respondents are asked to choose, hypothetically, between different mating cues, the factual individual acts and resulting aggregated patterns can hardly be predicted by this information.

With regard to mating practices, survey data is unable to focus on processes of interaction in their origins and sequential development, and the data does usually not contain information about potential and rejected potential mates. Thus, based on results of observed (inter)actions, it is hardly possible to draw 'causal' conclusions, such as interpreting an existing couple as the realization of past mate preferences.

Consequently, the question emerges regarding the extent to which surveys are adequate methodical instruments for acquiring data about unintended consequences of human agency, for example in the case of a specific (partner) market. Assortative mating processes – which describe the macro-phenomenon of actors mating with each other hierarchically according to their market value or their resources, for example – can hardly be modeled by using subjective statements of preferences.

Thirdly, there are the general problems affecting online surveys (see for example Couper and Coutts 2006: 217; Welker and Wenzel 2007). Online surveys cannot truly be thought of as a function of a random sampling process, which is a precondition for statistical inference. In the given case, the problem is at least twofold: (1) for this platform, a random self-assignment to the questionnaire is unlikely. Zillmann et al. (2013) show that processes of survey participation on the particular platform which is analyzed throughout this work are essentially a function of a user's perceived mate value. Users with a low mate value see the survey on online dating as an opportunity to learn something about the partner market, about the 'rules of the game', and about themselves. People who, in contrast, are confident that they will find a partner do not see a web questionnaire as an object of particular relevance. This leads to a non-random sub-population of the dating platform in which, in particular, overweight women and men with low educational status are represented disproportionately. Quite apart from the purely socio-demographically marginal distribution of such a sample, the substantive constructs – such as mating preferences, the structure of self-perceived potential, normative attitudes, etc. – are also affected by non-random participation. The impact of market position on users' willingness to participate in the online survey has been addressed in several works (Schmitz 2009; Zillmann et al. 2013).

Another problem is simultaneously the most and the least severe (at least from the perspective of the logics of inference). Any statistical insights refer only to the population of the platform under investigation, and not to (a) all dating platforms (b) the internet in general or (c) all offline mating markets (Schmitz 2009). This has practical implications, such as the legitimacy of the 'significance ritual' of statistical models being called into question. This also leads to a theoretical problem: what can we infer for any social context outside the particular platform? Consequently, all conclusions should be accorded the status of "substantiated hypotheses" (ibid.). Nevertheless, from a more abstract point of view, the analysis of a single specific context has traditionally been a rewarding approach for sociology.

Such studies were able to make remarkable sociological insights by not restricting themselves to questionnaires as the apparent 'gold standard' of empirical research, but by combining and integrating the most diverse techniques. The scientific constraints which accompany the analysis of one particular, necessarily limited, social context can only be compensated for when the context is reconstructed without methodological bias. This means that subjective information (such as that surveyed via standardized and unstandardized questions) can represent only one element of a comprehensive research approach. A mating market, for example, is defined by objective chance structures, and the field perspective emphasizes the social dimensionality of these chance structures. The objectification, in the broadest sense, of a context is a necessary prerequisite for the analysis of all social fields.

Observing the Users' Practices: Web-Generated Process Data

Due to technical necessities, Bourdieu essentially drew on questionnaire data for the construction of social space. However, Bourdieu actually criticizes the "undisputed pre-eminence" of the "royal technique" of the questionnaire in the practice of empirical research, and postulates that "epistemological primacy should […] be given to methodical and systematic observation" (Bourdieu and Passeron 1991: 44). This methodological postulate motivates our utilization of observational data from a dating platform. The way in which online dating works represents great potential for analyzing the data structure itself, as discussed above. Using the records of incoming and outgoing events, a user's contact network can be quantitatively assessed, as can each user's potential for success, and ultimately how profile characteristics relate to this potential. Furthermore, profile characteristics can be interpreted as resources signalized on the partner market. The record of dyadic interaction patterns between users enables an interpretation of the relationship of these resources in the context of mating theories. The objectivity of the market, which is often hard to grasp for a traditionally Bourdieusian, questionnaire-based sociology, can thus be assessed by reconstructing the user's objective chance structure and the practices of (reciprocal) classification involved.

Whereas any method involving surveys or questionnaires can directly influence an interviewee's answers, the automatic registration of electronic observation data can be characterized as non-reactive or unobtrusive. This means that the effects of observation and surveyance (e.g. social desirability, the guinea pig effect, interviewer influence, etc.) distort the data less severely. Log file data do not have the problem of unit or item nonresponse. The high level of automation in the data collection process leads to greater *data reliability*, when compared to survey data. The costs of data collection are also relatively low, as great amounts of data can be collected with minimal investment in personnel and time. Furthermore, log file data are, unlike survey data, completive, and – because the data include every actor in this specific context of digital interaction – not subject to the logic of random samples in the way survey research is. Any missing data can be put down to insufficiently precise definition of the events to be recorded, or of the method by which the data are stored. A data population can be developed efficiently, without the need to rely on complicated and error-prone processes of transcription. Despite all this, log file data must still undergo thorough checks regarding quality and plausibility.

The established sociological practice is to derive the variables under analysis from theoretical constructs. When using log file data, this is only possible if the intended objects of analysis were defined and programmed before their collection. However, process-generated data from a privately-funded internet platform are usually derived from non-operationalized constructs, and therefore will not automatically correspond to fields of theoretical interest (see e.g. Janetzko 2008).

In contrast to stated preferences, as outlined above, this data is close to the principle of Samuelson's (1947) theory of "revealed preferences". This approach – much like the acquisition of web-generated process data – aims to make conclusions regarding preferences based on the observation of selection acts (Schmitz 2009). Take the aforementioned example of revealed preference in online mate choice. We cannot directly derive true mating preferences from the observation of contacts online, as specific strategic mechanisms may lead some users to show adaptive behavior. Based solely on objective events, it is simply impossible to reconstruct any subjectively intended meaning in a way that might be of interest to sociologists – the events can be, at best, interpreted behavioristically. This means that, in certain contexts, the validity of a recorded construct may suffer in comparison to that of a survey. Although it is the case that log files encompass all actors and actions (or at least those that were defined as relevant beforehand), and therefore differ fundamentally from principally sample-reliant surveys, the problem of representativity cannot be disregarded. Valid questions can also be asked regarding exactly *which* analytical entity the completely recorded observation data are supposed to represent.

Web-Generated Process Data in the Present Study

The database extractions were made available to us by the dating service provider – henceforth 'the provider' – at regular intervals, approximately every 6 months.[3] The data were anonymized as SQL files, a procedure overseen by the data protection agent of the provider. In order to convert the data into a format readable by standard statistical software, the files first had to be uploaded incompletely to a MySQL database, and then exported in STATA and SPSS as CSV files for further analysis. In consultation with the provider's technical experts, code books for the process data were also created. As part of this project, a database was also created with process data comprising profile and interaction data for the years 2004 through 2010 (final database dump 14.4.2010). Table 6.1 gives an ideal-typical overview of the dyadic nature of the recorded data. The observational data recorded in online dating

---

[3] A comprehensive overview of the process data is given in Schmitz 2009.

Table 6.1 Data structure of HTTP status messages

ID S	ID R	Dyad no.	Contact no.	Mail	Time	Sex S	Sex R	Age S	Age R	Edu S	Edu R
17,172	9249	1430	1	0	01.07.2012.13:15.26	M	F	45	42	Abitur	Abitur
9249	17,172	1430	2	0	01.07.2012.18:42.19	F	M	42	45	Abitur	Abitur
17,172	9249	1430	3	0	02.07.2012.08:33.01	M	F	45	42	Abitur	Abitur
...											
17,172	9249	1430	15	1	02.07.2012.22:17.49	M	F	45	42	Abitur	Abitur

Reading example: Sender 17,172 (male of 45 years) contacts receiver 9249 (female of 42 years) at 01.07.2012.13:15.26. The constitute the dyad number 1430, whose last observed event is message number 15 at 02.07.2012.22:17.49

contain 'revealed' partner preferences, by logging contacts, and dyadic development, by logging interactions. Typically, users explore the profile database of the site, viewing other users' profiles and, upon finding another user appealing, will try to get in contact using a messaging function common to most dating sites. This kind of relational data, combined with the user profiles, allows for a detailed temporal reconstruction of the process of contact formation and interaction between potential mates on an observational level. For instance, it is possible to retrace which other user profiles a given user looked at, and which profiles he or she subsequently chose to contact via email. Table 6.1 also shows how the act of a sender (IDS) contacting a respondent (IDR) on a specific date (Time) is stored. After a certain amount of time had elapsed, the respondent sent a message as a reaction to the sender's initial contact.

Profile Data

In co-operation with the dating service provider, we were able to add further information on the website's users to the standard profile information – as outlined in Chapter 7 – in particular adjusting socio-demographic profile attributes to demographical standards. We were, for example, able to fully realize the response categories for familial status and educational level. We also added specifications of further education to the basic education rubric. The provider also followed our suggestion to transform many open questions, such as those regarding date of birth or number of children, into closed questions. This reduced the vulnerability of the profile information to mistakes and invalid answers considerably. Another suggestion of ours was also implemented, namely that the various response fields on the profile information page were pre-set to 'Please select one option', and the category 'Not specified' was made available as a separate option. This made it possible to differentiate between deliberate withholding of information and inadvertent omission of specific questions. We were also able to integrate comprehensive item sequences regarding users' lifestyles and social capital into this optimized profile system.

Relational Data Integration

The data collected was stored in a relational database consisting of data tables comprising relations (a) between users, (b) between the *attributes* of the users and (c) between the various data sources. In Schmitz (2009), data integration was examined in a complementary context, that is to say, regarding the mutual complementation of data from multiple informational sources, in order to compensate for blind spots inherent to the particular data types. A constitutive element of Bourdieu's relational methodology is the integration of different kinds of data and information, so that potential blind spots or weaknesses can be eradicated. The different data types collected on the digital partner market enable a more comprehensive reconstruction of the habitual practices of mate selection than has until now been possible. A major advantage of this data is that we can combine both subjective perceptions (for example, of actors' own structures of opportunity) and objective conditions (e.g. objective market value) (see Chapter 3). Thus, it is possible to observe practices of reciprocal classification on dating sites for all observed characteristics such as cultural goods and lifestyles, age, occupation, etc.

Qualitative Interviews

In research on online dating, a great number of scientists apply either quantitative or qualitative methods. As part of the relational methodology, the phenomenological perspective of agents is an important aspect of practice, for the social space in question, and for the processes taking place in it. Thus, the distinction between 'quantitative' and 'qualitative' is abandoned in favor of a relational or 'triangulating' integration. For that reason, several semi-structured, guideline-based interviews were conducted comprising several guiding questions. The interviews were conducted over various instant messengers – such as Chat City, ICQ, freenet-Community, MSN, or Skype. Also, the chat system of the dating platform analyzed here was utilized for the recruitment of respondents. The interviews lasted between 45 min and 2 h. The names of all respondents were changed for privacy reasons. Some selected findings of these interviews are mobilized in this book in order to highlight several arguments of this work (cp. Chapter 3).

Relational Methods

Usually, the quantitative social science approach assesses mating preferences and mating choices in the tradition of methodological individualism, and is augmented by ideas from exchange theory *sensu* Blau (cp. Chapter 3). In their recent standard *Handbook of Marriage and the Family*, Acock and Washburn (2013: 65 ff.) give an overview of methods ranging from simple regression to regression models with different outcome scales, to multilevel and survival models. In doing so, they tacitly persuade the reader to accept equating the world of quantitative methods with the narrow family of regression models. This also applies to the case of online research, where traditional methods are transmitted without reflecting upon their underlying methodological implications (Lewis 2015: 20). In this narrow notion of 'structure', the medium is seen as an innovative way of applying traditional methods of questioning. As a consequence, the object's specific attributes and ultimately the nature of the data are not sufficiently considered. Observational data on contact practices online is mostly interpreted with regard to a narrow conception of the underlying subjective meaning of observed contact acts of the average user.

The logic of techniques known from offline research, and their use in the practice of empirical mate selection research, corresponds to the philosophy of epistemology underlying them. In the simplest cases, logistical regressions are able to model, for example, the preference-guided behavior of an average individual, with ordinal regressions modeling the preference order. Although helpful in many specific research situations (and indeed used in some analyses in this book), the classically-applied regression model is often more appropriate to the world view of the individualistic paradigm than to social reality. Bourdieu and Passeron (1991: 46) are critical in this regard, postulating

> that one can successively isolate the action of the different variables from the complete system of relations within which they act, in order to identify the intrinsic efficacy of each of them, this technique [i.e. regression] makes it impossible to identify the efficacy that a factor may derive from its insertion in a structure and even the specifically structural efficacy of the system of factors.

A particular problem of such "causal" approaches for "analyzing interdependent processes" is that the researcher must focus "on one of the interdependent processes" and consider it "the dependent one" (Blossfeld and Mills 2001). In models of this kind, the particular relations

> between a dependent variable (political opinion) and so-called independent variables such as sex, age and religion, tend to dissimulate the complete system of relations that make up the true principle of the force and form specific to the effects recorded in such and such particular correlation (Bourdieu quoted in Rouanet et al. 2000: 7).

Another core difference between relational methodology and individualist methodology is that the former does not assume theoretical and statistical independence of the analyzed entities. Even the modern 'causal' approaches (most famously nowadays perhaps fixed and random-effects regressions) assume the independence of entities, reducing causality to 'averaged internal mechanisms' of artificially separated actors.

> Although statistical methods in sociology have grown increasingly sophisticated, they continue to treat individuals as independent units. The very assumption of statistical independence, which makes these methods so appropriate for […] categorical analysis, detaches individuals from social structures and forces analysts to treat them as parts of a disconnected mass (Wellmann 1988: 38).

As a consequence, individualistic methods fail to reveal causality between the agents, that is, *relational causality*. This also applies to modern mate choice research. Quantitative research perceives "online dating" as providing us "with a near-ideal market environment that allows us to observe the individual's choice sets and their actual mate choices" (Hitsch et al. 2010: 3). In fact, the new methodologies of online dating research are essentially understood as a means to control for structural distortion by analytically differentiating between "opportunity structure and [...] preference among daters at the interaction level" (Lin and Lundquist 2013: 188). Two aspects of relational methodology which are of utmost relevance for the structural analysis of (digital) dating platforms shall be addressed: the relational structure of the social space and the relational structure of interactions.

The Geometric Construction of Space

The preceding reflections on the status of relationalism in Bourdieu's research program indicate that objects and classes are not *a priori* postulated at the beginning of a research project, but need to be (re-)constructed as a relational fields or spaces. For him, "statistical analysis [...] is the only means of manifesting the structure of the social space" (Bourdieu 1985: 725). Consequently, Bourdieu neither defined *a priori* the structural axes of the space or the forms of capital – for example for the purpose of using them as 'independent' variables in regression models – nor did he postulate the existence of fields or space in purely speculative terms. Within the methodology of social space and field theory the construction is

> clearly a geometric one: the distance between individuals is defined on the basis of their properties (positions or views), whereby the real social and symbolic distances between them become formalized, and the different aspects of the variations between individuals can be examined within a Euclidean space (Lebaron 2012: 129, o.t.).

As a consequence of relational methodology, Bourdieu favored geometric data analysis, a family of techniques which transfers empirical data into a relational and spatial representation. He predominantly applied correspondence analysis, which is a multivariate statistical technique for the analysis of categorical data and its transformation into latent dimensions, which can be visualized in the form of spaces. This geometric method of data analysis was developed by the French statistician Jean-Paul Benzécri and his colleagues (1973). It is a part of the French approach referred to as "analyse des données" or "tabular analysis" (cp. Lebart et al. 1984; Le Roux and Rouanet 2004; Lebaron 2015). In the last decades, correspondence analysis has developed from a technique primarily utilized in the French academic field to a popular approach used in many national contexts and scientific disciplines (Beh and Lombardo 2012: 137), ranging from natural sciences to social sciences and communication studies. In the course of this development, several contributions have been made which discuss the formal foundations of correspondence analysis (e.g. Lebart et al. 1984; Greenacre 1984; Blasius and Greenacre 1994; Le Roux and

Rouanet 2004). In this chapter, we will give an overview of the basic ideas of correspondence analysis from the perspective of applied data analysis in the social sciences.

The classical variants of correspondence analysis are simple correspondence analysis (CA) and multiple correspondence analysis (MCA). CA is particularly suitable for the bivariate case, that is, when two cross-tabulated variables constitute a contingency table, but also for stacked tables. MCA is appropriate for multivariate data, where the associations between more than two variables are to be analyzed. Like principal component analysis, correspondence analysis constructs latent dimensions, which underlie the statistical associations between the categories of the analyzed manifest variables. The goal of correspondence analysis is to reduce the complexity of the observed data into a lower-dimensional space of latent variables, thus providing a reference system for the comparison of all variable categories. In contrast to comparable multivariate techniques, correspondence analysis makes few a priori assumptions about the data structure. Whereas in principal component analysis the base for the construction of latent factors is the correlation structure between variables, in correspondence analysis the associations between a data table's rows and columns are transformed into latent dimensions. In the case of CA, the Euclidean distances between row and column categories are not defined; multiple correspondence analysis allows researchers to interpret the emerging dimensions as a common Euclidean space. Thus, all categories of all variables or 'modalities' can be interpreted in such a way that similar categories are close to each other and dissimilar categories are distant to each other. Likewise, the units carrying the information (e.g. respondents of a survey) can also be located within the same latent space: units with similar 'profiles' are close to each other and units with dissimilar profiles are distant to each other. With the MCA solution, the space of categories and the space of individuals (units) can be interpreted as a common space. In consequence, MCA cannot only be understood as a principal component analysis for categorical data due to the identification of latent dimensions, but also as being similar to cluster analysis, as it assigns average positions to categories and units in a low-dimensional space. When interpreting the spatial solution, correspondences – i.e. the common occurrence of material conditions and subjective categories in contingency tables – play a central role.

Such spatial solutions can be used for the identification of classes of actors in the social space, which exhibit specific relations of material and subjective characteristics. In this way, MCA allows us to interpret manifest characteristics against the background of the latent concept of habitus. Overall, this particular technique of geometric data analysis ensures "a strong fit between social ontology, methodology, and theory" (Wacquant 2013: 6) and when,

> "Having taken into account the full range of efficient agents" […] and "properties" […] one can use correspondence analysis to reveal the "structure of positions", and thus "the structure of the distribution specific interests and powers" which underlie, and explain "the strategies of agents" (Bourdieu 2000: 102).

This method is also subject to ongoing further development. In Bourdieu's *Distinction*, the construction of the habitus was undertaken heuristically and manually, and in his final works, he attempted, via the integration of cluster and correspondence analyses, to depict these densities within the social space (see Bourdieu 1999). However, due to the conceptual fuzziness of the term habitus, the analysis of hard clustering procedures is inadequate. For this reason, finite mixture models will be applied within this work in order to model probability densities in space. This enables the objectification of several mechanisms which have been discussed by Bourdieu in merely theoretical terms. First, latent classes of mating dispositions will be derived corresponding to Bourdieu's concept of habitus as fuzzy probabilities within the social space. In this way, potential partner dispositions are modeled as bundles of preferences, and thus applied to the social space. Second, latent regression classes will be used to objectify relations between variables within habitus, using the example of differential habitus-specificity of (ir-)rationality in consideration of one's own mating chances and deceptive practice. Thirdly, a dyadic class model will be applied in order to operationalize reciprocal classification processes. As the latter method is new development of ours, it shall be discussed in detail.

A Finite-Mixture Model of Dyadic-Classification

Due to their underlying individualist epistemology, most quantitative empirical analyses of mating offline and online have ignored the expressly mutual character of couple formation as a sequence of reciprocal selections (Willoughby and Caroll 2010; Schmitz 2012). For example, as Schulz (2010: 506, o.t.) sees structure as the "structurally predetermined contact opportunities of the actors" on an online dating platform, it is assumed that opportunities "can be controlled for any point in time". In doing so, individualistic models tends to ignore the fact that two structured agents are socially and thus statistically dependent (or rather non-independent) without living together, or knowing each other, or indeed affecting each other directly in any way. The mechanism involved can be referred to as 'common fate' (cp. Kenny et al. 2006), that is, the historical and social conditions prior to the situation of encounter already structure the agents in such a way that their interaction will show a systematic statistical relation.

Often, first contacts in online dating are analyzed using (logistic) regression models, which implies a violation of model assumptions given non-independence. The dyadic nature of mating is reduced then to a unified entity, in order to maintain the individualistic conceptualization and conventional empirical modeling – but at the price of the irrevocable loss of the insights of exchange theory. This approach represents a reciprocal model in name only, in that the specifically reciprocal character of the interactions is obscured by (a) the uni-directionality of the regression, (b) the generalization of a supposedly average individual, and (c) the reduction of the process character to a choice act.

In the context of online dating, dyadic interactions are either ignored, or at best only examined in greatly simplified form, be it by means of random-intercept models or 'generalized estimating equation' models (e.g. Lin and Lundquist). For the individualistic paradigm, the so-called multilevel models, or random effects, may be perceived preferred methods, in order to model the nested data structure of, say, multiple senders within receivers, or vice versa. Interaction here becomes a bilateral act and yet is analyzed by uni-directional regression models. Lin and Lundquist, for example, claim that they "extend previous studies using online dating data by examining both the initiating and reciprocating behaviors" (2013: 207). However, this does not adequately treat the problem of reciprocally nested data. The problem of dyadic non-independence cannot be managed with the methodical panacea of our times – simple random-effects or 'multilevel' models – as the nesting is not unique: sender A can be nested in receiver B, B can be nested in A and both can be nested in a common dyad. Furthermore, it is difficult to model several variables at the same time. Finally, different logics of choice and interactions can hardly be elaborated on the basis of this technique. Traditional applications of individualistic regression models are unsuitable both for the data structure itself and for theoretical reasons. As can be derived by the arguments given in the theory section, it is unsatisfactory to model dyadic interactions empirically as a sequence of uni-directional regression models.

Here, log-linear models might be seen as a first step towards a promising quantifying approach: 'It takes two to marry', and for that reason most authors have used log-linear or harmonic mean models. Such models correctly use marriages as the unit of analysis, rather than individuals, but make it difficult to include multiple covariates in the model. From a methodological perspective, "such models are preferable, but if the prime concern is to test theories, their advantage is not so obvious" (Kalmijn 1998: 419). Thus, log-linear analysis does, theoretically, provide the potential to model data based on interaction processes. However, the number of variables, and the presence of low cell frequencies, poses a difficulty for computational and practical methods.

Apart from the restrictions of classical statistical methods, the more severe problem is the underlying theoretical foundation which conceals the role of 'structure' in empirical analyses. In contrast to individualistic approaches, the social space paradigm does not assume isolated decisions and actions of isolated actors, but emphasizes the relational mechanisms underlying every interaction of agents. The social space can thus be seen as meta-mechanism for the common fate of two interacting parties. The proposed elaboration of the habitus-field perspective on mating processes treats agents as reciprocally classifying each other and their characteristics. Methodologically speaking, agents represent reciprocally classifying entities that must themselves be classified by the scientific observer. Like social classes, emerging dyadic configurations can be assessed by analyzing the "structure of relations between all the pertinent properties" (Bourdieu 1984: 106). This view avoids *a priori* definitions of which particular resource is generally relevant for the development of couples, and instead motivates empirical analyses of which trait-relations may underlie reciprocal classification processes.

These considerations lead to the methodological postulate of observing interactions instead of individual practices. The task is not to model average agents with unidirectional contacting (as a regression model would suggest), but to find out which typical agent configurations emerge and survive. This dependence structure of dyad members cannot only be regarded as a statistical problem, but also as a source of substantial variation that needs to be modeled and interpreted. Analyzing the process of assortative mating thus means, in practice, observing and reconstructing dyadic agent configurations, and hence the configurations of their characteristics.

The most explicit analysis implementing dyadic data can be found in the work of Kenny et al. (2006), who analyzes dyads from a socio-psychological point of view. He describes dyadic data as a specific empirical structure of "non-independence" between two actors. The idea here is that (potential) partners are not independent of each other, neither statistically nor theoretically. He names several possible mechanisms that generate this statistical association within two partners: the aforementioned common fate, reciprocal affection, and compositional effects that affect encounters. His works essentially treat the socio-psychological question of reciprocal affection or common fate, and rather neglect the causal influence of 'pre-dyadic' mechanisms, which may be subsumed under 'assortative meeting'. Kenny et al. (2006: 291) postulate that "different sources of non-independence require different analysis strategies". The core idea of dyadic data analysis is to utilize the actor-partner 'non-independence', instead of ignoring it. The proposed models are specific multilevel models and specific structural equation models. These models "incorporating dyad-level latent variables decompose the associations among the observed variables into dyad-level relations" (Woody and Sadler 2005: 152).

There are two ways of interpreting these dyad-level latent variables: the common fate conceptualization, as already mentioned above, and the dyadic entity or dyadic personality conceptualization. Whereas the common fate conceptualization utilizes a dyad-level latent variable to represent external forces affecting both dyad members, the dyadic personality conceptualization interprets the dyad-level latent variable as a dyadic entity. The dyad has a recursive effect on each actor, for example, emerging norms may re-impact on the actors themselves.

Woody and Sadler formulate a criticism of Kenny's conception of common fate, and Gonzalez and Griffin's (1995) conception of dyadic personality, which reduce dyad-level variance of similarity between dyad members. In the context of interpersonal theory, they suggest including dyad-level variables that are based on dissimilarity as well. From a theoretical point of view, this recommendation can, consequently, be fulfilled in such a way that dyad-level variance should be modeled according to (a) similarity, (b) dissimilarity, (c) the absence of both, and (d) any combination of a-c. The problem is that, even now, no models of this kind exist in the social sciences, although they are relatively easy to derive.

From a statistical point of view, it is evident that both the random effect models and the structural equation models are only specific elements of a generalized linear latent and mixed model (cp. Skrondal and Rabe-Hesketh 2004). This means that an approach reducing dyadic associations to a latent metric variable can be replaced by the modeling of latent categorical variables or latent classes (Magidson and Vermunt 2004). Just as in finite mixture modeling with individual data, a latent categorical factor is measured by manifest variables, but the same information is used twice. This 'general latent variable-model' with K categorical latent variables and 2*J manifest 'mixed-mode' variables is a probabilistic classification of dyadic interactions. The joint density of the observed indicators, f(y), represents a mixture of class-specific densities with class-specific mean vectors and co-variance matrices. The C-unobserved categorical variables (Classes) can be identified by maximum likelihood estimation and information criteria such as the Aikake information criterion (AIC).

Whereas in traditional dyadic models the latent variable is specified as (a) parametric with the (b) assumption of a normal distribution, using (c) continuous manifest variables in a (d) confirmatory approach, the dyadic latent class model is characterized by (i) a non-parametric latent variable, (ii) without an assumption of (normal) distribution, (iii) using different scales of manifest variables in a (iii) confirmatory or explanatory way. The proposed finite mixture classification approach is similar to the logic of the modified common fate model of Griffin and Gonzalez (1995; see also Kenny et al. 2006). The conceptual difference is that the latent dyadic variable is conceived of less as the causal precursor to the manifest indicators, but rather as a latent representation of the dyadic constellations. This perspective takes into account the fact that couples often do not have the possibility to influence each other, but are similar or dissimilar due to selection effects, as in assortative mating. The dyadic co-variance therefore has a 'pre-dyadic origin' and requires a model without causal effects between manifest variables based on the 'compositional-effect assumption'. The difference is that we do not necessarily interpret dyadic classes as active entities. Consequently, the statistical association between partners due to composition through selective encounter may be referred to as 'Latent Classes as Dyadic Compositions'. The assignment of entity status is dependent on a theoretical and empirical justification, on a case-to-case basis, as is usual within the framework of generalized statistics. This interpretation of a latent variable as a representation rather than a cause is very much in line with Rabe-Hesketh's discussion of the ontological status of a latent variable (Skrondal and Rabe-Hesketh 2004: 2ff.). The striking advantage of the fact that the common dyadic models and the proposed dyadic latent class model are both part of the same statistical family is that they can be tested against each other. Consequently, one can decide on an empirical basis whether the idea of a generalized type of dyadic relations is more appropriate than the relational expectation of multiple dyad relations.

Thus, I propose to model agent configurations, applying the statistical dependency of the dyads involved, with a finite mixture model in order to identify typical dyadic association patterns. The identification of typically occurring dyads is effected by means of the manifest (dis)similarity in characteristics between the interacting users. For this purpose, each characteristic is used once for each dyad member, aiming for a statistical optimum of categorical latent classes. This approach is thus very similar to a structural equation model for dyadic data (Kenny et al. 2006). The proposed multivariate classification of dyadic data is a way to reduce the complexity of interactions and to facilitate a structural analysis. In contrast to traditional cluster analysis techniques, the latent class classification predicts probabilities of class membership. One can statistically determine the optimal number of classes, and predict the probabilities of variable values within these classes. The proposed dyadic extension of this basic principle consists of a classification of observed interactions of two individuals. Consequently, not classes of individual users are identified, but classes of dyads. Chapter 7 will present an empirical construction of reciprocal classification, as proposed in Chapter 5, by applying this model of dyadic classification. Overall, in contrast to models centered on the average actor and her free choice, the relational methodologies of geometric data analysis and dyadic classification will do justice to the complexity of the data structures, and, in doing so, allow for a systematical consideration of sociological core concepts such as structure, power, and dominance into the analyses of mating processes. The subsequent chapter will discuss important aspects of the genuine structuration of online mating processes.

References

Acock, A. C., & Washburn, I. (2013). Quantitative methodology for family science. In G. W. Peterson & K. R. Bush (Eds.), *Handbook of marriage and the family* (pp. 65–89). New York: Plenum Press.

Becker, G. S. (1993). *A treatise on the family*. Cambridge, MA: Harvard University Press.

Beh, E. J., & Lombardo, R. (2012). A genealogy of correspondence analysis. *Australian & New Zealand Journal of Statistics, 54*(2), 137–168.

Benzécri, J. P. (1973). *L´analyse des données: L´analyse des correspondances*. Michigan: Dunod.

Bergström, M. (2014). *Au bonheur des rencontres. Sexualité, classe et rapports de genre dans la production et l'usage des sites de rencontres en France*. Institut d'études politiques de Paris, PhD Thesis in Sociology.

Blasius, J., & Greenacre, M. J. (1994). *Correspondence analysis in the social science. Recent developments and applications*. New York: Academic.

Blasius, J., & Schmitz, A. (2013). The empirical construction of Bourdieu's social space. In M. Greenacre & J. Blasius (Eds.), *The visualization and verbalization of data* (pp. 205–222). London: Chapman & Hall.

Blau, P. M. (1964). *Exchange and power in social life* (9th ed.). New York: Wiley.

Blossfeld, H.-P., & Mill, M. (2001). A causal approach to interrelated family events: A cross-national comparison of cohabitation, nonmarital conception, and marriage. *Canadian Studies in Population, 28*(2), *Special Issue on Longitudinal Methodology*, 409–437.

Bourdieu, P. (1984). *Distinction: A social critique of the judgement of taste*. London: Routledge and Kegan Paul.

Bourdieu, P. (1985). The social space and the genesis of groups. *Theory and Society, 14*(6), 723–744.

Bourdieu, P. (1987). *Die feinen Unterschiede. Kritik der gesellschaftlichen Urteilskraft*. Frankfurt am Main: Suhrkamp.

Bourdieu, P. (1989). Social space and symbolic power. *Sociological Theory, 7*(1), 14–25.

Bourdieu, P. (1991). In J. B. Thompson (Ed.), *Language and symbolic power*. Cambridge, MA: Polity.

Bourdieu, P. (1993a). *Sozialer Sinn-Kritik der theoretischen Vernunft*. Frankfurt am Main: Suhrkamp.

Bourdieu, P. (1993b). Über einige Eigenschaften von Feldern. In P. Bourdieu (Ed.), *Soziologische Fragen* (pp. 107–130). Frankfurt am Main: Suhrkamp.
Bourdieu, P. (1998). *Praktische Vernunft. Zur Theorie des Handelns*. Frankfurt am Main: Suhrkamp.
Bourdieu, P. (1999). Une révolution conservatrice dans l'édition. *Actes de la recherche en sciences sociales, 126–127*, 3–28.
Bourdieu, P. (2000). *Pascalian meditations*. Oxford: Polity Press.
Bourdieu, P. (2005). *The Social Structures of the Economy*. Cambridge: Polity Press.
Bourdieu, P., & Passeron, J. C. P. (1991). *The craft of sociology*. Berlin: de Gruyter.
Bourdieu, P., & Wacquant, L. J. D. (1992). *An invitation to reflexive sociology*. Chicago: Polity Press.
Bourdieu, P., Darbel A., Rivet J.-P., & Seibel, C. (1963). *Travail et travailleurs en Algérie*. Recherches méditerranées, Documents Nr. 1, Paris & Den Haag: Mouton.
Couper, M. P., & Coutts, E. (2006). Online-Befragungen. Probleme und Chancen verschiedener Arten von Online-Erhebungen. In A. Diekmann (Ed.), *Methoden der Sozialforschung* (pp. 217–243). Wiesbaden: VS Verlag.
Greenacre, M. J. (1984). *Theory and applications of correspondence analysis*. London: Academic.
Griffin, D., & Gonzalez, R. (1995). Correlational analysis of dyad-level data in the exchangeable case. *Psychological Bulletin, 118*(3), 430–439.
Hitsch, G. J., Hortaçsu, A., & Ariely, D. (2010). What makes you click? Mate preferences in online dating. *Quantitative Marketing and Economics, 8*(4), 393–427.
Janetzko, D. (2008). Nonreactive data collection on the internet. In N. Fielding, R. M. Lee, & G. Blank (Eds.), *The SAGE handbook of online research methods* (pp. 161–176). London: Sage.
Kalmijn, M. (1998). Intermarriage and homogamy: Causes, patterns, trends. *Annual Review of Sociology, 24*, 395–421.
Kenny, D. A., Kashy, D. A., & Cook, W. L. (2006). *Dyadic data analysis*. New York: The Guilford Press.
Le Roux, B., & Rouanet, H. (2004). *Geometric data analysis. From correspondence analysis to structered data analysis*. Dordrecht: Kluwer.
Le Roux, B., & Rouanet, H. (2010). *Multiple correspondence analysis. Sage series of quantitative applications in the social sciences*. London: Sage.
Lebaron, F. (2002). *Pierre Bourdieu: Economic Models against Economism*. Retrieved from http://olivier.godechot.free.fr/hopfichiers/lebaron-second-draft-edited.pdf.
Lebaron, F. (2009). How Bourdieu "quantified" Bourdieu: The geometric modelling of data. In K. Robson & C. Sanders (Eds.), *Quantifying theory: Pierre Bourdieu* (pp. 11–29). Wiesbaden: VS Verlag.
Lebaron, F. (2012). Grundzüge einer geometrischen Formalisierung des Feldkonzepts. In S. Bernhard & C. Schmidt-Wellenburg (Eds.), *Feldanalyse als Forschungsprogramm* (pp. 123–150). Wiesbaden: VS Verlag.
Lebaron, F. (2015). *Pierre Bourdieu, geometric data analysis and the analysis of economic spaces and fields*. Forum for Social Economics. 09.07.2015.
Lebart, L., Morineau, A., & Warwick, K. M. (1984). *Multivariate descriptive statistical analysis. Correspondence analysis and related techniques for large matrices*. New York: Wiley.
Lewis, K. (2015). Studying online behavior: Comment on Anderson et al. *Sociological Science, 2*, 20–31.
Lichbach, M. (2003). *Is rational choice theory all of social science?* Michigan: University of Michigan Press.
Lin, K.-H., & Lundquist, J. (2013). Mate selection in cyberspace: The intersection of race, gender, and education. *American Journal of Sociology, 119*(1), 183–215.
Magidson, J., & Vermunt, J. K. (2004). Latent class models. In D. Kaplan (Ed.), *The Sage handbook of quantitative methodology for the social sciences* (pp. 175–198). Thousand Oaks: Sage.

Rabe-Hesketh, S., Skrondal, A., & Pickles, A. (2004). Generalized multilevel structural equation modelling. *Psychometrika, 69*(2), 167–190.
Rouanet, H. (2002). Lebaron Frédéric, Le Hay Viviane, Ackermann Werner, Le Roux Brigitte: Régression et analyse géométrique des données: réflexions et suggestions. *Mathématiques & Sciences Humaines, 40*(160), 13–45.
Rouanet, H., Ackermann, W., & Le Roux, B. (2000). The Geometric Analysis of Questionnaires: the Lesson of Bourdieu's La Distinction. *Bulletin de Méthodologie Sociologique, 65*(1), 5–18.
Samuelson, P. A. (1947). *Foundations of economic analysis. Harvard economic studies: Vol. 80.* Cambridge: Harvard University Press.
Schmitz, A. (2009). Virtuelle Zwischengeschlechtlichkeit im Kontext relationaler Methodologie. Überlegungen zu einer Soziologie der digitalen Partnerwahl. In H.-G. Soeffner (Ed.), *Unsichere Zeiten. Herausforderungen gesellschaftlicher Transformationen; Verhandlungen des 34. Kongresses der Deutschen Gesellschaft für Soziologie in Jena 2008*. Wiesbaden: VS Verlag.
Schmitz, A. (2012). Elective affinities 2.0? A Bourdieusian approach to couple formation and the methodology of E-dating. *Social Science Research on the Internet (RESET), 1*(1), 175–202.
Schulz, F., Skopek, J., & Blossfeld, H.-P. (2010). Partnerwahl als konsensuelle Entscheidung. Das Antwortverhalten bei Erstkontakten im Online-Dating. *Kölner Zeitschrift für Soziologie und Sozialpsychologie, 62*(3), 485–514.
Skopek, J. (2011). *Partnerwahl im Internet: Eine quantitative Analyse von Strukturen und Prozessen der Online-Partnersuche*. Wiesbaden: VS Verlag.
Skrondal, A., & Rabe-Hesketh, S. (2004). *Generalized latent variable modeling: Multilevel, longitudinal, and structural equation models. Interdisciplinary statistics series.* Boca Raton: Chapman & Hall/CRC. Retrieved from http://www.loc.gov/catdir/enhancements/fy0646/2004042808-d.html.
Wacquant, L. (2013). Symbolic power and group-making: On Pierre Bourdieu's reframing of class. *Journal of Classical Sociology, 13*(2), 274–291.
Welker, M., & Wenzel, O. (2007). Online Forschung 2007. Grundlagen und Fallstudien. Neue Schriften zur Online-Forschung, Band 1, Köln: Herbert von Halem.
Wellmann, B. (1988). Structural analysis: From method and metaphor to theory and substance. In B. Wellmann & S. D. Berkovitz (Eds.), *Social structures: A network approach* (pp. 19–61). Cambridge: Cambridge University Press.
Wendt, A. (1999). *Social theory of international politics*. Cambridge: Cambridge University Press.
Willoughby, B. J., & Carroll, J. S. (2010). Sexual experience and couple formation attitudes among emerging adults. *Journal of Adult Development, 17*(1), 1–11.
Woody, E. Z., & Sadler, P. (2005). Structural equation models for interchangeable dyads: Being the same makes a difference. *Psychological Methods, 10*, 139–158.
Zillmann, D. (2016). *Von kleinen Lügen und kurzen Beinen. Selbstdarstellung bei der Partnersuche im Internet*. [About little lies and small legs. Self-Presentation in Online Dating.] Wiesbaden: VS Verlag (forthcoming).
Zillmann, D., & Schulz, F. (2009). *Das Internet als Heiratsmarkt. Ausgewählte Aspekte aus Sicht der empirischen Partnerwahlforschung*. Ifb-Materialien 4/2009. Bamberg.
Zillmann, D., Schmitz, A., & Blossfeld, H.-P. (2011). Lügner haben kurze Beine. Zum Zusammenhang unwahrer Selbstdarstellung und partnerschaftlicher Chancen im Online-Dating. *Zeitschrift für Familienforschung, 23*(3), 291–318.
Zillmann, D., Schmitz, A., Skopek, J., & Blossfeld, H.-P. (2013). Survey topic and unit nonresponse. Evidence from an online survey on mating. *Quality and Quantity, 48*(4), 2069–2088.

Chapter 7
Empirical Analyses

The Online Dating Market and the Social Space

In this chapter, the Bourdieusian approach will be applied to observational and questionnaire data from a major German dating site. Firstly, by analyzing life-style indicators using multiple correspondence analysis, it will be shown that the dating site can be interpreted as a digital emanation of the 'offline' German social space rather than as an autonomous field. As physical attributes correspond to this social space, the idea that 'erotic capital' manifests as an independent structuring factor on a digital partner market will be dismissed. In a second step, an Eigen-value operationalization of chances for attention and exchange will be presented. Finally, using users' interaction events, it will be shown that both objective and subjective chances are to be understood as functions of the users' positions in the social space.

The Online Space of Lifestyles

Given the importance that self-portrayal, lifestyle indicators, general appearance, and linguistic expressions play in online dating, this context of encounter can be understood as being particularly structured on a symbolic basis. Within this market of symbolic goods, users and their profile representations become symbolic goods and objects of competition. The first question then is whether this symbolic good market can be understood as a digital representation of the (German) social space, or whether it has a relative autonomy from offline society to such a degree that there are specific forms of capital which are constituent for it. In offline research, the structure of the German social space has been shown to follow the findings of Bourdieu's analysis in that the dominant structuring dimensions (according to the particular data) are economic and cultural capital, both in the late 1990s (cp. Blasius and Winkler 1989) and the mid-2000s (Blasius and Mühlichen 2010). Given the fact that the dating platform in question includes all social strata of German society (cp. Chapter 2), and is little affected by selection bias, one might expect that the capital structure familiar from offline society will also manifest itself in this data. In the light of the assumed or factual peculiarities of the specific digital dating market, one also might expect an autonomous subspace (or even 'field') to prevail, one which does not display the same spatial structure as the offline social space. One may think that– due to the digital nature of the dating market and due to its primary goal, namely 'mating' – those symbols and resources are placed in the foreground which play a major role for mating practices, thus breaking with the logics of offline society. For example, following the media discourse, physical appearance could be expected to be of major relevance for this sphere. When users search for a partner, they may skim superficially over profiles and in doing so prioritize physicality, assigning particular relevance to profile pictures (cp. Hakim 2011).

In order to assess the question of the platform's overall capital structure, a construction following the Bourdieusian framework (cp. Chapter 6) will be presented. For this purpose, a data set from the relational database – consisting of profile information, web-questionnaire information, and web-generated process data – will be analyzed (N=756). The lifestyle items, (which, due to the importance of self-portrayal in profile pictures and textual self-descriptions, seem to be of particular relevance in online dating) comprise the classical indicators, familiar from *Distinction*, such as preferences for food, furniture, clothes, and so on (cp. Bourdieu 1984). Furthermore, the respondents' perception of their own attractiveness, their own estimation of their potential for success with the opposite sex, and the stated use of deceptive profile pictures were recorded. The questionnaire variables also include socio-demographic information and the participants' height and weight, enabling the construction of the Body Mass Index. The information regarding physical attractiveness underwent a principal component analysis, which identified a one-dimensional factor. The latent variable thus extracted was divided into quintiles, from 0 (low physical capital) to 4 (high physical capital). This indicator was paired with the respondents' gender, resulting in 5 groups each for men and women. Combined with the traditional lifestyle items, this variable was analyzed using multiple correspondence analysis. Firstly, Figure 7.1 shows the results without the physical indicators.

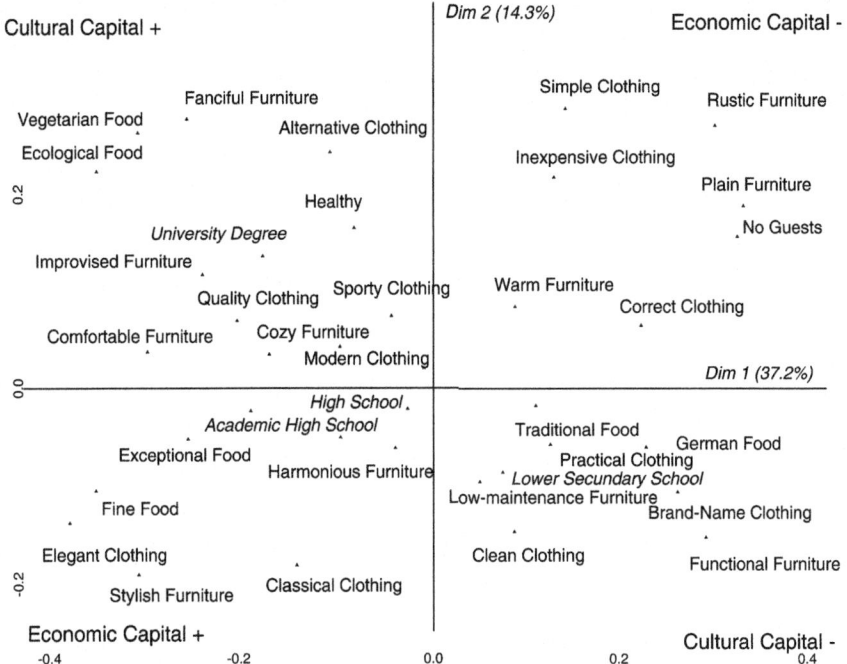

Fig. 7.1 The space of lifestyles

The visualization of the social space yields a two-dimensional structure, familiar from offline analyses of the German society (cp. Blasius and Winkler 1989). The upper right corner of the graph is characterized by simple and inexpensive clothing, and rustic and plain furniture, whereas fine food and elegant clothing and furniture can be found in the opposite quadrant. This oppositional relation can be interpreted as revealing a dimension of *economic capital*. At right angles to this dimension, a contrast between, in the upper left, ornate furniture, vegetarian and organic food, and alternative clothing, and, in the lower right, practical clothing and functional furniture, can be identified. This oppositional relation can be interpreted as users' *cultural* capital. The latter interpretation can be supported by passively projecting educational degree, which systematically varies with cultural capital. A first finding, thus, is that – from the viewpoint of the space of lifestyles – the capital structure of a typical (German) online dating market reflects the capital structure of offline (German) society.

Erotic Capital as Dimension of the Digital Partner Market?

Although not shown in the last graph, the indicator of physicality has been used as an active variable, and thus is constitutive for the constructed social space. The idea is that if physicality is indeed relevant enough for online partner markets such that it becomes a structuring variable, it should impact on the overall structure of the space (cp. Chapter 4). Following Hakim (2011), this relevance should show itself in such a way that a dimension of "erotic capital" emerges.

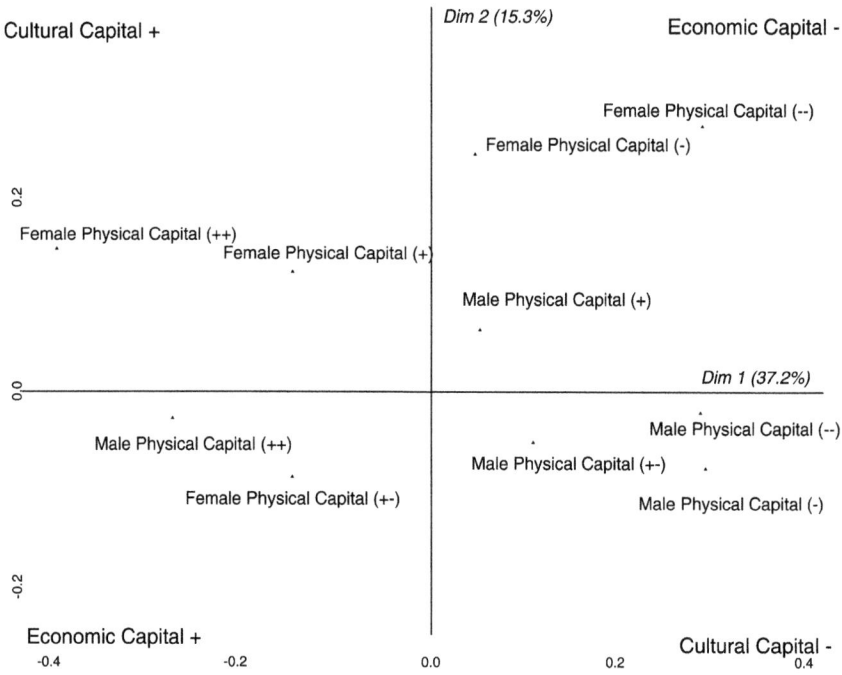

Fig. 7.2 Physicality within the social space

However, no third axis was identified statistically; the space can be sufficiently described by way of economic and cultural capital (cp. Figure 7.2). The distribution of the manifestations of physical attributes within the social space can be described as a clearly gender-specific function of economic and cultural capital, from right to left. Female attractiveness is associated with high overall capital (especially cultural capital), whereas low female attractiveness is associated with low economic capital. Male attractiveness, in contrast, more uniformly corresponds to high overall capital.

These findings correspond to Bourdieu's remarks on physicality in the social space; he argues that "the most sought-after bodily properties (slimness, beauty etc.) are not randomly distributed among the classes" (Bourdieu 1984: 207), but constitutive for class habitus (cp. Chapter 5). The dimension of erotic capital which Hakim (2011) suggests as being independent from other societal dimensions is actually subsumed by manifestations of the habitus (and its bodily emanation, 'hexis') which can essentially be explained as being determined by economic and cultural capital. 'Liveliness', 'charm', and the other indicators in Hakim's model of 'erotic capital' are, from this perspective, primarily to be thought of as class-specific phenomena: physical capital is a partial manifestation of actors' positions in the social space, their hexis, and their lifestyles. Nevertheless, the physicality portrayed in profile pictures is an important element of communication online, and part of the bundle of symbolic goods which users exhibit therein.

Whereas this analysis describes the online dating market as a representation of German society as a whole, we shall now focus on the partner market by analyzing how objective chances on the dating market relate, and indeed contribute, to this digital social space.

The Structure of Chances for Awareness and Exchange

As argued in Chapter 3, the exact notion of what the term 'partner market' actually means is rather unclear. A Weberian definition has been derived by emphasizing the competition for opportunities of exchange and awareness as the core elements of partner markets. The question, however, is: how should these structures of opportunity be constructed empirically? Apart from spontaneous constructions derived from *ad hoc* definitions (e.g. 'education *is* mate value', etc.), some attempts at an empirical construction of mate value can be found in the literature. Pawloski and Dunbar (1999) calculate a mate value for each cohort by dividing the proportion of users seeking individuals of a given age (the demand for individuals of that age) by the proportion of users of that age in a sample (the supply). The ratio of these two is thus a measure of the relative selection pressure placed on individual age cohorts, in the same sense that selection ratios are used in foraging ecology. Some authors propose surveying the self-perceived mate value of an actor as a measure (Penke and Denissen 2008; Brase and Guy 2004). Gigerenzer and Todd (291 ff.) discuss the allocation of 'offers and rejections' as an adaptive heuristic for learning one's own mate value. That would first mean counting possible romantic partners. However, as already mentioned, actors searching for a mate will also consider the mate value of the potential mate. The sheer number of offers from potential mates is simply too vague a measure, as the offering *alteri* themselves may well vary in their mate value. We call this the 'Cocotte problem': contacts from actors with a low market value are worth less than contacts from actors with a high market value. Consequently, a Weberian mate value of *ego* shall be conceptualized as a function of the quality and quantity of his or her contacting network (cp. Schmitz 2009). This can be illustrated with a simplified ingoing contact graph (Figure 7.3):

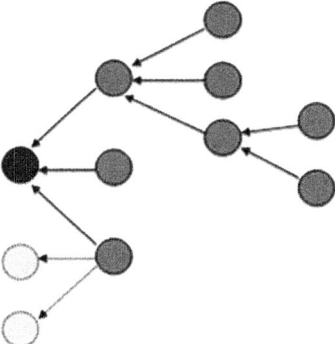

Fig. 7.3 Ego's ingoing contact network

The amount of incoming contacts increases *ego's* (dark) mate value. A higher *alter* mate value stemming from a high number of ingoing contacts results in a higher mate value of *ego*. The increase of *ego's* mate value declines relative to *alter's* outgoing contacts. To put it in layman's terms: it is good for one's mating chances to get a lot of offers; it is even better if the offers are from potential mates who also have good mating chances; and, finally, the more exclusive the attention that *ego* gets from *alter*, the better it is for *ego's* mating chances.

The eigenvector centrality indicator 'rank or status prestige' fits with this methodological consideration, as this network measure is a function of the rank or status of actors in a network (Bonacich 1987). For example, a man who is contacted by many high-ranked women has a higher rank than a man who is the target of exclusively low-ranked women. A user's rank therefore increases every time he or she is contacted, but it increases more the higher the rank of the choosing partner. This 'mate prestige' indicator (MP) can be formulated as:

$$MP_{IN}(A) = (1-d) + d \cdot \sum_{i=1}^{n} \frac{MP_{IN}(T_i)}{C_{IN}(T_i)}$$

with

$MP_{IN}(A)$ the mate prestige value of individual A
$MP_{IN}(T_i)$ the mate prestige of individuals T_i, who contacted A
$C_{IN}(T_i)$ the total number of contacts that were established by T_i
d a damping factor between 0 and 1

Hence, *ego's* prestige is a function of the ranks of the actors that contact *ego*. The computation implies an iterative optimization problem that can be solved with an eigenvector centrality algorithm.[1]

---

[1] From a relational point of view, the latent phenomenon of mate value cannot just be represented by the quantity and quality of ego's contact network (that is, the value of the offers), but must also take into account the fact that the ego himself contacts alteri who can react to this offer in a permissive or dismissive way. I call this the 'Casanova problem': Ccontacts from actors whose activities

Contrary to one common way of understanding information regarding objective or subjective mate value, the observed interactional data allows the chance structure to be objectified as such. The *a priori* definition of mate value with one or many variables (such as equating education or age with mate value) is transcended by this relational conceptualization, defining the unit of chances as a genuinely social entity.

However, this eigenvalue indicator is anything but independent from social impacts. What Bourdieu states for the sociology of markets in general also applies to the realm of (digital) partner markets: "it is not prices that determine everything, but everything that determines prices" (2005: 77). Thus, in order to illustrate the societal logics behind this indicator, it will be used as a dependent variable in a regression model with conventional socio-demographic predictors (cp. Schmitz 2014). Table 7.1 gives the results.

Table 7.1 Regression model of users' mate value (centrality)

	b	sig
Female	0.592	***
Age	0.021	***
Age (sq.)	−0.001	***
BMI	0.000	
BMI (sq.)	0.001	*
Education (ord.)	0.059	***
Age*Female	−0.007	***
BMI* Female	−0.008	***
Education* Female	−0.014	*
Profile Picture (y)	0.166	***
Intercept	−1.481	***
adj. R^2	0.06%	
N	15,455	

Quoted from Schmitz (2014). Note that the significance level is only of heuristic value given the non-sample nature of the data. Dependent variable is the user's Eigen-Centrality.
Legend: *$p \leq 0.05$; **$p \leq 0.01$; ***$p \leq 0.001$

The model illustrates that, on average, women display a more advantageous chance structure than men. Furthermore, age overall positively affects the average chance structure but it operates in a curvilinear way: beyond an optimal age, the mate value declines. In accordance with offline findings, the interaction terms show that the female chance structure becomes worse with older age and higher BMI. For men, a higher educational level positively affects the chances of being contacted, whereas a higher educational level impairs the female chance structure, which

---

are more widely distributed are worth less than from those who concentrate on one person. Therefore, an important indicator of ego's mate value is the value operationalized by means of accepted and rejected offers. Again, this indicator of appeal is meaningful only when augmented with the value of those that accept or reject ego's offer.

points to the gender-specificity of the value certain societal resources possess. For both sexes, the presence of a profile picture increases the chances for attention. Overall, it is clear that dating sites produce differential awareness chances (or symbolic capital), and thus exchange chances (or social capital) for its users. These findings are in line with offline research on the (gendered) value of mating traits, thus indicating that the chances for awareness and exchange online are strongly dependent on the societal conditions, as is the case in the offline world.

In order to take a closer look on the social conditions of chances on the partner market the objective eigenvalue indicator, subjectively perceived chances (as compared to offline chances)[2] and reported number of meeting users offline will be classified into five categories and passively projected in the social space as constructed before. Figure 7.4 shows that the passively projected chances for attention and exchange vary with the overall capital volume in much the same that way physical capital did in the first analysis, thus supporting the interpretation of objective 'romantic' chances as a function of the social space. The objective (dis)advantages associated with one's symbolic goods, and hence with one's position in this symbolic good market, seem to be directly associated with capital volume, and especially with cultural capital.

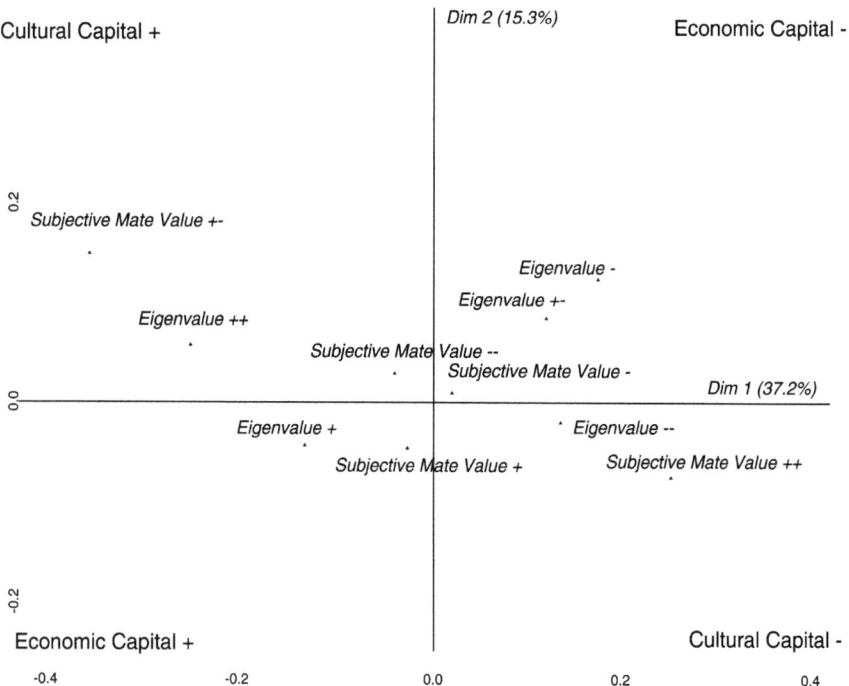

Fig. 7.4 Subjective and objective mate value within the social space

---

[2] The items are: 'How likely do you think you are to find a partner on this platform?' and 'How likely do you think you are to find a partner at all?'

The subjectively assessed mate value, however, does not correspond to overall capital in the same way. High overall capital, and cultural capital in particular, is associated with high objective chances for attention, average subjective mate value, and average count of offline meetings. Low overall capital (especially cultural capital) is associated with low objective – that is, actual – chances, but high subjective – that is, self-assessed – chances of finding a partner online. The middle position of the social space seems to be associated with low self-assessed mate value. Whereas the chance structure as operationalized via contact networks directly mirrors offline users' objective chances with regard to their specific positions and the associated symbolic goods, users seem to differ as to how they perceive their chances online. This might point to a differential interplay between the online dating market and the users' habitus. Low cultural capital might be associated with overestimating one's chances online (maybe due to an unfiltered belief in advertisements claiming that everyone has a chance). High cultural capital, in contrast, might be associated with a certain modesty, be it conscious or unconscious, thus understating one's actual chances. Lastly, low perceived chances online being associated with the middle position in the space could be a function of parts of the middle-class habitus having a sense (and disposition) for the prevailing competition, the ordinariness of the symbolic goods they offer, and the scarcity of partners conforming to optimal standards.

We can corroborate this habitus-based interpretation by inspecting the number of potential partners from the website met offline. The reported number of communication partners met offline is less of a linear function of overall capital but seems to correspond to economic capital, with few successful events for those with low economic capital, an average number for those users with average economic capital (but high cultural capital), and a comparatively large number of meetings for those who possess high economic capital. The fact that low economic and overall capital is associated with very few offline meetings is hardly surprising, as it has already been argued that unfavorable capital endowment is a problem in gaining attention. Thus, the disadvantages associated with these positions in the social space are reinforced by poor prospects of finding a partner online. The higher average number of users who met offline, located in the middle position of the social space, might be explained by a rational habitus which feels compelled to find the best possible partner and thus to realize multiple romantic appointments offline. In conclusion, revealing the structural logics of the digital partner market precludes us from assuming the existence of an 'average user' and an overall situational essence as characteristics for the digital dating market. As an agent's habitus is the expression of objective and subjective social conditions, prior to any contingent (in this case, online) experience, the social space constructed so far thus suggests that the actors on this digital partner market are fully socialized and structured subjects, rather than mere market participants. The following analysis will continue constructing the social space and the habitus by taking a closer look at the mating dispositions and rationalities relevant in the context of mating.

The Relational Structure of Mating Preferences

The previous chapter argued that the habitus perspective is a promising way to conceive of the relational logics of users on the dating platform analyzed here. The question addressed in this chapter will be whether different mating preferences are independent of each other – as a traditional economic model might assume explicitly, or traditional mating research does implicitly when it comes to modeling – or whether they are actually empirically interdependent, as predicted by habitus theory. Also, we will pursue the issue as to which patterns of preference interdependence can be empirically observed. First, a relational extension of mating preferences will be discussed using the example of age preferences in mating. It will be shown that no universal age-based homophily can be observed, but that age preferences are a function of the user's own age. Applying multinominal regression models, age preferences will be then revealed as being confounded with other preferences, and as being functions of the user's market position. As a further step towards a relational conceptualization of mating preferences, the habitus perspective will be applied afterwards. Using finite mixture classification analyses of different stated absolute and relational mate preferences, it will be shown that all surveyed partner preferences are confounded. We will argue that they display a pattern which fits better with Bourdieu's concept of mating dispositions as bundles of preferences, dislikes, and indifferences than with an (implicit) assumption of independent mating preferences. In the last step, by relating the latent class results to the previously constructed social space, it will be shown that mating dispositions systematically correspond to the social space. The findings will highlight the differential character of mating dispositions. In doing so, they will also support a relational rather than a generalized interpretation of homophily: for male users of the lower classes, homophily manifests as a 'romantic taste of necessity', whereas women who possess high cultural capital, but also high overall capital, show a dispositional complex of homophily and hyperphily.

Relational Mating Preferences: The Case of Age Preferences

An assumption underlying large parts of empirical research on mating preferences is that (homophilious) mating preferences operate independently in influencing choice acts, or that specific traits possess a certain level of causal primacy, or – at least within the modeling process – that one particular preference sufficiently approximates the actual processes underlying mate choice. This assumption leads to a great deal of research specializing on the impact of e.g. educational preferences, or preferences for attractiveness, income, etc. on acts of mate choice. The assumption of singularly operating preferences seems particularly appropriate in the case of online dating, given the situation of choice, choice sets, and induced rationality. When applying the individualistic mate choice paradigm, it could be expected that dating site users, relative to participants in traditional partner markets, are more able to realize their specific mate preferences without interferences of structural influences as exerted by third parties or institutional restrictions (see Chapter 3). As argued before, the concept of habitus in contrast emphasizes the interdependence between seemingly different (mating) preferences as well as between these preferential systems and the social space. Subsequently, we shall motivate a Bourdieusian extension of the preferential approach, starting with the case of age preferences, which will be subsequently related to other mating preferences and positions in the social space.

Even though age is a central variable in assortative mating (Hollingshead 1950; Klein 1996; Skopek et al. 2011), research on the role of age in mate selection is rare. Scholars studying age in assortative mating often rely on presumed preferences for similarity in age, and take patterns of age homogamy in existing couples as evidence for such preferences. Age patterns of marriage partners have also often been explained in terms of societal norms regarding an acceptable age difference in a couple (e.g. Lewis and Spanier 1979; Spanier and Glick 1980). In order to assess the appropriateness of the two generalized mechanisms of homophily and norms, observational and questionnaire data of the platform has been analyzed by Skopek et al. (2011). Utilizing a sample of 10,427 senders of first contacts (65.42 % male) who sent an average of 11.12 contacts (12.75 for men vs. 8.02 for women), they disclose 'revealed age preferences' by reconstructing men's and women's choices to calculate the degree of age-related homophily and heterophily in the selection of potential mates. For men, age homophily was particularly high in young age groups: over 50 % of first-time e-mails from men aged up to 25 were sent to women of similar age. However, the degree of men's homophilic contacts then declines strongly, although it remains higher than expected given the marginal distributions of the platform's population. In contrast, women's age homophily increases over age, starting with relatively low values in women younger than 25 (a maximum of 30 %) and then oscillating considerably higher than expected at around 40 % for higher ages. Also, whereas a sub-group of women increasingly contacts younger males, men generally showed less propensity towards older women.

Overall, it becomes clear that, whereas the average male chance structure increases with age, female potential rapidly diminishes as they age. This 'differential decline of mate value' represents different challenges for aging women and men. Whereas women are increasingly looking for men in the same age group, they are increasingly less favored by exactly these men. Skopek et al. (2011) also identify a high degree of competition for women of an optimal age in the digital partner market. Men compete amongst each other for a very specific segment of the female population, which will necessarily result in a lot of men being unable to realize this preference. This can be seen as a force for *preference adaption* from the perspective of market-endogenous effects. Subsequently, having illustrated the age-dependent reaction to a potential partner's age in men and women, and the gender-specific opportunity structures thus created, Skopek et al. (2011) assess the impact of this relational structure on the subjective level. The question arises as to whether the reported patterns of male and female choices regarding age were relevant for men's and women's subjective age preferences. Multinomial-regression analyses of stated relational age preferences support this idea (cp. Figure 7.5).

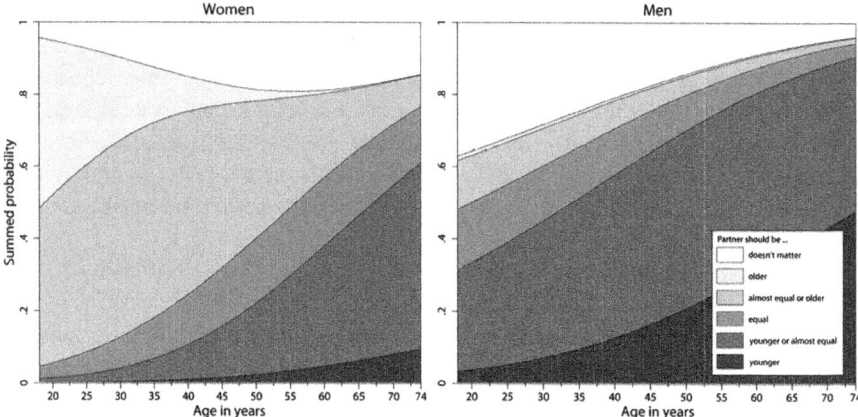

Fig. 7.5 Conditional effect of age on preference outcomes in men and women (Quoted from Skopek, Schmitz, and Blossfeld (2011))

It was shown that their own age significantly influences men's preferences for female age. Holding other variables constant, a one unit increase in men's age makes their preference for a younger woman (Outcome 1) more likely over remaining outcomes. Similarly, the probability of a preference for women of a younger or almost equal age (Outcome 2) increases with age, although the effect was stronger on Outcome 1, because the odds of Outcome 1 over Outcome 2 themselves increase significantly for each year. In contrast, other preferential outcomes become less likely with age. Discrete changes suggest that the loss in probability is largest for the indifference preference (Outcome 6). Figure 7.5 plots the conditional effect of age on probabilities in order to visualize this finding. Very much in line with prior results, there is a distinct age-graded shift in men's preference for younger women. Older men increasingly prefer younger women and are less interested in the indifference outcome (6 = doesn't matter).

Analyses of females' stated relational preferences show a stable disposition towards slightly older men until women reach the age of 45, when they begin to show a highly diverse pattern of age preferences. One interpretation here is that women are systematically encouraged to act to counter their increasingly disadvantageous situation on the partner market. Some female users maintain their high aspirations with regard to optimal male age, whereas some compromise by accepting or even seeking out men younger than themselves. In conclusion, using the example of age preferences in mating, we can empirically corroborate the hypothesis that (in this case, age-related) homophily can be characterized as a phenomenon of particular segments of the digital partner market, and is itself a socially variable disposition rather than a general principle of mating.

Applying relational reasoning, Skopek et al. (2011) pursue the question as to whether age preferences interrelate with other preferences relevant in mating. Their analysis shows that the more attractiveness was preferred as an important partner trait, the higher the probability of desiring a younger (or 'younger or almost equal') female partner became, relative to other outcomes, and the lower the probability of indifference became ('age of partner doesn't matter'). There was a similar effect for women: the more attractiveness was rated as a relevant partner feature, the more likely women were to state a preference for younger or almost equal partners. Also, the more women emphasized education as an important partner feature, the stronger their age preference shifted from equal and 'doesn't matter' to 'almost equal or older' or older men. Thus, women's age preferences seem to be confounded with preferences for educational (and hence economic) status. However, there was also an effect for men: the stronger the preference for female educational status, the less likely there was to be a preference for younger women compared to other preferences. Interestingly, men tended to shift to 'doesn't matter' rather than to the older category. Thus, a high absolute preference for education seems to be associated with age preferences for women, but not for men. Furthermore, men, but not women, showed a greater indifference toward a potential partner's age when they had a high absolute preference for education. As a consequence, one can dismiss the idea of homophily operating as the dominant principle of generating structural homogeneity (cp. Lin and Lundquist 2013: 207). Not only does the market-level age homogeneity of interacting couples emerge without a universal age-based homophily, but age preferences themselves cannot be separated from the dispositional systems they are embedded in.

Due to the specific situations men and women create for each other, Skopek et al. (2011) also hypothesize that the capital endowment of men and women will impact on their mating preferences. Within the analysis they show that the better an average male user's resource set was, the higher his aspirations will be. A high level of education significantly increases the probability of Outcome 1 over all other outcomes. There was a difference of about +7.7 percentage points in the probability of Outcome 1 for a hypothetical man (see above) with a high compared to a medium level of education. In contrast to men, female odds in favor of Outcome 1 compared to the remaining outcomes were reduced (albeit just on a 10% level of significance for most contrasts), and odds in favor of Outcome 6 were increased for more highly educated women. This means that, compared to women with a medium level of education, more highly educated women preferred younger men less often and were more frequently indifferent about the age of their partner. Skopek et al. (2011) interpret this finding to mean that age preferences might be the outcome of an adaptive cognitive process reflecting one's chances on the mating market.

This work was a first step in the direction of thinking of mating preferences as relational concepts, as it could be shown that mating preferences interrelate with each other as well as with the actors' resource endowment. Also, homophily in mating was shown to be a socially variable logic, rather than a constant. As it has been argued in Chapter 5, this finding can be generalized from the relational perspective of Bourdieu's theory. Mating preferences do not manifest themselves as mutually distinct attitudes, but rather as dispositions – that is, as coherent patterns of perception and evaluation. Also, following the habitus concept, mating dispositions can be expected to correspond not only to a partner market position, but to a user's position in the social space prior to any experience on a dating site. For example, the interdependencies between age preferences and resource endowment (and thus market position) cannot be traced back to short term experiences on the digital dating markets, but to processes of early habitus formation. This includes the internalization of parental roles, peer groups, social fields etc., which together form one's habitus during socialization. In conclusion, there is ample evidence that a more consequent relational approach to mating phenomena might be promising.

Structured Systems of Mating Preferences

Subsequently, we shall assess whether mating preferences manifest as interdependent preferential systems, as predicted by the habitus perspective. For this purpose, ordinally scaled items for the subjective importance of mating traits, as well as relational mating preferences and the user's gender, will be analyzed applying a finite mixture modeling approach (cp. Chapter 6), which provides probability-based types of mating preference interdependencies, or *relationship dispositions*. The statistical optimum of the model yields 5 classes, which is itself a substantial finding, as only a one-class solution would conform to the assumption of independent single preferences. Furthermore, the interrelation of mate preferences reveals a systematic pattern of co-variances between the different mating preferences.

Class 1 (27.38%) consists of male respondents who particularly value humor, intelligence, and attractiveness. Zodiac sign, religion, and income are not important in this group's view. With regard to relational preferences, Class 1 can be characterized as having a strong indifference towards female occupational status and income. The desired age of a future female partner is lower or the same, whereas preferred education does not show a clear pattern. The questionnaire items asking whether a woman should be older, younger, or the same age, and have a higher, lower, or equal educational status also were often answered with 'doesn't matter'.

Class 2 (23.48%) consists of female users who assign considerable value to male humor and intelligence, and, to a similar extent, to education and occupational status as well. Male income and occupational status are less relevant than the other categories for women of this class. Remarkably, all relational mating preferences essentially show the pattern of desiring a man with a higher educational level, age, occupational status, and income than themselves. The 'doesn't matter' category is also widely used, indicating a certain element of indifference within this female preference system.

Class 3 (19.42%) consists of male respondents who value humor and intelligence, similar to male Class 1, but who ascribe even more importance to female attractiveness and youth. With regard to relational preferences, this male class barely uses the 'doesn't matter' category, but does use the 'same' and 'same or lower' categories more than Class 1 males. Education, in particular, is an aspect of homophily in this class, but hyperphily and hypophily are also present to a non-negligible extent in this preferential system. For men of Class 3, female occupational status and income are ideally equal or lower than their own, and relational age preferences show an especially clear structure of hypophily (i.e. of desiring younger women).

Class 4 (16.17%) consists of male respondents who consistently pursued the lowest requirements in a female partner; "humor" was the only category to display a high aspiration level similar to that of the other classes. Accordingly, the relational preferences of these men are essentially given with the 'doesn't matter' category. There is solely a weak manifestation of a preference for younger females in this class.

Class 5 (13.55%) consists of female users who can be characterized by consistently high mating aspirations: male humor, intelligence, attractiveness, income, education, age, and occupational status are subjectively judged as being highly important traits in a future partner. The questions on relational mating preferences were almost never answered with the 'doesn't matter' category, but instead with a consistent and clear hyperphilous preference structure. Male occupational status and income in particular, but also education and age, are desired to be higher than one's own for women of Class 5. Again, a tendency of homophilous preferences is also present in this female class. Table 7.2 gives a simplified overview.

Table 7.2 Latent classes of mating preferences and underlying dispositional principles

	Class 1 (M)	Class 2 (F)	Class 3 (M)	Class 4 (M)	Class 5 (F)
Single preferences	Humor, Intelligence, (lower) Age, (same) Education	Humor, Intelligence, (higher) Age, (higher) Education, (higher) Occupational Status, (higher) Income	Humor, Intelligence, (lower) Age, (lower/same) Occupational Status, (lower/same) Income, (same) Education	Humor, (lower) Age	Humor, Intelligence (higher) Education, (higher) Age, (higher) Occupational Status, (higher) Income
	Physical attractiveness		Physical attractiveness		Physical attractiveness
Latent dispositions	Lifestyle aspirations & indifference	Hyperphily	Hypophily & homophily	Low aspirations & indifference	High aspirations & hyperphily

Male Class 1 ('Lifestyle Aspirations & Indifference') can be seen as being relatively undemanding, except with regard to cultural traits such as female intelligence and humor, and female attractiveness and youth. Male Class 3 ('Hypophily & Homophily') also values female attractiveness and youth, and cultural traits, but is also characterized by general hypophilous and homophilous mating preferences. Male Class 4 ('Low Aspirations & Indifference') also values humor, but otherwise has generally low aspirations and a strong pattern of preferential indifference, except regarding female youth. Female Class 2 ('Hyperphily') is characterized by its generally strong hyperphily, and preferences for cultural traits in men. Female Class 5 ('High Aspirations & Hyperphily') displays the highest mating aspirations over all single traits (including male physicality), and also a strong overall pattern of hyperphily. The two female dispositional classes are particularly characterized by their high appreciation for male intelligence, humor, education, and age. Women in both classes prefer older men with a better occupational status and higher income than their own, thus characterizing themselves as consistently hyperphilous. Even with regard to male education, they express a preference for a man of a higher status, relative to a man with equal educational status. The male classes show consistent preferences for female humor, intelligence, and age. They also more frequently express indifference, especially with regard to resource aspects such as income and occupational status (male classes 1 and 4). Men ascribe relatively little value to a potential partner's economic capital, going so far as to desire women who possess a lower income or occupational status. Furthermore, lifestyle, which according to Bourdieu is the core trait relevant in mating, turns out to be of universal importance in mating dispositions. All users are particularly keen on a partner with a good sense of humor (albeit with low values in class 4), and on an intelligent partner. Humor, intelligence, and education – which can be thought of as elements of cultural capital – constitute a preferential pattern, which underlies the single subjective mating preferences. Nevertheless, it must be taken into account that the meaning of cultural skills like 'intelligence' and 'humor' varies according to social class (see e.g. Kuipers 2006).

This analysis shows that the assumption and modeling of mating preferences as single entities has at least 5 shortcomings: (1) not all agents perceive the same elements of social reality as the same set of alternatives; (2) agents possess complex preferential systems, meaning that educational preferences, for instance, cannot be separated from other mating preferences; (3) homophily is not the dominant pattern of mating preferences; (4) homophily occurs systematically alongside hyperphily and hypophily for all variables; (5) some actors are indifferent towards mating preferences, but this preferential indifference can actually be interpreted as one element of a preferential, or rather dispositional, system. The analysis or assumption of solitary mating preferences should be approached with caution, even in this potentially promising field of application – that is, despite the fact that online dating represents a particularly good setting for actors to reflect upon their mating preferences. Our findings so far support the conceptualization of mate choice acts as resting on preferential systems rather than singular preferences, thus favoring the concept of mate choice as a generalized by-product of the habitus. As it has been shown that age preferences correspond to market positions, the next section shall address the extent to which the latent classes of mating dispositions vary according to their social preconditions, that is, the social space.

The Positional Character of Mating Dispositions

As argued in Chapter 4, most models of rational choice, not only in the case of mate choice, are characterized by a lack of conceptualization of the situational and pre-situational – i.e. social and historical – conditions of action. In particular, the question of the socio-historical differential conditions of perception and evaluation in analytically separate situations is emphasized as a conceptual desideratum for the MAS approach. When applying the Bourdieusian concept of habitus, mating preferences cannot only be thought of as dependent on one another, but also – to a crucial extent – on the social space. This is to say that one can expect that the different preferential systems, as elaborated in the last section, will vary according to the social space. Taking preferences for age as an example, it has been shown that these preferences vary according to market position, measured by market-relevant traits such as education. In this section, Bourdieu's fundamentally relational approach – in which the differing "spaces defined by preferences" (Bourdieu 1984: 208) are defined according to their common structure, that is, the amount and structure of the forms of capital involved – will be implemented for further investigation.

Let us examine the dispositional classes which were synthesized in the previous section from different relationship preferences, and proceed to apply them to the model of social space as constructed in the previous chapter. The latent classes are projected into this space passively, which results in their average positions without an impact of the original structuration of the geometric space (see Figure 7.6).

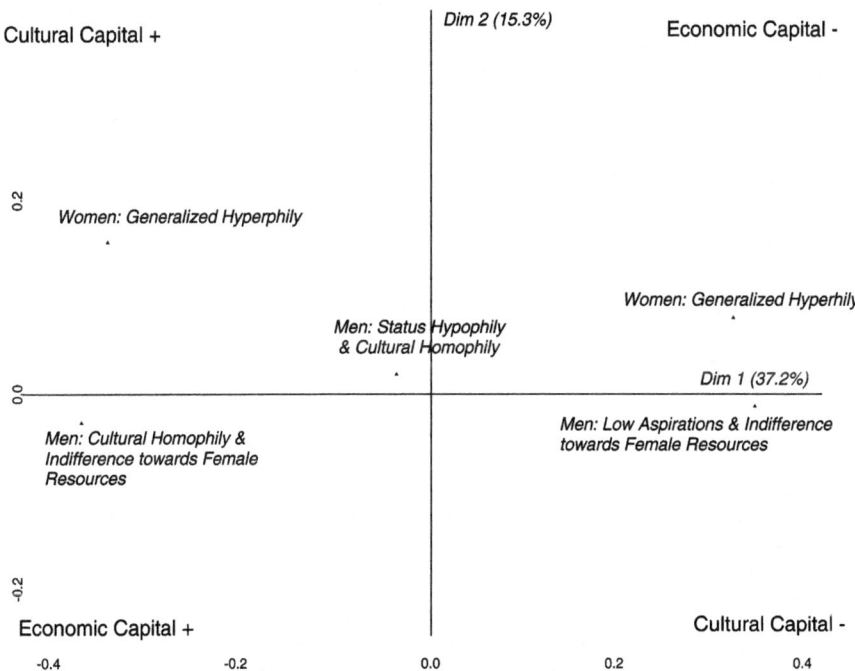

Fig. 7.6 Classes of mating dispositions within the social space (*Source*: own illustration. Calculations are based on the survey and observation data from a German online dating website, 2009. N = 756.)

The results are as follows: the latent dispositional classes ascertained in the previous section vary considerably in their positions in the social space representation of the dating platform's market structure (a complete independence of the dispositional classes and their spatial location would result in the accumulation of all classes at the intersection of the axes). It can thus be seen that systems of mating preferences vary *non-coincidentally* with the users being investigated. The empirical pattern is in line with Bourdieu's concept of habitus: latent *Class 1*, the class of men with high lifestyle aspirations and a particular indifference towards other female mating traits (except for youth and looks) can be located in an advantageous position of high capital volume, and of high cultural capital in particularly. Apparently, their upper-class habitus, which is characterized by a generally 'disinterested interest', manifests here in the form of little interest in a female partner's control over societally-rewarded resources (income, status, etc.). This interest is empirically accompanied by a particularly strong lifestyle homophily, a fact which tends to conceal the underlying objective implications – namely that men in this group are nevertheless more likely to form a relationship with a female partner of the same social class (given their youth and attractiveness).

Female *Class 2* can be located on the right-hand side of the social space illustration, as those users possess little economic and cultural capital. Their habitus is evidently characterized by a disposition towards higher male status: women in this preferential class systematically prefer men with higher status with regard to income, age, education, and occupation. Homophilous tendencies are, in this female class, consistently insignificant. The relational mating preferences of the habitus of the female Class 2 point to a strong dispositional *hyperphily*. Thus, these women can be characterized by a systematic hyperphily, which indicates that they might see the (digital) partner market as a means of social advancement.

Male *Class 3* can be located in the middle of the social space, indicating an average capital endowment. Their preference system can be characterized by systematic economic hypophily and cultural homophily, which points to the presence of traditional gender roles in their habitus.

Members of male Class 4 possess little economic and cultural capital, and a low total capital volume. Due to their consistently undemanding preferences and their general indifference, their habitus can be interpreted, in the context of mate choice, as a romantic "taste of necessity" (Bourdieu 1984: 6): apart from a preference for female youth and a low level of educational homophily (which actually means here that a potential female partner should not be better educated than themselves), men in this class seem simply to be satisfied with those women who are available. Men of this social class seem to have internalized their offline chance structure and are thoroughly satisfied if they can realize any partnership with a younger woman who does not have a higher social status than themselves. Obviously, lower-class men seem to be prone to becoming the disadvantaged participants of the partner market, not only because they can hardly meet the relationship demands of women with similar backgrounds. The restricted conditions of existence and the backgrounds of these users – that is, their social class – manifest themselves in regard to relationship dispositions; they are affected by necessities in the same way as they are on other markets. Nevertheless, as Figure 7.4 reveals, this position is also associated with high subjectively-assumed chances of finding a partner online, a pattern which could be interpreted as a manifestation of a frictional relation between habitus and market: these users may believe in the applicability of advertisements claiming that everyone has a chance, thus mistaking the market for a sphere of equal opportunities, and themselves for the 'average user' able to take advantage of them.

Class 5, consisting of women with especially demanding mating preferences, is located in an advantageous socio-spatial position in the space. These women, who possess high cultural capital, but also high overall capital, display even higher standards regarding potential partners than women from Class 2. This may seem surprising from the perspective of economic exchange: even if they themselves have a strong set of resources, women in this class desire partners with superior symbolic and material resources in the key social values. From a Bourdieusian perspective, this strong tendency for hyperphily can be thought of as a female disposition for submissiveness: only in culturally legitimate symbolic subordination can this female habitus realize its suitable societal status. The highly demanding nature of these preferences actually represents a disposition for submissiveness, and hence a manifestation of male domination within women's dispositions. In general, men consistently show mating dispositions for female youth and beauty, as biological and psychological research has frequently substantiated. It should be also taken into account, however, that the male interest in female youth is accompanied by the desire for women with explicitly lower status (Class 3) or at least indifference (Class 1), which amounts to an implicit devaluation of female economic capital. In sum, combined with the female habitus' disposition for higher status in their male partners, the partner market brings agents together whose various forms of dispositions and emanating practices reproduce societal male dominance and women's objectified status.

This analysis undermines empirically the central arguments for a relational expansion of the individualist notion of mating preferences: the dispositional character of relationship preferences precipitates in the systematic interrelation with and correspondence to the social space. Also, mating dispositions were shown to depend on the general relational position of the actors on the partner market. The relational mating perspective leads us to expect that the conditions which form the system of relationship preferences are not merely a function of the structural logic of the theoretical construct 'partner market': the different systems of mating dispositions, as well as their relations to actors' objective position in the market, are the result of socialization processes, which essentially take place before they enter the (digital) partner market, as argued in Chapter 5. In the following section, we will assess how users from different social classes reproduce the socio-spatial conditions in their practice of using the digital partner market.

The (Dis-) Positional Character of Rationalities in Mating

In the next section, the issue of rationality and strategies in mating-related agency will be assessed using the example of deceptive practices in online dating. The realm of deception and trust represents one of the core issues in current research on online dating and online interaction in general. Again, the relational position of the user will be utilized for an explanatory model of deception. Using latent class regression models, it will be demonstrated that the position in the social space affects not only the quality and quantity of deceptive practices, but also corresponds to different causally adequate rationalities involved in deceptive practices. Thus, the example emphasizes the fact that rationality (in mating) can be understood more as a function of the user's position in the social space than a general principle of (mate) choice.

Deceptive Practices and Market Position

In this section, the issue of rationality and strategies in mating-related agency will be assessed using the example of deceptive practices in online dating. The realm of deception and trust represents one of the core issues in current research on online dating and online interaction in general. Many authors emphasize psychological traits or the nature of online dating as key mechanisms in deceptive practices (see e.g. Hall et al. 2010; Phillips et al. 2011).

Zillmann et al. (2011) apply a relational perspective in order to assess deceptive practices as a function of the partner market rather than as an outcome of psychological traits. This emphasis on the relational market position of the users, within the market's rules and norms, represents a transformation of the fundamentally individualistic approach, inasmuch as deceptive practices are not ascribed primarily to the individual or psychological characteristics of the users, but to the user's market position. The overall situation on the digital partner market is characterized by a high level of competition for chances for attention and contact: all actors are required to present themselves as attractive and interesting as possible, in order to be contacted by other actors or to receive a reply to their own contacts. Those actors, however, who are endowed with relatively poor market-relevant resources are the ones most likely to resort to strategies of deception to increase their chances for attention and contacts. The theoretical discussion of partner market's conventions regarding the acceptable quantity and quality of untruthfulness led Zillmann et al. (2011) to postulate two rational strategies of compensation. In the assumption that actors are aware of the conventions in force on the partner market, it would seem to be a natural strategy only to deceive to a conventionally acceptable degree, i.e., to a limited extent in various characteristics, and never to stray too far from the truth regarding one particular attribute. Apart from the obvious effect of specific deception in a trait where a user sees himself or herself as less than optimal, a hypothesis of non-specific compensation practices was also derived. As the average user can only legitimately compensate his or her specific weaknesses to a certain degree, users are systematically motivated to further enhance their potential for attention and subsequent exchange in this highly competitive environment by optimizing multiple profile attributes.

Using data from the online survey discussed earlier, Zillmann et al. (2011) analyze whether patterns of misrepresentation in users' profiles can be detected, and which of the actors' characteristics influence the observable patterns of reported untruthfulness. Categorical regression models show that men with a low educational status have the highest probability – compared to men with intermediate or high levels of education – of making dishonest statements regarding their educational status. For women, in contrast, the effect was u-shaped: both women with low educational status and women with high educational status are more likely than women with an intermediate educational status to describe their educational status untruthfully (see also Zillmann 2016).

Also, with increasing weight, both men and women exhibit an increasing likelihood of being dishonest regarding their weight, and the taller a man is, the less likely he is to lie about his height in his user profile. The analyses also support the hypothesis of unspecific compensation. For education, it seems that men with low educational status, when compared to men with intermediate and high status, have a greater tendency to be untruthful with respect to their weight. The effect of education is reversed for women; highly educated women have a higher probability of lying about their weight, compared to women with intermediate and low educational status, and keeping weight constant. Furthermore, men with low educational status have, compared to men in the intermediate and high status groups, an increased tendency to lie about their height. The study shows that whereas men attempt to compensate for disadvantageous educational status with their height and age, women use physical attractiveness as a counterweight for perceived or actual weaknesses in their educational status.

This explanatory model, which in principle could also be applied to offline processes, was promising for the context of the virtual partner market. As argued before there is (a) an unusually high level of competition for attention, (b) deception is considered a common practice, (c) users are required to avoid competitive disadvantages, and (d) the assumption prevails that the technical and social situation of online dating induces a particular kind of rational disposition, including the need for reflection upon one's mate value and prospects for success. The assumption is that typical users consciously attempt to increase their attention potential, calculating their exchange potential dependent on their subjectively perceived partner market value. The lower the perceived chances for exchange as a function of one's perceived set of resources, the greater the probability that the user will engage in deception, both regarding the 'defective' attribute itself and regarding other characteristics. The foundation of this calculation, at least according to this model, is the subjective comparison of one's own set of resources with anticipated expectations on the partner market, taking the normative limits of legitimate deception into account, as well as the trade-off between utility and success probabilities.

The analysis assumes that users reflect upon their reflection of chances for attention and exchange – following the Weberian definition of market value as outlined in Chapter 3 – taking this assumption the basis for a general logic underlying practices of deception. Although a relational market perspective is utilized, the approach applied so far assumes an average actor and a universal logic of practice. This inflexible assumption can fundamentally be relativized with recourse to the concept of habitus.

An OLS Regression of Deceptive Practices

Using the example of deceptive practices, we will empirically examine the plausibility of a model of one universal logic of practice. Although every interpretation of statistical models is restricted, in that we do not know the actual subjective intentions of the actors involved, a generalizing average actor-model seems even more restricted, as the scope for possible subjective dimensions is especially limited here. If, for example, we observe that many users tend to select profiles according to a particular trait (such as age), it is not possible to establish that the same subjective logics are involved (see also Chapter 4). The same applies to the realm of deceptive practices in online dating. The empirical analysis will proceed in two steps. First, a traditional regression model of all stated deceptions will be discussed. In the next step, a latent class regression model (Vermunt and van Dijk 2001) will be applied to the data in order to identify the potentially different types of rationality underlying practices of deception.

Using the same data which formed the basis for the analysis of Zillmann et al. (2011), the logarithmized number of every surveyed characteristic where deception was recorded and modeled will be used as dependent variable in OLS regression model. For this purpose, the following indicators will be analyzed, by way of counting when users admitted to employing deceptive practices: education, age, occupational status, income, (authentic) profile picture, and gender. Gender, body mass index, education (ordinally scaled), age, and interaction terms are used as independent variables in the model. Table 7.3 reports the results of the model, showing that the effects essentially correspond to the results of Zillmann et al. (2011): women report that they deceive less often than men; education is weakly associated with deception, especially for men; age correlates negatively with deception for both sexes, but it shows a curvilinear increase, which indicates a slight increase of deception from a certain age. Accordingly, this model, where various profile attributes potentially subject to deception are assessed, also conforms to the interpretation presented before (or is "causally adequate" (Weber 1978: 11)).

Table 7.3 OLS – model with logarithmized count of deceptive practices

	b	sig.
Sex (Male=0)	−1.28	***
BMI	−0.05	***
Education (ord.)	−0.29	***
Age	−0.03	**
BMI*Sex	0.03	**
Education*Sex	0.14	**
Age*Sex	0.00	*
Age (sq.)	0.01	**
Intercept	3.38	***

Source: Online survey of users of a large German online dating portal; N=2113; own calculations

In the next step, model 2 additionally includes the subjectively perceived potential for attention on the dating site, and the subjectively perceived potential for finding a partner in general, in order to test the interpretation that subjective calculations underlie the deceptive practices of the actors directly. Both variables are Likert-scaled from 1 to 5. The expectation which can be deduced from the aforementioned generalized assumption of rationality is that, with increasing potential for attention and exchange, the number of deceptive practices should diminish. The effects of the market value indicators should also diminish in explanatory significance, if not disappear entirely, as the market position effect was conceptualized as taking effect by way of subjective perception and reflection.

Table 7.4 OLS – model with logarithmized count of deceptions incl. subjective chances

	b	sig.
Subjective chances for		
Attention (online)	−0.03	–
Exchange (long-term)	0.14	***
Resources		
Sex (Male=0)	−1.22	***
BMI	−0.05	**
Education(ord.)	−0.24	***
Age	−0.03	**
BMI*Sex	0.02	**
Education*Sex	0.12	**
Age*Sex	0.00	*
Age (squared)	0.00	**
Intercept	3.24	***

Source: Online survey of users of a large German online dating portal; N=2113; own calculations

However, the empirical effects of model 2 question this assumption (see Table 7.4): (a) with an increase in subjectively perceived potential for exchange, the average number of deceptions actually *increases*; (b) subjective potential for attention online has *no independent effect beyond* the subjectively perceived potential for general exchange chances (i.e. finding a mate); (c) indicators of market value continue to function as strong predictors of dependent variables, *despite* the control of the central assumed theoretical mechanism.[3] Overall, this finding challenges our previous conceptualization of deception as a function of the anticipated relation between chances for (online) attention and (long-term) success.

A Latent Class Regression Model of Mate Value and Deceptive Practices

Using the example of deception, the question assessed now is whether a reflective rationality can be seen as being universally induced by the special conditions of online dating, or whether individual users' rationalities can be better understood as working differently. From a habitus perspective, the specific question is as to whether there are different rationalities at work behind practices of deception, or whether partner market participants act in the same reflective, utility-maximizing way. To analyze this problem in a meaning-adequate way (Weber 1978: 12), the most appropriate method would involve a qualitative reconstruction of the user's perceptions; however, the alternative presented in the following section again uses the survey data analyzed above. Although no differentiated qualitative data was recorded for the assessment of this problem, this quantitative framework at least enables a corroboration of the idea of the 'differential logics' underlying deceptive practices. This operation can thus show that more potential causally adequate interpretations than only one single universal rationality can be assumed. To approach the question of the differential logics of practice upon which deception on the digital partner market might be based, we will again present an integration of the two empirical modeling traditions of finite mixture classification and geometric data analysis. In the first step, the relation between subjective potential for attention and exchange on the one hand and deceptive practices on the other hand will be statistically classified. The intention is to investigate whether the assumption of an average actor is empirically valid or whether an empirical typology of multiple causally adequate patterns of rationality can be identified within the sample. In the second step, it will be examined whether and to what extent these classes of subjective relations of chances and practice empirically correspond to the social space as previously constructed.

---

[3] This result is extremely stable, appearing both in models of the probability of individual profile deception and in models with several traits. This effect did not disappear when the influence of resources on self-perceived market value was specified using a structural equation model approach, nor did it disappear when the survey drop-out mechanism was modelled with Heckman correction models. Zillmann et al. 2013 present a description of the selective survey participation of the particular data.

To answer the first question, the dependent variable – the logarithmized number of deceptions – will be analyzed again using OLS regression, albeit only using the two variables of subjective perception (the subjective assessment of potential for attention online and the subjective assessment of general romantic exchange chances) as independent predictors. However, a statistical differentiation of this regression model is conducted based on the *parameters of these two independent variables*; this means that the analysis is actually examining whether empirically different types of statistical associations between deceptive practices on the one hand, and chances for attention and exchange on the other, can be identified. This procedure of latent class regression (Vermunt and van Dijk 2001) can be thought of as a non-parametric random effect model, thus conforming to the multilevel and parametric random effect models so prevalent in current social science research, albeit without the assumption of a continuous, normally distributed random effect parameter. Just as in conventional finite mixture modeling, this process identifies a statistical optimum of latent classes of regression associations.

Table 7.5 yields the results of the non-parametric latent class regression model. The optimal solution here is three classes, and this 3-class pattern was remarkably robust over a range of different models. The first substantive insight is that the relation between deceptive practices and subjective potential chances *cannot* be generalized for all users, as not one but three classes are identified. Class 1, with 32 % of all users, represents a type where neither subjective chances for attention online nor subjective chances for exchange in general affect the extent of deceptive practices. Class 2, comprising 41 % of all users, conforms more to the rationality mode assumed by Zillmann et al. (2011): users in this class tend to reduce their deceptive practices with increasing perceived potential for attention online. However, Class 2 also *increases* deceptive practices with increasing general exchange chances. Class 3 (26.80 %), in contrast, increases deceptive practices as a function of both perceived potential for attention and exchange. Furthermore, the respective intercepts indicate that Class 2 shows the highest base level of deception, Class 3 the lowest, and Class 1 a medium base level.

Table 7.5 Latent class regression of deception as function of subjective chances

	Class 1 (32.03%)	z	Class 2 (41.17%)	z	Class 3 (26.80%)	z	Wald
Subjective chances for							
Attention (online)	0.0005	0.37	−0.1295	−2.56	0.92	16,4888	273,6951
Exchange (longterm)	−0.001	−0.65	0.1651	3.15	1.00	20,682	434,0551
Intercept	−0.007	−5.21	1.2493	24.26	−0.27	−11,1127	847,6516

Source: Online survey of users of a large German online dating portal; N = 2113; own calculations

Accordingly, assuming a generalized rationality underlying deception is not causally adequate for all interviewees. Although no meaning-adequate insights can be derived from this, or indeed any quantitative model, an interpretation of the possible meaning underlying these patterns shall be proposed: Class 1 does not show any particular reflective relation between its own perceived mate value and deceptive practices; members of this class do not seem to ask themselves the question as to the relation between potential for attention and potential for exchange. What could expected to be the logic of all users, from a generalizing point of view, can actually be found for Class 2. This class reduces deceptive practices as a result of attention received online, whereas the stated confidence in generally finding a partner encourages deceptive practices independent of subjectively assessed chances for attention. Class 3 also tends to engage in a great deal of deceptive practices if the potential for finding a partner is low. However, high levels of attention do not lead to these users refraining from deception but, conversely, to even more intensive deceptive practices. One possible interpretation here is that the effect of long-term exchange chances operates in the same way as in Class 2, while the effect of potential for attention is different. Perhaps an actual attention event does not represent enough of a 'safe chance' for the initiation of a relationship for these users, and instead requires further deceptive self-presentation to maintain an initial contact beyond the early stages of merely being perceived by a potential partner.

Up to this point, a classificatory modeling of the systematic difference in the relation between subjective potential and deceptive practice has been introduced, which means that the model of rationality assumed by Zillmann et al. (2011) can be differentiated by taking into account the fact that different rationalities underlie deceptive practices. We shall now proceed to relate these classes of rationality to the social space as constructed before.

Rationality Types Within the Social Space

The next question will be whether the empirical typology of rationalities as identified before can also be thought of – as one might expect from a Bourdieusian perspective – as a function of the social space, or if the empirical relationship between rationality type and position in the social space is unsystematic. This would result in an empirical concentration of the classes at the *origo* of the diagram. For this purpose, the three statistically identified probability types of causally adequate rationalities will be differentiated by gender and then passively projected onto the social space as described above. The projection clearly shows that the gender-specific 'subjective chance – deceptive practice' relations, or causally adequate rationality types, are by no means independent from the social space (see Fig. 7.7).

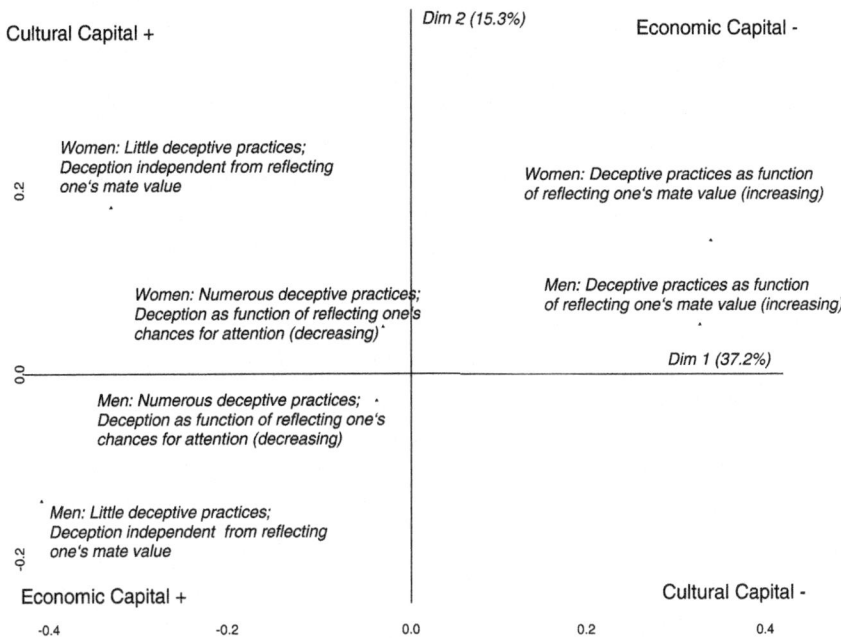

Fig. 7.7 Passive projection of rationality-deception types and illustrative variables (*Source*: own illustration. Calculations are based on the survey and observation data from a German online dating website, 2009. N = 765)

Clearly, men and women with an advantageous chance structure in the sense of capital volume tend to belong to rationality Class 1. Class 2 is empirically associated with an average position in the social space, whereas Class 3 displays a disadvantageous position in the space. From a habitus perspective, the finding of socially variable rationality is unsurprising: Class 1 is unlikely to show a reflexive approach to deception, simply because it is neither necessary nor expedient for these users to behave strategically in a rationalist sense. These users already have greater than average potential for success on the partner market and will find it less necessary than other users to contemplate their specific market situation. Apart from the advantage of a high mate value, they also have "the easy relation of those who are in their element, who have the laws of the market on their side" (Bourdieu 1993: 85). In this context of self-presentation in online dating, one is reminded of Bourdieu's description of the *upper classes*' talents for "casualness, grace, facility, elegance, freedom, in a word, naturalness" (Bourdieu 1984: 339). This casualness is apparent in the way that, among other things, users belonging to this class consider their own potential to be merely 'average', a fine example of understatement. The habitus of privileged men and women can be characterized via an 'objective utility' – not just in mating – which seems to manifest itself in everyday interaction as informality and not in form of subjectively expected utilities. However, this class's practice of self-presentation certainly implies, quantitatively, a level of deception as an element of their habitual self-presentation, albeit more as an almost involuntary matter of course than as the result of particular strategic calculation. This shows that the most privileged members of a particular society cannot be described according to a subjective instrumental rationality in dealing with the issue of deceptive self-presentation. They are, in contrast, characterized by a relative absence of subjective rationality, a disposition which ensures the objective rationality for these users.

The particular rationality characteristic for users of Class 2 can also be explained with recourse to habitus: users in this class are located in a middle position of the social space, thus literally representing the middle class in the broadest sense. Bourdieu sees their position as being "characterized above all by opportunities for social advancement – opportunities which may be small objectively, but which can be magnified and indeed realized by an absolute desire for advancement" (Krais and Gebauer 2002: 45, o.t.). The "pretentious" taste of the middle class is impelled to overcome "reality" by "appearance" and "bluff", and especially "middle-class men are obsessed with both the Goffmanesque question of the best theatrical presentation and with the effort to compensate for their lack of economic capital and connection to the world of legitimate culture by means of an ascetic rigidity and assiduity" (Joppke 1986: 70). According to Bourdieu, a considerable part of the middle class is practically predisposed to develop a disposition towards the world which largely corresponds to the idea of a rationally and reflectively choosing actor. On the digital partner market, too, the assumption of a reflective approach to personal potential for attention and to utility-maximizing logic as the driving force behind deceptive practices seems to be causally adequate for this habitus. The regression parameters give the impression of a particular form of calculation – one which lets actors engage in 'safe' deception up to a certain point and then leads them to reduce the deception strategically after an actual attention event occurs. This also explains the fact that there is a higher number of actually realized dates in this segment: the habitus of this class of users seems to move them to consider – in much the same way that voices from critical sociology assume to be the case for all users – the principal problem of online dating to be the maximization of utility in the search for a partner. One might say that the 'locus of instrumental rationality' underlying acts of deception can be shown to be the central position of the mating market and the social space. The fact that users in the central section of the social space actually consider their potential to be relatively low also supports this theory: the competitiveness of the online dating market seems to be felt particularly acutely by these user, just as competitiveness can be seen as a characteristic of middle class culture.

Class 3 users are more likely to deceive the greater their potential for attention and exchange is; this highlights the specific situation of users from the lower classes in which attention does not correspond to a potential relationship, but instead involves further deception so as not to lose the attention of the potential partner in question. Remarkably, however, the users in this class, males in particular, dramatically overestimate their potential for finding a mate. Their position in the space shows that their subjectively perceived probabilities of realizing a relationship are grossly overestimated – in fact they have the worst chances of all users, a fact which manifests itself in the disadvantageous Eigen-Value centrality and the low number of actual offline dates. Whereas the habitus of the middle classes is broadly compatible with the specific situation of online dating, for Class 3 users, the situations generated by the digital partner market seem to result in habitus friction, and corresponding unrewarding practices, which result from the incongruence of the objective situation and their internalized dispositions.

Although conducted on a quantitative basis, this empirical example challenges the attempt to generalize any (bounded) rationality as being the universal principle of deceptive practices on the partner market. Applying a differentiated view to the data, it cannot be inferred that each analytically-defined market participant in a situation of mate choice genuinely and subjectively orientates his agency in the same manner towards a future 'romantic' outcome.

In contrast to the picture of online dating as implying a specific logic of (hyper-rationally) choosing a potential partner (cp. Žižek 2010; Illouz 2007; Whitty 2008), no general logic of deception (as a result of the medium itself) which appears equally relevant for all users (cp. Hancock et al. 2007; Toma et al. 2008; Toma and Hancock 2010) can be claimed. Practices of deception, which are often analyzed as formally similar and comparable, must rather be interpreted as differing in the form and content of their respective rationalities. By pretending to possess more symbolic capital than is in fact the case, agents may try to achieve an advantage in the highly competitive market. However, this must not be understood as the result of a universal instrumental rationality, and of an "action being the product of a calculation of chances and profits" (Bourdieu 2000: 138) – supposedly universally induced by the digital partner market – but rather as a systematic emanation of habitus-based practice. Some users may assess their chances very much in line with the individualistic model, whereas others follow an opposing logic, and some do not evaluate their own chances on the partner market at all in the context of deceptive practices. Evidently, for certain locations in the social space, the assumptions of MAS seem to be more valid than for other positions. As argued before, online daters act according to different situational logics, which can be defined by their external market position, as well as by internalized conceptions of themselves, potential partners, and the market's principles. Thus, users may 'solve' different problems in contacting potential partners, problems which are always dependent on the users' particular life courses, which structure their perception and self-perception.

After having demonstrated the (dis)positional nature of mating preferences, and the dubiousness of assuming a universally prevailing rationality – even on the rationality-inducing digital partner market – in the next section, another step is made towards a Bourdieusian sociology of couple formation. If mating preferences and rationalities are indeed best described as relational systems dependent on structural conditions prior to the dating market, the user's interactions can be also expected to exhibit a structural logic, as they are constituted by the encounter of agents and their habitus being structured in every respect. We can therefore expect that reciprocal classification processes (see Chapter 5) will manifest in various constellations, rather than in one or two typical modes.

Structured Reciprocal Classification in Mating Interactions

In the previous analyses, we corroborated the theoretical idea that mating chances, mating preferences, and mating rationalities can be understood as being genuinely structured and as structuring the online dating market. We shall now discuss the issue of the structural dimension of mating interactions. Theoretically, online dating data allows partner market research to observe interactions, and thus to assess which principles underlie dyadic constellations. However, both traditional mate choice research and social space theory tend to under-conceptualize the variability of mating interactions. The choice perspective has difficulties abstracting from the average actor and average actor relations, and thus in conceptualizing systematically different resource relations. As a consequence, and due to the transfer of monadic statistical models to a situation of dyadic interactions, the observation of interaction data is often interpreted under the assumption of general underlying logics, such as the logics of exchange. Habitus theory overemphasizes the impact of the social space on the process and outcome of interactions, and thus (inter)-subjective variations and processes in mating. This is related to its specific statistical approach, which usually constructs the social space as a space of agents and not as a space of interactions. In this chapter, the concept of mating as reciprocal classification practices – as motivated in Chapter 5 – will be mobilized in order to reveal the structural variations which underlie the exchange of messages on a dating site. A finite mixture model of dyadic classification, as proposed in the chapter on methodology, will be applied to the first, sixth, and last observed contacts. It will be shown that different dyadic constellations emerge in the process of reciprocal classification online. Given these findings, we reject the idea that any generalized logic in mating interactions (such as educational homophily, lifestyle affinity, exchange, or utility maximization) can be understood as the one single meta-principle of interaction in mating.

Lifestyle Homogeneity as a Process

Viewing "acts of co-option" (Bourdieu 1984: 241) primarily from a perspective of dispositions for lifestyle similarity, Bourdieu was not particularly interested in the processual and intersubjective character of mating, or the gender-specific resources taking effect in form of reciprocal evaluation and rating practices. Hence, a superficial reception of Bourdieu's work might suggest a quasi-deterministic model of mating (cp. Schmitz 2012). One may conclude that, similar to the process of selecting a cultural commodity, men (or women) choose women (or men) with similar positions and lifestyles in the social space (Nagel et al. 2011). The result of such an oversimplified process or 'mode 1' interaction (cp. Chapter 5) would be nothing but *ab ovo* homogeneous couple configurations – that is, exclusively dyads comprising agents with the same lifestyle. The following analysis will illustrate the limitations of this view. First, and following the orthodox interpretation of Bourdieu (Schütze 2008; Streib 2015: 20), dyadic lifestyle similarity will be analyzed by deriving the average correlation between the cultural capital of sender and receiver for each contact event. Figure 7.8 shows the average correlations of the cultural capital of sender and receiver of a message for each contact event, from the first observed contact to the last observed contact. Obviously, lifestyle appears as a strong sorting mechanism, as the average correlation moves from a near zero correlation at the first observed contact to a correlation of .4 at the 22th interaction event.

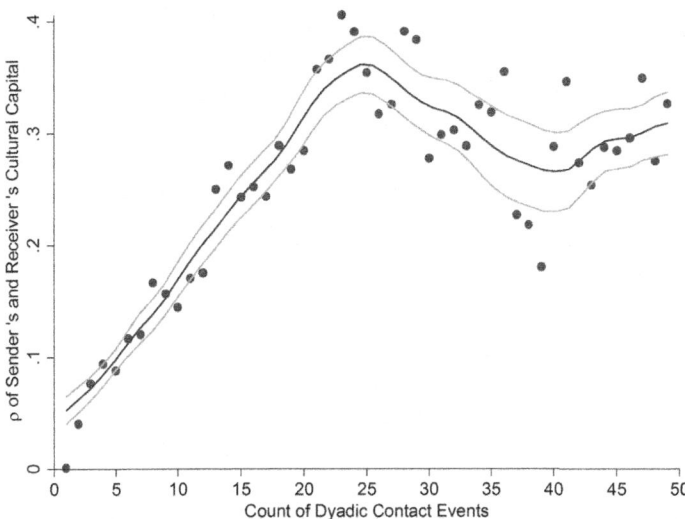

Fig. 7.8 Correlation between sender's and receiver's cultural capital (n=21,048 (Initiated Dyads). A *dot* indicates the correlation coefficient ρ for the particular interaction length (1–50). Example: the correlation of sender's and receiver's cultural capital is approximately zero for first contact events and approximately 0.4 for 22nd events. The *black line* represents a local polynomial smoothing plot. The *gray lines* indicate the confidence intervals (Quoted from Schmitz 2012))

However, the relation between the sender's and the receiver's cultural capital is far from deterministic, even at the peak of the interactional chains: only 16% ($r=0.4$) of the variance of the receiver's cultural capital can be explained by the sender's cultural capital. Hence, there is still considerable variance between the cultural capital of two interacting users. Furthermore, the average inclination of correlations says nothing about the reciprocal dimension of the process. For example, it is sufficient if one actor in a dyad has a disposition for lifestyle similarity to explain the emerging pattern. Another mechanism to be taken into account is the fact that lifestyle similarity may be a by-product of other preferences (as argued in Chapters 4 and 5). Finally, there is considerable leeway for heterophily, and the question is whether there are further mechanisms and logics implied (such as relations of dominance, manifest exchange, latent equivalency, etc.) that may contribute to generating couple configurations.

A Dyadic Finite Mixture Model of First and Last Observed Contacts

As argued in Chapter 5, the concepts of social space and habitus allow us to specify the logic of a mating situation as being the interplay of two (or more) agents' habitus with one another, and thus as confrontations of structured positions and dispositions. The conceptualization of mating as reciprocal classification processes analytically incorporates different inter-subjective principles, such as lifestyle similarity preferences, (gender-specific) heterophilious dispositions, and relational equivalency preferences. These principles are understood as (conscious, unconscious, partially conscious, etc.) reciprocal orientations relevant in particular dyadic constellations.

Regarding objective capital endowment as associated with the agent's habitus, processes of reciprocal classification can be understood as comprising different classes of manifest similarities and dissimilarities between two interacting agents. In Chapter 5, the question of 'who chooses whom' was reformulated to the question: how do classified agents classify themselves and each other into classes of agents? This consideration motivated the dissection of the aggregated interaction process into different empirical dyadic configurations using a dyadic, rather than monadic, statistical technique. In Chapter 6, we proposed modeling agent configurations, applying the statistical dependency of the agents involved, with a finite mixture model (Vermunt and Magidson 2003) in order to identify typical dyadic association patterns. Within this approach, the statistical identification of typically occurring dyads is effected by means of the manifest (dis)similarity in characteristics between the interacting users. In this way, the way in which the process of classification works in the agents' practice can be generalized for an understanding of how reciprocal classification works: similar to the way Bourdieu's concept of class condenses agents into fuzzy groups which are defined by probabilities, interactions can be reduced to a finite number of classes of probability. Consequently, it is not classes of individual users which are to be statistically identified, but classes of dyads.

A first analysis was conducted by Schmitz (2012), who used records of interaction events and integrated profile information following the theoretical extension of mating as classificatory mechanism of classified agents and the statistical model of dyadic class analysis. For this purpose, each profile characteristic was used once for each dyad member and an optimum of categorical latent classes was identified. In doing so, the potential for observing and modeling the statistical dependencies between the users interacting on the platform was utilized, rather than treating statistical interdependencies between sender and receiver as a nuisance. The analysis was restricted to the profile characteristics sex, age, education, and lifestyle of the interacting users, and to the first and the last recorded contact.

From a simplified Bourdieusian perspective of homophily, one could expect that the only dyads to emerge in such a model will be homogeneous with regard to the variables used, i.e. that a variable value (e.g. a certain lifestyle) of the sender determines the same variable value of the receiver of a contact. If this was the predominant pattern, the analysis would lead to a class of homogeneous dyads (a class with lifestyle A of sender and receiver, a class with lifestyle B of sender and receiver etc.). This was labeled 'mode 1 process' in Chapter 5. Another expectation may be that all possible dyadic configurations, and no classes, emerge – meaning that the sender's characteristics do not determine what kind of receiver he or she contacts. If we were to observe this, neither the homophily model, nor an equivalency or exchange model, nor relations of submission and domination, or any other logics could be derived from dyadic class analysis.

However, Schmitz (2012) shows that the users create several classes of interaction which are multi-faceted in the first contacts, but which (a) reduce in number and (b) become increasingly distinct and stable up to the last observed interaction event. Within this process of *cumulative decomposition*, the structure of the dyadic classes showed that no one single mating trait (such as age, education, or lifestyle, etc.) was uniformly preferred by an 'average user' in the moment of first contact. On the contrary: as all modeled variables showed a strong covariance with regard to their systematic intersections in different agents (and their classes), reciprocal classification practices generated multi-dimensionally structured dyadic classes.

For example, it was shown that the very significance of lifestyle itself varies according to age and sex. Older women seemed to be more discriminating regarding the lifestyle and education of a potential partner, right from the outset. Thus, a stable dyadic class with older, well-educated, and demanding women with considerable cultural capital and men representing the symbolic goods of the upper class was identified. Younger women of the sample, by contrast, were characterized by a preference for manifest similarities, and also by the fact that they remain in relatively stable dyadic classes with more highly educated men with high cultural capital. The analysis also showed that the various reciprocal classification processes impact on the relative value of the symbolic goods, as well as on the men and women presenting them in their profiles. For example, less well-educated men are rated down on the dating market, but less-educated women are not.

A Dyadic Finite Mixture Model of 6th Contacts

The intention of the following section is to further illustrate the scope of structure within reciprocal classification processes. Whereas in the model put forward in Schmitz (2012), first contact events and last observed contacts were compared, this section addresses dyadic classification in more detail. For this purpose, data containing sixth contacts – that is, a dyadic interaction length of six – will be analyzed.[4] This enables an emphasis on the different empirical constellations which 'survived' the early stages of contacting and answering, but for which the relationship had usually not yet been transferred to email or telephone. Again, the statistical model applied is the dyadic class finite mixture model. The variables used are gender, age, body mass index, high school diploma, qualification, job position, and cultural capital (as measured by a dimension of lifestyle practices yielded by correspondence analysis).[5] Furthermore, several indicators were derived from the process-generated data itself: distance in kilometers between two users, the length of the interaction chain (number of exchanged messages), number of parallel interactions,[6] length of time on the dating platform,[7] desired relationship status, and mate value (derived from the network indicator as described in this chapter).

Whereas an approach involving testing hypotheses is indeed possible (for example by restricting the parameters of the model in a certain way), we do not want to test hypotheses regarding the emergence of couple constellations here. Rather, this analysis of dyadic classes shall further illustrate the manifold manifestations of structure within different reciprocal classification practices. The resulting dyadic classification model of sixth contacts yields an optimum of eight classes, according to the lowest classification error.[8] Table A.1 (Appendix) reports the profiles parameters for the dyadic classes.

Dyadic Class 1 (21.02%) is characterized by considerable differences between the sender and receiver of the particular contact event. The male initiator of the sixth interaction event has a lower educational level and occupational qualifications than the female receiver (e.g. male vocational apprenticeship compared to female university degree). Men of this class also possess a low educational level and low qualifications overall. The sender and receiver of this dyadic class differ according to age (men are on average 34, and thus 7 years older than women of this dyadic class), BMI (women have a 'more favorable' figure), cultural capital (female capital being higher than male), and chance structure (female mating chances being exceptionally high and male chances being exceptionally low). The average number of subsequent interactions is 0.4, meaning that the average dyadic constellation of this class ends after less than one additional contact.[9] This 'moribund' dyadic class is particularly

---

[4] The average dyadic length is 1.9, with a standard deviation of 2.2.

[5] Although formal education is an emanation of cultural capital in the Bourdieusian sense, this analysis focuses on the question of whether cultural capital, as measured via lifestyle differences, shows a pattern independent from formal education.

[6] This was measured as interactions with more than one user in a day. This variable is only used for one actor per dyad as it determined the variable value of the dyadic partner in all models.

[7] However, this is not necessarily a sign of long-term stabilization, but may just as well represent a sign of insufficient motivation to change the communication medium (email, telephone etc.).

[8] A solution with more classes represents better fits, but the size of the resulting classes is negligible both empirically and substantively.

[9] Alternatively – and this is less plausible given the findings of the previous analysis, which showed that women consistently 'disprefer' men with lower status than themselves – the interaction is transferred to email, telephone, or even face-to-face meetings.

remarkable as it is the quantitatively largest class, even though five interaction events have already taken place. Apparently, and as discussed in Chapter 5, the mere dissimilarity of two users is not sufficient for an immediate contact termination, as the interacting parties still need to recognize and act upon this (habitus) dissimilarity during the process of communication (or the disutility of continuation, as others would put it).

Dyadic Class 2 (16.25%) shows another pattern; this constellation consists of female users with an average age of 44 and male users with an average age of 47, with a striking similarity in their (comparably high) education and qualifications. Additionally, the cultural capital and objectified mate value of men and women in this class are particularly homogeneous. This pattern may be interpreted as consequence of straightforward homophily, but given the previous analyses of stated dispositions (which established that women with high objective mate value and overall capital configuration tend to have a systemtic hyperphilious disposition) it might be better understood as *hyperphily in disguise*. The average interaction length amounts to 4.5 subsequent contacts, which points to a comparably high probability of stabilization and subsequent interaction. In this dyadic class, not only does habitual similarity seem to condition the dyad's survival, but a male status advantage – as indicated by higher male age and higher occupational status – is also inherent. This dyadic class points to a nascent logic of exchange between male economic capital (to the extent to which it is legitimate to interpret occupational status as a proxy for economic capital) and female traits (e.g. a comparatively good figure). Remarkably, habitual congruency of two agents in the sense of lifestyle similarity is accompanied by habitual complementarity, which may involve a (probably subjectively unconscious) objective exchange.

Dyadic Class 3 (15.2%) contains the oldest users of the platform, with men aged 49 and women 44 on average. Men in this constellation show average to low educational qualifications, and possess little cultural capital, whereas women show average values for cultural capital and slightly above-average formal education. Men in this class are likely to have a vocational apprenticeship and differ from their female communication partners in that they are also disproportionately often self-employed, which points to a systematic potential male economic advantage. This dyadic class does not imply habitus similarity by means of cultural capital, but nevertheless shows a non-negligible dyadic interaction length. A possible interpretation is that this 'mode 2 constellation' (see Chapter 5) combines users with a rational habitus and a disposition towards exchange rationality (and is thus a particularly good example for MAS); another interpretation is that the interacting parties themselves reciprocally provide the situational conditions for recourse to instrumental rationality.[10] Women in dyadic Class 3 are relatively old, possess a disadvantageous chance structure, and hence have an objective inducement to lower their sights when it comes to lifestyle affinities. Nevertheless, their corresponding communication partners possess a relative economic advantage, which could make them appear to

---

[10] Of course, the interplay of these analytically distinct mechanisms cannot be neglected.

be acceptable partners in the context of rational comparison. Another fact that may be interpreted as manifestation of rational conduct in mating is that the interacting parties tend to live relatively close to each other, which enhances the expected probability of success of a specific relationship.

Another interpretation can be applied to *dyadic Class 4* (11%) with women aged 38 and men 43 on average: higher qualifications, education, and cultural capital for women are accompanied by higher male occupational status and lower (institutionalized) cultural capital, both in terms of relative and absolute comparison. Remarkably, the mate value indicator for men and women in this class is strikingly similar. This class has the highest interaction length (16 interactions in total) and communicates over the largest geographic distance (average of 234 km). Couples surviving the sixth interaction and eventually realizing an offline relationship may well be understood as being the result of (conscious or unconscious) exchange mechanisms.

Dyadic Class 5 (10%) contains the youngest users of the platform – with men aged 26 on average and women 22 on average. Women display all educational levels, but contact men with *Abitur*[11] disproportionately often, while contacting men with the lowest level of secondary education less frequently. Furthermore, these interacting parties have similar cultural capital but different chance structures on the platform (which is due to the advantageous youthfulness and appearance of these women). Accordingly, this class can be characterized by similarity in habitus, which again could be understood as objective exchange between female attractiveness and male status. However, this does not necessarily lead to the establishment of a relationship, as one can tell from the comparably low probability of dyadic 'survival'.

Dyadic Class 6 (10%) contains older men (49) and women (42), with the men having, on average, a higher educational level and better qualifications, but different job profiles (men show higher probabilities of being self-employed – be it in trade, industry, or professional services); women have a BMI particularly conforming to standards of what some may label as female 'erotic capital'. In addition, men and women of this dyadic class share similar amounts of cultural capital. The dyadic interaction length averages four further contacts. Accordingly, the conditions for the emergence of this constellation seem to be founded in both lifestyle affinity and latent equivalency of (symbolic) capital.

A similar logic applies to *dyadic Class 7* (8.4%) which consists of male users aged 32 on average and female users aged 27 on average; men of this class interact with women of the same or lower educational level. In addition, women are more often not (or not yet) in full-time work and men are more often self-employed. This points to a logic of exchange between male economic status and female youth and attractiveness, which is both encouraged and at the same time concealed by a particular similarity of lifestyles.

Dyadic Class 8 (7%) contains users with accumulated disadvantages: both men and women of this dyadic class show a particularly weak structure of success

---

[11] The Abitur is Germany's highest level of secondary education and a prerequisite for university admission.

chances, which can be traced back to the disadvantageous BMI of the women and to low male educational levels. In addition, these women are comparatively old (43) and have a high probability of belonging to the working class or being unemployed, which is commensurate with very low cultural capital. Moreover, while this class is characterized by a considerable interaction length, it is restricted to a smaller geographic environment, which can be interpreted in this case as an expression of geographical and socio-spatial restrictions. The 'taste of romantic necessity', previously discussed with regard to preferential systems, seems to manifest itself here in the form of the increased likelihood of survival for those dyads which actually take up an unfavorable position in the partner market or the social space in general.

In conclusion, a dyadic class analysis of sixth contacts establishes that, even within the early process of interaction, agents cumulatively decompose the market through practices of reciprocal classification. In doing so, a strong assortative mating can be observed, mediated not by one single core variable, but by several traits and their interrelations. Accordingly, the variety of classification practices cannot be reduced to general homophilious lifestyle preferences, but also comprise dissimilarity preferences which foster (partially) dissimilar couple configurations, while nevertheless contributing to the creation of homogeneity in the aggregate. One must then interpret Fig. 7.8 in such a way that emerging dyadic lifestyle homogeneity results from selective extinction of heterogeneous configurations, rather than from homophilious (lifestyle) preferences. Likewise, 'macro-homogeneity' in education or any other singular variable must be understood as the result of diverse classification practices, practices which cannot be reduced to a single class of preferences or 'micro-behaviour'. Another result yielded by dyadic class analysis is the fact that the strong pattern of emerging cultural similarity shown for the overall process for some dyadic classes turns out to be accompanied by a difference in male (higher) and female (lower) economic capital and female youthfulness and attractiveness. Exchange in mating must be interpreted as a question of market segments, as only some dyadic constellations show corresponding patterns of complementary resources, and – requiring time as they do – these patterns do not manifest in first contact events but in the subsequent process. This pattern would have been overlooked when applying unidirectional regression models and looking for 'average causalities'. These findings are in line with the theoretical derivations that 'elective affinities' in mating imply gender specific dissimilarity dispositions: it is not general lifestyle affinities, but the complementarity of male and female mating dispositions which characterize their particular habitus. On the whole, the different objective and subjective logics involved in interactions reproduce aggregate patterns, the material and symbolic differences between couples, and gender differences within couples on the level of the digital partner market.

Thus, the practice of restricting the interpretation of choice acts in online dating to any single general meaning (such as one mating preference, e.g. educational degree, age, income etc.) is inadequate. Whereas it is common in current analyses of online and offline dating when using web-generated process data to interpret contact behavior with reference to one prevailing subjective logic, the model of reciprocal classification – in contrast – highlights the necessity of conceptualizing several interactional logics underlying individual and dyadic classification practices in mating.

Of course, the possible underlying classification logics of the objectively emerging classes can only be assumed given the 'objective' nature of the data. The problem is exacerbated in the context of romantic interaction, where two agents bring in their specific practical meanings. For example, questions arise as to whether the observation of educationally similar contacts in online dating are actually the result of educational homophily, whether genuine exchange calculations are made by both potential partners in heterogeneous constellations, whether one of the practical logics applies to one of the interacting parties, whether the observed (dis)similarity is a one-sided or two-sided by-product, etc. Regardless of these questions, however, it is indisputably reasonable to consider different and simultaneous causally adequate explanations, a potential which is hardly provided by the method and methodology of the mate choice paradigm (e.g. when trying to identify average exchange logics in analyses of first contact events).

Overall, the selected empirical evidence of this chapter supports the insight that online dating is a partner market which is highly structured and structuring in its outcomes over a range of different traits. The market itself follows the structural logics of the German offline society with regard to both economic and cultural capital. Women's and men's objective structures of opportunity on the market can be understood as a function of the social space and social class. Mating preferences show a relational interdependency to each other and to the positions in the social space. Also, rationality in mating can be understood as a question of habitus and position, rather than as a universal model of human agency or a general characteristic of digital partner markets. Finally, just as mating preferences, rationalities, and resources etc. are best understood as relational in the sense that they constitute structured patterns, interactions themselves are also to be recognized as highly structured (and ultimately structuring) processes. In the subsequent chapter, we shall reflect on the implications of this generality of structuration and discuss our findings in the context of a Bourdieusian theory of mating processes.

References

Blasius, J., & Mühlichen, A. (2010). Identifying audience segments applying the "Social Space" approach. *Poetics, 38*(1), 69–89.

Blasius, J., & Winkler, J. (1989). Gibt es die „feinen Unterschiede"? Eine empirische Überprüfung der Bourdieuschen Theorie. *Kölner Zeitschrift für Soziologie und Sozialpsychologie, 41*, 72–94.

Blossfeld, H. P., & Timm, A. (2003). *Who marries whom? Educational systems as marriage markets in modern societies* (European studies of population, Vol. 12). Dordrecht: Kluwer.

Bonacich, P. (1987). Power and centrality: A family of measures. *American Journal of Sociology, 92*(5), 1170–1182.

Bourdieu, P. (1984). *Distinction: A social critique of the judgement of taste*. London: Routledge/Kegan Paul.

Bourdieu, P. (1993). *Sociology in question. Theory, culture and society*. London: Sage. Retrieved from http://www.loc.gov/catdir/enhancements/fy0656/93086215-d.html

References

Bourdieu, P. (1998). *Practical reason: On the theory of action*. Cambridge: Polity Press.
Bourdieu, P. (2000). *Pascalian meditations*. Cambridge: Polity Press.
Bourdieu, P. (2005). Principles of an economic anthropology. In N. J. Smelser & R. Swedberg (Eds.), *The handbook of economic sociology* (2nd ed., pp. 75–89). Princeton: Princeton University Press.
Brase, G. L., & Guy, E. C. (2004). The demographics of mate value and self-esteem. *Personality and Individual Differences, 36*(2), 471–484.
Gigerenzer, G., & Todd, P. M. (Eds.). (1999). *Evolution and cognition. Simple heuristics that make us smart*. New York: Oxford University Press. Retrieved from http://www.loc.gov/catdir/enhancements/fy0640/98051084-d.html
Hakim, C. (2011). *Erotic capital: The power of attraction in the bedroom and the boardroom*. New York: Basic Books.
Hakim, C. (2013). *The new rules of marriage: Internet, playfairs, and erotic power*. London: Gibson Square.
Hall, J. A., Park, N., Song, H., & Cody, M. J. (2010). Strategic misrepresentation in online dating: The effects of gender, self-monitoring, and personality traits. *Journal of Social and Personal Relationships, 27*(1), 117–135.
Hancock, J. T., Thoma, C., Ellison, N. (2007). The truth about lying in online dating profiles. In *Proceedings of the ACM conference on human factors in computing systems* (pp. 449–452). Springfield.
Hollingshead, A. B. (1950). Cultural factors in the selection of marriage mates. *American Sociological Review, 15*(5), 619–627.
Illouz, E. (2007). *Cold intimacies: The making of emotional capitalism* (1st ed.). Cambridge: Polity.
Joppke, C. (1986). The Cultural dimensions of class formation and class struggle: On the social theory of Pierre Bourdieu. *Berkeley Journal of Sociology, 31*, 53–78.
Klein, T. (1996). Der Altersunterschied zwischen Ehepartnern. Ein neues Analysemodell. *Zeitschrift für Soziologie, 25*(5), 346–370.
Krais, B., & Gebauer, G. (2002). *Habitus*. Bielefeld: Transcript.
Kuipers, G. (2006). *Good humor, bad taste. A sociology of the joke*. Berlin/New York: De Gruyter.
Lewis, R. A., & Spanier, G. B. (1979). Theorizing about the quality and stability of marriage. In W. Burr, I. Reiss, R. Hill, & F. Nye (Eds.), *Contemporary theories about the family: General theories and theoretical orientations* (pp. 268–294). New York: Free Press.
Lin, K. H., & Lundquist, J. (2013). Mate selection in cyberspace: The intersection of race, gender, and education. *American Journal of Sociology, 119*(1), 183–215.
Nagel, I., Ganzeboom, H. B. G., Kalmijn, M. (2011). Bourdieu in the network: The influence of high culture and popular culture on network formation in secondary schools. In J. Rössel & G. Otte (Eds.), *Lebensstilforschung* (pp. 424–446). Sonderheft 51, Kölner Zeitschrift für Soziologie und Sozialpsychologie.
Pawlowski, B., & Dunbar, R. I. M. (1999). Impact of market value on human mate choice decisions. *Proceedings of the Royal Society of London B, 266*, 281–285.
Penke, L., & Denissen, J. J. (2008). Sex differences and lifestyle-dependent shifts in the attunement of self-esteem to self-perceived mate value: Hints to an adaptive mechanism? *Journal of Research in Personality, 4*(42), 1123–1129.
Phillips, M. C., Meek, S. W., & Vendemia, J. M. C. (2011). Understanding the underlying structure of deceptive behaviors. *Personality and Individual Differences, 50*(6), 783–789.
Schmitz, A. (2009). Virtuelle Zwischengeschlechtlichkeit im Kontext relationaler Methodologie. Überlegungen zu einer Soziologie der digitalen Partnerwahl. In H. G. Soeffner (Ed.), Unsichere Zeiten. *Herausforderungen gesellschaftlicher Transformationen*; Verhandlungen des 34. Kongresses der Deutschen Gesellschaft für Soziologie in Jena 2008. Wiesbaden: VS Verlag.
Schmitz, A. (2012). Elective affinities 2.0? A Bourdieusian approach to couple formation and the methodology of E-Dating. *Social Science Research on the Internet (RESET), 1*(1), 175–202.
Schmitz, A. (2014). The online dating market: Theoretical and methodological considerations. *Economic Sociology, 16*(1), 11–25.

Schütze, Y. (2008). Die feinen Unterschiede der Liebe. *Leviathan, 36*(1), 76–84.

Skopek, J., Schmitz, A., & Blossfeld, H. P. (2011). The gendered dynamics of age preferences – Empirical evidence from online dating. *Zeitschrift für Familienforschung, 23*(3), 267–290.

Spanier, G. B., & Glick, P. C. (1980). Mate selection differentials between Whites and Blacks in the United States. *Social Forces, 58*(3), 707–725.

Streib, J. (2015). Explanations of how love crosses class lines: Cultural complements and the case of cross-class marriages. *Sociological Forum, 30*(1), 18–39.

Toma, C. L., & Hancock, J. T. (2010). Looks and lies: The role of physical attractiveness in online dating self-presentation and deception. *Communication Research, 37*(3), 335–351.

Toma, C. L., Hancock, J. T., & Ellison, N. B. (2008). Separating fact from fiction: An examination of deceptive self-presentation in online dating. *Personality and Social Psychology Bulletin, 34*(8), 1023–1036.

Vermunt, J., & Magidson, J. (2003). Latent class models for classification. *Computational Statistics and Data Analysis, 41*(3–4), 531–537.

Vermunt, J. K., & van Dijk, L. A. (2001). A non-parametric random-coefficient approach: The latent class regression model. *Multilevel Modeling Newsletter, 13*, 6–13.

Weber, M. (1978). *Economy and society*. In G. Roth & C. Wittich (Eds.). Berkeley: University of California Press

Whitty, M. T. (2008). Liberating or debilitating? An examination of romantic relationships, sexual relationships and friendships on the net. *Computers in Human Behavior, 24*(5), 1837–1850.

Zillmann, D. (2016). *Von kleinen Lügen und kurzen Beinen. Selbstdarstellung bei der Partnersuche im Internet*. [About little lies and small legs. Self-presentation in online dating.] Wiesbaden: VS Verlag (forthcoming).

Zillmann, D., Schmitz, A., & Blossfeld, H. P. (2011). Lügner haben kurze Beine. Zum Zusammenhang unwahrer Selbstdarstellung und partnerschaftlicher Chancen im Online-Dating. *Zeitschrift für Familienforschung, 23*(3), 291–318.

Žižek, S. (2010). Time of the monsters. A call to radicalness. *Le Monde diplomatique* 12.10.2010

Chapter 8
Online Dating – A Unified and Unifying Symbolic Good Market

This last chapter will combine the lines of argumentation and provide a conclusive sociological understanding of the phenomenon 'online dating'. Applying a Bourdieusian notion of 'structure', we will argue that the social distances between agents of different social classes, otherwise maintained by social, geographic, and institutional segregation in a largely direct way, are consolidated in digital partner markets in a particularly immediate way. In the 'hyper-focus' online dating, users – socially classified before even entering the market – classify themselves, their symbolic goods and their potential partners in the course of their practices and interactions. It is under the conditions of numeric abundance of potential partners from all social classes where the scarcity and hierarchy of symbolic goods already operative in the offline world come to light and can unfold their full force. A dating platform is a partner market with a unique efficacy, as it allows symbolic capital to operate very efficiently in its function of converting the users' capital endowments. In the aggregate, users thereby create a particularly structured market, which reinforces the relations of societal domination also effective outside of the online dating market. In contrast to reductionist theories of individual choice, that conceive of the market's structure as condition and outcome of individual preferences only, the Bourdieusian conceptualization helps us to understand the role of relational structuring practices. Given the fact that habitus is operative even in the supposedly structure-free sphere of online dating, this work makes a case for a sociological approach that remains sensitive to the aggregated effects of reproduction strategies in a realm closest to the idea of freedom of action.

The Ongoing Unification of the Market of Symbolic Goods

In contrast to a widespread spontaneous impression, this particular context of online interaction was shown to be both fundamentally structured and structuring in regard to its socio-structural conditions, processes, and outcomes. Social structure, which is often seen as attenuated in online dating – due to the absence of the direct influence of third parties, social networks, and institutional arrangements – is in fact consistently and diversely present in the digital partner market, its users, their interactions, and the emerging assortative structure. Analyzing survey and observational data from a major German dating site, it was demonstrated that online dating users display categories of perception and systems of romantic preferences which correspond systematically with their position within the partner market and thus with their societal position itself. Each user participates actively with their habitus in this digital meeting context as a fully socialized subject, and thus becomes part of a nexus of relations of mating dispositions, strategies, (ir)rationalities, practices, and hence of all the social preconditions of mating also relevant in offline mating.

In fact, in non-specialized online dating platforms with profile-based free choice in which agents from virtually all social classes participate (cp. Skopek 2011; Zillmann 2016), the users and their traits, practices, and dispositions are uniquely subject to comparison, mutual referencing, and conforming to romantic standards. This comparability contains, in particular, all the symbolic emanations of class-based habitus such as self-presentation, use of language, practices of flirtation, use of deceptive strategies, dealing with the artificiality of the 'unromantic situation', digital competencies, and so on. If the term 'focus' labels contexts where agents meet and – among many other things – mate, then online dating can be unequivocally conceived of as a *hyper-focus*, virtually (in its twofold meaning) throwing together the symbolic goods which have always been effective in the offline manifestation of the social space.

As argued in Chapter 5, the unification of the *symbolic good market* is not a new phenomenon resulting from supposed idiosyncrasies of the digital medium. Bourdieu (2008) demonstrated, using the example of the rural region of Béarn in the 1960s, that improved infrastructure and the economic development of France as a whole led to a structural expansion of the national marriage market, but not to the emergence of a generalized increase in the 'level of freedom' of mate choice. On the contrary, as a consequence of the convergence of previously distant partner markets, the agents' symbolic goods were subject to manifold processes of symbolic standardization and hierarchization.

Consequently, the modernization of the French state further increased the relations of symbolic domination and social inequality between different social classes, with the marriage market being one of the social forces involved. The unification of the market of symbolic goods, in the case of France, must be understood as a result of the long-term transformations of society exerted by modernization. Processes of technologization, improving infrastructure, individualization, and rationalization, etc., are still taking place today. In our times, these societal developments appear in the form of pronounced digitalization and marketization of the social, for which online dating markets are perhaps one of the best examples. Well-known mechanisms of hierarchizing agents' chances according to their symbolic goods are particularly efficient on a dating site, with its profile design, and in particular the potential for and necessity of direct comparisons of these profiles, fostering a clear visibility of society's class structure.

It is for these reasons that mechanisms of symbolic hierarchization are particularly characteristic in the modern case of a digital partner market. Here, the users' differentially structured dispositions come into contact with one another, a fact which activates particular rationalities, fosters particular interactional logics, and ultimately precipitates in differentially structured dyadic classes. When configuring their profiles, ranging from pictures, hobbies, and likes and dislikes to socio-structural indicators, users of a dating site are forced to reveal their symbolic goods and to expose them and themselves to direct comparison with the goods as advertised by their competitors. Thus, online dating enables a particularly efficient "labour of representation" including "theatralization and aestheticization" which is – already constitutive for offline life – "directed towards manifesting the agent's social conditions" (Bourdieu and Passeron 1977: 197). Users with little symbolic capital can hardly avoid unfavorable comparisons between their symbolic resources and those of other, better-equipped users. When lower-class users present their symbolic goods, this leads to their objective evaluation and ultimately devaluation, resulting – for them – in a low probability of finding a partner. The social and code-related architecture fosters the adaptation to a perceived or assumed standard (like confirming to a certain body shape). As a consequence, behind the exposition of the most innocent lifestyle dispositions, there prevails a simultaneous devaluation of all the symbolic goods which are constitutive for the position of the lower classes in the social space.[1]

Digital Classification Practices

The unification and the implied standardization of symbolic goods is not limited to the symbolic value of profile characteristics, but refers equally to the ways online daters make use of this technology by means of interacting with communication partners. As it was shown for the case of age and lifestyle-related practices of classification in mating, and as others have been showing for educational level (Skopek 2011; Skopek et al. 2011) or ethnic background (e.g. Potarca and Mills 2013), users exhibit practices of 'free choice' which will result in couple configurations familiar from offline contexts. But online dating is not a mere digital facsimile of offline partner markets. A constitutive part of this hyper-focus, which operates with little physical co-presence, is the particular relevance of visual self-portrayal and linguistic expression. The importance of profile pictures (or rather of creating an image of oneself which conforms to attractiveness standards) has a particularly immediate impact on the quality and quantity of users' chances for attention. Of course, physical appearance is a decisive factor for offline mating as well, but in the digital sphere there is little chance for a user's more intangible qualities to shine if they have

---

[1] Given the increase of educational expansion in Western societies, mate choice research should analyze which different milieus and lifestyles are hidden behind formally identical educational attainments.

already been rejected as a result of their profile picture. This is one reason some dating site providers have the default setting of blurred profile picture, which can be un-blurred as soon as one thinks that another user might be promising, usually as a consequence of a promising exchange of messages. One way or another, under the terms of computer-mediated communication in the platform's chat system, a particularly strong linguistic structuration of the interaction process can be identified. In a particular immediate way, different sociolects, which have been acquired offline, collide within reciprocal classification processes online.

Just like in offline mating, the symbolic goods demonstrated while using the chat system – which further display the form and competencies of expressing oneself in written messages – have their distinctive value defined in relation to the alternative advertized goods on the partner market, thus generating a clear 'distinction profit' for those users who have the least to lose from such comparisons. One could say that, in online dating, the bourgeois, which is "characterized by distinguished distance, prudent ease and contrived naturalness", and the working class, which "manifests itself in the tendency to […] shun the bombast of fine words and the turgidity of grand emotions through banter, rudeness and ribaldry" (Bourdieu and Passeron 1977: 116) experience a particular reciprocal intensification of their class affiliations. This extent of actualization is usually not found in relatively homogenous offline foci such as bars, university seminars, parties, balls, etc. Just as the ways of speaking and writing are specific to habitus, modes of decoding are dependent on capital endowment and constitutive elements within practices of reciprocal classification and, ultimately, for class reproduction.

Moreover, and in contrast to most everyday situations offline, on the digital dating market, the representatives of the lower classes are not merely abstract presences, but become concrete reality inasmuch as the architecture of online dating insinuates that they are potential mates, which fosters practices of distinguishing and distinction. These are less likely to occur offline, where most social interaction take place within more socially homogeneous settings. Users from the upper and middle classes report in qualitative interviews that they prefer those potential partners who "can take what is written on board and who can adequately react to it, that is, that they are oriented towards dialog in their communication" and do not use "street slang"; they prefer those users "who can keep up with them", for example by "visiting the theatre" and "liking to read books", in contrast to "talking about TV soap operas" and "wanting an early personal meeting". They complain about those who make "always the same spelling mistakes", or that a chat partner "always makes a smiley without a colon". However, statements like these not only occur in interviews, but become part of the dyadic communication process itself, where the unusual context of encounter and the urge to compare are particularly pronounced. Dismissively referring to third parties and their "disgraceful", "uninspired" or "brash" communication practices while chatting with a promising potential partner serves not least to establish a 'stylistic' consensus, transforming ineligible users into objects of strategic communication.

For those who can afford the capacity to believe in romance when searching for their significant other, the 'insignificant others' become not merely something to be ignored, but instead an appreciated *insufferable* other. The overt cultural differences between sender and receiver underline the uniqueness of the rejecting user and his or her actual ideal partner. Online dating, effective at generating additional symbolic distinction, implies a selective integration of the underclass into the dyadic communication process even more efficient than it is the case in offline foci. It facilitates both the inclusion and exclusion of the ineligible classes as constitutive parts of the reciprocal classification process. And whereas class-specific flirting practices in their respective offline contexts are seldom subject to sanction and stigmatization, they are particularly effective in online dating at generating additional symbolic distinction profit for the most privileged users, who gain a rewarding conversational gambit and a distraction from the embarrassment of taking the first step. Thus, online dating not only – similar to the traditional love letter – promotes processes of idealizing (Ben-Ze'ēv 2004: 19) an unknown communication partner, but also of de-idealizing other users and ultimately hierarchizing the symbolic goods of the users according to standards defined by the privileged.

Habitus-specific practices of deception in profile presentation and communication, which constitutes a core issue in online dating research (cp. Zillmann et al. 2011; Zillmann 2016), represent another striking example of the considerable comparability and standardization of symbolic goods on the digital partner market. Those users with little symbolic capital are particularly subject to the effects of the devaluation of their symbolic goods: they are forced to 'optimize' their own symbolic capital in order to be perceived at all, thus recognizing the legitimacy of the symbolic goods of those actors who already have higher success chances on the online and offline partner market. Practices of posting particularly flattering photos, the glossing over of negative traits, or direct lies lead to even more intense competition for the most desired resources, doubling the competitive advantage of the upper classes: they are not merely blessed with better resources from the outset – they are also able, being less subject to the necessity of deception, to distance themselves from those users who are forced to engage in deception to increase their success chances. This leads to an additional moral differential on the market, intensifying the symbolic hierarchy of the social classes. The reduced probability of being exposed as a deceiver is accompanied by a clear moral superiority, even when compared to the middle positions in the social space, who display a particular rationality and thus unease in their practices of self-presentation and interaction. The symbolic goods of the most privileged are not only advantageous even before entering the partner market; these users experience an additional increase in value because the users from the middle and lower classes, recognizing and respecting the symbolic hierarchies, engage in deception according to the ideals they share regarding attractive partners – ideals, however, which are defined by the resources de facto monopolized by users from the upper classes. As a consequence, not only are the symbolic goods of the privileged users rewarded, but the legitimacy of their dominant cultural arbitrariness is further reinforced, due to the fact that their lifestyle and ways of coping with the dating situation constitute the reference system for the standardization of the plurality of the different mating practices. Online dating may well be thought of as a striking case of what Richard Sennett describes as the tyranny of intimacy in contemporary society, where "the test of whether people are being authentic and 'straight' with each other is a peculiar standard of market exchange in intimate relations" (Sennett 2002: 8). However, users of a dating site are capable to different degrees of avoiding and profiting from this tyranny.

In turns out that the technical and social conditions of a dating site as analyzed throughout this book imply a differential operation between the habitus of members of different classes, and thus a tendency of the market to operate to the advantage of the advantaged. Subscribing to a dating platform and thereby transcending the digital divide does not lead to a universal 'digital dividend', for 'the user', as the distribution of profit varies socially. The users – socially classified before even entering the market – classify themselves and their potential partners in the course of their practices and interactions, creating a particularly structured market, and recreating and reinforcing relations of societal domination that already exist outside of the online dating market.

It is a restriction of the partner market analyzed here that it only includes heterosexual couple constellations. However, reciprocal classification practices are equally constitutive for all types of interactions, including those outside the standards of heteronormativity. Thus, whereas this work chose a non-specialized heterosexual dating platform, future research may well utilize the proposed approach in the context of homosexual dating, as well as in analyzing particular niches of the partner market (such as dating sites for particular religious affiliations, ethnic groups, etc.).

Equal Opportunity as Illusion and Symbolic Violence

One can state without doubt that classification practices on the digital partner market reproduce the positional and dispositional hierarchies between the social classes and the sexes in many ways. The idea should be dismissed that increased opportunities for free mate choice and romantic self-fulfillment – as they are theoretically provided by online dating – are actually realized in the practices of 'the user'. Processes of reciprocal classification on a dating site lead to a systematic hierarchization of the chances for attention and exchange which can hardly be identified in this pure form in any offline market. Whereas geographical and social segregation represent relatively intact foci for specific social groups in the offline context, providing a certain number of potential partners for all members of the social group in question, the hyper-focus online dating is characterized by the selective provision of 'romantic advantages' for users privileged even before registering to the dating platform. Thus it is certainly not the case – as frequently assumed by both laymen and some scientists – that only 'losers' are forced to use the internet to find a partner, neither can online dating adequately be described by general "superior outcomes" (Finkel et al. 2012: 28). Just as differential cumulative advantages and disadvantages can emerge in any market, the losers and winners are reproduced as such on the digital market. This is of genuine sociological interest, precisely because the analysis of an online market provides a clear picture of the users' habitual distinctions that reflect their socialization both off and online, without spatial and social limitations interfering with the symbolic classification of mating value.

As has been shown, the potential for realizing one's own predicted chances of finding someone is not a question of the medium itself, but of the user's social class background. In online dating, the disadvantage of users with low capital is further increased: not only do they have objectively poor prospects, but in addition, they are led to believe in the promises of an efficient search for a perfect match, and thus overestimate their chances (not least as a result of a comparison with their offline chances and advertisement slogans). Believing in their chances online, these users tend to engage in 'illegitimate' strategies such as sending, or responding to, contacts en masse. Users with low chances for attention clearly experience the low value of the symbolic goods they embody – if only via their low probabilities of receiving a reply – which in itself already has plenty of potential to reinforce their sense of class position. Even worse, trying to utilize the virtual possibilities of strategic adaptation to one's market value is not a promising approach; the compensatory strategy made possible by the technical and social conditions of a dating platform to increase the amount of contacted profiles is a conspicuous example. Such practices impede possible success, as the blatancy of impersonal messages contributes to symbolic devaluation relative to those men, who possess the distinctive cultural capital of addressing individuality in a market operating via goods rather than persons.

In the light of these considerations, online dating is not characterized by chances for everyone, but in fact by the scarcity of chances for attention, which reflects the relative scarcity of symbolic goods. For the upper classes, online dating is, to a degree, a means of revealing the distinctive value of their symbolic goods. Every time the personal happiness of the disadvantaged is realized by 'realizing their homophily', the objective social distances between the classes are realized and reproduced. Due to the persistent claims in the dating industry's advertising that there is 'someone for everyone', however, the individual user is led to ignore the structural implications of his or her 'personal choice'. Ultimately, the disenchanted user, infected with the self-made man ideology and the rhetoric of 'every Jack will find his Jill', is confronted with the additional burden of being forced to attribute lack of romantic success to herself. These mechanisms of symbolic dominance and symbolic violence, resulting from practices often reduced to 'free choice', further contribute in the reproduction of societal class structure.

Re-Traditionalizing Effects of Modern Technology: The Case of Gender

The ubiquitous reciprocal evaluation, classification, standardization, and hierarchization of symbolic goods and their carriers on the digital partner market manifests itself not least with regard to gender relations. A trait sought by most men is female youthfulness and attractivity, a disposition which contributes in defining the female exchange value towards physicality. On the digital partner market, even more intensively than in traditional markets, the female body becomes a criterion for selection, whereas societal power resources such as education or income are neglected by most male users of the dating platform, independent from their class background. As men show highly selective patterns, excluding women above a certain age, body mass, and with unappealing profile pictures, those women not conforming to standards of attractiveness are forced to compensate for this 'deficit' by showing feminity with respect to behavioral and linguistic aspects. As the female habitus is structured by the societal relations of power and domination, a tendency to anticipate stereotypical male expectations regarding can be expected to become (re)-activated. A particularly striking example of the structuration of female dispositions can be seen in the fact that upper class women deceive with regard to their social status, not by feigning higher education or occupational status, but by concealing (or even downgrading) their academic degrees in an act of anticipating men's unwillingness to accept their own inferiority (cp. Zillmann et al. 2011; Zillmann 2016). It is a particular perfidy of the partner market that upper class women are not only less able to capitalize on their potentially superior economic and cultural capital than men, but that the representation of their symbolic goods contributes to the subversion of their romantic prospects. However the high aspirations and standards of women with an advantageous capital endowment must also – indeed, especially – be understood as internalized subordination to male domination, which is not reduced but rather promoted in this market. In the course of messaging they only accept offers from men who have at least the same economic and cultural capital. This is often misunderstood as further evidence for the generality of the homophily principle, but the recurring finding of (educational) homogeneity, which is derived from the observation of the educational degrees shown in the profiles, must be interpreted as hyperphily in disguise. The analysis of stated preferences revealed that women with high economic and cultural capital do show a systematic and strong pattern of hyperphily. Thus, upper class women, although having an advantageous position in the social space, are nevertheless disposed to symbolize their social status through the relational superiority of a man.[2]

Women from the upper classes, whose economic and educational resources are rewarded to a lower degree on the market (or even have a negative impact, which explains the female tendency to conceal higher education), thus by necessity compete with (younger) women from lower strata, who are encouraged to invest in their physicality in order to approximate their ideal of hyperphily. On the market level, this reinforces the status of the (youthful) female body as a legitimate object of romantic exchange.

Trapped in the same structure, societal power relations manifest in men in the form of a complementary complicity. It is a peculiarity of the male habitus, which is hardly separable, to implicate a disposition which tends to consider the female body a symbolic good and to display only subordinate interest in women with a

---

[2] Further research may profit from this consideration, for example by relaxing the strong assumption of homophily in analysing homogeneity developments within international comparisons.

higher volume of economic, cultural, and ultimately symbolic capital. In the light of the market character and the role of erotic charisma in online dating, it is not far-fetched to expect a certain (re-)activation of deeply rooted representations of the female body as a symbolic good within men's dispositional systems. The promises of freedom from normative restrictions (Kauffmann 2011) and erotic ideals (Bühler-Illieva 2006), which may lure (female) users into entering the digital partner market, are anything but fulfilled. Social control in the sense of direct influence by the family and peers (Kauffmann 2011) may indeed be suspended online, but control in the sense of feedback to one's characteristics is more direct and intensive than in any offline context. The social and code-based architecture fosters the adaptation to perceived or assumed standards (like confirming to a certain body shape), to an extent that self-portrayal may be better described self-disciplining for some users. Consequently, the operation of erotic charisma clearly does not serve as "women's trump card in mating and marriage markets" (Hakim 2010: 510), but as mechanism of the re-traditionalization and reproduction of gender relations. If a class of users can be said to profit from the advantages yielded by online dating, it is upper class men who can, due to their symbolic capital, easily and promisingly enter different segments of the partner market.

Whereas gender and class have been given analytical priority in this work, the impression should be avoided that the underlying mechanisms are restricted to these categories. Just as male and female mating dispositions, which are deeply rooted in patterns of perception and practices, are actualized on the online dating market and further reinforce the structure of domination between the sexes, all dispositional categories can be expected to be impacted by the 'hyper-focus' online dating. Further research should focus on other emanations of re-traditionalization regarding, for example, ethnic, religious, or ideological categories, which can be expected to also experience particular (re)activation in digital dating markets.

Acquired Digital Space and Physical Space

As a consequence of the described mechanisms inherent to this digital sphere, the structure of the overall social space – society – tends to retranslate itself into the offline physical space (cp. Bourdieu 1996: 10). Just as the physical space is socially structured through practices of closeness and distance, the digital space (which in fact turns out to be an analytical sub-category of the social and the physical space) is genuinely structured by the distances reproduced in the course of reciprocal classification practices.

The habitus of the dating site's users provide, to (socially) different degrees, the conditions of realizing the theoretical possibilities and coping with the challenges of online dating with consequences that resemble the historical case of the French region of Béarn: "Whereas the most advantaged may extend the geographical and social range of their marriages [...] the least advantaged may be condemned to extend their geographical area to compensate for the social restriction of the social area in which they can find partners" (Bourdieu 2008: 184). Like the urbanites in Bourdieu's analysis, male online dating users of the upper class "can choose between several hierarchized markets", whereas the peasant, like the members of the lower classes in online dating, "is confined to his own area, and has to compete even here with rivals who are better endowed, at least symbolically" (ibid. 183). The geographically bound nature of the lower classes familiar from offline research (cp. Bozon and Heran 2006) is reproduced under the conditions of digitality. And, like Bourdieu's analysis of the rural marriage market, online dating offers a particular opportunity for women from lower social classes to escape from their local marriage markets, by providing an enlarged field of eligibles compatible to their hyperphilous disposition, i.e. to 'marry upwards'. Also, as dyadic class analysis revealed, the combination of geographic proximity and proximity in the sense of belonging to the lower classes seems to work as an efficient principle for couple emergence.

For example, male members of the lower classes, in contrast to their privileged competitors, struggle to maintain a lasting online interaction, and, even if they manage to do so, will often end up with a female partner from the same disadvantaged class. For them, male domination manifests as a 'romantic taste of necessity', which could be misunderstood as mere homophily, but which is the result of internalized societal position resulting from being lower class males. The consequences clearly manifest in the way the access of the disadvantaged agents is limited to partners in close geographical and social proximity.

Accordingly, the frequently invoked digital relativization of physical proximity between agents is itself relativized by the social origin of the users: whereas some are able to attract partners from further afield, others are restricted to their position in the social and thus in the physical space. The debate regarding the space-boundedness of the lower classes (Bauman 2005: 32) repeats itself in the 'place-free' sphere of a dating platform: it is the digital space that engenders re-placement in a social and a geographical sense.

Structuration Trough Neutralization of Structure

Overall, one may think that "online dating has fundamentally altered the romantic acquaintance process" (Finkel et al. 2012: 23), but one cannot claim that the offline effects of this digital partner market can be discussed in terms of a diminished relevance of class structure and gender relations. The shortsighted perception that social structures are strongly relativized online in general, and in the digital partner market in particular, cannot only be justifiably rejected: in fact, the exact opposite of this misconception holds true. The very principle of the unification of the (rural or digital) symbolic good market lies in the neutralization of "social mechanisms" as traditionally yielded by offline conditions, which structure offline mating processes (Bourdieu 2008: 181). In contrast to offline foci such as specific bars, educational institutions, geographic places etc., agents and thus cultures from the most diverse societal positions collide in the online dating market. On a dating site like the one analyzed here, where users can participate free of charge, the geographical and institutional segregation which is known from the offline partner market, is strongly relativized and even reversed. A remarkably direct confluence of users from different social classes and their respective internalized systems of classification can be observed, a confluence of agents with the common purpose of finding a mate, which cannot be observed in any offline context in this pure form. In the absence of reliability of expectations – as they prevail in familiar social settings due to shared norms, due to the established regulation of the processes of mating, and due to the fact that, predominantly, potential partners from the same class are encountered – online dating can be characterized by a comparably strong activation and relevance of aesthetic and moral structures, that is, the dispositions of the users' habitus. In contrast, in homogeneous foci such as specific educational institutions, bars, or other locations, the issue of status hierarchies is less evident to those looking for a mate, since the lower variance of encountered habitus creates less habitual friction and necessitates less active aesthetic and moral distinctions.

The social distances between agents of different social classes and different partner markets – otherwise maintained by social, geographic, and institutional segregation in a largely direct way – is consolidated in online dating in a particularly immediate way, comprising profile presentation and practices of usage and interaction. Not despite but precisely because of the frequently invoked relativization of offline structure, the incorporated structuration of habitus is particularly brought to the fore. The relativized relevance of structure, in the sense of institutional and geographical market segmentation as emphasized by the individualistic view, is subverted by the increased significance of structured habitus coming into force through the users' practices. Thus, in online dating, similar to the historical case described by Bourdieu, "the price of the freedom" from offline social structures "that results from direct interaction between the parties, who are no longer subject to family pressures and economic or ethical considerations" is accompanied by "submission to the laws of the market of individuals abandoned to their own resources" (Bourdieu 2008: 181). Socialized agents enter a partner market which intensifies the mechanisms of assortative mating via its technical and social structure, by way of providing particularly efficient technologies, vast opportunities, and inherent necessities of reciprocal classification practices, thus generating a particular standardization and hierarchization of the symbolic goods and the users advertising these goods. The standardization is further supported by the dating sites, whose services include supporting their customers not only in presenting their profile, but also in how to write the first message, when to reveal which aspects of the self, right up to tips on how to behave in the first face-to-face meeting. To the extent users are affected by the imperatives of the partner market, the anonymity of the dating platform acts as a *panopticon* in the Foucauldian sense.

In online dating, the principle of structuration through structural neutralization becomes particularly visible. A dating platform is a partner market with a unique efficacy, as it allows symbolic capital to operate very efficiently in its converting function of the users' capital endowments. The digital dating market efficiently translates any capital into symbolic capital by way of each user's categories of perception, which manifest in recognizing the symbolic goods of specific users and in disregarding those of others.

At the same time, a constitutive momentum of the reality of the (digital) partner market is the claim for the rejection of market principles which contributes to the operation of a market of symbolic goods: not standardized but special, not staged but authentic. The successful collective suppression of the arbitrariness of the social preconditions of the realisability of these general demands is itself a constitutive factor in the market's efficiency.

Areas of Rationality

At first glance, when trying to grasp the logics of an online dating market, one must agree with Eva Illouz, who states that "[n]ever before in history have men and women of different social classes, religions, races met as if on a free, unregulated market where attributes – of beauty, sexiness, social class – are rationally and instrumentally evaluated and exchanged." (Illouz 2012: 242). However, the inherent problem, often claimed to be universal, of having to continually optimize oneself in order to find a partner seems to be a particular issue of the representatives of the middle classes. This implies a distinction profit for all those who appear comparatively genuine in their communication, as exemplified using the case of the different rationalities behind deceptive practices. Also, in online dating, the upper class has "the privileges of the dominant," and has all the freedoms to "move in their world as a fish in water", which "resides in the fact that they need not engage in rational computation in order to reach the goals that best suit their interests" (Bourdieu 1990: 108).

In online dating, rationality does not just precipitate as special case of practice, which is especially prevalent in the middle classes, but also as delusive normative orientation for those users whose habitus is not predisposed for coping with the market, and as a distinction symbol for those who consider it unromantic to recognize the unromantic conditions of its practice. Reconstructing "the condition of love more markedly from the standpoint" of "middle-class lifestyles" (Illouz 2012: 10), then may suggest a false generalization of the situational logics and rationalities specific to the middle classes. Take, for example, the short-sighted strategy of users with little economic and cultural capital, who tend to expect gains from increased deception. This rationalization must be understood as the outcome of internalized previous conditions and the situational logics online dating generates for them. Here, rational conduct must be understood as a maladaptation towards the situation.

Overall, online daters are confronted with the contradiction between romantic ideals and rational calculation to very different degrees. It may well be that – theoretically – all users are confronted with the problem of the unnatural and unromantic dating situation online, but the relational constitution of the digital dating market directs their attention to the structural logics of the social space. Rationality in mating and the rationality of the market are best understood as areas within the social space, addressing the dispositional schemes and situational logics of specific classes of users.

The Structure of Digital Partner Choice

The 'hyper-focus' online dating, like many other late modern societal developments, embodies a dialectic structuration, one which simultaneously generates both social unification and social separation. From this point of view, the methodological advantage of online dating is not, as often emphasized by the most diverse scientists (disagreeing in everything but their reverence for the subject), that structures are relativized, and mating preferences or the crisis of romance can be observed in their purest form, but that the operation of habitus and thus of social structure can be observed especially overtly (cp. Schmitz 2012). It is in circumstances of numerical abundance of potential partners from all social classes where the scarcity and hierarchy of symbolic goods become clearly evident.

The reduced significance of social barriers on the internet in general and on online dating platforms in particular makes online dating not just a paradigmatic partner market, but a research context which allows us to establish the scientific significance of social structure where it is frequently thought to have the least influence. It may be understood as a tacit division of labor that other authors seem to overemphasize structure in the sense of the market's inner logic. However, what research on mate choice has observed in the last few years are not the dysfunctional excesses of an autonomous market, but the specific and emphatic conspicuousness and intensification of structural principles which have always been constitutive for society.

Whereas large parts of the mate choice paradigm, which has been labeled as MAS (mating as agency in structures) throughout this work, as a consequence of the underlying individualistic epistemology, start with the assumption of a relativization of structure in an attempt to highlight and to analytically grasp the innovation of the digital medium, the relational perspective genuinely understands the processes of structuration of online dating as generic mechanisms of social reproduction. It may seem counterintuitive from an individualist viewpoint that the striking significance of class structure on dating sites is actually produced by the diminished relevance of structure in its geographic and institutionalized sense.

Observing class reproduction in online dating will only come as a surprise when one associates online dating with a lack of structure in the sense of the traditional micro-macro-distinction. Focusing on structure in the sense of opportunities, direct external influences, etc. and seeing structure as controllable on a dating site leads to ignoring the deeper principles of structure, such as the genuine structure of habitus and the indirect effects which structured agents exert on each other. The discontinuation of opportunity structures – as it appears from the individualist view – results in the fact that the relational structure becomes particularly virulent and immediate, a fact which is not seen when structure is located outside the subject. The vast majority of traditional and current (online) partner market research applies a sharp analytical differentiation between an ostensibly average subject of mate choice on the one hand and structures on the other, which are reduced to structures of opportunity (e.g. mate choice sets) or restrictions (e.g. geographic distances or institutional settings as mechanisms of preventing the encounter of two actors). Accordingly, research on online dating is practically compelled to treat this context of encounter as a particularly good example for the effects of intentions and preferences on mate choice. Due to the inherent dichotomizing conception, traditional mate choice research is led to interpret patterns of homogeneity – in education, income, age, etc. – as outcomes of (homophilious) preferences rather than as a manifestation of social structure itself.

The fact that social structuration of the habitus manifests itself even without the direct impact of offline structure, is an irrefutable argument for a notion of structure which includes agents and their habitual practices. In contrast to the mate choice framework, drawing on methodological individualism and variants of rational choice, the concept of habitus enables a conceptualization of 'structure' in a seemingly structure-free space, as the social space structures the agents' habitus and is thus seen as prior to any physical (geographic or digital) space. Modes and results of the acquisition of any space are seen as a function of the agents' habitus, which themselves are structured in every respect.

Applying the habitus perspective, the users' different material and symbolic forms capital are understood as genuinely incorporated conditions, which define the users' habitus with all the socially differential consequences for the agents' patterns of perceiving, evaluating, and interacting with potential partners. Our empirical findings established that cultural and economic capital do not work as mere resources of the user, but structure the user's dispositions and practices themselves: Capital in contrast to resource is not only what an agent possesses but likewise by what he or she is *possessed*. Thus, a Bourdieusian approach which transcends the traditional actor-structure opposition allows us to establish the significance of social structure even where it is frequently thought to have the least influence. The absence of search frictions – as economists might put it – distorting market mechanisms is not interpreted as an absence of structure, but as the very opposite: the operation of social structure in its purest form.

It may seem a paradox that the intensity of market mechanisms outlined here cannot be taken as evidence for the suggestion that online dating (or any other partner market) represents a relatively autonomous sphere from the rest of society. One may well label online dating a paradigmatic partner market, but the goods traded here are not specific to the partner market, but rather symbolic ones, whose meaning and value essentially feed on structural conditions prior to and exogenous from the market. The strong homology between the digital dating market and the offline social space, and thus the striking heteronomy of the digital dating market, manifests in the 'hyperfocusing' of societal conditions, reinforcing the transformation of cultural differences between users into a cultural hierarchy. As these processes of social reproduction are far from being endogenous occurrences in an autonomous social sphere, the consequences of this digital partner market are also highly structured, which manifests in the stratification of dyadic classes, emerging in the early phases of encounter, in the homogeneous constellation of couples surviving the online phase, and ultimately in the reproduction of the logic of the social space within the (digital) partner market. Dating platforms can be said to contribute to traditional existing mechanisms of social inequality and domination in manifold ways, which can hardly be assessed taking contingent singular preferences or choices as an analytical basis, assigned to the 'average user'. It may best be interpreted in terms of the relational structures of mating dispositions, strategies, interaction, and chances, whose interrelations come to light in a particularly clear manner in the digital context, which neutralizes structural factors previously ensuring relative autonomy and cultural particularism for the social classes offline.

The Mate Choice Paradigm as Special Case of Practice Theory

As it has been shown throughout this work, even online dating – which is particularly close to what one might see as a theoretical concept of a partner market – is thoroughly and consistently structured in its operation, and structuring in its effects. Consequently, the analysis of traditional offline partner markets may profit from a stronger consideration of structure in the relational sense as proposed here. The relational approach outlined throughout this work does anything but exclude traditional mate choice research: relations between preferences and their general societal background was shown to be a relational extension of preference and is compatible with previous research, as well as with the concept of dispositions; strategies and rationalities have been conceptualized as special cases of habitus and practice; exchange was shown to be a particular logic of reciprocal classification, and the partner market was conceptualized as social space.

The example of mate choice shows that Bourdieu's theory is anything but an "antithesis of rational choice theory" (Lunt 2006: 329). On the contrary, "far from being the founding model, economic theory (and rational action theory which is its sociological derivative) is probably best seen as a particular instance, historically dated and situated, of field theory" (Calhoun 1993: 85f.). Likewise, the MAS paradigm and its variations may well be understood as special cases of a generalized theory of practice, as provided for in Pierre Bourdieu's work. However, the argumentation thus far should not suggest that a Bourdieusian approach to mating represents a mere reformulation of traditional mate choice perspectives in terms of practice theory, or an elaborated version of the Blau space. It is up to future research to apply the Bourdieusian approach to other, traditional and modern, meeting contexts and technologies.

Although a single dating platform has been analyzed within this work, our considerations also apply to the overall digital partner market with its different niches: the habitus also manifests in the 'choice' of particular dating platforms, which themselves are socially hierarchized. The same applies to mobile dating (cp. Schmitz and Zillmann 2016). Future research may build on this work by assessing the structural manifestations within and between offline, online, and mobile markets. In doing so, the artificial distinction between offline and online should be dismissed in favor of a relational view of the totality of the partner market, independent from the technological form of its particular singular manifestations. In final consequence, however, practices, strategies, preferences, and markets, usually being assigned to the narrow realm of mating, must be seen as being embedded within an overall relational system of dispositions and social fields.

Applying a Bourdieusian approach, processes of rationalization, marketization, individualization, and technologization can be understood as transformations of the social space, where online dating is both an emanation and a contributing instance of rationalization, individualization, and modernization. Ongoing societal changes regarding, for example, the transformation of romance are then not seen as effects of online dating; instead, analyzing a dating platform reveals societal processes which are inherent to rationalization, individualization, marketization, and all the other emanations of modernization in the classical Western sense.

In the light of this consideration, online dating cannot be reduced either to a neutral methodological medium for the scientific observation of well-known facts, or to a mere threat to romance. Digital partner markets must be understood as one further sign of the strengthened nomos of the economic field (Lebaron 2001) within the field of power. In fact, the economic nomos manifests in form of two intimately linked social facts: increasingly market-driven tendencies in intimacy and the dominant ways of investigating intimacy as a question of the subjects' choice acts. Not only is the phenomenon of online dating, and the forms of rational practice thus fostered, an emanation of modernization processes, but the specific ways this modern phenomenon is analyzed are anything but devoid of historical and social implications.

In conjunction with the same societal processes of economization, individualization, and rationalization, theories of rational choice and methodological individualism have developed and expanded their claim to power within the field of social sciences. In generalizing their scientific world view, and thus in generalizing the characteristics of the logics traditionally assigned to Western modernity, choice theorists describe a world in individualist and rationalist terms; in doing so they contribute to the legitimacy of a concept of man as being subject to rationalist imperatives. Accordingly, the same applies for modern theories of 'mate choice', whose axiomatic distinction between action and structure also represents the dominant approach to the scientific conceptualization of online dating. Whereas the dominant (mate) choice paradigm represents fertile tool for empirical research in general, and for the analyses of online dating markets in particular, it also runs the risk of obfuscating the fact that their specific underlying epistemology and methodology is contingent on specific historical and social conditions. Future research may hence apply a field perspective by analyzing the diachronic genesis and transformation of mating dispositions as effects of different social fields on the agents' habitus.

A field-analytical approach may also prove useful in tracing the influences of the economic field on the prevalent orthodoxies of the scientific sphere, such as the practice of rationalist re-construction of 'mate choice' and 'partner markets'. This could extend into a fruitful cultural comparison of how different partner markets operate and how offline partner markets are transmitted to online dating in different cultural contexts. In doing so, one must reflect on the question of how these markets are conceptualized by different paradigms of research. This represents one way to establish the extent to which rational choice perspectives are appropriate, and the extent to which rationality can be assigned to a characteristic of the medium itself. Such research efforts would bring about an analytical reorientation, which would absolve rationality from being the sole *explanans* by revealing its status as a historically and culturally variable *explanandum*.

References

Bauman, Z. (2005). *Liquid life*. Cambridge: Polity Press.
Ben-Ze'ev, A. (2004). *Love online: Emotions on the internet*. Cambridge: Cambridge University Press. Retrieved from http://www.loc.gov/catdir/description/cam032/2003055129.html
Bourdieu, P. (1990). *In other words. Essays towards a reflexive sociology*. Stanford: University Press.
Bourdieu, P. (1996). *Physical space, social space and habitus*. Lecture at the University of Oslo.
Bourdieu, P. (2008). *The Bachelors' Ball*. Chicago: University of Chicago Press.
Bourdieu, P., & Passeron, J. C. P. (1977). *Reproduction in education, society and culture*. Beverly Hills: Sage.
Bozon, M., & Heran, F. (2006). *La formation du couple*. Paris: La Découverte.
Bühler-Illieva, E. (2006). *Einen Mausklick von mir entfernt. Auf der Suche nach Liebesbeziehungen im Internet*. Marburg: Tectum.
Calhoun, C. (1993). Habitus, field, and capital: The question of historical specificity. In C. Calhoun, E. LiPuma, & M. Postone (Eds.), *Bourdieu: Critical perspectives* (pp. 61–88). Chicago: University of Chicago Press.
Finkel, E. J., Eastwick, P. W., Karney, B. R., Reis, H. T., & Sprecher, S. (2012). Online dating: A critical analysis from the perspective of psychological science. *Psychological Science in the Public Interest, 13*(1), 3–66.
Fiore, A. (2004). *Romantic regressions: An analysis of behavior in online dating systems*. Doctoral dissertation, Institute of Technology, Massachusetts.
Geser, H., & Bühler, I. (2006). *Partnerwahl online*. Retrieved from http://socio.ch/intcom/t_hgeser15.pdf
Hakim, C. (2010). Erotic capital. *European Sociological Review, 26*(5), 499–518.
Hodgson, G. M. (2002). *How economics forgot history: The problem of historical specificity in social science*. New York: Routledge.
Illouz, E. (2012). *Why love hurts. A sociological explanation*. Cambridge: Polity Press.
Kauffmann, J. C. (2011). *Sex@amour: Wie das Internet unser Liebesleben verändert*. Konstanz: UVK.
Lebaron, F. (2001). Toward a new critique of economic discourse. *Theory, Culture & Society, 18*(5), 123–129.

Lee, S. (2008). *Preferences and choice constraints in marital sorting: Evidence from Korea.* Working Paper.

Lunt, P. (2006). Rational choice theory versus cultural theory. On taste and social capital. In M. Altmann (Ed.), *Handbook of contemporary behavioral economics: Foundations and developments* (pp. 326–339). New York: M. E. Sharpe.

Potarca, G., & Mills, M. (2013). *Racial homophily and exclusion in online dating preferences: A cross-national comparison.* Unpublished working paper.

Schmitz, A. (2012). Elective affinities 2.0? A Bourdieusian approach to couple formation and the methodology of E-Dating. *Social Science Research on the Internet (RESET), 1*(1), 175–202.

Schmitz, A., & Zillmann, D. (2016). Online dating as a social sciences research tool. In F. X. Olleros, & M. Zhegu (Eds.), *Research handbook of digital transformations.* Cheltenham: Edward Elgar (forthcoming).

Schmitz, A., Witte, D., & Gengnagel, V. (2016). Pluralizing field analysis: Toward a relational understanding of the field of power. *Social Science Information/Information sur les sciences sociales* (forthcoming).

Sennett, R. (2002). *The fall of public man.* London: Penguin.

Skopek, J. (2011). *Partnerwahl im Internet: Eine quantitative Analyse von Strukturen und Prozessen der Online-Partnersuche.* Wiesbaden: VS Verlag.

Skopek, J., Schmitz, A., & Blossfeld, H. P. (2011). The gendered dynamics of age preferences – Empirical evidence from online dating. *Zeitschrift für Familienforschung, 23*(3), 267–290.

Zillmann, D. (2016). *Von kleinen Lügen und kurzen Beinen. Selbstdarstellung bei der Partnersuche im Internet* [About little lies and small legs. Self-presentation in online dating]. Wiesbaden: VS Verlag (forthcoming).

Zillmann, D., Schmitz, A., & Blossfeld, H. P. (2011). Lügner haben kurze Beine. Zum Zusammenhang unwahrer Selbstdarstellung und partnerschaftlicher Chancen im Online-Dating. *Zeitschrift für Familienforschung, 23*(3), 291–318.

Appendix

Table A.1 Profile parameters for dyadic classes

	Cluster1	Cluster2	Cluster3	Cluster4	Cluster5	Cluster6	Cluster7	Cluster8
Cluster size	0.21	0.16	0.15	0.11	0.11	0.10	0.08	0.07
Sender female	0.00	0.99	0.00	0.99	0.99	0.00	0.00	0.88
Sender male	0.99	0.00	0.99	0.00	0.00	0.99	0.99	0.11
Receiver female	0.99	0.00	0.99	0.00	0.00	0.99	0.99	0.11
Receiver male	0.00	0.99	0.00	0.99	0.99	0.00	0.00	0.88
Sender age (Mean)	34.02	44.04	49.21	38.22	22.43	49.70	32.04	41.31
Receiver age (Mean)	27.92	47.03	44.76	43.09	26.88	43.83	27.81	43.76
Sender Bmi (Mean)	24.25	22.74	26.29	22.36	21.13	25.08	24.33	28.06
Receiver Bmi (mean)	18.22	29.97	20.31	27.69	26.36	19.72	20.75	30.35
Sender school								
High school (Academic secondary)	0.17	0.36	0.07	0.33	0.22	0.73	0.45	0.01
High school (Lower secondary)	0.40	0.18	0.52	0.12	0.22	0.02	0.17	0.48
High school (Vocational secondary)	0.39	0.44	0.40	0.48	0.35	0.22	0.35	0.40
No secondary qualifications	0.02	0.00	0.00	0.03	0.02	0.01	0.00	0.03
Still in school	0.00	0.00	0.00	0.02	0.16	0.00	0.01	0.06

(continued)

Table A.1 (continued)

	Cluster1	Cluster2	Cluster3	Cluster4	Cluster5	Cluster6	Cluster7	Cluster8
Receiver school								
High school (Academic secondary)	0.28	0.40	0.22	0.16	0.41	0.24	0.25	0.05
High school (Lower secondary)	0.17	0.14	0.30	0.45	0.10	0.10	0.18	0.43
High school (Vocational secondary)	0.50	0.45	0.46	0.37	0.41	0.65	0.42	0.42
No secondary qualifications	0.00	0.00	0.00	0.00	0.01	0.00	0.01	0.07
Still in school	0.02	0.00	0.00	0.00	0.04	0.00	0.12	0.01
Sender education								
College degree	0.15	0.43	0.05	0.36	0.08	0.78	0.21	0.00
Completed apprenticeship	0.71	0.49	0.90	0.53	0.39	0.18	0.60	0.90
PhD	0.00	0.03	0.00	0.01	0.03	0.02	0.01	0.02
No further education	0.05	0.01	0.02	0.07	0.07	0.00	0.06	0.04
Still in further education	0.05	0.02	0.00	0.00	0.41	0.00	0.09	0.02
Receiver education								
College degree	0.30	0.49	0.39	0.12	0.16	0.25	0.30	0.16
Completed apprenticeship	0.45	0.50	0.55	0.78	0.61	0.74	0.28	0.74
PhD	0.03	0.00	0.00	0.01	0.01	0.00	0.00	0.04
No further education	0.01	0.00	0.04	0.08	0.02	0.00	0.04	0.02
Still in further education	0.19	0.00	0.01	0.00	0.17	0.00	0.36	0.02
Sender occupational position								
Salaried employee	0.36	0.48	0.39	0.68	0.61	0.39	0.48	0.18
Laborer	0.31	0.18	0.28	0.10	0.05	0.03	0.00	0.49
Civil servant	0.01	0.02	0.03	0.05	0.00	0.03	0.07	0.04
Career professional (doctor, lawyer, etc.)	0.02	0.07	0.01	0.02	0.11	0.14	0.08	0.00
Self-employed (business, trades, services)	0.23	0.19	0.15	0.05	0.07	0.39	0.13	0.05

(continued)

Table A.1 (continued)

	Cluster1	Cluster2	Cluster3	Cluster4	Cluster5	Cluster6	Cluster7	Cluster8
Alternative civilian service	0.00	0.00	0.00	0.00	0.00	0.00	0.02	0.02
Unemployed	0.03	0.03	0.09	0.09	0.11	0.00	0.03	0.19
Independent agriculturer	0.02	0.00	0.01	0.00	0.01	0.00	0.00	0.00
Receiver occupational position								
Salaried employee	0.49	0.38	0.68	0.38	0.43	0.72	0.64	0.26
Laborer	0.24	0.02	0.13	0.36	0.29	0.06	0.04	0.40
Civil servant	0.01	0.05	0.02	0.00	0.04	0.00	0.00	0.00
Career professional (doctor, lawyer, etc.)	0.10	0.05	0.07	0.00	0.01	0.00	0.07	0.00
Self-employed (business, trades, services)	0.11	0.47	0.06	0.23	0.18	0.13	0.06	0.20
Alternative civilian service	0.00	0.00	0.00	0.00	0.01	0.00	0.00	0.00
Unemployed	0.01	0.00	0.00	0.00	0.00	0.05	0.16	0.12
Independent agriculturer	0.00	0.00	0.00	0.01	0.01	0.01	0.00	0.00
Sender cultural capital (mean)	0.16	0.28	−0.65	0.25	0.20	0.21	0.22	−0.46
Receiver cultural capital (mean)	0.50	0.32	0.07	−0.18	0.35	0.27	0.35	−0.73
Differences in kilometers (mean)	200.54	181.18	129.26	234.28	196.50	200.71	166.61	68.23
Number of interactions (mean)	6.45	10.53	10.56	16.78	9.52	10.16	15.39	10.97
Sender Eigen-vector centrality (Mean)	0.9	1.4	1.1	1.8	2.2	1.2	1.1	0.8
Receiver Eigen-vector centrality (Mean)	2.4	1.5	1.6	1.7	1.1	1.6	1.8	1.0

Source: logfile data of dyadic 6th contacts of a major German dating platform. Sample of active users. Controls: type of message sent (standardized message or free text); desired form of relationship; time spent on platform

Bibliography

Acock, A. C., & Washburn, I. (2013). Quantitative methodology for family science. In G. W. Peterson & K. R. Bush (Eds.), *Handbook of marriage and the family* (pp. 65–89). New York: Plenum Press.
Adloff, F., & Wacquant, L. (2015). For a sociology of flesh and blood questions to Loïc Wacquant. In F. Adloff, K. Gerund, & D. Kaldewey (Eds.), *Revealing tacit knowledge: Embodiment and explication* (pp. 185–196). Bielefeld: Transcript Verlag.
Alexander, J. C., Giesen, B., Münch, R., & Smelser, N. (Eds.). (1987). *The micro-macro link* (1st ed.). Berkeley: University of California.
Alpern, S., & Reyniers, D. (2005). Strategic mating with common preferences. *Journal of Theoretical Biology, 237*(4), 337–354.
Alterovitz, S. S. R., & Mendelsohn, G. A. (2013). Relationship goals of middle-aged, young-old, and old-old internet daters: An analysis of online personal ads. *Journal of Aging Studies, 27*(2), 159–165.
Andersen, S. H., and Lars, G. H. (2010). The rise and fall of divorce – A sociological adjustment of Becker's model of the marriage market. FOI Working paper. Retrieved from https://core.ac.uk/download/files/153/6480754.pdf
Anderson, E. (1993). *Value in ethics and economics*. Cambridge, MA: Harvard University Press.
Anderson, A., Goel, S., Huber, G., Malhotra, N., & Watts, D. J. (2014). Political ideology and racial preferences in online dating. *Sociological Science, 1*(1), 28–40.
ARD/ZDF-Onlinestudie. (2012). Retrieved from http://www.ard-zdf-onlinestudie.de/index.php?id=388
Arkes, H. R., & Ayton, P. (1999). The sunk cost and Concorde effects: Are humans less rational than lower animals? *Psychological Bulletin, 125*(5), 591–600.
Arkes, H. R., & Blumer, C. (1985). The psychology of sunk cost. *Organizational Behavior and Human Decision Processes, 35*, 124–140.
Aspers, P. (2007). Theory, reality, and performativity in markets. *American Journal of Economics and Sociology, 66*(2), 379–398.
Axelrod, R. M. (1984). *The evolution of cooperation*. New York: Basic Books.
Baker, A. J. (2005). *Double click: Romance and commitment among couples online*. Cresskill: Hampton Press.
Bauman, Z. (2005). *Liquid life*. Cambridge: Polity Press.
Beck, U. (1992). *Risk society: Towards a new modernity. Theory, culture and society*. London: Sage.
Beck, U., & Beck-Gernsheim, E. (2002). *Individualization. Institutionalized individualism and its social and political consequences*. London: Sage.

Beck, U., Bonß, W., & Lau, C. (2004). Entgrenzung erzwingt Entscheidung: Was ist neu an der Theorie reflexiver Modernisierung? In U. Beck & C. Lau (Eds.), *Entgrenzung und Entscheidung: Was ist neu an der Theorie reflexiver Modernisierung?* (pp. 13–64). Frankfurt am Main: Suhrkamp.

Becker, G. S. (1974). A theory of marriage. In T. W. Schultz (Ed.), *Economics of the family: Marriage, children, and human* (pp. 299–344). Chicago: University of Chicago Press.

Becker, G. S. (1976). *The economic approach to human behavior.* Chicago: University of Chicago Press.

Becker, G. S. (1993). *A treatise on the family.* Cambridge, MA: Harvard University Press.

Becker, G. S. (1996). *Accounting for tastes.* Cambridge, MA: Harvard University Press.

Beh, E. J., & Lombardo, R. (2012). A genealogy of correspondence analysis. *Australian & New Zealand Journal of Statistics, 54*(2), 137–168.

Belot, M., & Francesconi, M. (2007). Can anyone be "The" One? Field evidence on dating behavior (Working Paper (17)). Colchester: ISER.

Benzécri, J. P. (1973). *L´analyse des données: L´analyse des correspondances.* Michigan: Dunod.

Ben-Ze'ēv, A. (2004). Love online: Emotions on the internet. Cambridge: Cambridge University Press. Retrieved from http://www.loc.gov/catdir/description/cam032/2003055129.html

Bergström, M. (2011). Casual dating online. Sexual norms and practices on French heterosexual dating sites. *Zeitschrift für Familienforschung, 23*(3), 291–318.

Bergström, M. (2014). *Au bonheur des rencontres. Sexualité, classe et rapports de genre dans la production et l'usage des sites de rencontres en France.* Institut d'études politiques de Paris, PhD Thesis in Sociology.

Bertilsonn, M. (1986). Love's labour lost? A sociological view. *Theory, Culture & Society, 3*(2), 19–35.

Blasius, J., & Greenacre, M. J. (1994). *Correspondence analysis in the social science. Recent developments and applications.* New York: Academic Press.

Blasius, J., & Mühlichen, A. (2010). Identifying audience segments applying the "social space" approach. *Poetics, 38*(1), 69–89.

Blasius, J., & Schmitz, A. (2013). The empirical construction of Bourdieu's social space. In M. Greenacre & J. Blasius (Eds.), *The visualization and verbalization of data* (pp. 205–222). London: Chapman & Hall.

Blasius, J., & Winkler, J. (1989). Gibt es die "feinen Unterschiede"? Eine empirische Überprüfung der Bourdieuschen Theorie. *Kölner Zeitschrift für Soziologie und Sozialpsychologie, 41*, 72–94.

Blau, P. M. (1964). *Exchange and power in social life* (9th ed.). New York: Wiley.

Blau, P. M. (1977). *Inequality and heterogeneity: A primitive theory of social structure* (1st ed.). New York: Free Press.

Blau, P. M. (1987). Contrasting theoretical perspectives. In J. C. Alexander, B. Giesen, R. Münch, & N. Smelser (Eds.), *The micro-macro-link* (pp. 71–85). Berkely: University of California Press.

Blau, P. M. (1989). Reciprocity and imbalance. A citation classic commentary on exchange and power in social-life by Blau, P. M. *Current Contents/Arts & Humanities, 25,* 16.

Blau, P. M., & Duncan, O. D. (1967). *The american occupational structure.* New York: Wiley.

Blau, P. M., Beeker, C., & Fitzpatrick, K. M. (1984). Intersecting social affiliations and intermarriage. *Social Forces, 62*(3), 585–606.

Blossfeld, H.-P. (1995a). Changes in the process of family formation and women's growing economic independence: A comparison of nine countries. In H.-P. Blossfeld (Ed.), *The new role of women: Family formation in modern societies* (pp. 3–32). Boulder: Westview Press.

Blossfeld, H.-P. (Ed.). (1995b). *The new role of women: Family formation in modern societies.* Boulder: Westview Press.

Blossfeld, H.-P. (1996). Macro-sociology, rational choice theory, and time. A theoretical perspective on the empirical analysis of social processes. *European Sociological Review, 12*(2), 181–206.

Blossfeld, H.-P. (2009). Educational assortative marriage in comparative perspective. *Annual Review of Sociology, 35,* 513–530.

Blossfeld, H.-P., & Drobnic, S. (2001). Theoretical perspectives on couples' careers. In H.-P. Blossfeld & S. Drobnic (Eds.), *Careers of couples in contemporary societies. From male breadwinner to dual earner families* (pp. 16–50). New York: Oxford University Press.

Blossfeld, H.-P., & Mill, M. (2001). A causal approach to interrelated family events: A crossnational comparison of cohabitation, nonmarital conception, and marriage. *Canadian Studies in Population, 28*(2), Special Issue on Longitudinal Methodology, 409–437.

Blossfeld, H.-P., & Müller, R. (1996). Sozialstrukturanalyse, Rational Choice Theorie und die Rolle der Zeit: Ein Versuch zur dynamischen Integration zweier Theorieperspektiven. *Soziale Welt, 47*(4), 382–410.

Blossfeld, H.-P., & Timm, A. (1997). *Das Bildungssystem als Heiratsmarkt: Eine Längsschnittanalyse der Wahl von Heiratspartnern im Lebenslauf* (Sonderforschungsbereich 186, Vol. 43). Bremen: University of Bremen.

Blossfeld, H.-P., & Timm, A. (2003). *Who marries whom? Educational systems as marriage markets in modern societies* (European studies of population, Vol. 12). Dordrecht: Kluwer.

Bok, S. (1979). *Lying. Moral choice in public and private life*. New York: Random House.

Bokek-Cohen, Y., Peres, Y., & Kanazawa, S. (2007). Rational choice and evolutionary psychology as explanations for mate selectivity. *Journal of Social, Evolutionary, and Cultural Psychology, 2*(2), 42–55.

Bonacich, P. (1987). Power and centrality: A family of measures. *American Journal of Sociology, 92*(5), 1170–1182.

Boudon, R. (1986). *Theories of social change*. Oxford: Polity Press.

Bourdieu, P. (1973). Cultural reproduction and social reproduction. In R. K. Brown (Ed.), *Knowledge, education, and cultural change: Papers in the sociology of education* (pp. 71–112). London: Tavistock.

Bourdieu, P. (1974). *Zur Soziologie der symbolischen Formen*. Frankfurt am Main: Suhrkamp.

Bourdieu, P. (1977). *Outline of a theory of practice* (Cambridge studies in social anthropology, Vol. 16). Cambridge: Cambridge University Press.

Bourdieu, P. (1983a). Ökonomisches Kapital, kulturelles Kapital, soziales Kapital. In R. Kreckel (Ed.), *Soziale Welt Sonderband* (Soziale Ungleichheiten) (Vol. 2, pp. 183–198). Göttingen: Schwartz.

Bourdieu, P. (1983b). Unpublished interview with Maria Iser. In M. Iser (Ed.), *Der Habitus als illegitimer Normalfall gesellschaftlicher Reproduktion. Die soziale Bedeutung von symbolischer Gewalt und strukturgesteuertem Lernen und Handeln in der Theorie von Pierre Bourdieu* (pp. 242–279).

Bourdieu, P. (1984). *Distinction: A social critique of the judgement of taste*. London: Routledge/ Kegan Paul.

Bourdieu, P. (1985). The social space and the genesis of groups. *Theory and Society, 14*(6), 723–744.

Bourdieu, P. (1986). The forms of capital. In J. Richardson (Ed.), *Handbook of theory and research for the sociology of education* (pp. 46–58). New York: Greenwood.

Bourdieu, P. (1987a). *Die feinen Unterschiede. Kritik der gesellschaftlichen Urteilskraft*. Frankfurt am Main: Suhrkamp.

Bourdieu, P. (1987b). What makes a social class? On the theoretical and practical existence of groups. *Berkeley Journal of Sociology, 32*, 1–17.

Bourdieu, P. (1988). Vive la Crise!: For heterodoxy in social science. *Theory and Society, 17*(5), (Special Issue on Breaking Boundaries: Social Theory and the Sixties), 773–787.

Bourdieu, P. (1989). Social space and symbolic power. *Sociological Theory, 7*(1), 14–25.

Bourdieu, P. (1990a). *In other words. Essays towards a reflexive sociology*. Stanford: University Press.

Bourdieu, P. (1990b). *The logic of practice*. Cambridge/Oxford: Polity Press/B. Blackwell.

Bourdieu, P. (1993a). *Sociology in question. Theory, culture and society*. London: Sage. Retrieved from http://www.loc.gov/catdir/enhancements/fy0656/93086215-d.html

Bourdieu, P. (1993b). Sozialer Sinn-Kritik der theoretischen Vernunft. Frankfurt am Main: Suhrkamp.

Bourdieu, P. (1993c). Über einige Eigenschaften von Feldern. In P. Bourdieu (Ed.), *Soziologische Fragen* (pp. 107–130). Frankfurt am Main: Suhrkamp.
Bourdieu, P. (1996a). *Physical space, social space and habitus*. Lecture at the University of Oslo.
Bourdieu, P. (1996b). On the family as a realized category. *Theory, culture & society, 13*, 19–26.
Bourdieu, P. (1996c). *State nobility. Elite schools in the field of power*. Stanford: Stanford University.
Bourdieu, P. (1996d). *The rules of art: Genesis and structure of the literary field*. Stanford: Stanford University Press.
Bourdieu, P. (1997). Wie eine soziale Klasse entsteht. In P. Bourdieu (Ed.), *Der Tote packt den Lebenden* (Schriften zu Politik & Kultur, Vol. 2, pp. 102–129). Hamburg: VSA.
Bourdieu, P. (1998a). *Practical reason: On the theory of action*. Cambridge: Polity Press.
Bourdieu, P. (1998b). *Praktische Vernunft. Zur Theorie des Handelns*. Frankfurt am Main: Suhrkamp.
Bourdieu, P. (1999a). Une révolution conservatrice dans l'édition". *Actes de la recherche en sciences sociales, 126–127*, 3–28.
Bourdieu, P. (1999b). *The weight of the world. Social suffering in contemporary society*. Stanford: Stanford University Press.
Bourdieu, P. (2000). *Pascalian meditations*. Cambridge: Polity Press.
Bourdieu, P. (2001). *Masculine domination* (1st ed.). Cambridge: Polity Press.
Bourdieu, P. (2002a). *Le bal des célibataires*. Paris: Seuil.
Bourdieu, P. (2002b). On marriage strategies. *Population and Development Review, 28*(3), 549–558.
Bourdieu, P. (2004). *Science of science and reflexivity*. Chicago: University of Chicago Press.
Bourdieu, P. (2005a). Principles of an economic anthropology. In N. J. Smelser & R. Swedberg (Eds.), *The handbook of economic sociology* (2nd ed., pp. 75–89). Princeton: Princeton University Press.
Bourdieu, P. (2005b). *The social structures of the economy*. Cambridge: Polity Press.
Bourdieu, P. (2008). *The Bachelors' ball*. Chicago: University of Chicago Press.
Bourdieu, P. (2010). Sociologists of belief and beliefs of sociologists. *Nordic Journal of Religion and Society, 23*(1), 1–7.
Bourdieu, P. (2014). The future of class and the causality of the probable. In A. Christoforou & M. Lainé (Eds.), *Re-thinking economics: Exploring the work of Pierre bourdieu* (pp. 233–269). London/New York: Routledge.
Bourdieu, P., & Chartier, R. (2011). *Der Soziologe und der Historiker*. Wien: Turia + Kant.
Bourdieu, P., & Passeron, J. C. P. (1977). *Reproduction in education, society and culture*. Beverly Hills: Sage.
Bourdieu, P., & Passeron, J. C. P. (1991). *The craft of sociology*. Berlin: de Gruyter.
Bourdieu, P., & Thompson, J. B. (1991). *Language and symbolic power*. Cambridge: Polity.
Bourdieu, P., & Wacquant, L. J. D. (1992). *An invitation to reflexive sociology*. Chicago: Polity Press.
Bourdieu, P., Darbel, A., Rivet, J.-P., & Seibel, C. (1963). *Travail et travailleurs en Algérie* (Recherches méditerranées, Vol. 1). Paris/Den Haag: Mouton.
Bozon, M. (1991). Women and the age gap between spouses: An accepted domination? population. *An English Selection, 3*, 113–148.
Bozon, M., & Heran, F. (1989). Finding a spouse: A survey of how french couples meet. Population. *An English Selection, 44*(1), 91–121.
Bozon, M., & Heran, F. (2006). *La formation du couple*. Paris: La Découverte.
Brase, G. L., & Guy, E. C. (2004). The demographics of mate value and self-esteem. *Personality and Individual Differences, 36*(2), 471–484.
Brehm, S., Miller, R. S., Perlman, D., & Campbell, S. (2002). *Intimate relationships* (3rd ed.). Boston: McGraw-Hill.
Breiger, R. L. (2000). A tool kit for practice theory. *Poetics, 27*(2–3), 91–115.
Bühler-Illieva, E. (2006). *Einen Mausklick von mir entfernt. Auf der Suche nach Liebesbeziehungen im Internet*. Marburg: Tectum.

Burgess, R. L., & Huston, T. L. (1979). *Social exchange in developing relationships*. New York: Academic Press.

Burrell, C. (2004). *Online dating. Info 311 Term Project*. University of Washington School of Information. Retrieved from http://www.jaamati.info/portfolio/human/info311/Online_Dating.pdf

Buss, D. M. (1989). Sex differences in human mate preferences: Evolutionary hypotheses tested in 37 cultures. *Behavioral and Brain Sciences, 12*(1), 1–49.

Buss, D. M. (2006). Strategies of human mating. *Psychological Topics, 15*(2), 239–260.

Buss, D. M., & Barnes, M. (1986). Preferences in human mate selection. *Journal of Personality and Social Psychology, 50*(3), 559–570.

Butler-Smith, P., Cameron, S., & Collins, A. (1998). Gender differences in mate search effort: An exploratory economic analysis of personal advertisements. *Applied Economics, 30*(10), 1277–1285.

Buunk, B. P., Dijkstra, P., Kenrick, D. T., & Warntjes, A. (2001). Age preferences for mates as related to gender, own age, and Involvement level. *Evolution and Human Behavior, 22*(4), 241–250.

Calhoun, C. (1993). Habitus, field, and capital: The question of historical specificity. In C. Calhoun, E. LiPuma, & M. Postone (Eds.), *Bourdieu: Critical perspectives* (pp. 61–88). Chicago: University of Chicago Press.

Cameron, C., Oskamp, S., & Sparks, W. (1977). Courtship american style: Newspaper ads. *The Family Coordinator, 26*(1), 27–30.

Caplan, S. E. (2003). Preference for online social interaction: A theory of problematic internet use and psychosocial well-being. *Communication Research, 30*(6), 625–648.

Carol, S. (2016). Like will to like? Partner choice among Muslim migrants and natives in Western Europe. *Journal of Ethnic and Migration Studies, 42*(2), 261–276.

Caspi, A., & Gorsky, P. (2006). Online deception: Prevalence, motivation, and emotion. *Cyberpsychology & Behavior, 9*(1), 54–59.

Çelikakso, A., Nekby, L., & Rashid, S. (2010). Assortative mating by ethnic background and education among individuals with an immigrant background in Sweden. *Zeitschrift für Familienforschung, 22*(1), 65–88.

Chambers, D. (2013). *Social media and personal relationships. Online intimacies and networked friendship*. Basingstoke: Palgrave.

Chiswick, B. R., & Houseworth, C. (2011). Ethnic intermarriage among immigrants: Human capital and assortative mating. *Review of Economics of the Household, 9*(2), 149–180.

Coleman, J. S. (1986). Social theory, social research, and a theory of action. *American Journal of Sociology, 91*(6), 1309–1335.

Coleman, J. S. (1990). *Foundations of social theory*. Cambridge: Harvard University Press.

Collins, R. (1990). Stratification, emotional energy, and the transient emotions. In T. D. Kemper (Ed.), *Research agendas of the sociology of emotion* (pp. 27–67). Albany: State University of New York Press.

Collins, R. (2004). *Interaction ritual chains*. Princeton: Princeton University Press.

Cooper, A., and Sportolaria, L. (1997). Romance in cyberspace: Understanding online attraction. *Journal of Sex Education and Therapy, 22*(1), Special Issue: Sexuality and the Internet, 7–14.

Corijn, M. (2003). Who marries whom in Flamish Belgium? In H.-P. Blossfeld & A. Timm (Eds.), *Who marries whom? Educational systems as marriage markets in modern societies* (pp. 37–55). Dordrecht: Kluwer.

Couper, M. P., & Coutts, E. (2006). Online-Befragungen. Probleme und Chancen verschiedener Arten von Online-Erhebungen. In A. Diekmann (Ed.), *Methoden der Sozialforschung* (pp. 217–243). Wiesbaden: VS Verlag.

Crossley, N. (2010). *Towards relational sociology. International library of sociology*. New York: Routledge.

de Campos, S. L., Otta, E., & de Oliviera Siqueira, J. (2002). Sex differences in mate selection strategies: Content analyses and responses to personal advertisements in Brazil. *Evolution and Human Behavior, 23*(5), 395–406.

de Munck, V. C. (1998). *Romantic love and sexual behavior: Perspectives from the social sciences.* Westport: Praeger.
de Paulo, B. M., Kashy, D. A., Kirkendol, S. E., Wyer, M. M., & Epstein, J. A. (1996). Lying in everyday life. *Journal of Personality and Social Psychology, 70*(5), 979–995.
de Singly, F. (1987). Théorie critique de l'homogamie. *L'Année sociologique, 37*, 181–205.
Degele, N. (2002). *Einführung in die Techniksoziologie.* München: Fink.
Diekmann, A., & Wyder, D. (2002). Vertrauen und Reputationseffekte bei Internet-Auktionen. *Kölner Zeitschrift für Soziologie und Sozialpsychologie, 54*(4), 674–693.
Donath, J. S. (1999). Identity and deception in the virtual community. In M. A. Smith & P. Kollock (Eds.), *Communities in cyberspace* (pp. 29–59). London/New York: Routledge.
Donati, P. (2010). *Relational sociology: A new paradigm for the social sciences. Ontological explorations.* London: Routledge.
Dröge, K., & Voirol, O. (2011). Online-Dating: zwischen romantischer Liebe und ökonomischer Rationalität. *Zeitschrift für Familienforschung, 23*(3), 337–357.
Dupré, J., & O'Neill, J. (1998). Against reductionist explanations of human behaviour. *Aristotelian Society Supplementary, 72*(1), 153–171.
Durkheim, E. (1964). *The division of labor in society.* New York: The Free Press.
Durkheim, E. (1973). *Emile Durkheim on Morality and Society.* Chicago: University of Chicago Press.
Durkheim, E. (1992). *Professional ethics and civic morals.* London: Routledge.
Durlauf, S. N., & Blume, L. (2008). *The new Palgrave dictionary of economics* (2nd ed.). Basingstoke/Hampshire/New York: Palgrave Macmillan.
Eastwick, P. W., & Finkel, E. J. (2008). Sex differences in mate preferences revisited: Do people know what they initially desire in a romantic partner? *Journal of Personality and Social Psychology, 94*(2), 245–264.
Edwards, J. (1969). Familial behavior as social exchange. *Journal of Marriage and the Family, 31*(3), 518–526.
Elder, G. (1969). Appearance and education in marriage mobility. *American Sociological Review, 34*(4), 519–533.
Elias, N. (1978). *What is sociology?* New York: Columbia University Press.
Elias, N. (1997). *Über den Prozess der Zivilisation. Soziogenetische und psychogenetische Untersuchungen: Erster Band: Wandlungen des Verhaltens in den weltlichen Oberschichten des Abendlandes* (Suhrkamp Taschenbuch Wissenschaft 159 20th ed.). Frankfurt am Main: Suhrkamp.
Ellison, N., Heino, R., & Gibbs, J. (2006). Managing impressions online: Self-presentation processes in the online dating environment. *Journal of Computer – Mediated Communication, 11*(2), 415–441.
Ellison, N. B., Lampe, C., & Steinfield, C. (2009). Social network sites and society: Current trends and future possibilities. *Interactions, 16*(1), 6–9.
Elster, J. (1986a). *An introduction to Karl Marx.* Cambridge: Cambridge University Press.
Elster, J. (1986b). *Rational choice.* New York: New York University Press.
England, P., & Farkas, G. (1986). *Households, employment, and gender: A social, economic, and demographic view.* New York: Aldine Publishing Co.
Esser, H. (1993). *Soziologie. Allgemeine Grundlagen.* Frankfurt am Main/New York: Campus.
Esser, H. (1999). *Soziologie: Spezielle Grundlagen. Band 1: Situationslogik und Handeln.* Frankfurt am Main: Campus.
Federal Statistical Office of Germany. (2014). Pressemitteilung Nr. 185 vom 28.05.2014. https://www.destatis.de/DE/PresseService/Presse/Pressemitteilungen/2014/05/PD14_185_122.html
Feld, S. L. (1981). The focused organization of social ties. *American Journal of Sociology, 86*(5), 1015–1035.
Feld, S. L. (1982). Social structural determinants of similarity among associates. *American Sociological Review, 47*, 797–801.
Ferguson, T. (1989). Who solved the secretary problem? *Statistical Science, 4*(3), 282–289.

Finkel, E. J., Eastwick, P. W., Karney, B. R., Reis, H. T., & Sprecher, S. (2012). Online dating: A critical analysis from the perspective of psychological science. *Psychological Science in the Public Interest, 13*(1), 3–66.

Fiore, A. (2004). *Romantic regressions: An analysis of behavior in online dating systems. Doctoral dissertation.* Cambridge, MA: Institute of Technology.

Fiore, A. T., & Donath, J. S. (2005). Homophily in online dating: When do you like someone like yourself? In G. van der Veer (Ed.), *CHI '05. Extended abstracts on human factors in computing systems* (pp. 1371–1374). New York: ACM.

Fiore, A., Taylor, L. S., Mendelsohn, G. A., & Hearst, M. (2008). Assessing attractiveness in online dating profiles. In Association for Computing Machinery (Ed.), *Proceedings of the SIGCHI conference on human factors in computing systems* (pp. 797–806). New York: ACM.

Fiore, A., Taylor, L. S., Zhong, X., Mendelsohn, G. A., & Cheshire, C. (2010). Who is right and who writes: People, profiles, contacts, and replies in online dating. *Proceedings of the Annual Hawaii International Conference on System Sciences, 43*, 1–10.

Flap, H. (2002). No man is an island: The research programme of a social capital theory. In O. Favereau & E. Lazega (Eds.), *New horizons in institutional and evolutionary economics. Conventions and Structures in Economic Organization. Markets, Networks and Hierarchies* (pp. 29–59). Cheltenham: Elgar.

Fligstein, N., & McAdam, D. (2012). *A theory of fields.* Oxford: University Press.

Foucault, M. (1978). *The history of sexuality volume I. An introduction [La volonté de savoir].* New York: Random House.

Freese, J. (2009). Preferences and the explanation of social behavior. In P. Hedström & P. Bearman (Eds.), *Oxford handbook of analytic sociology* (pp. 94–114). Oxford: Oxford University Press.

Frey, B. S., & Eichenberger, R. (1996). Marriage paradoxes. *Rationality and Society, 8*(2), 187–206.

Gardner, M. (1960). Mathematical games. *Scientific American, 202*(1), 150–153.

Geser, H., & Bühler, I. (2006). *Partnerwahl online.* Retrieved from http://socio.ch/intcom/t_hgeser15.pdf

Gibbs, J. L., Ellison, N. B., & Heino, R. B. (2006). Self-presentation in online personals: The role of anticipated future interaction, self-disclosure, and perceived success in internet dating. *Communication Research, 33*(2), 152–177.

Gibbs, J. L., Ellison, N. B., & Lai, C.-H. (2011). First comes love, then comes Google: An investigation of uncertainty reduction strategies and self-disclosure in online dating. *Communication Research, 38*, 70–100.

Giddens, A. (1984). *The constitution of society. Outline of the theory of structuration.* Berkeley/ Los Angeles: University of California Press.

Giddens, A. (1991). *Modernity and self-identity: Self and society in the late modern age.* Stanford: Stanford University Press.

Giddens, A. (1992). *The transformation of intimacy: Sexuality, love and eroticism in modern societies.* Cambridge: Polity.

Gigerenzer, G., & Todd, P. M. (Eds.). (1999). *Evolution and cognition. Simple heuristics that make us smart.* New York: Oxford University Press. Retrieved from http://www.loc.gov/catdir/enhancements/fy0640/98051084-d.html

Goffman, E. (1959). *The presentation of self in everyday life.* New York: Doubleday Anchor Books.

Goldstein, J. R., & Harknett, K. (2006). Parenting across racial and class lines: Assortative mating patterns of new parents who are married, cohabiting, dating or no longer romantically involved. *Social Forces, 85*(1), 121–143.

González-Ferrer, A. (2006). Who do immigrants marry? Partner choice among single immigrants in Germany. *European Sociological Review, 22*(2), 171–185.

Gower, J. C., Sugnet, L. G., & Le Roux, N. J. (2010). *Understanding biplots.* New York: Wiley.

Greenacre, M. J. (1984). *Theory and applications of correspondence analysis.* London: Academic Press.

Greenwald, A. G., & Banaji, M. R. (1995). Implicit social cognition: Attitudes, self-esteem, and stereotypes. *Psychological Review, 102*(1), 4–27.

Griffin, D., & Gonzalez, R. (1995). Correlational analysis of dyad-level data in the exchangeable case. *Psychological Bulletin, 118*(3), 430–439.

Guillory, J. (2000). Bourdieu's refusal. In N. Brown & I. Szeman (Eds.), *Pierre Bourdieu: Fieldwork in culture* (pp. 19–44). New York: Rowman & Littlefield.

Gustavsson, L., Johnsson, J., & Uller, T. (2008). Mixed support for sexual selection theories of mate preferences in the Swedish population. *Evolutionary Psychology, 6*(4), 575–585.

Habermas, J. (1981). *Theorie des kommunikativen Handelns*. Frankfurt am Main: Suhrkamp.

Hakim, C. (2010). Erotic capital. *European Sociological Review, 26*(5), 499–518.

Hakim, C. (2011). *Erotic capital: The power of attraction in the bedroom and the boardroom*. New York: Basic Books.

Hakim, C. (2013). *The new rules of marriage: Internet, playfairs, and erotic power*. London: Gibson Square.

Hall, J. A., Park, N., Song, H., & Cody, M. J. (2010). Strategic misrepresentation in online dating: The effects of gender, self-monitoring, and personality traits. *Journal of Social and Personal Relationships, 27*(1), 117–135.

Haller, M. (1981). Marriage, women, and social stratification: A theoretical critique. *American Journal of Sociology, 86*(4), 766–795.

Hancock, J. T., Thoma, C., & Ellison, N. (2007). The truth about lying in online dating profiles. In *Proceedings of the ACM conference on human factors in computing systems* (pp. 449–452). New York: ACM.

Harrison, A. A., & Saeed, L. (1977). Let's make a deal: An analysis of revelations and stipulations in lonely hearts advertisements. *Journal of Personality and Social Psychology, 35*(4), 257–264.

Hassebrauck, M. (1990). Wer sucht wen? Eine inhaltsanalytische Untersuchung von Heirats- und Bekanntschaftsanzeigen. *Zeitschrift für Sozialpsychologie, 21*(2), 101–122.

Hedström, P. (2005). *Dissecting the social: On the principles of analytical sociology*. Cambridge: Cambridge University Press.

Hedström, P., & Bearman, P. S. (Eds.). (2009). *The Oxford handbook of analytical sociology*. Oxford: University Press.

Heiner, R. A. (1983). The origin of predictable behavior. *The American Economic Review, 73*(4), 560–590.

Hertog, E. (2012). *Hedged bets: Preferences for future marriage partners' earning power in contemporary Japan*. Unpublished working paper.

Hirschmann, E. C. (1987). People as products: Analysis of a complex marketing exchange. *The Journal of Marketing, 51*(1), 98–108.

Hitsch, G. J., Hortaçsu, A., & Ariely, D. (2005). *What makes you click: An empirical analysis of online dating*. Retrieved from https://www.aeaweb.org/assa/2006/0106_0800_0502.pdf

Hitsch, G. J., Hortaçsu, A., & Ariely, D. (2010a). Matching and sorting in online dating. *American Economic Review, 100*(1), 130–163.

Hitsch, G. J., Hortaçsu, A., & Ariely, D. (2010b). What makes you click?—Mate preferences in online dating. *Quantitative Marketing and Economics, 8*(4), 393–427.

Hodgson, G. M. (2002). *How economics forgot history: The problem of historical specificity in social science*. New York: Routledge.

Hodgson, G. M. (2009). Choice, habit and evolution. *Journal of Evolutionary Economics, 20*(1), 1–18.

Hodgson, G. M. (2010). Markets. In J. B. Davis & W. Dolfsma (Eds.), *The Elgar companion to social economics* (pp. 251–266). Cheltenham/Northampton: Edward Elgar.

Hogan, B., Li, N., & Dutton, W. H. (2011). *A global shift in the social relationships of networked individuals: Meeting and dating online comes of age*. Paper of the "Me, My Spouse and the Internet" project. Retrieved from http://blogs.oii.ox.ac.uk/couples/

Hollingshead, A. B. (1950). Cultural factors in the selection of marriage mates. *American Sociological Review, 15*(5), 619–627.

Homans, G. C. (1961). *Social behavior: Its elementary forms*. New York: Harcourt Brace & World.

Homans, P., & Aden, L. (1968). *The dialogue between theology and psychology* (3rd ed.). Chicago: University of Chicago Press.
Huber, G., & Malhotra, N. (2013). *Dimensions of political homophily: Isolating choice homophily along political characteristics*. Working paper. Retrieved from http://huber.research.yale.edu/materials/38_paper.pd
Huckfeld, R. R. (1983). Social contexts, social networks, and urban neighborhoods: Environmental constraints on friendship choice. *American Journal of Sociology, 89*(3), 651–669.
Huinink, J., & Feldhaus, M. (2009). Family research from the life course perspective. *International Sociology, 24*(3), 299–324.
Huston, T. L. (2000). The social ecology of marriage and other intimate unions. *Journal of Marriage and the Family, 62*(2), 298–320.
Illouz, E. (2007). *Cold intimacies: The making of emotional capitalism* (1st ed.). Cambridge: Polity.
Illouz, E. (2012). *Why love hurts. A sociological explanation*. Cambridge/Malden: Polity Press.
Illouz, E., & Finkelmann, S. (2009). An odd and inseparable couple: Emotion and rationality in partner selection. *Theory and Society, 38*(4), 401–422.
Jackson, J., Halberstadt, J., Jong, J., & Felman, H. (2015). Perceived openness to experience accounts for religious homogamy. *Social Psychological and Personality Science*. Advance online publication.
Janetzko, D. (2008). Nonreactive data collection on the internet. In N. Fielding, R. M. Lee, & G. Blank (Eds.), *The SAGE handbook of online research methods* (pp. 161–176). London: Sage.
Joas, H. (2007). *Lehrbuch der Soziologie*. Frankfurt am Main: Campus.
Joinson, A. N. (2004). Self-esteem, interpersonal risk, and preference for e-mail to face-to-face communication. *Cyberpsychology & Behaviour, 7*(4), 472–478.
Joppke, C. (1986). The cultural dimensions of class formation and class struggle: On the social theory of Pierre Bourdieu. *Berkeley Journal of Sociology, 31*, 53–78.
Kalmijn, M. (1991). Status homogamy in the United States. *American Journal of Sociology, 97*(2), 496–523.
Kalmijn, M. (1994). Assortative mating by cultural and economic occupational status. *American Journal of Sociology, 100*(2), 422–452.
Kalmijn, M. (1998). Intermarriage and homogamy: Causes, patterns, trends. *Annual Review of Sociology, 24*, 395–421.
Kalmijn, M., & Flap, H. (2001). Assortative meeting and mating: Unintended consequences of organized settings for partner choices. *Social Forces, 79*(4), 1289–1312.
Kara, A. (2009). Implications of multiple preferences for a deconstructive critique and a reconstructive revision of economic theory. *Journal of Economic and Social Research, 11*(1), 69–78.
Karch, I., Schaefer, K., Pflitsch, D., & Wiechers, H. (2013). *Vom Dating zum Traualtar. Wie viele der Hochzeitspaare haben sich im Internet kennen gelernt?* Retrieved from http://www.single-boersen-vergleich.de/presse/studie-2013-vom-onlinedating-zum-traualtar.pdf
Katz, A. M., & Hill, R. (1958). Residential propinquity and marital selection: A review of theory, method, and fact. *Marriage and Family Living, 20*(1), 27–35.
Kauffmann, J. C. (2011). *Sex@amour: Wie das Internet unser Liebesleben verändert*. Konstanz: UVK.
Kaupp, P. (1968). *Das Heiratsinserat im sozialen Wandel*. Stuttgart: Ferdinand Enke.
Kenny, D. A., Kashy, D. A., & Cook, W. L. (2006). *Dyadic Data Analysis*. New York: The Guilford Press.
Kenrick, D. T., & Keefe, R. C. (1992). Age preferences in mates reflect sex differences in human reproductive strategies. *Behavioral and Brain Sciences, 15*(1), 75–91.
Kincaid, H. (1995). *Philosophical foundations of the social sciences: Analyzing controversies in social research*. Cambridge: Cambridge University Press.
Klein, T. (1996). Der Altersunterschied zwischen Ehepartnern. Ein neues Analysemodell. *Zeitschrift für Soziologie, 25*(5), 346–370.
Klein, T. (2011). "Durch Dick und Dünn." Zum Einfluss von Partnerschaft und Partnermarkt auf das Körpergewicht. *Kölner Zeitschrift für Soziologie und Sozialpsychologie, 63*, 459–479.

Kling, R. (1996). *Computerization and controversy: Value conflicts and social choices* (2nd ed.). Boston: Academic Press.
Kok, J. (2007). Principles and prospects of the life course paradigm. In *Virtual knowledge studio for the humanities and social sciences*. Retrieved from https://www.cairn.info/revue-annales-de-demographie-historique-2007-1-page-203.htm
Krais, B., & Gebauer, G. (2002). *Habitus*. Bielefeld: Transcript.
Kroneberg, C. (2006). *The definition of the situation and variable rationality: The model of frame selection as a general theory of action* (Sonderforschungsbereich 504, No. 06–05). Mannheim: University of Mannheim.
Kroneberg, C., & Kalter, F. (2012). Rational choice theory and empirical research: Methodological and theoretical contributions in Europe. *Annual Review of Sociology, 38*, 73–92.
Kuhn, T. S. (1962). *The structure of scientific revolutions*. Chicago: University of Chicago Press.
Kuipers, G. (2006). *Good humor, bad taste. A sociology of the joke*. Berlin/New York: De Gruyter.
Kurzban, R., & Weeden, J. (2007). Do advertised preferences predict the behavior of speed daters? *Personal Relationships, 14*, 623–632.
Lamaison, P., & Bourdieu, P. (1986). From rules to strategies: An interview with Pierre Bourdieu. *Cultural Anthropology, 1*(1), 110–120.
Latour, B. (1987). *Science in action: How to follow scientists and engineers through society*. Cambridge: Harvard University Press.
Lawson, H. M., & Leck, K. (2006). Dynamics of internet dating. *Social Science Computer Review, 24*(2), 189–208.
Le Roux, B., & Rouanet, H. (2004). *Geometric data analysis. From correspondence analysis to structered data analysis*. Kluwer: Dordrecht.
Le Roux, B., & Rouanet, H. (2010). *Multiple correspondence analysis. Sage series of quantitative applications in the social sciences*. London: Sage.
Lebaron, F. (2001). Toward a new critique of economic discourse. *Theory, Culture & Society, 18*(5), 123–129.
Lebaron, F. (2002). *Pierre Bourdieu: Economic models against economism*. Retrieved from http://olivier.godechot.free.fr/hopfichiers/lebaron-second-draft-edited.pdf
Lebaron, F. (2009). How Bourdieu "quantified" Bourdieu: The geometric modelling of data. In K. Robson & C. Sanders (Eds.), *Quantifying theory: Pierre Bourdieu* (pp. 11–29). Wiesbaden: VS Verlag.
Lebaron, F. (2012). Grundzüge einer geometrischen Formalisieurng des Feldkonzepts. In S. Bernhard & C. Schmidt-Wellenburg (Eds.), *Feldanalyse als Forschungsprogramm* (pp. 123–150). Wiesbaden: VS Verlag.
Lebaron, F. (2015). Pierre Bourdieu, geometric data analysis and the analysis of economic spaces and fields. *Forum for Social Economics*. 09.07.2015.
Lebart, L., Morineau, A., & Warwick, K. M. (1984). *Multivariate descriptive statistical analysis. Correspondence analysis and related techniques for large matrices*. New York: Wiley.
Lee, S. (2008). *Preferences and choice constraints in marital sorting: Evidence from Korea*. Working Paper.
Lee, S. (2015). Effect of online dating on assortative mating: Evidence from South Korea. *Journal of Applied Econometrics, 30*(7).
Lenton, A. P., & Stewart, A. (2008). Changing her ways: The number of options and mate-standard strength impact mate choice strategy and satisfaction. *Judgment and Decision Making, 3*(7), 501–511.
Lewin, K., & Cartwright, D. (1952). *Field theory in social science: Selected theoretical papers* (1st ed.). London: Tavistock.
Lewis, K. (2015). Studying online behavior: Comment on Anderson et al. *Sociological Science, 2*, 20–31.
Lewis, S. K., & Oppenheimer, V. K. (2000). Educational assortative mating across marriage markets: Non-Hispanic Whites in the United States. *Demography, 37*(1), 29–40.
Lewis, R. A., & Spanier, G. B. (1979). Theorizing about the quality and stability of marriage. In W. Burr, I. Reiss, R. Hill, & F. Nye (Eds.), *Contemporary theories about the family: General theories and theoretical orientations* (pp. 268–294). New York: Free Press.

Lichbach, M. (2003). *Is rational choice theory all of social science?* Michigan: University of Michigan Press.

Lichter, D. T., Anderson, R. N., & Hayward, M. D. (1995). Marriage markets and marital choice. *Journal of Family Issues, 16*(4), 412–431.

Lin, K.-H., & Lundquist, J. (2013). Mate selection in cyberspace: The intersection of race, gender, and education. *American Journal of Sociology, 119*(1), 183–215.

Lindenberg, S. (2001). Social rationality versus rational egoism. In J. H. Turner (Ed.), *Handbook of sociological theory* (pp. 635–668). New York: Springer.

Lindenberg, S. (2013). Social rationality, self-regulation, and well-being: The regulatory significance of needs, goals, and the self. In R. Wittek, T. Snijders, & V. Nee (Eds.), *The handbook of rational choice social research* (pp. 72–112). Palo Alto: Stanford University Press.

Lizardo, O. (2014). Taste and the logic of practice in distinction. *Sociologický ústav*, AV ČR.

Luhmann, N. (1973). *Zweckbegriff und Systemrationalität*. Frankfurt am Main: Suhrkamp.

Luhmann, N. (1987). *Love as passion. The codification of intimacy. Translated by Jeremy Gaines*. Cambridge, MA: Harvard University Press.

Luhmann, N. (1995). *Social systems*. Stanford: Stanford University Press.

Luhmann, N. (1997). *Die Gesellschaft der Gesellschaft*. Frankfurt am Main: Suhrkamp.

Luhmann, N. (2011). *Einführung in die Systemtheorie. Herausgegeben von D. Baecker*. Heidelberg: Carl-Auer Verlag.

Lunt, P. (2006). Rational choice theory versus cultural theory. On taste and social capital. In M. Altmann (Ed.), *Handbook of contemporary behavioral economics: Foundations and developments* (pp. 326–339). New York: M. E. Sharpe.

Mäenpää, E. (2015). Socio-economic homogamy and its effects on the stability of cohabiting unions. In The Population Research Institute Väestöliitto (Ed.), *Finnish yearbook of population* (pp. 32–34). Turku.

Magidson, J., & Vermunt, J. K. (2004). Latent class models. In D. Kaplan (Ed.), *The Sage handbook of quantitative methodology for the social sciences* (pp. 175–198). Thousand Oaks: Sage.

Mare, R. D. (1991). Five decades of educational assortative mating. *American Sociological Review, 56*(1), 15–32.

Martin, J. L. (2003). What is field theory? *American Journal of Sociology, 109*(1), 1–49.

Marx, K., & Engels, F. (1848). Manifesto of the communist party. In K. Marx & F. Engels (1969, 1.ed.), *Selected works* (pp. 98–137). Moscow: Progress Publishers.

Marx, K., & Engels, F. (1976). *Collected works – volume six*. New York: International Publishers.

Mayntz, R. (2004). Mechanisms in the analysis of social macro-phenomena. *Philosophy of the Social Sciences, 34*(2), 237–259.

McAdam, D., Tarrow, S., & Tilly, C. (2001). *Dynamics of contention*. Cambridge: Cambridge University Press.

McPherson, M. (1983). Ecology of affiliation. *American Sociological Review, 48*, 519–532.

McPherson, J. M., & Ranger-Moore, J. R. (1991). Evolution on a dancing landscape: Organizations and networks in dynamic Blau space. *Social Forces, 70*(1), 19–42.

Miller, G. F., & Todd, P. M. (1998). Mate choice turns cognitive. *Trends in Cognitive Sciences, 2*(5), 190–198.

Moucha, P., Pflitsch, D., & Wiechers, H. (2012). *Der online dating markt 2011–2012*. Retrieved from http://www.singleboersen-vergleich.de/presse/online-dating-markt-2011-2012-de.pdf

Mu, Z., & Wu, X. (2015). *Residential concentration and marital behaviors of Muslim Chinese*. Population Studies Center Research Report 15.

Münch, R. (1987a). The interpenetration of microinteraction and macrostructures in a complex and contingent instituional order. In J. C. Alexander, B. Giesen, R. Münch, & N. J. Smelser (Eds.), *The micro-macro Link* (pp. 319–337). Berkeley: University of California Press.

Münch, R. (1987b). *Theory of action: Towards a new synthesis going beyond parsons*. London/Boston: Routledge & Kegan Paul.

Münch, R. (1991). *Dialektik der Kommunikationsgesellschaft*. Frankfurt am Main: Suhrkamp.

Münch, R. (2002). *Soziologische theorie. Band 2: Handlungstheorie*. Frankfurt am Main: Campus.

Murstein, B. (1970). Stimulus – value – role: A theory of marital choice. *Journal of Marriage and the Family, 32*(3), 465–481.
Nagel, I., Ganzeboom, H. B. G., & Kalmijn, M. (2011). Bourdieu in the network: The influence of high culture and popular culture on network formation in secondary schools. In J. Rössel & G. Otte (Eds.), *Lebensstilforschung* (pp. 424–446). Sonderheft 51, Kölner Zeitschrift für Soziologie und Sozialpsychologie.
Oppenheimer, V. K. (1988). A theory of marriage timing. *American Journal of Sociology, 94*(3), 563–591.
Ormel, J., Lindenberg, S., Steverink, N., & Verbrugge, L. M. (1999). Subjective well-being and social production functions. *Social Indicators Research, 46*(1), 61–90.
Parsons, T. (1937). *The structure of social action*. New York: Free Press.
Pawlowski, B., & Dunbar, R. I. M. (1999). Impact of market value on human mate choice decisions. *Proceedings of the Royal Society of London B, 266*, 281–285.
Peggs, K., & Lampard, R. (2001). (Ir)rational choice. A multidimensional approach to choice and constraint in decisions about marriage, divorce and remarriage. In M. S. Archer & J. Q. Tritter (Eds.), *Rational choice theory. Resisting colonization* (pp. 93–110). New York: Routledge.
Penke, L., & Denissen, J. J. (2008). Sex differences and lifestyle-dependent shifts in the attunement of self-esteem to self-perceived mate value: Hints to an adaptive mechanism? *Journal of Research in Personality, 4*(42), 1123–1129.
Peter, F., & Spiekermann, K. (2011). Rules, norms, commitments. In I. C. Jarvie & J. Zamora-Bonilla (Eds.), *The sage handbook of the philosophy of social sciences* (pp. 216–238). Thousand Oaks: Sage.
Phillips, M. C., Meek, S. W., & Vendemia, J. M. C. (2011). Understanding the underlying structure of deceptive behaviors. *Personality and Individual Differences, 50*(6), 783–789.
Popper, K. R. (2002). *The poverty of historicism*. London: Routledge.
Postman, N. (1992). *Technopoly: The surrender of culture to technology*. New York: Vintage Books/Random House.
Potarca, G., & Mills, M. (2013). *Racial homophily and exclusion in online dating preferences: A cross-national comparison*. Unpublished working paper.
Rabe-Hesketh, S., Skrondal, A., & Pickles, A. (2004). Generalized multilevel structural equation modelling. *Psychometrika, 69*(2), 167–190.
Regan, P. C., Levin, L., Sprecher, S., Christopher, F. S., & Cate, R. (2000). Partner preferences: What characteristics do men and women desire in their short-term sexual and long-term romantic partners? *Journal of Psychology & Human Sexuality, 12*(3), 1–21.
Reimer, T., & Rieskamp, J. (2007). Fast and frugal heuristics. In R. F. Baumeister & K. D. Vohs (Eds.), *A sage reference publication. Encyclopedia of social psychology* (pp. 347–349). Los Angeles: Sage.
Robinson, L., & Halle, D. (2002). Digitization, the internet, and the arts: eBay, Napster, SAG, and e-Books. *Qualitative Sociology, 25*(3), 359–383.
Roscoe, P., & Chillas, S. (2014). The state of affairs: Critical performativity and the online dating industry. *Organization, 21*(6), 797–820.
Rosenbaum, E. (2000). What is a market? On the methodology of a contested concept. *Review of Social Economy, 58*(4), 455–482.
Rosenfeld, M. J. (2005). A critique of exchange theory in mate selection. *American Journal of Sociology, 110*(5), 1284–1325.
Rosenfeld, M. J. (2010). *Meeting online: The rise of the internet as a social intermediary*. Draft. Retrieved from http://web.stanford.edu/~mrosenfe/Rosenfeld_How_Couples_ Meet_PAA_ updated.pdf
Rosenfeld, M. J., & Thomas, R. J. (2012). Searching for a mate: The rise of the internet as a social intermediary. *American Sociological Review, 77*(4), 523–547.
Rouanet, H. (2002). Lebaron Frédéric, Le Hay Viviane, Ackermann Werner, Le Roux Brigitte: Régression et analyse géométrique des données: réflexions et suggestions. *Mathématiques & Sciences Humaines, 40*(160), 13–45.

Rouanet, H., Ackermann, W., & Le Roux, B. (2000). The geometric analysis of questionnaires: The lesson of Bourdieu's La distinction. *Bulletin de Méthodologie Sociologique, 65*(1), 5–18.

Samuelson, P. A. (1947). *Foundations of economic analysis*. Harvard economic studies (Vol. 80). Cambridge: Harvard University Press.

Sanchez, L., Manning, W. D., & Smock, P. J. (1998). Sex-specialized or collaborative mate selection? Union transitions among cohabitors. *Social Science Research, 27*(3), 280–304.

Sautter, J. M., Tippett, R. M., & Morgan, S. P. (2010). The social demography of internet dating in the United States. *Social Science Quarterly, 91*(2), 554–575.

Scharlott, B. W., & Christ, W. G. (1995). Overcoming relationship-initiation barriers: The impact of a computer-dating system on sex role, shyness, and appearance inhibitions. *Computers in Human Behavior, 11*(2), 191–204.

Schmitt, D. P., Jonason, P. K., Byerley, G. J., Flores, S. D., Illbeck, B. E., O'Leary, K. N., & Qudrat, A. (2012). A reexamination of sex differences in sexuality: New studies reveal old truths. *Current Directions in Psychological Science, 21*(2), 135–139.

Schmitz, A. (2009). Virtuelle Zwischengeschlechtlichkeit im Kontext relationaler Methodologie. Überlegungen zu einer Soziologie der digitalen Partnerwahl. In H.-G. Soeffner (Ed.), *Unsichere Zeiten. Herausforderungen gesellschaftlicher Transformationen; Verhandlungen des 34. Kongresses der Deutschen Gesellschaft für Soziologie in Jena 2008*. Wiesbaden: VS Verlag.

Schmitz, A. (2012). Elective affinities 2.0? A Bourdieusian approach to couple formation and the methodology of E-dating. *Social Science Research on the Internet (RESET), 1*(1), 175–202.

Schmitz, A. (2014). The online dating market: Theoretical and methodological considerations. *Economic Sociology, 16*(1), 11–25.

Schmitz, A., & Riebling, J. (2013). Gibt es erotisches Kapital? Anmerkungen zu körperbasierter Anziehungskraft und Paarformation bei Hakim und Bourdieu. *Gender- Zeitschrift für Geschlecht, Kultur und Gesellschaft, Special Issue, 2*, 57–80.

Schmitz, A., & Zillmann, D. (2016). Online dating as a social sciences research tool. In F. X. Olleros & M. Zhegu (Eds.), *Research handbook of digital transformations*. Cheltenham: Edward Elgar (forthcoming).

Schmitz, A., Klein, D., Skopek, J., Schulz, F., & Blossfeld, H.-P. (2009). Die Integration von Befragungs- und Prozessdaten einer Online-Kontaktbörse. [The integration of survey and process generated data of an online dating site.] Sozialwissenschaftlicher Fachinformationsdienst soFid. *Methoden und Instrumente der Sozialwissenschaften, 2009*(1), 31–44.

Schmitz, A., Sachse-Thürer, S., Zillmann, D., & Blossfeld, H.-P. (2011). Myths and facts about online mate choice. Contemporary beliefs and empirical findings. *Zeitschrift für Familienforschung, 23*(3), 358–381.

Schmitz, A., Witte, D., & Gengnagel, V. (2016). Pluralizing field analysis: Toward a relational understanding of the field of power. *Social Science Information/Information sur les sciences sociales* (forthcoming).

Schoen, R., & Wooldredge, J. (1989). Marriage choices in North Carolina and Virginia, 1969–71 and 1979–81. *Journal of Marriage and the Family, 51*(2), 465–481.

Schroedter, J. H., & Kalter, F. (2008). Binationale Ehen in Deutschland. Trends und Mechanismen der sozialen Assimilation. In F. Kalter (Ed.), *Migration und integration* (Sonderheft 48 der KZfSS, pp. 350–379). Wiesbaden: VS Verlag.

Schulz, F. (2009). Bildungshomophilie im Onlinedating. In Deutsche Gesellschaft für Soziologie (Ed.), *Konferenzband der DGS zum Soziologentag in Jena*. DGS Tagung 2009, Jena.

Schulz, F. (2010). *Verbundene Lebensläufe: Partnerwahl und Arbeitsteilung zwischen neuen Ressourcenverhältnissen und traditionellen Geschlechterrollen*. Wiesbaden: VS Verlag.

Schulz, F., Skopek, J., & Blossfeld, H.-P. (2010). Partnerwahl als konsensuelle Entscheidung. Das Antwortverhalten bei Erstkontakten im Online-Dating. *Kölner Zeitschrift für Soziologie und Sozialpsychologie, 62*(3), 485–514.

Schütze, Y. (2008). Die feinen Unterschiede der Liebe. *Leviathan, 36*(1), 76–84.

Schwartz, C. R. (2013). Trends and Variation in Assortative Mating: Causes and Consequences. *Annual Review of Sociology, 39*, 451–470.

Scott, J. (2000). Rational choice theory. In G. K. Browning, A. Halcli, & F. Webster (Eds.), *Understanding contemporary society. Theories of the present* (pp. 126–138). London: Sage.
Searle, J. R. (1969). *Speech acts: An essay in the philosophy of language*. Cambridge: Cambridge University Press.
Sen, A. K. (1977). Rational fools: A critique of the behavioral foundations of economic theory. *Philosophy & Public Affairs, 6*(4), 317–344.
Sennett, R. (2002). *The fall of public man*. New York: Penguin Books.
Simmel, G. (1890). *On social differentiation*. Leipzig: Duncker & Humblot.
Simmel, G. (1983). Soziologie: Untersuchungen über die Formen der Vergesellschaftung. In *Gesammelte Werke* (6th ed., Vol. 2). Berlin: Duncker & Humblot.
Simmel, G. (1985). *Schriften Zur Philosophie und Soziologie der Geschlechter*. Frankfurt am Main: Suhrkamp.
Simmel, G. (2008). *Gesamtausgabe*. Frankfurt am Main: Suhrkamp.
Simon, H. A. (1956). Rational choice and the structure of the environment. *Psychological Review, 63*(2), 129–138.
Simpson, J. A. (1987). The dissolution of romantic relationships: Factors involved in relationship stability and emotional distress. *Journal of Personality and Social Psychology, 53*(4), 683–692.
Skopek, J. (2011). *Partnerwahl im Internet: Eine quantitative Analyse von Strukturen und Prozessen der Online-Partnersuche*. Wiesbaden: VS Verlag.
Skopek, J., Schulz, F., & Blossfeld, H.-P. (2009). Partnersuche im Internet. Bildungsspezifische Mechanismen bei der Wahl von Kontaktpartnern. *Kölner Zeitschrift für Soziologie und Sozialpsychologie, 61*(2), 183–210.
Skopek, J., Schmitz, A., & Blossfeld, H.-P. (2011a). The gendered dynamics of age preferences – Empirical evidence from online dating. *Zeitschrift für Familienforschung, 23*(3), 267–290.
Skopek, J., Schulz, F., & Blossfeld, H.-P. (2011b). Who contacts whom? Educational homophily in online mate selection. *European Sociological Review, 27*(2), 180–195.
Skrondal, A., & Rabe-Hesketh, S. (2004). *Generalized latent variable modeling: Multilevel, longitudinal, and structural equation models. Interdisciplinary statistics series*. Boca Raton: Chapman & Hall/CRC. Retrieved from http://www.loc.gov/catdir/enhancements/fy0646/2004042808-d.html
South, S. J. (1991). Sociodemographic differentials in mate selection preferences. *Journal of Marriage and the Family, 53*(4), 928–940.
Spanier, G. B., & Glick, P. C. (1980). Mate selection differentials between whites and blacks in the United States. *Social Forces, 58*(3), 707–725.
Sprecher, S., Sullivan, Q., & Hatfield, E. (1994). Mate selection preferences: Gender differences examined in a national sample. *Journal of Personality and Social Psychology, 66*(6), 1074–1080.
Sritharan, R., Heilpern, K., Wilbur, C. J., & Gawronski, B. (2010). I think I like you: Spontaneous and deliberate evaluations of potential romantic partners in an online dating context. *European Journal of Social Psychology, 40*(6), 1062–1077.
Stauder, J. (2008). Opportunitäten und Restriktionen des Kennenlernens. Zur sozialen Vorstrukturierung der Kontaktgelegenheiten am Beispiel des Partnermarkts. *Kölner Zeitschrift für Soziologie und Sozialpsychologie, 60*(2), 266–286.
Stauder, J. (2011). Regionale Ungleichheit auf dem Partnermarkt? Die makrostrukturellen Rahmenbedingungen der Partnerwahl in regionaler Perspektive. *Soziale Welt, 62*, 41–69.
Stevenson, B., & Wolfers, J. (2007). Marriage and divorce: Changes and their driving forces. *The Journal of Economic Perspectives, 21*(2), 27–52.
Stewart, S., Stinnett, H., & Rosenfeld, L. B. (2000). Sex differences in desired characteristics of short-term and long-term relationship partners. *Journal of Social and Personal Relationships, 17*(6), 843–853.
Stigler, G. J., & Becker, G. S. (1977). De Gustibus non est Disputandum. *The American Economic Review, 67*(2), 76–90.

Stovel, K., & Fountain, C. (2009). Matching. In P. Hedström & P. S. Bearman (Eds.), *The Oxford handbook of analytical sociology* (pp. 365–390). Oxford: University Press.
Streib, J. (2015). Explanations of how love crosses class lines: Cultural complements and the case of cross-class marriages. *Sociological Forum, 30*(1), 18–39.
Surra, C. A., & Boelter, J. M. (2013). Dating and mate selection. In G. W. Peterson & K. R. Bush (Eds.), *Handbook of marriage and the family* (pp. 211–232). New York: Springer.
Swedberg, R. (2011). The economic sociologies of Pierre Bourdieu. *Cultural Sociology, 5*(1), 67–82.
Thibaut, J. W., & Kelley, H. H. (1959). *The social psychology of groups*. New York: Wiley.
Timm, A. (2004). *Partnerwahl- und Heiratsmuster in modernen Gesellschaften. Der Einfluss des Bildungssystems*. Wiesbaden: DUV.
Todd, P. M., & Miller, G. F. (1999). From Pride to Prejudice and Persuasion. In G. Gigerenzer & P. M. Todd (Eds.), *Evolution and cognition. Simple heuristics that make us smart* (pp. 287–308). New York: Oxford University Press.
Todd, P. M., Penke, L., Fasolo, B., & Lenton, A. P. (2007). Different cognitive processes underlie human mate choices and mate preferences. *Proceedings of the National Academy of Sciences of the United States of America (PNAS), 104*(38), 15011–15016.
Toma, C. L., & Hancock, J. T. (2010). Looks and lies: The role of physical attractiveness in online dating self-presentation and deception. *Communication Research, 37*(3), 335–351.
Toma, C. L., Hancock, J. T., & Ellison, N. B. (2008). Separating fact from fiction: An examination of deceptive self-presentation in online dating. *Personality and Social Psychology Bulletin, 34*(8), 1023–1036.
Valkenburg, P. M., & Peter, J. (2007). Who looks for casual dates on the internet? A test of the compensation and the recreation hypotheses. *New Media & Society, 9*(3), 455–474.
van Dijk, J., & Hacker, K. (2003). The digital divide as a complex and dynamic phenomenon. *The Information Society, 19*(4), 315–326.
Vermunt, J., & Magidson, J. (2003). Latent class models for classification. *Computational Statistics and Data Analysis, 41*(3–4), 531–537.
Vermunt, J. K., & van Dijk, L. A. (2001). A non-parametric random-coefficient approach: The latent class regression model. *Multilevel Modeling Newsletter, 13*, 6–13.
Wacquant, L. (2013). Symbolic power and group-making: On Pierre Bourdieu's reframing of class. *Journal of Classical Sociology, 13*(2), 274–291.
Wacquant, L. (2016). A concise genealogy and anatomy of habitus. *The Sociological Review, 64*(1), 64–72.
Walster, E., Walster, G. W., & Berscheid, E. (1978). *Equity. Theory and research*. Boston: Allyn & Bacon.
Wang, H., & Lu, X. (2007). Cyberdating: Misinformation and (Dis)trust in online interaction. *Informing Science Journal, 10*, 1–15.
Weber, M. (1922). *Wirtschaft und Gesellschaft: Grundriß der verstehenden Soziologie* (Grundriß der Sozialökonomik, Vol. 3). Tübingen: Mohr.
Weber, M. (1946). *From Max Weber: Essays in sociology*. New York: Oxford University Press.
Weber, M. (1947). *The theory of social and economic organization*. New York: Simon and Schuster.
Weber, M. (1968). *Economy and society: An outline of interpretive sociology*. New York: Bedminster Press.
Weber, M. (1978). In G. Roth & C. Wittich (Eds.), *Economy and society*. Berkeley: University of California Press.
Weber, M. (2003). *General economic history*. Mineola: Dover Publications.
Weber, M., & Roth, G. (1978). *Economy and society: An outline of interpretive sociology*. New York: University of California Press.
Welker, M., & Wenzel, O. (2007). Online Forschung 2007. Grundlagen und Fallstudien. Neue Schriften zur Online-Forschung, Band 1, Köln.

Wellmann, B. (1988). Structural analysis: From method and metaphor to theory and substance. In B. Wellmann & S. D. Berkovitz (Eds.), *Social structures: A network approach* (pp. 19–61). Cambridge: Cambridge University Press.
Wendt, A. (1999). *Social theory of international politics*. Cambridge: Cambridge University Press.
Wetzel, D. (2012). "Ich hab ihn…? Poststrukturalistische Zugänge zu Emotionen/Affekten bei der Online-Partnerwahl". In Deutsche Gesellschaft für Soziologie (Ed.), *Konferenzband der DGS zum Soziologentag in Jena*. DGS Tagung 2009.
Wetzel, D. J. (2013). *Soziologie des Wettbewerbs. Eine kultur- und wirtschaftssoziologische Analyse der Marktgesellschaft*. Wiesbaden: VS Verlag.
White, H. C. (1981). Where do markets come from? *American Journal of Sociology, 87*(3), 517–547.
White, H. C. (1992). *Identity and control: A structural theory of social action*. Princeton: Princeton University Press.
White, J. M. (2013). The current status of theorizing about families. In G. W. Peterson & K. R. Bush (Eds.), *Handbook of marriage and the family* (pp. 65–89). New York: Springer.
Whitty, M. T. (2007). The art of selling one's self on an online dating site: The BAR approach. In M. T. Whitty, A. J. Baker, & J. A. Inman (Eds.), *Online matchmaking* (pp. 57–69). Basingstoke: Palgrave Macmillan.
Whitty, M. T. (2008). Liberating or debilitating? An examination of romantic relationships, sexual relationships and friendships on the net. *Computers in Human Behavior, 24*(5), 1837–1850.
Wiesenthal, H. (1987). Rational Choice – Ein Überblick über Grundlinien, Theoriefelder und neuere Themenakquisition eines sozialwissenschaftlichen Paradigmas. *Zeitschrift für Soziologie, 16*(6), 434–449.
Wiik, K. A., & Holland, J. A. (2015). *Partner choice and timing of first marriage among children of immigrants in Norway and Sweden*. Discussion Papers No. 810 of the Research Department, Statistics Norway.
Willis, J., & Todorov, A. (2006). First impressions: Making up your mind after a 100-Ms exposure to a face. *Psychological Science, 17*(7), 592–598.
Willoughby, B. J., & Carroll, J. S. (2010). Sexual experience and couple formation attitudes among emerging adults. *Journal of Adult Development, 17*(1), 1–11.
Winch, R. F., Ktsanes, T., & Ktsanes, V. (1954). The theory of complementary needs in mate-selection: An analytic and descriptive study. *American Sociological Review, 19*(3), 241–249.
Winter, L., & Kron, T. (2009). Fuzzy thinking in sociology. In R. Seising (Ed.), *Views on fuzzy sets and systems from different perspectives: Philosophy and logic, criticisms and applications* (pp. 301–320). Berlin/Heidelberg: Springer.
Witt, U. (1991). Economics, sociobiology and behavioral psychology on preferences. *Journal of Economic Psychology, 12*(4), 557–573.
Witte, D. (2014). *Auf den Spuren der Klassiker. Pierre Bourdieus Feldtheorie und die Gründerväter der Soziologie*. Konstanz/München: UVK.
Wood, D., & Brumbaugh, C. C. (2009). Using revealed mate preferences to evaluate market force and differential preference explanations for mate selection. *Journal of Personality and Social Psychology, 96*(6), 1226–1244.
Woody, E. Z., & Sadler, P. (2005). Structural equation models for interchangeable dyads: Being the same makes a difference. *Psychological Methods, 10*, 139–158.
Yancey, G., & Emerson, M. O. (2014). Does height matter? An examination of height preferences in romantic coupling. *Journal of Family Issues* forthcoming.
Yang, C. (2009). Looking online for the best romantic partner reduces decision quality: The moderating role of choice-making strategies. *Cyberpsychology & Behavior, 13*, 1–4.
Yoder, S. (2014). *How online dating became a $2 billion industry. Fiscal times*. Retrieved from http://www.thefiscaltimes.com/Articles/2014/02/14/Valentines-Day-2014-How-Online-Dating-Became-2-Billion-Industry

Yurchisin, J., Watchravesringkan, K., & McCabe, D. B. (2005). An exploration of identity re-creation in the context of internet dating. *Social Behavior and Personality: An International Journal, 33*(8), 735–750.

Zafirovski, M. (1999). What is really rational choice? Beyond the utilitarian concept of rationality'. *Current Sociology, 47*(1), 47–113.

Žakelj, T., Kocon, D., Švab, A., & Kuhar, R. (2015). Internet dating as a project: The commodification and rationalisation of online dating. *Journal Družboslovne razprave, 78*, 7–24.

Zillmann, D. (2016). *Von kleinen Lügen und kurzen Beinen. Selbstdarstellung bei der Partnersuche im Internet.* [About little lies and small legs. Self-presentation in Online Dating.] Wiesbaden: VS Verlag (forthcoming).

Zillmann, D., & Schulz, F. (2009). *Das Internet als Heiratsmarkt. Ausgewählte Aspekte aus Sicht der empirischen Partnerwahlforschung.* Ifb-Materialien 4/2009. Bamberg.

Zillmann, D., Schmitz, A., & Blossfeld, H.-P. (2011). Lügner haben kurze Beine. Zum Zusammenhang unwahrer Selbstdarstellung und partnerschaftlicher Chancen im Online-Dating. *Zeitschrift für Familienforschung, 23*(3), 291–318.

Zillmann, D., Schmitz, A., Skopek, J., & Blossfeld, H.-P. (2013). Survey topic and unit nonresponse. Evidence from an online survey on mating. *Quality and Quantity, 48*(4), 2069–2088.

Žižek, S. (2010). Time of the monsters. A call to radicalness. *Le Monde diplomatique* 12.10.2010.

Printed by Printforce, the Netherlands